# Empire of No Meaning

- this book indexes intense verbs
- what he is _running away from_ is most important, yet never mentioned (Name) Genre

- an inventory that becomes a parody

The publication of this book was assisted by a bequest
from Josiah H. Chase to honor his parents,
Ellen Rankin Chase and Josiah Hook Chase,
Minnesota territorial pioneers.

# Empire of Meaning

## The Humanization of the Social Sciences

*or, French name-dropping !*

François Dosse

*Translated by Hassan Melehy*

University of Minnesota Press
*Minneapolis*
*London*

The University of Minnesota Press gratefully acknowledges financial assistance provided by the French Ministry of Culture for the translation of this book.

Originally published as *L'empire du sens: L'humanisation des sciences humaines.* Copyright Éditions La Découverte, Paris, 1995.

Published by the University of Minnesota Press
111 Third Avenue South, Suite 290
Minneapolis, MN 55401-2520
http://www.upress.umn.edu

Printed in the United States of America on acid-free paper

**Library of Congress Cataloging-in-Publication Data**

Dosse, François, 1950–
    [Empire du sens, Humanisation des sciences humaines. English]
    Empire of meaning : the humanization of the social sciences /
François Dosse : translated by Hassan Melehy.
        p.    cm.
    Includes bibliographical references and index.
    ISBN 0-8166-2964-1 (hardcover: alk. paper)
    1. Social sciences—Philosophy.   I. Title.
H61.15.D67   1998
300'.1—dc21                                                              98-26755

The University of Minnesota is an equal-opportunity educator and employer.


10  09  08  07  06  05  04  03  02  01  00  99      10  9  8  7  6  5  4  3  2  1

To Paul Ricoeur,
*en respectueux hommage*

# Contents

# Acknowledgments

I would first of all like to thank François Gèze, who suggested that I undertake this book. It was he who had the intuition of a common gestation in the social sciences and who did me the honor of trusting me to complete this research project.

I would also like to thank the following scholars, who agreed to answer my questions. Their testimony was an essential contribution to the completion of this project.

Daniel Andler, philosopher, Center for Research in Applied Epistemology (CREA), University of Paris X

Luc Boltanski, sociologist, École des Hautes Études en Sciences Sociales (EHESS)

Alain Caillé, sociologist, University of Paris X, *La Revue du MAUSS*

Michel Callon, sociologist, Center for the Sociology of Innovation (CSI), École des Mines

Roger Chartier, historian, EHESS

Bernard Conein, sociologist, University of Paris VIII

Dany-Robert Dufour, philosopher, University of Paris VIII

Jean-Pierre Dupuy, philosopher, CREA, Stanford University

Pascal Engel, philosopher, CREA, University of Caen

Olivier Favereau, economist, University of Paris X

Jean-Marc Ferry, philosopher, Free University of Brussels (ULB)

Marcel Gauchet, historian and philosopher, EHESS, *Le Débat*
Bruno Latour, sociologist, CSI, École des Mines
Pierre Lévy, philosopher, University of Paris X
Gérard Noiriel, historian, EHESS, *Genèses*
Patrick Pharo, sociologist, EHESS
Louis Quéré, sociologist, EHESS
Isabelle Stengers, philosopher, ULB
Laurent Thévenot, economist, CREA, EHESS
Michel Trebitsch, historian, Institute for the History of the
    Present Time (IHTP)
Francisco Varela, biologist, University of Paris VII

I also thank the entire *EspacesTemps* group, whose collective reflection has greatly contributed to my work on this project, especially
Christian Delacroix, who always provided me with valuable sugges-
tions. The annual seminar on the theme "What Do the Social Sciences
Examine?" organized by *EspacesTemps* since 1992, provided impor-
tant material for this project. The following people participated in this
seminar from 1992 to the end of 1994: Sylvain Auroux, Luc Boltanski,
Robert Bonnaud, Alain Boyer, Alain Caillé, François Dosse, Marcel
Gauchet, Maurice Godelier, Jacques Guilhaumou, Denis Hollier, Jean-
Luc Jamard, Bruno Latour, Bernard Lepetit, Jacques Lévy, Louis Quéré,
Isabelle Stengers, and Laurent Thévenot.

I also thank those who took on the difficult task of reviewing this
work and greatly helped me with their useful suggestions and correc-
tions: Christian Delacroix, François Gèze, Jacques Hoarau, and Marc
Saint-Upéry.

# Introduction

According to the dominant depictions of the day, the French intellectual scene seems to be divided into two very distinct poles: on the one side, a few media-friendly philosophers endlessly solicited to give their opinions on the most diverse subjects; and, on the other, a completely atomized community of scholars in the social sciences, more and more locked into their technicality and incapable of giving birth to a common language that might interest society and participate in the public debate. This apparent sequestering in fact hides a profound evolution— underground, so barely perceived—that seems to augur a new mode of being of intellectual life in France.

The disappearance of the guiding thinkers and the end of the great unifying paradigms have not left behind them a void, but rather an intense activity, abounding and complex. Meanwhile, this effervescence is hardly perceptible, and this lack of visibility essentially maintains a very different functioning of research, a more collaborative one. The American detour, which has seen the expatriation of numerous scholars across the Atlantic for fruitful periods of research, teaching, and intellectual exchange, has doubtless been decisive in hatching networks of scholars who conduct dialogue among themselves on the basis of relatively confidential projects. The effect of this evolution is that research has gained in rigor but lost its radiance in the City.[1] Furthermore, projects today circulate in the mode of pointed articles— reworked, commented on, discussed, within the confines of conferences or specialists' journals. This progressive professionalization of the social sciences will not fail to evoke the habitus that has for a long time been characteristic of scholars in the exact sciences.

The study undertaken here has the objective of putting in evidence the richness of research in progress by giving it greater visibility. This project must allow itself to be situated in the maze of networks of a more and more complex puzzle, in order to discern a certain number of transversal axes of coherence.

The principal corpus of this study is quite evidently constituted by the many projects in the social sciences that have appeared in recent years. Their fertility is not limited to the list of interviews done, which have served only as guidelines for orientation in the various laboratories and networks of scholars.

The maturation of research, more collaborative than before, brings about the appearance of "family resemblances," in Ludwig Wittgenstein's expression, beginning with the diverse filiations and heritages of each. Reconstituting several biographical paths appeared important to us in this regard, in order to make the new, gestating cartography perceptible. The scholars interviewed, nevertheless, must not be considered as "representatives" of some list of top prizewinners. They are simply emblematic of the new modes of elaboration of knowledge. They thus allow the opening of entryways into an entire intellectual field whose major trait is precisely a more collective method of functioning. The structuralist period often privileged a powerful theoretical matrix that encompassed knowledge through totalization on the basis of very individualized pivots; the current situation is more allied with a gradual, constant process of translation, founded on a new ethic of intellectual labor.

The other great transformation in progress is the reconciliation of the relations between the exact sciences, the social sciences, and philosophy. Now, it seems very much that the social sciences, as a third culture, hybrid and in tension, are in the process of playing a major role in this recent and promising pacification.

Can one, for all that, speak of the emergence of a "new paradigm"? At the outset of this inquiry, it was more modestly a question of putting in evidence several convergences, of bringing to the surface what were still only implicit crossovers, of favoring the departure from the ivory towers, and of contributing to the redynamization of transdisciplinary confrontation. Now, this inquiry in the heart of the contemporary French social sciences truly led us to discover, at its completion, if not a new paradigm that had emerged fully armed from chaos and poststructuralist uncertainty, at least a new intellectual configuration that brought together the diverse positions of its protagonists around several lines of force.

Marcel Gauchet already saw this phenomenon in 1988, when he described in *Le Débat* the "change of paradigm in the social sciences" marked by a greater attention to the explicit, reflected role of action.[2] For my part, I finished my *History of Structuralism*[3] in 1992 by reporting a departure from that false alternative that has long split the social sciences between the deification and the dissolution of the subject: I evoked the birth of a new paradigm, that of a dialogic, of a communicative action that could represent both a real path of emancipation as a social project and a fertile framework in the domain of the social sciences. This study invites the systematic exploration of that particular configuration.

What does one term this new paradigm? As we have said, it does not rely on rigid criteria that would come to replace, term for term, the themes and schemes of structuralism, but on what Wittgenstein called "family resemblances": pertinent traits that allow areas of research to resonate among themselves, step by step, areas different in their origins and their declared objectives, without for all that the need to postulate, in the final analysis, a common epistemological core or an ineluctable philosophical convergence. In the first place, then, it is appropriate to specify that this intellectual configuration involves a plural reality and not a school assigned to a specific place. It puts to work fertile theoretical synergies that doubtless express the unavoidable necessities of the intellectual conjuncture rather than the a priori orientations of a new grand program of research toward unifying or federating origins. In this regard, the inquiry conducted, fully engaged in defending the fertility of current research, respected as much as possible the word of the actors, the literalness of their works. It is on the scale of the proliferation of these many quests that one may measure the potential richness of what is happening today in the social sciences.

In the second place, this study does not aim for exhaustiveness: that would make no sense, as the situation itself is far from finished. Indeed, it is not a matter of elaborating a catalog of innovations. The partiality of the choices is also strongly proclaimed, and so the result can only be partial. There was no question of doing a "state of . . . ," but of illustrating certain characteristic orientations of the transformations in progress. The latter, in my view, are articulated around four poles of a constellation in motion: the galaxy of the disciples of Michel Serres, notably with the CSI (Center for the Sociology of Innovation); the cognitivist orientation, with the CREA (Center for Research in Applied Epistemology);[4] the pragmatic/conventionalist perspective, which is nourished by the work of the new sociology and by the renewed interrogation of the standard model of economics; and finally the partisans of a reglobalization of the discourse of the social sciences through the political, which essentially involves the disciples of Claude Lefort.

This change of configuration—this mutation of the intellectual landscape—is above all an attempt to respond to a certain feeling of exhaustion of the meaning of historical experience, as Olivier Mongin has rightly perceived.[5] Before the crisis of the great unitary paradigms (functionalism, Marxism, structuralism), as well as, alongside it, holistic and determinist responses to social questions—whether by the intermediary of the total state or that of the invisible hand of the market—the new theoretical approaches place, on the pragmatic resourcefulness of the theory of action, a dynamization of the "workshops of practical reason" and, more generally, one might say, a "humanization of the social sciences." It is not for all that a matter of a pure and simple return to the subject or to a form of precritical humanism, but of a reequilibration, of a change of scale that allows one to ask, on the level of the individual, what "being together," or the social bond, is based on. This reequilibration passes through the reevaluation of the force of the weak bonds—the invisible, ineffable bonds that maintain the humanity of the human being. This attention to the mediations, to the effectiveness of the bond, is therefore well inscribed in a true pragmatic turn that federates these diverse approaches—whatever their various reorientations, whatever models of intelligibility they favor: the anthropology of networks, hermeneutical understanding, cognitivist decoding, and so on. This pragmatic turn accords a central position to action endowed with meaning, rehabilitates the intentionality and the justifications of the actors in a reciprocal determination of doing and saying. The social is then no longer conceived as a thing; it is no longer the object of reification, for the actor and the observer are both held in a relation of interpretation that implicates intersubjectivity.

The end of French exceptionalism has allowed this pragmatic reorientation. During the period in which our national provincialism dominated, the genuine intellectual debate had a tendency to take place elsewhere, between Anglo-Saxons and Germans, between analytic and Continental philosophy. The activism of numerous scholars—and this study precisely retraces the paths of some, as well as their efforts at mediation and disclosure—has permitted an appropriation, an assimilation, and an adaptation of thematics that have long remained foreign to the French intellectual field. Thanks to these people, France is emerging from its provincialism and can claim to participate fully in the current debate on the international level.

The pragmatic turn is also situated in a median space between explanation and understanding, in the search for a third way between the prevalence of pure lived experience and the priority of conceptualization, envisioned as the recollection of a meaning not postulated but discovered by way of the resources mobilized by intersubjectivity. The turn equally implies a major shift in the attribution of cognitive competencies, which are no longer considered the sole privilege of the scientific stance. Evidently, this reevaluation of the actors' competencies involves the renewed interrogation of the notion of "epistemological break" that is at work in the studies of the philosophy of science from the 1970s. The scholar is invited, more modestly, to conduct a "clarification," as Wittgenstein wished, and no longer to effect an artificial separation between judgments of fact, depending solely on scientificity, and judgments of value, which are proscribed.

This pragmatic and interpretive reorientation, of course, once again takes up the preoccupations of classical writers who are sometimes revered at a distance, such as Max Weber, or blatantly neglected, such as Georg Simmel. It nonetheless does it on the new basis of the backlash of the epistemological crisis in the so-called hard sciences. It begins with the principle of incompleteness, with an indeterminacy of its object, which becomes the very means to prop up a pertinent vision of social coordination, always fluctuating in time and caught between opacity and transparency. The determinations have become weak in the new paradigm that seeks, in contrast to what was done before, to defatalize, to avoid the impasses of determinism. It allows the liberation of a reflexive moment of analysis on the basis of the crises of the scientific models. We are witnessing a genuine transformation: the terms *structure, reproduction, static, combinatory, invariant, universal,* and *binary logic* are being effaced, in favor of the notions of organizing chaos, fractal, event, process, meaning, complexity, self-organization, construction, strategy, convention, autonomy, enaction . . . It is therefore certainly a question of a radical, renewed interrogation of the ideal of objectivism and determinism. The new configuration allows the revival of old but too often ignored traditions. German critical philosophy of history at the turn of the century, and then the phenomenological currents, by placing understanding and the question of meaning at the heart of their procedure, contributed to this redefinition of a new objectivity, indissociable from intentionality and intersubjectivity. And ethnomethodology broke with the indifference to everydayness by giving itself the task of restoring the effective dynamic of the processes of action in the course of being completed.

The social sciences have entered the age of what Anthony Giddens terms a double hermeneutic,[6] as a complementary process of translation and interpretation that accords a prevalence to the present. The present has become the imposing category hanging over our sphere of experience and invites a memorial and symbolic rereading of the past.

This interpretive and pragmatic paradigm opens new and pacified relations with philosophy. After celebrating the cutting of the umbilical cord that bound them to philosophy, the social sciences are beginning to notice that they can revisit the philosophical tradition in a fertile way. With philosophy no longer claiming the crowning position, the social sciences can draw resources from contact with it.

In addition, the philosophical dimension of the social sciences is more than ever an imperative, because it is the only means of preserving interpretive pluralism, the plurality of possibilities, of available worlds. It makes possible the reopening of a space of investigation by avoiding sterile alternatives: freedom/constraint, individual/society, universalism/relativism, substantialism/hermeneutics, and so on—so many pairs that have long haunted and impoverished work in the social sciences.

To grasp the forms of action, the new projects take an interest in the phenomenological and hermeneutic tradition, which permits them to define a paradigm of interpretation that thematizes doing within saying.[7] They also use the works of analytic philosophy in order better to grasp the will of the actors in the very effectuation of the action. The social fact is perceived as a semantic fact, bearing meaning. Jürgen Habermas's theory of communicative action, as well as the works of cognitive science, are mobilized to recapture social actions as facts at once psychological and physical. The notion of the dialogic, introduced by Mikhail Bakhtin, elegantly informs the new research of the fact of the accent placed on the polyphonic character of discourse, on its enunciative heterogeneity.

A new alliance, in the form of a triad, is taking shape among the exact sciences, the social sciences, and philosophy, in the pacified relations that are no longer based on the deportation of concepts and the savage practice of interdisciplinarity, but on codisciplinarity or transdisciplinarity. This new theoretical pluralism must invest "science as it is," not by importing into it ready-made modelizations, but by taking seriously what the players of the sciences say about them and by conducting a discourse compatible with scientific discoveries. It is on this condition that the transdisciplinarity based on the search for the meaning of human action, in all its dimensions, can respond to the pressing interpellations of our current situation.

With humility, let us not forget that we will always be closer to the smoke than the crystal.[8] The reorientation that is being elaborated once again opens the field of experience of the past and the present, the entire realm of action, to the problematization of the social sciences.

Action: this is doubtless the guiding word of the crystallization in progress. This new sensibility is not emerging on just any shore. It is manifestly that of a generation strongly marked by a movement that it traversed, that of May '68. It is in the course of these "events" that an everyday was born. It was called . . . *Action.*

Would the new paradigm be the expression of the true thought of 1968, finally liberated from its shackles, some ready-to-think items whose radical movement has been adorned so as to express itself? One cannot really postulate it, as too many discontinuities separate us from the configuration of the 1960s. The current movement is notably situated in radical rupture with the hypercritical posture, the philosophy of suspicion that was that of May '68. Meanwhile, the will to make "sense," after having made a "sign," is really the common point of those who work today for the renewal of the social sciences.

When I began my inquiry, I did not intend to use criteria of age to draw up the list of scholars that I wished to meet. Only in the course of working on the book did I notice that I was dealing with a generational phenomenon.

The very notion of a paradigm evokes that of a moment, which must be doubly stated: as an exit from structuralism, and as the delayed effect of a generation marked by May '68. This generation finally seems to have found the words and mental equipment to pursue its quest for meaning without teleology, to express its sensitiveness to historicity without historicism, and its taste for acting without activism.

The disturbance in progress is also the occasion for a great intellectual and generational meeting with a philosopher who traversed the previous period in the shadows, precisely because he incarnated the philosophy of action and meaning: Paul Ricoeur. One may find him all over the deployment of the multiple facets of the new paradigm as the essential resource of the present orientations.

To take the measure of the current turn and to gauge the potentialities offered—such is the ambition of this book, which intends to make audible to the citizen the current stakes of research by tracing the contours of the theoretical space common to the innovative practices that are still very widely flourishing. It must therefore contribute, according to the secret hope of the author, to rethinking the social bond in the modern City.

# Part I

## *Itineraries*
### *One Generation*

The new configuration of the social sciences that has emerged in France since the late 1980s shows, beyond its abundance and the plurality of its poles, a true generational unity. Each author certainly has her or his particular trajectory, discernible in its own coherence. Nonetheless, a tacit bond is the basis of a common identity, that of belonging to a poststructuralist intellectual space. This generation, between forty and fifty years old, was barely out of adolescence in May 1968, and we should not be surprised to find among most of its representatives an acute sense of engagement, the concern for the social. This relation to the world has of course changed since that date, and the various evolutions are many. Still, a common sensibility binds all the itineraries. It is not really a common paradigm, but rather one quest for meaning, one horizon of reconciliation with democracy, a problematization of the relations of the individual to the political, a will to surpass the old artificial divisions between individualism and holism and thereby to break with the disciplinary pretensions. "Power to the imagination," they said in the late 1960s. Today, one can detect a common aspiration to opening, to decompartmentalization, to cutting across. From these exchanges, one may discern a certain number of innovative and common orientations. They are the fruit of opening the doors and windows, of engaging in dialogue on the most diverse fields of knowledge, and of departing from French provincialism.

Four poles, we have already said, structure this intellectual community in motion: the galaxy of Michel Serres's disciples, the cognitivist orientation, the pragmatic/conventionalist paradigm, and the attempt at reglobalization through the political. But the bridges between these diverse sites of research are numerous; some straddle these divisions all the more easily in that these four poles very often function in convergence. Let us retrace, in the inquiry, the singularity of each one. We will thus be able to reveal unexpected similarities in the history of ideas that is in progress.

# One

# The Galaxy of Michel Serres's Disciples

A heterodox philosopher under the patronage of Hermes, Michel Serres has, paradoxically, begun a school. His winding path, difficult to follow because of its singularity, did not really lend itself to the building of a chapel; the school is rather a veritable nebula that has fed on his daring. Alone, he has conducted a systematic labor of de-sacralization of the contemporary sciences by interrogating the efficiency of their models within the social sciences, but also at the heart of literature, notably on the thermodynamics at work in Émile Zola's *Rougon-Macquart*.[1]

Introduced early on to epistemology, Serres is one of those rare philosophers in France who have worked in mathematical logic, having discovered Bertrand Russell and Ludwig Wittgenstein in the 1950s. He retains some of its essential ideas, which he will never cease to rework in various forms: those of pluralism, of the prevalence of invention, and of the encyclopedic horizon of knowledge. A specialist in Leibniz, on whom he wrote his thesis,[2] he went to war against all foundational and hierarchical forms of scientific knowledge. In this sense, he broke with the tradition of French epistemologists—from the continuism of Comtian positivism to the discontinuism of the Bachelardian rupture.

His philosophical problem is not that of the break, but, on the contrary, that of circulation, of invention, which he tracks in its diverse scientific and poetic manifestations. The philosophy of Serres strives to circulate the messages at the very center of human experience. He has dedicated no fewer than five works to Hermes,[3] in which he multiplies all the possible connections, following the thread of an achronic time, a folded time in which displacement is the rule on the inside of a space of cross-links [*métissages*]: "This is the reason for my attraction to topology—the science of proximities and ongoing or interrupted transformations—and my attraction to percolation theory and to the notion of mixture."[4]

Serres the messenger, if he cultivates the art of solitude ("New ideas come from the desert, from hermits, from solitary beings"),[5] has nonetheless been heard. He has thus inspired numerous scholars to follow the winding path. They are in no case disciples, in the sense of having the task of diffusing a vulgate, but rather innovators who have adopted the gesture of Serres's philosophy, that of nomadism, wandering, indefinite circulation on the margins of inventiveness, as well as a functioning through networks beginning with discontinuous chains. One finds among them the practitioners of a new aggregate discipline: the anthropology of science (Michel Callon, Bruno Latour, and others), a chemist settled on terrains as diverse as thermodynamics, sociology, and hypnosis (Isabelle Stengers), a historian conquered by the modern technologies of communication (Pierre Lévy), and others. The path within this galaxy shows to what point the fertility of Michel Serres the smuggler seems far from having exhausted its effects.

## Innovation

One of the active sites of the work of decompartmentalization between disciplines appeared in the midst of the École des Mines in Paris, with the creation of the Center for the Sociology of Innovation (CSI)[6] in 1967, through the impetus of Pierre Laffitte. The current director of the CSI, Michel Callon, with his colleague Bruno Latour, has initiated an original direction of research that is tending to become a new branch of knowledge, a novel discipline: the anthropology of science and technology. It is situated at the intersection of sociology and the hard sciences. It is placed at the very heart of emerging scientific invention and there irrigates its diverse technological translations.

Having begun at the École des Mines in 1964, Michel Callon was involved in the Union des Grandes Écoles, a section of a UNEF[7] that was particularly active in the wake of the war in Algeria. The political effervescence of the 1960s in student circles incited him to turn to the economic and social sciences. Now, one of the original aspects of this school for engineers was to offer an advanced set of economics courses with Maurice Allais (who would win the Nobel Prize for economics in 1988). Certainly, Michel Callon, preparing for a degree in mining engineering, took the courses in mathematics, physics, and chemistry, but what was to become essential to his work took a marginal position: "Eighty percent of my life consisted of reading sociology, anthropology, and philosophy."[8] This bath in the social sciences, dominated at the time by the tutelary figure of Pierre Bourdieu, prompted Callon to specialize in this area. He sought to extend his studies in economics.

With his engineering diploma in hand in 1969, he seized the opportunity offered by the creation of the Center for the Sociology of Innovation, which had just been established by the adjunct director of the École des Mines, Pierre Laffitte. The CSI was one of three research centers founded at that time, along with a Center for Research in Economic Sciences with Maurice Allais and a Center for Research in Management. With the lack of sociologists at the École des Mines, Laffitte asked Alain Touraine to recommend to him a young scholar who was established and available. That is how Lucien Karpik was granted the directorship of the CSI, whose projects he would orient in three directions.

Karpik first began the study of the politics of large corporations, in the lineage of Alain Touraine, who had just published *The Self-Production of Society*.[9] In this book Touraine developed his characterization of society as "postindustrial." Shifting the analysis to the changes in modern societies, Touraine distinguished three constitutive components of their mode of historicity: knowledge in general, which includes all forms of relations with the world, notably those involving language; accumulation, by which one part of what is consumable is invested in production; and, finally, the cultural model, by which society grasps its own creativeness, valorizing the role of scientificity in the act of transforming nature. Thus, Touraine defined a "system of historicity's dominion over social practice"[10] specific to modern society, completely different from that of traditional, agrarian society, which had a colder historicity. In this schema, the corporation became the privileged site, as an intermediate level, in society's process of production. Karpik worked with this orientation, which allowed him to surpass the dualism opposing the logic of individuals to the market, in order to concentrate better on corporations as sites of a true power, at once autonomous, modeled by society, and capable of transforming the latter. Among the resources mobilized by corporations there figured, quite evidently, science and technology.

Michel Callon participated in this research program in the area of the leading corporations in the company of Jean-Pierre Vignolle and Thierry Chauveau. For two years, they worked in the field, going from corporation to corporation, practicing participatory observation, integrating themselves into the research laboratories, into the teams that made the strategic decisions. These three researchers divided the work among themselves. Vignolle worked on commercial functions, Chauveau on finances and production, and Callon concerned himself with "research and development" activities: "The choice of this subject marks a break with current sociology. It will profoundly mark subsequent research."[11]

The corporation was at the time no longer at the center of economic or sociological studies, and the ambition of the CSI was to make it a full-fledged actor in society. A living, heterogeneous entity, in constant tension between sometimes opposing forces, the corporation was analyzed as a perceptible sheet, proliferating in its ramifications, beginning with a grid of new analysis, "like that of the logic of action . . . , that of corporate government."[12] The CSI sought to restore the relations of competition among corporations as a strategic stake, beginning with the definition of products, commercial policies, and alliances with public powers.

Two other directions of research accompanied this one. The second was inspired by the sociologist Haroun Jamous, who had then just completed an important study on health-care reform.[13] He proposed to study the mechanism of public decision through a modelization of alliances between social and professional groups, in order to consider public decisions, thus relativizing Michel Crozier's functionalist theses on organizations.[14] The third axis of research was directed by Marie Moscovici. Her objective was to show that the Mertonian functionalist model of the analysis of science[15] did not correspond to the diversity of practices and contexts in which these scientific practices were deployed. So her group also completed a field study in a series of laboratories, as many public as private ones. They showed that there were differences, but no contradictions, between the ethos of academic science (the search for truth, for norms) and that of business. So research was conceivable according to diverse norms.

Seminars allowed a comparison of the experiments of the three groups and a testing of the reliability of the theoretical hypotheses. For Michel Callon, it was a fertile and educational four years, especially as "Karpik was an excellent pedagogue. He spent a great deal of time educating us in sociology."[16] Hence, the CSI could expand into many sites of production and research laboratories in a protected atmosphere, as its director, Karpik, was not very concerned with the problem of resources. Reworking Oscar Wilde's famous retort on the fact that he was already sad enough to be poor—if he had to complain about it too . . . , he deemed that one should never subordinate the imperatives of research to financial constraints. This attitude allowed the Center a respectable lack of concern, which nevertheless led to a serious crisis ten years later.

Callon was then still under the influence of Alain Touraine, whose seminar he attended until 1973. He was sensitive to the composite character of an international audience, especially Latin American, and to Touraine's capacity to find coherencies throughout the most diverse experiences, as he was in contact with the social and political movements of the day. Bourdieu's model did not play the same role, and "for studying the corporations, it offered us practically nothing."[17] The early 1970s were also very marked by the influence of Althusser, and Callon tried then "to combine Althusser on the one hand and Touraine on the other"[18] by testing the Althusserian concepts of the diverse strata of organization of corporations, distinguishing property relations, levels of appropriation, and so on. "We regularly and systematically read everything the Althusserians might have been writing to see how those concepts could be put into practice."[19]

## Translation

As they did for many, the years 1974 and 1975 marked a turning point for Michel Callon. The political climate was changing, and he took his distance from the conceptual instruments that he had used until then. He realized that the supply of available tools—whether Althusserian, Mertonian, or Tourainian—did not work to account for scientific research in progress or technological creations. The renewed interrogation of the old models was also born of a collaborative reflection conducted at the Center around a critical approach to science. For two years, a small group met regularly once a month, around the person who represented the critical current in France, the physicist Jean-Marc

Lévy-Leblond; he had published, with Alain Jaubert, *Autocritique de la science*,[20] a work in which he defended the idea that science played the role of a "spoiler of all-encompassing thought."[21] Around him were Callon, Pierre Thuillier—who was writing in *La Recherche*—the former Dominican Philippe Roqueplo,[22] Michel Volle, Claude Gruson, Luce Giard, Bernard Guibert, Alain Desrosières, Gérard Fourez, Pierre Papon, Liliane Stehelin, and the current editor of the "Repères" series from the publisher La Découverte, Jean-Paul Piriou.[23]

The positions within the group were not homogeneous, but it constituted a nonacademic critical and active movement, enjoying the funds of CORDES[24]—an organism tied to the Commissariat Général du Plan[25]—to finance a seminar dedicated to the influence of social relations on science. The general intention was to oppose a purely internalizing history of science that was content to research a genealogy of scientific discoveries, and to accord maximum attention to the labors that related to an external history, taking account of the social context, while distinguishing the task "from certain Marxist tendencies that wanted to reduce science to a socially constructed object."[26] At the intersection of the internalizing and externalizing approaches, this group of about twenty opened itself to new philosophical inspirations so as better to reengage in the study of scientific discoveries. It was the moment that translations of the German philosopher Jürgen Habermas were beginning to appear in France, and a seminar on him was given. Also discussed were the controversies among Karl Popper, Imre Lakatos, and Paul Feyerabend. Epistemology was the biggest topic of the internal discussions.

But one discovery was to be decisive for Michel Callon, that of the work of Michel Serres. Having attended Serres's seminar on the philosophical notion of *translation* (which would be the topic of volume 3 of *Hermès*),[27] Callon introduced it into the field of sociology. "That notion seemed absolutely illuminating to me."[28] It immediately brought him to understand a statistical work that was lost in confused explanations; he came to know why, in certain industrial sectors, innovations are more the work of researchers, whereas in others businesses are rather at the origin of new products: "There were either sectors where the operations were already in place, or sectors where, on the contrary, one had to construct all the chains of translation."[29] Therefore, it was careless and reductive to postulate the prevalence of one domain of explanation of innovation before the inquiry.

In 1976, Callon published, in a collective work, an article on the theme of translation;[30] there is no explicit reference to Serres in it because the influence was still only an oral one, but the notion of translation in sociology became central, defining an equivalence among heterogeneous objectives of particular actors. This notion had the function of surpassing the false alternative between internalism and externalism:

> It is a matter of a particular operation that we term translation, which transforms a particular problematic utterance into the language of another particular utterance. . . . Such a distinction renders any distinction between inside and outside useless, because the network has neither a center nor a periphery, but rather is a system of relations among problematic utterances that come, equally, from the social sphere, scientific production, technology, or consumption.[31]

Translation, nevertheless, does not imply an a priori equivalence, but simply a conjectural one.[32]

At a moment when the old models presented an impasse, and the new inspirations a beginning, Callon decided to take a decisive detour, to which we will return, toward the nascent British sociology of science. The resulting reorientation came to present innovation as a "total social fact"—to borrow Marcel Mauss's expression—and so to take into consideration not only the margins of science but its very content, neglected until then by the sociologist. Callon was then working on a project that he submitted to CORDES. It was the time of the first oil crisis, of the nuclear debate, and there were announcements that the internal combustion automobile would have to give way to the electric car. Callon seized the opportunity for an innovation that was being born, whose success or failure we do not yet know. He spent six months completing his research project on the electric car that seemed to involve, besides the technological disruptions represented by the abandonment of the internal combustion engine, many implications on the social level. Some already saw in it the advent of a society of cleanliness taking the place of the pollutive industrial society whose principal resource was petroleum: "I felt that it was a total innovation, and that in following that innovation I was going to look at society as a whole."[33]

Indeed, this inquiry implicated the fundamental research labs as much as the private enterprises and public powers. Therefore, it allowed movement from one place to another so as better to grasp the place of each protagonist, and thus to restore the elements of the controversy from within the very stage on which it was playing. The object Callon chose illustrated very well the watchword of the time, which concerned studying science as it was taking place and not science that had been completed. In the specific case of the electric car, the technological, political, and scientific uncertainty was maximal. Once accepted by CORDES, Callon got to work on the project in the solitude of the basic researcher. He established himself, so to speak, at his own expense at the CSI and undertook the study of archives, because work had begun on the car in 1965–66. And he spent time with the many players in this innovation, shared their everyday life in certain labs, met with mayors, town councillors, and public officials.

In parallel with this study of the electric car, which permitted the testing of the notion of translation—for he had to "bring together" elements as different and heterogeneous as the limits of the electrode, the requirements of the city center, the politics of EDF,[34] and the creation of a mode of equivalency among all the heterogeneous levels— Callon undertook a project on public policies regarding research. The opportunity for this study came to him through a meeting with a well-known chemist from Strasbourg: "He told me there was an important group project conducted by the Ministry of Research on macromolecular chemistry."[35] The chemist asked whether this public project had had some effect on the development of the discipline. Insofar as Callon was interested in the links between scientific content and social environment, the chemist proposed that he conduct this study. The economist Claude Gruson was also concerned with this project, because he had participated in the reconstruction of national accounting;[36] notably, he investigated the means at hand to facilitate the decisions of public officials and to avoid systematically having to delegate all the decisive choices to the scientists alone: "He asked what power the political could have on scientific policy, and I must say that this idea pleased me greatly."[37]

The stake was indeed decisive, and all the better perceived by Callon in that at the same time they were discussing Habermas's texts on science at the CSI seminar. Now, Habermas's critique of the progressive technicization of choices, which leads one no longer to realize that one is making decisions of a political order, responded well to the concern to give scientific policy instruments that were just as effective as those of economic and social policy. The critical work on science could find in this perspective a better balance between the political and the scientific. The latter passed through the construction of tools that allowed one to situate the workings of the various levels of the chain of production, from the research lab to its ultimate technological implications. To emerge from opacity, to bring back to the public scene the requests for funds, to restore transparency, and to open to discussion the possible choices—such was the ambition of Callon, armed with the twofold tool of the notion of translation borrowed from Michel Serres and that of communicative action borrowed from Habermas.

## The Meeting

It was when Callon published a rapid presentation of his two studies in *Le Progrès scientifique*—on electric cars and on the impact of public financing in the case of molecular chemistry—that he would meet with Bruno Latour, who would be decisive for the birth of the anthropology of science in France. Returning from San Diego via England in 1977, in this issue of *Le Progrès scientifique* Latour discovered a panoramic view of what was happening in France, and he was vitally interested in the orientations defined by Callon, whom he then met: "That was the beginning of a dialogue that has not since been interrupted."[38]

Their collaboration began with the publication of a small bulletin titled *Pandore*, whose objective was to begin to structure the area. It was a matter of circulating information and signaling the publication of works in a still eclectic realm that ranged from the ethnology of techniques to the management of research, passing through the sociology of science and cognitive psychology. *Pandore* was active for four years, from 1977 to 1981, and had a certain success, allowing the proliferation of meetings and favoring implicit convergences. The overflow of books and projects to signal required resorting to pseudonyms: "In certain cases we went as far as writing critiques of our own works. Thus, Bruno harshly criticized one of his own books. We had fun raising false controversies, getting indignant and taking colleagues to task."[39] The small financial support, at first from the Maison des Sciences de l'Homme and then from the CNRS (Centre National de la Recherche Scientifique), allowed them to distribute *Pandore* free of charge.

The second occasion for collaboration between Callon and Latour was when they coauthored an article.[40] Besides, the year 1981 was one of a political change that would contribute to unraveling a grave crisis that had been hatching for two years at the CSI. Unable to find an internal outlet with the tensions so high, it was necessary to start again at ground zero: "It was a second birth."[41] In these conditions, new axes of research were defined. Lucien Karpik, sick and tired of the internal conflicts, retired, and Callon assumed the responsibilities of directing the Center, which he still holds today.

## A Philosopher in the Field

For his part, Bruno Latour had his early education in the provinces, at Dijon, where he followed a very traditional curriculum that did not in the least prepare him to be the innovator he would become. Studying philosophy, beginning to read the classical texts, he was "removed from the world, as one can be at a provincial university."[42] Beginning his studies in 1967, he passed through May '68 in a climate where the shock was very much attenuated compared with Paris. As for the intellectual climate, in Dijon they were far from the structuralist effervescence. His teachers then were Jean Brun in epistemology and André Malet, the translator of Rudolph Bultmann; with the latter he did a lot of exegesis, and that gave him a good classical background. Taking the *agrégation* in philosophy in 1972, he was ranked first.[43] A year later, he left to do his military service in Africa, at Abidjan, as a research assistant for ORSTOM,[44] in order to conduct a study in the sociology of development.

Latour discovered late, in the field, the social sciences he had somewhat neglected in his early education. He spent two years in the Ivory Coast, during which he learned what anthropology was; he coordinated his research in industry with the courses he gave at the law school, where he taught social science. That is where he became imbued in the Marxist discourse on unequal development and underdevelopment, and above all where he enthusiastically discovered *Anti-Oedipus* by Gilles Deleuze and Félix Guattari. The object of the study he was assigned was to explain why the Ivory Coast managers did not succeed in replacing the French. On this occasion Latour discovered "an entire and completely racist literature on blacks in the factories."[45] It was in the African context that he began to consider that, with the same analytic categories, it would be possible to transpose a similar inquiry into a scientific laboratory.

At the same time, Latour was preparing a doctoral thesis that he would defend on his return from Africa, in 1975, on the theme "Exegesis and Ontology," directed by Claude Bruaire. In the tradition, this time, of his exegetical background, in this work he examined the notion of religious truth: "That played a very important role. I can't say what's left of it today, but I'm still interested in theological questions."[46] Paradoxically, his interest in the sciences derived from this examination of religious truth. After finishing his thesis, he tried to understand the basis of scientific truth, and that led him to move to another continent. From 1975 to 1977, he was in California: he dedicated those two years to a field study in a laboratory directed by a former professor from Dijon, the neuroendocrinologist Roger Guillemin, at the Salk Institute in San Diego. In California he found the full bloom of French modernity in the fields of philosophy and the social sciences. "I was able to catch up a bit on my reading."[47] It was the period in which French culture was beginning its successful exportation onto American soil, and notably at the University of California, San Diego, where Latour found Jean-François Lyotard, Michel de Certeau, Michel Serres, Paolo Fabbri, and Louis Marin. Fabbri, a semiotician and disciple of Algirdas Julien Greimas, would have at the time a great influence on Latour: "He played a considerable role."[48]

Although very skeptical about Greimas's semiotic square,[49] Latour intended to complete the intersection between semiotic analysis and ethnomethodology. This intertwining of the content of semiotic discourse, the social, and objects would constitute the theoretical matrix of his study in Professor Guillemin's neuroendocrinology lab (Guillemin would receive the Nobel Prize for medicine in 1977). Michel Serres would also have a great influence on Latour: "I was bedazzled to stumble across Serres, who was preparing his *Lucrèce*. It was a strong impression, the first time I had the impression while listening to someone of running into a true philosopher."[50] It was in the very Frenchified Californian context that, with Steve Woolgar, Latour published the results of his field study in 1979,[51] which allowed the conception of the possibility of a new discipline, the anthropology of science, founded on a materialist analysis of the production of science. "It was invented simultaneously in California by four other scholars who had the same idea at the same time, none of whom was Californian."[52]

Back in France in 1977, Latour found a position at the Conservatoire National des Arts et Métiers (CNAM), at a moment when a small research group was organized under the direction of Jean-Jacques

Salomon, STS (Sciences, Technologies, and Societies). But especially, he said, "I had the good luck to stumble across Michel Callon."[53] The meeting between the two scholars was one between the sociology of industry and technology, on the one hand, and the nascent anthropology of science, on the other. It allowed a convergence of these two directions, and Latour quite naturally joined the CSI in 1982.

## A Chemist in the Land of the Social Sciences

On December 2, 1993, an ironically Bonapartist date, Michel Serres awarded Isabelle Stengers the grand prize for philosophy of the Académie Française. He thus rewarded an only somewhat academic philosopher, who has always refused herself any form of enclosure in a mold and who cultivates a taste for transversality and nomadism. A true franc-tireur, she tirelessly denounces the capturing attempts among scientific disciplines in which each seeks to acquire a hegemonic position. Gathering honey from flowering flower beds and trampling on prohibitions, she is, according to her friend Bruno Latour, a "witch . . . the thorn and the pebble in the shoe. If you haven't resolved a problem with Isabelle, you've resolved nothing in the philosophy of science."[54] Enamored of risks, she also situates herself in the tradition of Michel Serres's orientations, realizing in fact the functions of Hermes, those of mediation and translation.

A chemist by training, she acquired a solid scientific education that makes her a philosopher who is "well-centered, who can radiate, move. She is sure to have a basis."[55] Her early education, which today she considers more as a source of cultural knowledge than of scientific competence, allows her easily to find the path of a true dialogue with scientists. Very interested in problems of temporality, she first came to know the historical model by way of her father, a historian by profession: "That obviously counted for me. For a long time, everyone, myself included, thought my destiny was set, that I would be a historian like my father."[56] But that was not counting on her taste for nomadism, her quest for new thoughts, her interest in new practices. Stengers's personal equation constantly brought her to lose fondness for the old models, in the manner of Nathanaël, the hero of André Gide's novel *Fruits of the Earth*.

Her itinerary, made up of breaks, is oriented toward the sciences as a form of escape with respect to an overly set destiny, and it is also a means for her to capture contemporaneity. "I had the impression that with history I would be too buried in the past and incapable of seizing the moment, the present and its stakes."[57] She chose chemistry, which she perceived as a science at a crossroads, a field of investigation that was still ill defined and, as a result, a terrain of multiple possibilities. In the course of her studies in chemistry, she discovered that the other scientific disciplines, notably physics, considered chemistry to be dated, on its way to disappearing as such. This apprehension of the conflictuality of the sciences was absolutely essential in her later positioning as a philosopher and historian of science: she would understand that there were strategies of conquest and major, almost military, stakes, with a history of science strewn with losers and whose protagonists were reduced to silence. The fact of having belonged to a minority science, which she discovered was a "serf," materially powerful but ideologically dominated, makes Stengers particularly sensitive to this dimension. Chemistry is an "almost mute science, without a voice, without a tradition to oppose to the physical or biological one."[58] She would retain from chemistry the essential notion of minority, which runs through all of her work, and would dedicate herself to, among other things, the history of that minority, therefore giving voice to a science reduced to silence.[59]

Thus, Stengers followed a classic curriculum in chemistry, through her *maîtrise* at Brussels, where she would have Ilya Prigogine as a professor. Her branching out came from the dissatisfaction felt on the inside of a too narrowly specialized and too functional training. She told herself that if a Kepler existed, she would not be able to recognize him and would even be bothered by his existence, which would come to disturb the canons of her discipline of origin. "I already had a social preoccupation, in the sense of wanting to know what the reproduction of a discipline involves."[60] Therefore, Stengers decided to give herself the academic means to locate the pioneer fronts, the true innovations. That could be done only in a situation of transversality.

In the early 1970s, she chose to study philosophy in order to become a philosopher of science. For the first time then she heard a word that seemed quite strange to her, *epistemology*. "It was the first word I didn't understand in my first course in philosophy."[61] Her attraction for the discipline, which was quite new to her, simply came from the fact that here was the only place one could reflect on the sciences without performing them. She finished her studies in philosophy in 1973, and considered herself a philosopher only after her academic training, when she started to read Gilles Deleuze: "It was the great moment of *Anti-Oedipus*,[62] but as for me, it was *Difference and Repetition*[63] that put me to work."[64] What seduced Stengers in the work of Deleuze was his capacity to engage—and to engage his reader—in a procedure of communication among zones that are normally compartmentalized: "His emotional life and professional work."[65] This decompartmentalization, which she was looking for precisely in the relation among the sciences, and which she discovered in the field of philosophy, allowed her to discover herself: "I am a philosopher."[66]

A philosopher now, Stengers retraced her steps and sought out her former teacher Ilya Prigogine. He did not yet have the Nobel Prize in chemistry that he would receive in 1977. He had just finished his scientific research on dissipative structures and was considering the problem of publishing his discovery. Stengers's arrival was an opportunity, because he needed precisely her abilities, her background in philosophy, to "put into words"[67] the material on dissipative structures. So he set her up with an office in his lab and a true collaboration began, which first involved articles in specialized journals, then the collective writing of a work that would have a wide reception, *La Nouvelle Alliance*, published in 1979.[68]

Nevertheless, Stengers did not get caught up in the success that could have made her a specialist in a particular domain of the epistemology of science, that of thermodynamics. She decided to explore new continents of knowledge and pursue her nomadism. She went to work with some friends in a sociology department, still pursuing the preparation of her thesis, which she would defend in 1982, on the construction of physicists' views of the world since Galileo and Newton, with particular emphasis on the problem posed to them by the chemical phenomenon. "I tried to show how the physicists' different views of the world were articulated, without being stated, around a new possibility of interpreting."[69] At the same time, she participated in an innovative project in sociology, centered on the shifting of society toward the salary-based form, which studied the redistributions induced by this change.

In 1982, Stengers left Brussels for Paris. She would work for almost four years on the preparation of the City of Sciences at La Villette, of which she has a very bad memory—it was a "near nightmare."[70] On the other hand, she found a pleasurable workplace in which she involved herself with passion, *L'Autre Journal,* edited by Michel Butel, who requested her collaboration. "My work for *L'Autre Journal* is one of the wonderful memories of my life."[71] In retrospect, La Villette made her love Belgium, to which she had the desire to return. She had the opportunity to return when Prigogine offered her a half-time position to collaborate on a second book.[72] Upon completion of this work, Stengers was finally hired as a tenured professor at the Free University of Brussels, where she still teaches today. But a new adventure presented itself when the psychoanalyst Léon Chertok asked her to work with him on hypnosis. "I like to get interested in a field only when I'm in the company of someone who belongs to it."[73] This meeting was particularly fertile. It very quickly led her to write a book on hypnosis with Chertok.[74]

This work was also at the origin of an original series and on the cutting edge of reflection on scientific innovation. This series was published by the department of communications of the Delagrange Laboratories (later Synthélabo, after the latter acquired Delagrange), and edited by Philippe Pignarre. The series bore a deliberately provocative title, "The Spoilers of All-Encompassing Thought,"[75] an expression borrowed from Jean-Marc Lévy-Leblond. As founder of the series, Pignarre was interested in scholars whose object was science "in the process of taking place." In 1989, after hearing Stengers speak about her book on hypnosis at the conference at Le Mans on the topic "Science and Philosophy," he asked her to give a presentation to three hundred psychiatrists invited by Delagrange. It was a success, and numerous participants expressed their wishes to obtain the text of the presentation. That is how the series was born. "Otherwise, it would never have been a well-conceived and well-elaborated project, but simply a meeting."[76] The first volume, then, was *L'Hypnose, blessure narcissique,* which appeared in 1990. This mode of publication-intervention corresponds perfectly with the refusal of academicism on the part of the laureate of the 1993 prize in philosophy of the Académie Française. She effectively views her books (also the case for *Drogues. Le défi hollandais,* with Olivier Ralet) as so much "risk taking."[77] Now, for Stengers risk has become the major criterion of discrimination between the true and the false sciences. She utilizes, with the notion of risk as a discriminating factor, an entirely new concept. The true creator, according to Stengers, invents risk, whereas the false creator is content to mime the other sciences.

## A Historian in the Universe of the Machine

The publication, under the editorship of Michel Serres, of *A History of Scientific Thought*[78] allowed for a true collective effort for three years. It was on this occasion that the study group on interdisciplinarity, meeting around Serres, could consolidate its friendly and intellectual ties. The two leaders were Stengers and Latour, in the tutelary presence of Serres. In this network there was another disciple of Serres, Pierre Lévy. An examiner of the world of information science and its effects on society, he is on the cutting edge of reflection on what he understands as a major anthropological transformation. His first book, *La Machine univers,*[79] won the prize of the Association Française des Informaticiens. His path, like those of the others, is at the very least unexpected, composite. He participates in the nomadism inherent in the network that gravitates around Serres.

Lévy first received classical training as a historian at Paris I, and that barely predisposed him to the study of the technosciences. Nonetheless, it was in the framework of this classical training that he followed the teaching of Serres on the history of science. For Lévy, this meeting was decisive. Serres played a "releasing"[80] role for him, whereas the philosopher was a lost figure in the history department. He certainly benefited from a sizable attendance that passionately followed his work in progress, but the actual number of students registered in his courses was pathetic: when Lévy got to his first class, there were only five there. Lévy the student was not certain then, as he had heard Serres's name frequently enough, that the Professor Serres who offered the courses was the same as the author of the numerous books he had read. "When I saw this grey-haired fellow, I told myself: 'It's him! It's the one who wrote the books.' I went to see him to ask where Michel Serres's course was being held, and he answered: 'Michel Serres? That's me.' His five students followed him, and he entered an amphitheater where three hundred people were waiting for him."[81]

During the course of his studies in history, which he pursued through the *maîtrise* in 1978, Lévy was more interested in the technical problems of the media of knowledge than in the themes of classical historiography in vogue at the time. He had a passion for quantitative geography, for computer cartography. In medieval history, what interested him was the use of computers, the use of databases. Serres asked him for an interpretive summary of the Nora-Minc report on the computerization of society, which had just been published. "All of that confirmed for me the idea according to which the intellectual technologies and the instruments they make possible—which are aids to memory, to imagination, to reflection, to visualization—were something central for cultural evolution in all its dimensions."[82]

His training as a historian and that which he obtained at the same time at the CNAM, to learn about information technology, predisposed him to make the connection between a particular technostructure and its social implications. Already, during his training as a historian, the apprenticeship in computing as a research tool interested him less than "reflecting on the way it transformed the very matter of research."[83] Very quickly, reflection on computing became Lévy's specialty; he was writing articles then for the journal *Terminal* (a journal of critical computer scientists). At Paris VII-Jussieu, he completed a DEA[84] in a department that was better suited to his centers of interest, "Computing and Society," and as soon as he got his diploma he taught this theme, presenting the many pedagogical, ergonomic, and juridical implications of this new area of activity.

Serres left to teach in the United States, at the University of California, San Diego, and Lévy turned to Cornelius Castoriadis, whose seminar he took at the École des Hautes Études en Sciences Sociales and with whom he did a new DEA on the theme "Ethnology and Computing." Then he began a thesis, under the direction of Castoriadis, to work on the idea of freedom in antiquity. Going back in time, Lévy was at first interested in the philosophical questions of the eighteenth century, then of the seventeenth century and of the Middle Ages, and he told himself that he had to explore Greek philosophy. "It was not a real thesis; it was for learning."[85] During this time, he continued to take Serres's seminar, when the latter returned from the United States; in this setting Lévy met Isabelle Stengers, for whom he had a profound admiration. "For me, Serres, Deleuze, and Guattari are the great ones. Isabelle is also great. She has a generosity that shows in an understanding of others, of the world, of a thinking that also takes place in her life."[86]

In Castoriadis's seminar, Lévy met Jean-Pierre Dupuy, the director of the CREA (Center for Research in Applied Epistemology), who was then starting a vast research program on the origins of the idea of self-organization. Lévy participated in this program for two years, studying the origins of cybernetics. He was then interested in Warren

McCulloch, who was the first to establish a link between neuronal functioning and logic circuits. As early as 1943, McCulloch, with Walter Pitts, had advanced the notion of formal neuronal networks. McCulloch asked how the brain thinks; he proposed the idea of a neuronal network undergoing stimuli and giving responses in the form of particular configurations of its output neurons.[87] According to Lévy, this scholar, who is unknown in France, is the founder of "connectionism," a theoretical approach that notably led to Jean-Pierre Changeux's *Neuronal Man*.

This project on the history of cybernetics led Pierre Lévy along the path of the one who is considered the pioneer in the area, Heinz von Foerster and his famous Biological Computer Laboratory, a center of interdisciplinary research at the University of Illinois: "It was the second generation of cybernetics. . . . They studied all the vital functions from the angle of a computer simulation or a network of automata."[88] What interested Lévy about von Foerster's project, and also about Jean-Pierre Dupuy and the CREA, was the mind-body relation, the question of what perception and memory are. Thanks to the paradigm of self-organization, of order through noise, the work of von Foerster marks a constitutive moment for the brand-new cognitive orientations.

If conceiving information technologies became Lévy's specialty, his originality resides mainly in transversality. In the fashion of Stengers and in the sphere of influence of Serres, he has ignored disciplinary boundaries. His reading of Gilles Deleuze and his meeting with Félix Guattari also played a big role, and here we are led back to the Deleuzian idea of a rhizome of knowledge with multiple ramifications.

## Two

# The Cognitivist Pole

*( never explained )*

The examinations of the very old body-mind dichotomy were to cause a new focus of research to emerge: that of cognitive science, which involves a plurality of disciplines. Among the representatives of this current, Jean-Pierre Dupuy is an early founder and organizer: today he directs one of the top places where cognitive science rubs elbows with philosophy and the social sciences, at the top of the Montagne Sainte-Geneviève,[1] the Center for Research in Applied Epistemology (CREA).

## The Fertility of Paradoxes

Jean-Pierre Dupuy started out as a brilliant *polytechnicien*. His future was completely laid out when, after finishing at the École Polytechnique at the top of his class, he was admitted into the Corps des Mines, one of the symbols of the French technostructure: "I was destined to become a public official or captain of industry."[2] A fast-forward to what became of his nine comrades in promotion in the Corps is revealing: the CEOs of Saint-Gobain, Rhône-Poulenc, and Ciments Lafarge, the number two at the Crédit Agricole, the CEO of SAGEM . . .[3] "I myself became the philosopher, so I'm quite marginal."[4] This choice, already unorthodox, came from a deep dissatisfaction in the face of, on the one hand, the discourse of the École Polytechnique according to which everything that is real is rational—a form of sub-Hegelianism—and, on the other, lived reality: "The first

contact with reality was hard . . . with the mediocrity of the bureau-
cratic tasks they assigned us."[5]

Dupuy then decided to make other choices than the completely
planned ones to which his training should have led him. He played
hooky, and he went through the hierarchy of the social sciences in de-
scending order. After a detour through mathematical economics, the
closest to his engineer's baggage, he came to adopt an "attitude of systematic criticism of everything I had believed, beginning with science
and technology. I had become an intellectual. What a road to travel! I
had believed in an abstract universal; I found myself plunged into the
most naive relativism, a nihilism of knowledge for which everything
was worthy, that is, nothing was worthy."[6]

This critical attitude would allow him to situate his research at
the point of articulation of two traditionally separate cultures: the literary culture to which he intended to direct himself as an intellectual
and the polytechnical culture that constituted his early scientific training. This double affiliation, the source of an internal tension that may
be found in all of Dupuy's works, allowed him to return to the classical splits between object and subject, nature and culture, and to trans-
gress disciplinary boundaries. He thus became a smuggler, as did all
the scholars in the nebula that formed around Michel Serres.

Quite obviously, he would not be the only one to attempt to move
mountains, and a series of meetings allowed him to carry out his conversion effectively. It took place in the context of the critical paradigm
of the 1970s. The principal inspiration came to him at the time from
Ivan Illich, with whom he had extremely close relations; he actively
participated in the projects of Illich's center, the CIDOC,[7] at Cuernavaca, Mexico. In addition, at Éditions du Seuil he was given the responsibility of editing an "Illichian" series, "Techno-critique." Dupuy
reworked Illich's radical critique of industrial society: he tracked
down the effects of counterproductivity in technocratic management;
denounced the facts that schools promoted unlearning, that medicine
caused illness, and that modern transportation immobilized; and finished with the paradox, worthy of Jacques Tati, that "people spend
more and more time trying to have more time."[8] Illich was trying to
break the counterproductive circle of modernity with a tragic language
of the religious, of the goddess of vengeance (Nemesis) who punishes
human beings who are guilty of immoderation (*hubris*). For his part,
Dupuy thought that one could give an answer to these dysfunctions in

terms of mechanism, of logical paradox. Even if today Dupuy holds that he went a bit too far in the direction of the critique of modernity, he does not deny this decisive contribution: "It is my work with Illich that gave me the taste for paradoxes that has never left me."[9]

Thanks to Illich, Dupuy had other decisive encounters, notably one with Heinz von Foerster, "a Viennese Jew," an émigré like Illich, and, as we have seen, the founder of a "second cybernetics," that of systems of organization. In 1976, von Foerster suggested, after learning at Cuernavaca of Illich's theses, to use the theory of automata to model counterproductivity. Dupuy, who participated in the meeting, was very attracted to this perspective, because it allowed the convergence of the critical paradigm and logic. Von Foerster advised him to see two biologists, Henri Atlan and Francisco Varela. Dupuy thus came back to his early training, and this was also the opportunity for an essential connection with a highly eminent study group, what has been called the "group of ten," of which Atlan was an active member.[10] This small circle met once a month from six P.M. to midnight, with an eye to transdisciplinary exchanges. Dupuy gave a presentation, "Von Foerster's Conjecture," to the "group of ten": "Only one of the participants understood the range of the project. . . . That was Henri Atlan. When he left, he told me, 'Basically, chance and meaning are only two sides of the same coin.'"[11]

At that time, Dupuy did not have a base of research: he was placed at Éditions du Seuil by Illich and Jean-Marie Domenach to edit the "Techno-critique" series. From his office at Seuil, for two years he organized a network of scholars from all disciplines who were interested in the theme of self-organization, in preparation for a conference that took place June 10–17, 1981, at Cerisy.[12] Thanks to this conference, Dupuy achieved the reconciliation that he was calling for because of his ties to the two cultures. Present there was what Pierre Rosanvallon, who attended the conference, would call the "galaxy of self-" (it was the time when there was much discussion of self-management, autonomy, and so on), in which the second left, having broken with party apparatuses and in search of a new culture, was having a dialogue with scientists. "All the areas of research are dissociable only with difficulty, and, for reasons as conceptual as they are sociological, they form a whole, a quasi discipline, supported by a quasi community."[13]

Among the participants at the conference was an author whose work had very strongly impressed Dupuy, René Girard. Dupuy had furthermore just published a book with Paul Dumouchel on the work of Girard.[14] A professor at Stanford University, in California, since the early 1960s, Girard had developed an anthropological theory of man conceived as a being of desire, a specular being whose mimetic behavior is at once the matrix of the social bond and the source of conflictuality.[15] In 1981, Girard had just been appointed at Stanford, moving from the East Coast to the West Coast of the United States. With considerable financial means at his disposal to plan research as he wished, he asked Dupuy to organize a conference on self-organization at Stanford similar to the one at Cerisy. Thus, in September of the same year, Dupuy invited the same participants, as well as some American scholars, to a conference in California on the theme "Disorder and Order." This meeting would have an important impact on the Stanford community; in 1984, Dupuy would be offered a teaching position at Stanford, which he still holds today.

Besides this "galaxy of self-," Dupuy participated in another study circle, that of the *Esprit* family. As he was close to Jean-Marie Domenach, he got to know Marcel Gauchet, who was then publishing his pieces on Tocqueville in the journal. He also met Claude Lefort. This intellectual proximity opened Dupuy to political philosophy and the Arendtian critique of modernity. Illich had introduced Dupuy to Hannah Arendt: "She was quite a discovery for me, especially her great book *The Human Condition*."[16]

## The Creation of the CREA

The political turning point in France in 1981 marked a major reorientation, as much on the theoretical as on the institutional level, for Jean-Pierre Dupuy. The two conferences at Cerisy and Stanford allowed him to turn the page of the 1970s and to carry on a less hypercritical relationship with modernity. And in the course of the Cerisy conference, in June 1981, a new adventure began over a bottle of Calvados. François Mitterrand had just been elected in May, the rose wave triumphed in June,[17] Jacques Attali had just been named special counsel to the president, and Henri Atlan was a close friend of Attali. All hopes were allowed: the world was going to change. The whole intelligentsia, up until then situated in critical opposition, all at once felt it was approaching the paths to power and the possibility of transforming ideas into material forces, as they said at the time. "A certain number of us were very excited at the idea of creating something."[18]

The objective was to occupy the site at the Montagne Sainte-Geneviève, which had become available when the École Polytechnique relocated to Palaiseau. "Finally, the Montagne brought forth not a mouse, but something much more modest than what we had in mind."[19] Besides, the completion was twofold: on the one hand, the CESTA,[20] which would become Jacques Attali's study center, and, on the other, the Science-Culture group, in which there were some former members of the "group of ten," as well as new researchers.[21] This group was essentially led by Jacques Robin, already the mainstay of the "group of ten," Henri Atlan, and Jean-Pierre Dupuy. An opportunity came up with the appointment of Jean-Marie Domenach as professor of humanities at the École Polytechnique: "Domenach said to me then, 'Why not create a research center tied to my chair at Polytechnique?' And this center was the CREA, of which I took the directorship."[22]

At the outset, there was that intellectual effervescence that came from the top of the Montagne Sainte-Geneviève and the fact that the École Polytechnique did not have a center for philosophical research. The CREA was destined to become this center. "From the beginning, we had two components, a hard one and a soft one."[23] Thus, there was cohabitation between a camp of physicists and mathematicians, who studied connectionist[24] systems and networks, and a camp of social, moral, and political philosophers. At the outset of the venture, the team that really made the CREA function was limited to Jean-Marie Domenach, Paul Dumouchel, a Canadian philosopher, and its director, Dupuy. "At that time, I was interested in logic without really having a background in the area."[25] Dupuy set up an intensive training period that lasted three years, during which the small team had logicians come to study the works of Kurt Gödel, Alan Turing, and others. This training period would lead to the addition of a logician to the CREA, Daniel Andler.

In turn, Andler rapidly proposed that scholars with whom he worked join the CREA, for the most part analytic philosophers: Dan Sperber, from anthropology, François Récanati, Pierre Jacob, Pascal Engel, and Joëlle Proust. A good part of the current CREA team was then in place. It quickly became involved in the vogue that cognitive science was enjoying. The focus on self-organization was effaced little by little to give place to the cognitivist paradigm, more directed toward connectionism.[26] It was the moment that the CNRS launched a study, in 1988, on the new field of research that cognitive science represented. In July 1989, Jean-Pierre Changeux renewed his relationship with the Ministry of Research, which was starting up a broad-ranging program in the area of cognitive science. The CREA was then split into two different teams, one centered on cognitive science and the other on social, moral, and political philosophy. Dupuy was uncomfortable at the rise in power of cognitive science—with the risks of everything getting in its way, "in particular within the sciences of humanity and society"[27]—and decided to modify the structure of the CREA and to fuse the two teams in 1990. "I'm happy with it, because since then there have really been interactions in all directions."[28] Dupuy's concern was really to avoid any form of reductionism, to preserve the connection between cognitive and social science that gives the CREA its originality and allows it to remain faithful to its early orientation in the study of complex phenomena, thereby preserving the margin of autonomy of these phenomena in arrangements characterized by their heterogeneity.

One can measure the price Dupuy paid for his conversion, in which he passed from a comfortable situation as an engineer to one of an intellectual engaged on all the innovative fronts of knowledge, by the number of necessary detours and the labor investments that it required.

## Autopoiesis

Von Foerster, we have said, had advised Dupuy to meet with biologist Francisco Varela. Originally from a small Chilean village perched at 3,200 meters on the cordillera of the Andes, Varela has had an itinerary rich in transdisciplinary crossings and marked by a spatial wandering. When he was six and a half years old, his family settled in Santiago, Chile. There he pursued his university studies and had a decisive meeting with the biologist Humberto Maturana, at first as a student and then as a colleague. His curriculum then was very strictly centered on biology, but Maturana, with whom he was preparing his DEA, favored the multiplicity of his investigations.

Varela received a scholarship that allowed him to pursue his education at Harvard University. So he left Chile in 1968 for the United States; but meanwhile he felt a profound dissatisfaction with the small response to his questionings, which one may qualify as cognitivist *avant la lettre*. He was already interested in the foundation of human cognition, in the way the brain functions. If he did not find a globalizing answer to these questions, the American experience was nonetheless very useful for him. At that time he took advantage of the courses on neurobiology, the seminar of the linguist Noam Chomsky, as well as courses on the ethology of primates and on artificial intelligence.

At twenty-three, he went back to Chile with the intention of contributing his knowledge to his country. His return to Santiago, one week before the election of President Salvador Allende, coincided with a privileged political moment, which allowed a glimpse into possible scientific development in the country. The work with Maturana on the theory of autopoiesis, which would become the axis of his program of cognitive research, dates from this period. But, in 1973, the coup d'état of General Pinochet required Varela to leave his country, along with many committed intellectuals. Without a visa for the United States and with great urgency, he left with his family and a hundred dollars in his pocket for Costa Rica: "It's a wonderful country, very democratic, and I was immediately given a job as a professor of biology."[29] In spite of the charm of this small country, Varela could not stay. He needed a larger framework in which to develop his innovative theses. It was at this time that he met Ivan Illich, who was interested in his manuscript on autopoiesis, and von Foerster, an old friend of Maturana.

Varela set out again for the United States, where he was offered a job in Colorado that he kept for five years. There, he pursued his research on the neurobiological aspects of sensorimotricity and broadened it to include questions of immunology. The results of his efforts were published in 1980.[30] "For the first time, I tried to give an explicit theorization of the question of biological autonomy in the broader sense."[31] In the meantime, the situation improved in Chile and Varela was offered a position at the University of Santiago. Homesickness won out over the perspective of a North American career, and he went back to Chile from 1980 to 1984. Here was the opportunity for him to work with Maturana once again. They wrote a book together that appeared in 1987,[32] and it was during this new period in Chile that the cognitivist problematic was really sketched out, notably with his participation in the two conferences on self-organization directed by Dupuy in Paris and at Stanford. Meanwhile, Varela lost, bit by bit, any hope of effectively contributing to the scientific development of his homeland. Once again he took his distance, in the literal sense, and left for Germany, where he was awarded a fellowship to work for a year at the Max Planck Institute. Dupuy convinced Varela to settle in France in 1986. He got him a position at the CREA, where the transdisciplinary and cognitivist vocation at the time perfectly suited the Chilean scholar.

## Epistemology

The adjunct director of the CREA, Daniel Andler, also came to cognitive science and philosophy on the basis of his original itinerary, because he came from the continent of mathematics. He finished his studies in mathematics at the moment the university opened its doors to young instructors in response to the needs of a student population in the middle of a demographic explosion. Andler began a DEA in mathematics at Orsay in 1967, and at the same time obtained a position as an assistant in mathematics. "I had decided to begin a specialization in mathematics. My curiosity then was of a second degree. I wanted to know what research in mathematics was."[33] This examination at a remove from its object, which one may already term a preoccupation with epistemology, led Andler to specialize in logic, in order to confront the concepts involved in the deployment of mathematical operations. In addition, Andler's curiosity surpassed this classical confrontation, because not only did he aspire then to work in philosophy, but he was also very attracted to literature. He even considered his hidden vocation as a writer to be the most important aspect of his personality. "I had a first vocation, which was literature; a second, philosophy; and a third, which wasn't really a vocation but an interesting job, and that was mathematics."[34]

In the early period, he nevertheless pursued his specialization in mathematical logic, in the theory of models in the tradition of the work of Alfred Tarski; that got him an invitation to the University of California, Berkeley, in 1969, where "my research work really began."[35] The Berkeley campus, an international model of the interdisciplinary spirit in the late sixties, would constitute a highly favorable framework for this beginning. Although Andler knew nothing about cognitive science at the time, little by little the link would be fortuitously made, starting with his thesis in the theory of models, on categoricity. This notion may also be found at the basis of the cognitive approach.

During the same period, at Berkeley, Andler passionately took Hubert Dreyfus's courses on phenomenology. "From those courses

I've kept a respect, and even an affection, for the players in that tradition."[36] The American philosopher Dreyfus held that the program of artificial intelligence (AI) was at an impasse. He contested the triumphalist theses of Edward Teigenbaum, according to which the intelligence of computers was unlimited. Andler would later translate the book in which Dreyfus put forth his critical positions.[37]

Once he obtained his doctorate from Berkeley, Andler returned to France. He then had a long period of transition during which he was dissatisfied with his academic competence in the area of mathematics. It took him until 1981 to escape indecision. The event that brought Andler to the path of philosophy was the Cerisy conference on Karl Popper in the summer of 1981. "I owe Popper my emergence from that preparatory phase. . . . Problematizing and nonessentialist conception opened the possibility for me to work in philosophy."[38] At Cerisy, Andler discovered a freedom of speech that, as a mathematician and beginner in philosophy, he had not yet authorized himself to have: "At the Popper conference, there were open questions, and so I could participate in the dialogue independently of my original labeling."[39] It was then that Andler assumed his status as a philosopher, translated Dreyfus, criticized the latter's arguments, and got involved in two related areas, cognitive science and analytic philosophy. When Dupuy requested his participation in a collaborative research program in the framework of the CREA, he finally acquired the institutional means necessary for his work in epistemology.

## The Philosophy of Mind

Also a researcher with the CREA, Pascal Engel is more classically situated in a philosopher's itinerary, evolving toward the positions of analytic philosophy. Engel is an alumnus of the École Normale Supérieure (ENS), rue d'Ulm, where he took Jacques Derrida's courses. He was then influenced by what is called poststructuralism or post-Nietzscheanism. "I thought of myself as a Deleuzian."[40] At the time, he took Michel Foucault literally when the latter announced that the century would be Deleuzian. So the mentors of his student life were Deleuze, Foucault, and Derrida. But "quickly enough I saw how their work led to a complete impasse."[41]

At the Sorbonne, in the framework of working on his *licence* in philosophy from 1972 to 1974, Engel had a professor of philosophy who would count a great deal in his coming conversion: Jacques

Bouveresse, the great Wittgenstein specialist.[42] The latter introduced him to logic and analytic philosophy. "With Bouveresse I saw that all those things were real problems at the very moment that I realized what an impasse poststructuralism was."[43] Engel later turned to analytic philosophy and plunged into the Anglo-American journals on the theme. "I remember that Althusser wanted the ENS to stop subscribing to those journals."[44]

The other professor who would count for Engel was Jules Vuillemin, who taught at the Collège de France and gave courses in the philosophy of mathematics, epistemology, and the philosophy of science. "With people like Vuillemin and Bouveresse, we had a canonical epistemology. They posed the problems in the manner of the traditional philosophy of science from the twenties."[45] What Engel would no longer tolerate was the split in principle between philosophy and science, which made philosophical discourse into either a repeat of scientific discourse or the deployment of skeptical and nihilist positions. He wondered how a philosopher could fail to be interested in the problem of truth. "When a philosopher reads philosophical theses, he wants to be able to ask himself the question, Is it true or false? What do I think of them and how would I reformulate the same theory or another one on the same subject?"[46]

With a certain number of other very isolated students at the time, Engel found in analytic philosophy the echo of this type of concern. For them it was not a matter of exoticism but of new blood. They began to work on Frege, Russell, and Quine. This small group included Alain Boyer, like Engel a student of Bouveresse; becoming a specialist in Karl Popper and the philosophy of the social sciences in 1975, he joined the CREA too. There was also François Récanati, a specialist in pragmatic linguistics, at the CREA; Pierre Jacob, who left early on to do his studies at Harvard; the logician Jacques-Paul Dubucs,[47] member of the Institut d'Histoire des Sciences—founded by Gaston Bachelard, and later directed by Georges Canguilhem; Jacques Hoarau,[48] also a philosopher, a disciple of Bouveresse. The interest in analytic philosophy of this whole group—to which must be added Claudine Engel-Tiercelin[49] and Ruwen Ogien, who did his thesis on logical empiricism—was awakened early enough by Jacques Bouveresse's 1971 work *La Parole malheureuse*.[50] The same year saw the publication, in the series "L'ordre philosophique," edited by Paul

Ricoeur and François Wahl for Seuil, of Claude Imbert's translations and commentaries of the decisive work of Gottlob Frege.[51]

But this group remained very isolated and little understood. Thus, when Althusser and Derrida asked Engel to give them a presentation on analysis, he was very excited; but he had to calm down when, after presenting analytic philosophy, the two masters reacted, with obvious misunderstanding, by asking Engel what he had to say about psychoanalysis. After completing the *agrégation,* Engel began a doctoral thesis with Bouveresse on proper names in Kripke,[52] then a *thèse d'État*[53] with Gilles-Gaston Granger on Donald Davidson's philosophy of language.[54] And he made his debut with Daniel Andler's team in the sanctuary of cognitivism, the CREA.

# Three

# The Pragmatist Pole

A third innovative direction in the social sciences, the examination of social action, brings together scholars from different disciplines—philosophers, sociologists, economists, historians—who have the same interpretive concern with practical reason restored on the basis of the observation and analysis of human experience.

This new current in the social sciences is strongly inspired by a philosophical detour, which is really indispensable. So we will not be surprised to find the privileged opportunity, in this new conjuncture, for a fertile dialogue among the social sciences, which seem to be seeking a philosophical horizon on the basis of their own problematization; and also for philosophers to turn resolutely to the elucidation of the social, even if the detour they produce remains very speculative.

## The Introduction of Habermas

Among the latter is the French specialist in the thought of Habermas, Jean-Marc Ferry. A precocious philosopher who found a passion for Kant at the age of sixteen, he followed a winding path that quickly made him sensitive to social questions. Ferry taught himself in preparation for the *baccalauréat*, alone in a small village outside Paris, near Mantes-la-Jolie. He was registered at the Center for Television Instruction at Vanves; his passion for philosophy led him to spend a great deal of time meticulously preparing papers, well beyond what was required. When he left secondary school, he registered at the

Institut d'Études Politiques, where he studied law and economic science from 1968 to 1972. At the same time, he did not completely give up his penchant for philosophy, because he participated in the seminars at the Collège de Philosophie that began in the early 1970s. At the outset, it was a matter of assuring a continuation of Jean Wahl's Collège Philosophique. In that circle at the time there was also Ferry's brother Luc, Alain Renaut, Barbara Cassin, and others. "In particular I took the seminars on German idealism."[1]

At the time, Ferry experienced a curious tension between his interests in philosophical speculation and his new professional activities. Indeed, he was led to assume the family business in the area of race-car engines. "I was trained then in a very technical area; there was an urgency, since I was on call from everywhere in France and abroad."[2] The philosopher had to turn his attention to the adjustment of piston ring play and valve clearances, the heat treatment of special alloys, and so on. His competence was not at issue in the difficulties the business would have; but the oil crisis was, as well as the decision of Pierre Messmer, the prime minister at the time, to cancel the car-racing season, symbolically marking the government's will to reduce energy consumption. The immediate effect was catastrophic for the business managed by the new promoter-philosopher Jean-Marc Ferry; nonetheless, he succeeded, even with the serious social crisis, to start again from ground zero and rebuild a profitable company within a year and a half. Once the balance was regained, he sold the family business and could return to his intellectual training.

He began a DEA in sociology at the University of Paris I with Pierre Birnbaum; he took the latter's course on the state and discovered the authors honored by sociology in this area. He was essentially interested then in the mode of functioning of investment capital and studied the international ramifications of the power of large firms. He quickly conceived the necessity of changing the scale of analysis, of no longer thinking in terms of national Keynesian policy in the face of crisis but of redistribution on the planetary scale. "I was thinking then about the necessity of a 'quaternary' sector to accommodate those excluded by large-scale production and automation; the principle of a universal allocation seemed a good idea to me."[3] At the time, this interest in the internal logic of economic policies and the study of its effects did not bear much relation to his involvement with the Collège de Philosophie, where he was working on the canonical texts of German idealism: Kant, Fichte, Hegel, Heidegger, Adorno, and so on.

In 1978, he came to a junction between these two apparently unrelated activities. The occasion presented itself when Ferry was entrusted with the responsibility of critically assessing two books by Habermas that had just been published by Payot in the series edited by Miguel Abensour, "Critique de la politique." The first book was Habermas's thesis, *The Structural Transformation of the Public Sphere,* which dated from 1961 and whose translation was therefore late; the other, a more recent work, *Legitimation Crisis,* dated from 1970. "We were just at the beginning of the reception of this philosopher."[4] The discussion of Habermas's theses at the time was mainly the result of the Marxist current, which saw him as a representative of the Frankfurt School pursuing the work of the criticism of technology and science as ideology. Ferry was more interested in the use Habermas made of the notion of crisis and its functioning in the late-capitalist system. This aspect of Habermas's thought especially enabled him to make the link between his two centers of interest, until then unconnected. "I found this theory of crises original and powerful."[5] It had the advantage of offering a globalizing vision. This vision was based on the idea of the deployment of crises in waves, which began at the economic level and continued through the creation of a global crisis of identity and morality, by way of an administrative crisis of rationality and a crisis of political legitimation.

So Ferry devoted his work for the DEA to Habermas. Then he pursued this research in the framework of a doctoral thesis directed by both Miguel Abensour and Évelyne Pisier. In February 1985, he defended his thesis on the work of Habermas in the Salle Louis-Liard at the Sorbonne.[6] Paul Ricoeur presided over the session; Ferry had recently met him to submit the results of his work. There was a very intense discussion on the relations between two traditions, that of the critique of ideologies, represented by the Frankfurt School, and that of the hermeneutics of traditions of Hans-Georg Gadamer.

Ferry shifted the lines of division by bringing together the two currents. With his thesis located in the heart of the German debate, Ferry had the ambition of accounting for the foundations of legitimacy in modern societies. In the course of this work, he discovered the importance of Karl Otto Apel, who had been the first, beginning in the 1950s, to grasp the importance of Charles Sanders Peirce and Charles

William Morris—not only as a founder of pragmatism and an essential agent in the "linguistic turn," but also as a philosopher proposing an ontology and a logic. Apel is situated in the continuity of the Kantian project of a transcendental philosophy—renewed most notably thanks to the "linguistic turn"—with his account of the major role of language in all ontology. All of Ferry's philosophical work belongs in this pragmatic perspective[7] initiated by Habermas and Apel; it is in line with the globalizing political ambition of the emergence of an ethic of discussion and argumentation on the planetary scale, and thus actively participates in the current change of paradigm in the social sciences.

## The End of "Bourdieusianism"

Among the representatives who today make up this new pragmatic current, Luc Boltanski has had a particularly interesting itinerary. He was in fact Pierre Bourdieu's closest disciple. At the outset, he worked every day with Bourdieu for five years, from 1970 to 1975. "And we were going to write a big book together, on 1968, revolution, social structures."[8] When *Distinction* appeared in 1979, he deemed that Bourdieu was then at the apogee of the deployment of his system of analysis, having become saturated to the point that he could no longer evolve but simply routinize his work. Boltanski vividly felt the inner tension of an intellectual project in which the left hand did not know what the right hand was doing, between the aim of a totally objectified world, without a subject, and a sociology that was supposed to account for the experience of social agents. When *Distinction* appeared, "I was in the middle of writing *Les Cadres*. I told myself that there was nothing left in that paradigm."[9]

In the early 1980s, Boltanski was not fully convinced by the theory of the habitus,[10] which gave him the feeling of being a "black box."[11] In this theory, the actor does not really have a free choice of strategy but is the prey of heterogeneous causal series that play on him and with him. The objective structures remain totally independent of the consciousness of the agents, and they are nonetheless interiorized by the latter who, in exteriorizing them, give them their full effectiveness. To account for this black box, Boltanski thought that one should turn to a cognitive psychology; but such a move seemed impossible to him. So Bourdieu seems to stumble on an aporia by oscillating constantly between a soft version of the habitus, which could be allied with the catchall notion of mentality, and a firmer version, according to which the habitus would determine all behaviors in all situations. "That means nothing; no one can defend such a position."[12]

When Boltanski published *Les Cadres*,[13] his work fit in well with the Bourdieusian perspective, but there were nonetheless visible reorientations. The notion of the habitus was completely absent from the book, to the great surprise of the English-language translator, who wondered, before reading it, how he was going to translate the concept: "What interested me in *Les Cadres* was working on and at the same time departing from naturalism."[14] The objective was to describe how a social group constitutes itself as a political entity. With this retreat, Boltanski reproached himself for not having been sensitive enough to a major dimension, the interrelation between the formation of social categories and that of the nation-state.

Even before the publication of *Les Cadres*, Boltanski was taking his distance from the paradigm of Bourdieusian sociology. He met Bruno Latour in 1978, on the latter's return from the United States, and a great intellectual complicity immediately formed between them; this tie has not subsequently weakened. "I was strongly impressed when I read his manuscript *Irréductions*, as well as his article on the Leviathan."[15] The other decisive meeting is the one Boltanski had, thanks to his friend Alain Desrosières, with the economist Laurent Thévenot. Beginning in 1981, they went to work together on a concrete problem, that of the socioprofessional categories of the INSEE.[16] To the volunteers who were undergoing continuous training, they proposed a two-day workshop to bring out their awareness of the reality of the social structure. The exercises took the form of games: the participants were to classify the census information sheets corresponding to the professions, find coherent sets, then designate a profession representative of a more general interest, and collectively discuss the pertinence of these regroupings. These exercises in social taxonomy allowed the tension to surface between the two possible modes of classification analyzed by cognitive psychologists:[17] nominalist, in the manner of Buffon, or realist, in the manner of Linnaeus. The fruit of this two-year project would be published in an article in English.[18] This research would, among other things, serve to show that the category of managers only formed late and over time, between 1936 and 1950, afterward becoming a major segment of the French social taxonomy.

But beyond the study of management, this collaborative project on the representation of socioprofessional categories enabled Boltanski and Thévenot to discover the reflexive competence of nonspecialists, of common sense, the capacity broadly shared in generalization that surpassed particular cases: "We worked on people's reflexivity."[19] This discovery shook up the sociological paradigm current until then, insofar as it postulated an overarching position for the sociologist, alone considered capable of making intelligible a social reality in which the agents would do nothing but undergo the various mechanisms of manipulation. Now, the collective generation of categorical classifications "showed that the actors were not passive, that they were not merely in bad faith."[20] Placing the reflexive capacities of common sense in evidence invited a renewed interrogation of the "great division," as Bruno Latour calls it, between the scientist and his or her object, between scholarly knowledge and common sensie. Ethnomethodology had already enabled the shifting of this radical separation.[21]

After this inquiry into socioprofessional categories, Boltanski became interested in the question of denouncing injustices. The idea for this research came to him from his study on managers, in the course of which he had encountered many who had been fired from their companies. "I was very struck by the moment of denunciation."[22] Boltanski, interested in the shape of paranoia analyzed by Lacan through the case of Aimée, then became concerned with the distinction people made between cases of denunciation viewed as political and cases viewed as pathological. Speaking with unionists, Boltanski quickly realized that there was no caesura between these two categories of analysis, but rather a constant social process of separation between the two levels and of an elaboration of the collective on the basis of the particular. This sociological study on the processes of generalization, of the socialization of protest, led Boltanski to question another postulate of sociology from the Bourdieusian paradigm: that of the naturally critical, distanced position of the sociologist who gives himself or herself the task of unveiling the normative position of common sense without ever clarifying his or her own normative point of view. It is a paradigm at once critical and axiologically neutral: "And that is absurd. Either one is axiologically neutral and not critical, or one is critical and has a normative position."[23]

For Boltanski, the posture of unveiling pretenses, the bad faith of the actor, implied the flattening of the normative positions of the sociologist. In this perspective, he questioned the epistemological break instituted in the entire tradition of the philosophy of science in France between scientific and common competence. It is a question of "attempting to define a procedure that can give us the means to analyze denunciation as such, and whose object is the critical work effected by the actors themselves."[24] Of course, it is not a matter of denying the contribution of the French epistemological tradition that has insisted on the difference between sensory experience [*expérience*] and the experiment [*expérience*] in the physical sciences. What science tells us about the structures of matter has nothing to do with the perception that we have of it, but a certain sociology has had the tendency to generalize and radicalize this principle so as better to distinguish a scholarly competence from the debris of common knowledge. It is this break in principles that was questioned by Boltanski.

Here we find the same concern as in the anthropology of science of Bruno Latour and Michel Callon, who underscore the necessity of considering "symmetrically" the winners and losers of the great controversies in the history of science. Boltanski's similar preoccupation comes down to shifting the critical position, which was until then the privilege of the sociologist, to the social actor, by thus symmetrizing the two positions. "The idea was that the actors 'perform' the world, and that they perform it through critique."[25] The field experiment effectively revealed the natural competencies of each person to pass from the particular to the general and vice versa.

Boltanski then gave himself the objective of forming a corpus to test his innovative hypotheses. He renewed contact with a certain number of the managers he had met in the course of preparing his first book and who had been involved in the questions of denunciation. Next he looked to the daily papers, with the idea that they would quite certainly have letters of denunciation preserved in the archives. This was the case for *Le Monde,* where he met Bruno Frappat, "a quite extraordinary guy who classified all of that and responded to everything."[26] For three months, then, Boltanski went to *Le Monde* every afternoon to read the archives. He was not allowed to take them out, and so on site he collected three hundred letters from a three-year period, on the basis of which he started a statistical processing "with the idea of producing a grammar of normality, of exploring the common sensibility of normality."[27] He situated this work in the Maussian perspective of the total social fact and of the exploration of the moral categories of common sense. This corpus enabled Boltanski to discover the critical capacity of the actors; he also humorously said at the time that he "could have been an adviser on denunciation."[28]

This study also corresponded with a moment in which the question of freedom of expression in the corporation was being debated. Boltanski wanted to show that this question should be related to the capacity or incapacity of the various forms of protest to reach the public sphere, according to their more or less great conformity with the grammar of denunciation. "My point of view was to open the possibility of expression, people's possibility of protesting."[29] Boltanski therefore involved himself in reading these denunciations according to the axis of the particular and the general, of the personal and the public. The most commonly denounced scandal is indeed that of the use of a social position in the service of the common good to advance personal interests. The other dimension to elucidate was people's constant concern, in the act of denunciation, with aggrandizing themselves to gain access through their protest to the public sphere of generalization. This idea of greatness would become essential in the new paradigm of Boltanski and Thévenot: they were struck by its importance, but also by its plurality, the fact that different forms of grandeur of a heterogeneous nature exist. It was thus with this study that they would escape the single axis of the particular and the general, by observing the multiplication of possible ways of passing from one point to another of grandeur. This project of pluralization around the construction of different "Cities" would lead to a fundamental work, *Les Économies de la grandeur.*[30]

## The Investment of Forms

Boltanski's reorientations are indissociable from those of Thévenot, who came from economics (after finishing at the École Polytechnique, he studied at the ENSAE[31] to become an administrator at the INSEE). Thévenot had, from this point of view, an itinerary similar to that of certain economists from the school of regulation, such as Robert Boyer or Michel Aglietta. For Thévenot, who was born in 1949, the choice to study economics was tied, as it was for his entire generation, to the desire to involve himself in social questions in a particularly effervescent climate, that of the late sixties: "The INSEE was an incredible political nesting ground. The entire leftist movement was represented there."[32] Very quickly, Thévenot developed a passion for questions of classification in social categories. Confronted with problems of a sociological order, he discovered the author who then dominated studies of that type, Pierre Bourdieu: "He was going the farthest in the problems of category."[33] Thévenot's elder, Alain Desrosières, played an essential role for him: he was also working at the INSEE and was already close to Bourdieu, who needed statistical data for his sociological modelizations. So Thévenot very quickly became an unorthodox economist. In the years 1975–77, he gained a background in sociology, which seemed to suit his expectations better.

When he became a member of Bourdieu's group, Thévenot met Boltanski, with whom he would conduct several highly fertile projects. "He was a complete 'Bourdieusian' then, but his was a very inventive mind that sought connections with psychology, and Bourdieu looked ill on that."[34] The moment of this meeting between the economist and the sociologist was quite propitious, because it corresponded with a questioning of the nomenclatures in use and thus with a possibility of rethinking them along different lines. The empirical work Boltanski and Thévenot undertook on representations, on the manner in which people spontaneously keep themselves at a distance in relation to official classifications, enabled them to make the link among statistical instruments, the state, and sociology.

On the basis of this study, Boltanski and Thévenot effected a major break with the Bourdieusian schema, as they took seriously the judgments and representations of those they studied. "That was related to taking distance from the philosophy of suspicion,"[35] which had the habit of seeking to unveil the actor's speaking, postulating that the truth was hidden behind it—whereas "one can't be totally outside. . . . One is on the lookout for people's competence."[36] Bourdieu's initial model of collective mutual representations was undone as the empirical study went along; in the course of it, the crucial importance of moral judgments showed through, taking shape behind the questions of classification.

At the same time, Thévenot returned in a new way to his original discipline, economics, with his research on "investments of form."[37] Here, he proclaimed a broadened definition of the notion of investment, "which could account for the entire range of operations of formation"[38] through institutional objects and techniques, misunderstood by classical economic theory. This work marked the emergence of a new field, that of the economics of convention. Since 1983,

Thévenot has cooperated with François Eymard-Duvernay in the framework of a research seminar at the INSEE. Thévenot planned a research project at the INSEE then, the results of which would be published in 1984 under the title *Économie et formes conventionnelles*.[39] This orientation, different from the one pursued by Pierre Bourdieu, is nonetheless strongly marked by a reflection on the notions of category. Now, Thévenot's orientation involving the "investment of forms" consists of investigating the cognitive character of material tools. Thus, Frederick Winslow Taylor's *Principles of Scientific Management*, dating from 1911, includes a whole repertory of instruments of formation whose adjustment must produce a certain number of mechanisms of scientific organization: the tool, the chassis, the slide rule, the chronometer, the measurement, the task, the written instructions, the price, the subsidy, the workers' training, the close collaboration between management and labor—that is, quite a varied list. ("There are workshop tools of production to be found; instruments, schemata, conventions, formulas drawn from the exact sciences; precepts attached to educational methods; arrangements for prescribing that are close to military uses; ways of remuneration used in industry; principles, advice, or examples for orienting one's way of acting.")[40]

This horizon would logically lead Thévenot to the CREA in the early 1980s. It was at Stanford, in the university cafeteria, that Jean-Pierre Dupuy proposed that Thévenot come to the CREA, which thus picked up the program in the economics of convention. This new orientation really emerged as a new school of economists, which would notably express itself as such in a special issue of the *Revue économique* on the economics of convention.[41]

## From within Orthodoxy

Among these economists, Olivier Favereau had a traditional economist's itinerary. He did his university studies at the school of economic sciences in Paris. Born in 1945, he took his DEA in 1969. But he already had an intellectual curiosity that exceeded the strict economics program, as he registered at the Political Science Institution, studied at the ENA[42] and, as he says, "the chance of my lifetime was to be one of the first to be failed at the ENA."[43]

In 1970, Favereau proposed a thesis in economic theory on the level of employment in a growing economy. This study would be for him the very terrain of experimentation in upsetting the paradigm;

that would delay the completion of his thesis, and he would not defend it until twelve years later, in late 1982. This exceptionally long period came from the fact that Favereau was dissatisfied with the classical instruments of economics: "I continually needed to go looking for other tools."[44] Even in the most sophisticated economics, he found only "monstrosities" on the descriptive level to account for the employment market. He then researched more realistic elements and discovered the American institutionalist trend,[45] which had put at the forefront the rules of regulation practiced by corporations in the management of their personnel. "What served me as a guiding thread on the theoretical plane was the idea of coordination by rules."[46]

This broadening of view in relation to the schema of classical economics had the advantage of being audible to orthodox economists, and thus Favereau could easily enter the circle of economists at the University of Paris I, without appearing to be too unorthodox a scholar who spoke to them esoterically, especially in view of the fact that he became friends with a small group led by Pierre-Yves Hénin, the current director of the CEPREMAP,[47] who made practical contributions to converting the circle of economists to mathematical economics. Favereau wrote his thesis with Hénin; thus he belongs in a certain way to orthodox economics in that he followed the movement of the discipline's formalization.

Taking note that marginal or unorthodox economists have failed to be understood and so have never succeeded in moving the corpus of classical economics, Favereau deemed that the best strategy consisted of situating himself within the orthodoxy of economic theory in order to examine a few isolated aspects of it and thus to measure the limits of their coherence. He proceeded on the basis of a rereading of Simon, Piore, Doeringer, and Keynes, and that enabled him to give credibility to new instruments of analysis.

Favereau was notably interested in the way in which Keynes's *General Theory* in fact contains two research projects: Keynesian discourse deliberately juxtaposes very conservative elements and a veritable reservoir of fundamentally heretical ideas that Keynes left hidden so as not to go against the milieu in which he wanted to produce effects. It may even be said that Favereau, exploring the Keynesian arguments from the inside,[48] would adopt this argumentative tension in order to shift in turn the boundaries of economics according to its own discourse. "That made me really attentive to the way of discussing, of working in a really weighty orthodoxy that at the same time had its power."[49] After his thesis and completion of the *concours d'agrégation,* Favereau right away became a professor in Mans for four years, and since 1988 has been at the University of Paris X-Nanterre.

## The Manifesto of Conventions

A major moment of crystallization of the reflection on rules, involving a small group of economists, would correspond to the publication of a special issue of the very old and canonical *Revue économique* devoted to the economics of convention.[50] In this publication, Favereau played the role of the one who would bring together very diverse studies, with the major asset of being recognized by his equals as a true economist and thus the possibility of being heard. For some time, Favereau had worked with François Eymard-Duvernay, Laurent Thévenot, Robert Salais, and the CREA, where for years he had taken all the seminars. He had even, after his *agrégation,* become a member of the teams of the CREA at the invitation of Jean-Pierre Dupuy. It was in the course of a lunch with Eymard-Duvernay and Salais "that we told each other we should try to take advantage of all the ties we had. It was Robert Salais's idea to propose a special issue of the *Revue économique* on the economics of rules and institutions."[51] Everyone then brought in another participant to prepare an issue completely devoted to this theme. Favereau requested the collaboration of Dupuy; Salais invited André Orléan; and Eymard-Duvernay secured the participation of Thévenot.

Now, what was prepared was much more than a mere journal issue—it was a common elaboration of the milestones in a new approach to economics. A true collective task was begun, and it lasted for more than a year. The authors had more and more meetings during which they presented to one another the state of progress of their articles, as they had the idea of producing a coherent issue. This concern for a collective presentation pushed Favereau to refuse the offer from the *Revue économique* to shoulder responsibility for the issue. Thus, the issue opens with a collaborative text, an introduction signed by the six authors: "The different research projects brought together in this issue have in common the development of the hypothesis . . . that the agreement of individuals, even when it is limited to the contract of a market exchange, is not possible without a common framework, without a constitutive convention."[52] At the last moment, the provisional theme of the economics of rules and institutions appeared to the group to be a little heavy, and seemed to give a poor account of the new venture that the publication of this issue enabled. At the last stage of work, Salais and Thévenot proposed to change the title, choosing "The Economics of Convention" ("L'économie des conventions"), which had a "respectable obscurity."[53] But, above all, it allowed the acknowledgment of the twofold aspect of rules, in the sense of regulation and of the procedures of construction of the rules themselves.

The adventure of the economics of convention was beginning. If the CREA as such did not, despite the presence of Dupuy and André Orléan, play a decisive role in the emergence of this issue of the *Revue économique,* it was important with regard to the economists to maintain the presence of a "respectable heterodoxy."[54] The scientific radiance of the CREA, the reference to the École Polytechnique, and the dynamism of cognitive science offered a guarantee to the economics of convention. This field in addition constituted one of the research foci of the CREA, which was an active party in the 1992 creation of a DEA in the economics of institutions involving three establishments of learning: the École des Hautes Études en Sciences Sociales, Paris X-Nanterre, and the École Polytechnique. The instruction in this DEA involves specialists in the economy of organizations, institutions, and conventions, as well as certain scholars of orthodox theory, because also taught there is the new microeconomics centered on contracts and incentives: "It's the first time the École Polytechnique is associated with a DEA in economics."[55] The seminars for this DEA take place at the Institut International de La Défense, where Thévenot and Favereau teach (these two had to give up, for innumerable reasons, their institutional affiliation with the CREA, although their intellectual adherence to the Center's research has not changed at all).

Favereau has also reorganized the economic research groups at Nanterre by creating one associated with the CNRS in 1993, the FORUM,[56] which allowed different groups to come together around common institutionalist perspectives. All these teams begin with the acknowledgment of empirical problems that must be resolved and with the necessity of submitting them to economic theory. Among these problems, the FORUM has taken up the study of the regulation of national economies in a space of multiple systems—of the transition toward a market economy, both in the Third World and in the economies of the former Communist countries—as well as that of the massive development of unemployment pretty much everywhere. "The idea is to give an explicit institutional form to the resurgence of institutionalism."[57] The problem cutting across the various fields of investigation is that of how a group, a corporation, a collectivity, or a country can mobilize its resources according to a new mode of collective initiation. One may find here the same concern as in the anthropology of science with the examination of the process of social creativity.

## The Importation of Ethnomethodology

Particular attention to social acting and its forms of enunciation may also be found in the work of sociologist Louis Quéré, who has contributed a great deal to the awareness in France of studies in ethnomethodology. In a think tank on the epistemology of the social sciences, little by little he sketched a "descriptive" program in sociology. Quéré began his intellectual life with clerical studies. As a seminarian, he was influenced by questions of hermeneutics, by a solid background in exegesis. At the same time, he became familiar with the social sciences; his teacher, Jacques Jullien, the current archbishop of Rennes, introduced him to anthropology, and in particular Claude Lévi-Strauss, between 1965 and 1968. The movement of May 1968 sounded the death knell of his career in the church, and Quéré then moved into the university.

He abruptly found himself in the Maoist current of the University of Rennes in the fall of 1968, in the department of sociology. He then traded the Marx of Calvez—the Jesuit specialist in Marx's thought[58]—for the "Althusserized" Marx of Nicos Poulantzas. During these effervescent years, the attraction of Paris prompted Quéré to leave Rennes to finish his studies in sociology at the Sorbonne. Next he turned to the École des Hautes Études en Sciences Sociales (EHESS), where Alain Touraine was, directing the Center for the Study of Social Movements. Under Touraine's direction, Quéré prepared a thesis on regionalist movements, which at the time represented the "secondary fronts" of a very hypothetical future revolution. His adherence to Touraine's positions brought him for the first time to distance himself from critical sociology, whether Bourdieusian or Althusserian. "It was Touraine's interest in the question of historicity that hooked me."[59] Indeed, Touraine had brought into focus, in order to understand the modernity of social conflicts, a "system of historical action," which he had explained in his 1973 work *The Self-Production of Society.* In it he defended a dynamic conception of the social system, in which the historical dimension of social organizations played a major role in grasping the "network of oppositions."[60]

At the same time, Quéré learned from the reflections on history of Claude Lefort and Marcel Gauchet, beginning with the journal *Textures.* Quéré was interested in the essentially cultural dimension of the regionalist movements, in the heart of which may be found the question of defending the language community. "I was interested in the question of what happens when one gets to the language of a community."[61] He was then struck by the artificiality of the political defense of a language in relation to the problem of its survival. The intellectuals engaged in the defense of normalized and codified regional languages seemed to be impotent in assuring their perpetuation in the people's everyday life. Putting this discord into evidence "counted in the maturation of my interest in questions of language."[62]

This interest in regional languages led Quéré back to his native region, Brittany. He was interested in the role of the great daily newspaper *Ouest-France,* a genuine regional institution, and scrutinized the relation the paper wove with its territory. The Althusserian instruments—such as the ideological state apparatus or simply the theory of reflection—were in no way illuminating, and it was Habermas who enabled him to open his inquiry to a new theoretical horizon.[63] The confrontation between Habermas and Gadamer held Quéré's attention as he sought a path between critical sociology and hermeneutics. He worked toward understanding the implication for the social sciences of the fact that their object was constituted through self-understanding. The particular situation of the social object credited with a language-based constitution posed the problem of the status of a hermeneutic procedure as a credible paradigm for sociology. This dimension led Quéré to take his distance from Tourainian sociology. "What was a problem for me in this type of procedure was that it didn't take into consideration the fact that one constituted the object itself by incorporating self-understanding."[64]

In the dynamic of these investigations, in the early eighties Quéré turned to ethnomethodology, which seemed to him to account even more for the dimension of language and the signification of the social object. This discovery of ethnomethodology alerted him to the necessity of interrogating the categories sociology used to study its object.

At the same time, Quéré shifted his investigative work toward the study of ordinary communication. The publication of his *Des miroirs équivoques*[65] represented "more or less the turning point"[66] for him. In it, he studied the modifications undergone by society when the structure of its symbolic and technical possibilities of communication are radically transformed. He attempted a synthesis between his own theoretical heritage, whose importance he recognized ("of the great contemporary figures in social and political thought—Habermas, Lefort, and Touraine in particular. This book is in debt to them"),[67] and new theoretical perspectives, those of the ethnography of communication, the studies of Erving Goffman,[68] and conversational analysis.

In 1982–83, Quéré began a "seminar in epistemology" at the Center for the Study of Social Movements at the EHESS, which would become a think tank for the elaboration of a new sociology. It would play a major role notably in the circulation of the theses of ethnomethodology. Scholars came to participate in the seminar: Patrick Pharo, Bernard Conein, Renaud Dulong, and Alain Cottereau. Here the texts of Harold Garfinkel and Harvey Sacks were translated and discussed, and the group complemented its reflection with a workshop publication, on grey note paper, the best known of which is the one devoted to ethnomethodological arguments.[69] Progressively, Quéré broke with the nomological model of Durkheimian sociology, that is, with the perspective of the construction of a social physics.

## From Interactionism to Ethics

Among this group of sociologists, Patrick Pharo was perhaps the most profoundly marked by the movement of May 1968: he had a period of social activism outside the university that lasted almost ten years, from 1968 to 1977, after finishing his studies in philosophy at the Sorbonne. Beginning in 1977, he continued his education, and did a doctoral thesis in the sociology of knowledge. In the course of his long detour, he had done fieldwork, notably as a professional counselor in employment agencies, then in the form of studies on the living conditions of workers and peasants. All this field experience led him to inquire into the "category of meaning in social analysis."[70] On the theoretical level, what is in his eyes most suggestive for the deployment of his work on the meaning of action may be found in Max Weber:[71] "In a certain way, I see my work as a small footnote to the first twenty pages of *The Theory of Social and Economic Organization* on the meaning of social activity."[72]

The return to theoretical sociology carried Pharo to the philosophical shores of the years of his early education. While deeming that Bourdieu and Lévi-Strauss represented the central contribution to the social sciences, he investigated the category of freedom, the place of consciousness, and returned to the "only discipline in which I was educated, phenomenology."[73] So he went back to the texts of Husserl, which remained for him the major repository of knowledge. But he was also interested in the extensions of the moral and political philosophy of Kant and Locke. Another philosophical trend with which he was not familiar interested him, insofar as it had already traced the path to the category of meaning: that of Frege, Russell, and Wittgenstein.

In the 1980s, Pharo participated, along with Louis Quéré, in the introduction of ethnomethodology in France. Meanwhile, he was more interested in the ethical than the epistemological dimension of reflection on the social sciences; he joined the Center for the Sociology of Ethics, created and directed by François-André Isambert (replaced since his retirement by Paul Ladrière), whose interests are very diverse (bioethics, law, analytic moral philosophy, and so on). He then became a specialist in the study of phenomena of "civility."[74] In addition to his very diverse empirical areas of interest, he is in the process of constructing a general sociology centered on the ethical dimension of the social bond, around two concerns: that of the problem of the normativity of law and that of the objectivity of signification, which poses the question of whether there is in action, feeling, and relation something on the order of the objective, and by what means it could be discovered.

## A Historicized Sociology in Search of a Language

Bernard Conein also participated in this group of pragmatist sociologists. Nonetheless, he was situated on the interface between the orientation defined by Louis Quéré and that of cognitive science. His path is made up of many ruptures and punctuated by continually new discoveries. An assistant to Nicos Poulantzas in sociology at the University of Paris VIII-Vincennes in 1970, he began to experience a true aversion for sociology and sought his salvation then among historians. He asked Robert Mandrou to direct a thesis on the massacres of September 1792 in the Paris region. Conein then plunged himself into the archives with a hypothesis in mind: to verify and apply the schema of Michel Foucault's *Discipline and Punish* to the Reign of Terror. He interpreted all the movements of popular public execution that occurred between 1789 and 1792 as the expression of punitive conceptions by the penal type of justice. "The executions were of this type, with the drawing and quartering of the bodies, but the archives had been carefully hidden by the Soboulians."[75] The idea was already to take into account, beyond the conflict among schools of interpretation over the Reign of Terror, the mental models of the various protagonists of the Revolution.

Conein chose a diverse jury for the defense of his thesis, which took place in 1978: Jean-Claude Passeron, Alain Touraine, Robert Mandrou, and Michel Vovelle. With the French Revolution as his object, Conein came across Régine Robin and Jacques Guilhaumou, who were at the cutting edge of discourse analysis in the field of history. He joined the research group that Michel Pêcheux[76] had set up, called Analyzing and Reading Archives. "This was at once very stimulating and a total intellectual failure."[77]

The tragic death of Pêcheux, who committed suicide in 1982, would bring on the immediate disappearance of his research group. Conein then found himself in a complex situation, because he felt behind as much in relation to sociologists as to historians.

Faced with admitting the failure of the instruments hitherto at his disposal, he undertook his pragmatic turn around 1981: "I began to read Searle and Austin."[78] At the same time, he discovered ethnomethodology, thanks to his friend Nicolas Herpin.[79] Herpin had drawn up a panorama of the main currents of American sociology in which he introduced ethnomethodology for the first time in France. He proposed that Conein get to know some of Sacks's unpublished lectures. "I began to read them and was really dazzled at that time."[80] Killed in a car accident in 1975, Harvey Sacks, the creator of conversational analysis, had left only scattered articles. Now, Herpin was in possession of numerous unpublished transcripts of Sacks's talks. It was at this time that Conein met Louis Quéré and Renaud Dulong. The latter provided a necessary connection, because he was at once a former member of Michel Pêcheux's research group and involved in research in the epistemology of the social sciences with Quéré. In this way, a study group was built on the texts of Sacks and Garfinkel.

Before starting the "grey journal," the group decided to organize a conference on the theme "Describing: An Imperative?"[81] The central question was why description did not have a status in sociology, whereas it did in linguistics. When the conference was about to begin, the organizing committee learned that Harold Garfinkel was in London and invited him to present his theses. "He arrived and, all at once, the conference was transformed by his presence."[82] After the conference, the small group that published the first issue of the journal *Problèmes d'épistémologie en sciences sociales* was formed. Conein was the most enthusiastic among the group about the possibilities that conversational analysis opened, whereas Patrick Pharo was somewhat removed, and Quéré "called himself Garfinkelian and not Sacksian."[83] Differences in interpretation came to light and made the appearance of unity in the camp of French ethnomethodology more tricky. Nonetheless, in 1986, Conein organized a conference with Michel de Fornel and Quéré on the topic "The Forms of Conversation," during which Garfinkel came again to present his theses. At the same time, Conein began a turn toward cognitive science, which would lead him to the construction of a "social cognition."

## The Mental Equipment of Historians

One may also detect this pragmatic turn among a certain number of historians. Gérard Noiriel belongs to this generation, which today is renewing the already traditional history through a concern to reconcile two traditions, that of comprehensive sociology and that of the historian's writing. He intends to promote a "subjectivist approach to the social."[84] In the wake of Lucien Febvre, he advocates a practical epistemology for the purpose of constructing an autonomous social history. The subjectivist paradigm allows for the recuperation of what a purely quantitativist approach removed. It must grant a full place to lived experience, for a long time the poor relative of the scientific aims of historians. "The subjectivist approach thus invites us to a whole critical task that aims to question anew the evidence of the everyday, to see in all the things that seem natural to us an arbitrary product of social history."[85]

This social history thus leads to a research program devoted to the modes of objectification of knowledge, to the various implications of the past in present society. In the beginning, Noiriel undertook a very classical thesis in social history: under Madeleine Rebérioux's direction, in the late 1970s he worked on the situation of steelworkers and on the miners of the Lorraine basin of Longwy between the wars.

This research, which unfolded at the moment of the great strikes of 1979–80 in the Lorraine region, gave Noiriel the opportunity for a first publication with the Maspero publishing house.[86] It was a political book that described the sudden disappearance of a world. At the time, Noiriel was a secondary school teacher in the region. He was therefore both a historian of what happened and an actor in his capacity as a teacher and communist militant: "That was decisive, insofar as I was at once working with the concept of the long period, for reasons that have to do with the admiration I had for Fernand Braudel."[87] Rather than brandishing the Little Red Book, Noiriel preferred the "little yellow book, Braudel's *On History.*"[88]

At the outset of this research, everything seemed quite coherent between his political engagement, his thesis at Paris VIII, and the very determined strikes of Lorraine. Nevertheless, he would quickly sense a profound discord between the scientific analyses of that crisis and what he was living on the inside of it: the diagnostics were content with a purely synchronic look, whereas to comprehend the extent of the mobilization and its forms, it was necessary to pass through history. In his eyes, the movement expressed a profound identity crisis, striking a group marked by immigration. "It was historically the first region opened to immigration since the beginning of the century."[89] This aspect would largely orient his subsequent studies, which would go beyond the limits of the Lorraine region.

The thesis, which he defended in 1982,[90] does not yet systematically explore the disparity he felt. It still remains classical in relation to what was then called social history, in the globalizing perspective that integrates the histories of technology and of labor, separating economic, social, and political history into three successive strata. The question to which Noiriel would later respond, as his thesis was limited to the period between the wars, is why the mobilization of this group of workers strongly marked by Italian immigration unfolded behind a whole, very nationalist symbolic, the cross of Lorraine, the children of Lorraine, and so on. "From that moment, I noticed that this problematic could function on the national level."[91] The French specificity seemed to him to be in the heterogeneous character of a working class less marked by the constitutive break of the industrial revolution than its English and German neighbors. In France, immigration was right away a necessary component to feed the labor market. Although the history of immigration was a little-explored field in

French historiography, Noiriel inhabited it brilliantly and published several works on the theme.[92]

Noiriel had no intention at all of deserting the terrain of social history, somewhat neglected for several years. On the contrary, he intended to surpass the restrictive conception of many studies in the area that limited social history to the history of social classes. "When I say social history, it means sociological history. . . . The paradigm of the layers of a cake no longer functioned, and I noticed that in the empirical work for my thesis."[93]

Noiriel realizes that social reality is not the mechanical derivative of a succession of categories, of "layers," separated from one another—the social, the political, the juridical, and so on; for the social actors are led to take into consideration these various levels at the same time. Thus, when the decree of 1888 required individuals, who until then traveled freely, to state their national identities, it involved a juridicopolitical phenomenon that penetrated to the deepest level of social identity, and therefore indicated that "the political is in the social."[94] Noiriel's analytic work has thus moved progressively toward the ways in which personal identities are structured. To do this, he installed the historian's projector, in the manner of sociologists, on the brim of the concrete and of social acting, by deconstructing the overarching position of the historical scholar so as better to restore the common competencies of the actors.

*Four*

# The Pole of Reglobalization
# through the Political

Among the efforts causing the horizon of the social sciences to move
in a new direction, there is a fourth focus that considers the political
as the means to rethink the social in a different way. It is not a matter
of a return to the old Lavissian[1] political history, but of a more philosophical approach to the political, broadly influenced by the reflection
on totalitarianism by the former Socialism or Barbarism current of
Claude Lefort and Cornelius Castoriadis.

## The Passion of Debate
In this movement was to be found, among others, Marcel Gauchet,
the editor in chief of the journal directed by Pierre Nora, *Le Débat*.
Gauchet discovered Socialism or Barbarism early on. In 1962, studying at the École Normale des Instituteurs in Saint-Lô, he was sixteen
when he met Didier Anger, an active militant at the emancipated
École. The very politicized atmosphere of the École Normale was polarized between the Communists and this small anti-Stalinist group in
which Gauchet counted the majority of his friends. He left La Manche
for the Lycée Henri-IV to prepare for the entrance examination at the
École Normale Supérieure of Saint-Cloud. But he reacted badly to
the confined atmosphere of the Parisian lycée, and so left to teach in La
Manche; at the same time, he took a course of studies in philosophy,
taking his *licence* and *maîtrise*.

The most important moment in Gauchet's itinerary occurred in

1966, when he was taking Claude Lefort's classes at the University of Caen. "With Lefort, I was bitten by the call to politics."[2] Lefort counted a lot for Gauchet—not only because Gauchet allowed him "to warn him of a few fatal errors from which I had no particular motive to escape,"[3] but more broadly on the intellectual level, because it determined his orientation and interest in philosophy in its political aspect. "I owe that impulse to him."[4] The primacy of the political drove Gauchet to a veritable craving for knowledge. He then began the preparation for three *licences* at the same time: in philosophy, history, and sociology. He sought to radicalize his break with the Marxist vulgate and deemed that Lefort remained too attached to Marx, who still represented the bulk of his teaching. For his part, Gauchet did not hesitate, as they said at the time, to throw out the baby with the bathwater; to complete the necessary break with Marxism, it was necessary to oppose an alternative to it. It was from the field of history that he saw the possibility of a genuine response, in conceiving a "theory of alternative history."[5] Evidently, May 1968 filled Gauchet with joy: he immediately saw in the movement the very expression of what he had been thinking. "I lived it in happiness and enthusiasm, naturally."[6] He fully participated in the movement in its dominant, spontaneous component, and always made the regular shuttle between Caen and Paris. He could only rejoice at the shaking of the institutional structures, whether Gaullist or Communist.

With May 1968, Gauchet began his involvement with journals. He has especially been known as the chief of *Le Débat* since 1980, but his interest and involvement in the activity of journals goes back to the immediate aftermath of 1968. In 1970, he met Marc Richir, who had directed a small Belgian journal of the generation of '68, *Textures*. Together they decided to start it again on a new basis, with Lefort and Castoriadis on the editorial board. *Textures* would last until 1976. In 1977, the opportunity to start a mass-market journal for the Payot publishing house presented itself; the team broadened to include Pierre Clastres and Miguel Abensour, and the journal *Libre* was created.

These two journals had a political end through their antitotalitarian engagement, and they aimed more broadly at favoring intellectual exchanges. Meanwhile, when *Libre* debuted in its venture, the intellectual configuration was modified to the point of very quickly making the enterprise unviable. The collapse of the French Communist Party, its sectarian withdrawal after the 1978 break with the Socialist

Party, as well as the bursting on the scene of the "new philosophers," created a new situation. For many, the antitotalitarian question became a closed case, but in a way that affected the very conditions of intellectual life: the "fluff-media" tended to be substituted for reasoned debate. Besides, "it was becoming clear that a certain type of intellectual had passed on."[7]

It was in this context that *Libre* disappeared and that a new venture began in 1980 with Pierre Nora and the launching of the journal *Le Débat* at the Gallimard publishing house. This new journal broke with anathema, exclusion, the style of cliques, to place itself better in the heart of the contemporary debates, without barring anyone, with the sole criterion of competence. Thus would Gauchet, with Nora, make *Le Débat* the echo chamber of the innovative orientations in the social sciences, beginning in the 1980s.

## Antiutilitarianism

Alain Caillé, another admirer of and participant in the journal, shares with Gauchet the strong impression made by Claude Lefort and attendance at the University of Caen in the 1960s. Caillé is situated at the intersection of economics and sociology, but the political dimension of phenomena remains on the horizon of his own research and the group he formed, to the point where in his last book he examines the "forgetting of the political" that condemns the social sciences to an impasse.[8]

After completing a doctorate in economics, Caillé registered for graduate work in sociology under the direction of Raymond Aron. "I wanted to do a thesis on planning as the ideology of bureaucracy."[9] He discovered then, in 1965, the Socialism or Barbarism articles on Soviet totalitarianism, particularly those of Lefort. He went to see Aron, who advised him to work on the subject with Lefort. While Caillé was waiting for a position as an assistant in economic science, one in sociology opened up at the University of Caen in 1967, and Lefort offered it to him. Trained in economics, he then found himself in sociology, even though he had just abandoned his idea of a thesis in sociology in order to return to his early background. "I followed both those tracks for a long time."[10]

This institutionally unstable position, which made peer recognition more delicate, prompted Caillé to play the "spoiler of all-encompassing thought" by constantly questioning and shifting the boundaries of thought and the disciplines. With Lefort and Gauchet, he conceived sociology in the broadest sense as a site of confluence, of convergence of the set of discourses conducted on society, in a perspective in which the field was cut off from neither philosophy nor economics. "We read the philosophers, the psychiatrists, Freud, ethnology, all at once—that was sociology."[11]

If he was close to Lefort, Caillé remained insensitive to the former's phenomenological considerations. Reflecting today on the influence that Lefort had on him, he judges it "considerable, but in the negative":[12] it played a major role in the affirmation of his critical thought, but without offering a constituted paradigm to be positively advanced. ("He implicitly conveyed to me a series of prohibitions, in the good sense of the term.")[13] Caillé situated his work in the tradition of the great classical sociology, that of Émile Durkheim and Max Weber. What attracted him to this sociology was precisely its capacity to answer the questions of political philosophy by other means than those of the philosophers. Finally, before fully devoting himself to sociology, Caillé defended a thesis in economics in 1974, on the ideology of economic rationality.

In the late 1960s, he had the impression of seeing the rebirth of a vulgar economism from the ashes, from the pen of sociologists as different as Raymond Boudon and Pierre Bourdieu. He decided to denounce this orientation, which in his eyes could only lead sociology to an impasse. He then defended an economic anthropology against the diverse forms of utilitarian reduction of social behavior.[14] Caillé surrounded himself with a small group that started, without support from any institution or publisher, the Bulletin du MAUSS in 1982. This journal was placed under the patronage of the master of French sociology that Marcel Mauss was, and was affirmed as the support of a research program defined by the very title of MAUSS (Mouvement Anti-Utilitariste dans les Sciences Sociales—Antiutilitarian Movement in the Social Sciences). Begun on the basis of this fortunate polysemy, the bulletin continues to have a workshop quality, poor circulation (with no more than five hundred readers), often defying in its typographical poverty the elementary rules of legibility. Nevertheless, it has played a very important role in questioning the utilitarian paradigm that was dominant in the social sciences during the 1980s.[15]

Caillé's journal contributed a lot to asking the old questions anew, the questions that had been repressed and totally forgotten since the writings of Durkheim, Mauss, and Polanyi. With regard to Marxism, Caillé, who had allied himself with it, turned his back on it beginning in the mid-1970s:

> I remember very well an episode that made an impression on me. I was giving my course in sociology at Caen in 1975, and I was still trying to say that one may criticize Marx, but in such and such a way. . . . At that moment, a long-haired guy, about thirty, whom I didn't know, came into the room, listened for fifteen minutes, and then declared, "Marx is dead! Let him die!" Then he got up and left. For me, he was the exterminating angel, or the herald. I finished my class, somewhat disturbed, and I said to myself he was right.[16]

Caillé would then devote himself to giving value to another language in the social sciences. To the dominant utilitarian reason, he would oppose the spirit of the gift according to Marcel Mauss's schema, that of giving/receiving/returning, this threefold relation finalized by the necessity of the social bond.

## The Trinity versus Stammering

The triangular relation, the ternary figure opposed to binary enclosure, is at the heart of the highly original work of Dany-Robert Dufour.[17] The question of the social bond is also found on the horizon of his research, but in a more symbolic than sociological sense. He did his university studies in 1966–70, in the department of art history at the University of Nancy. In these engaged years, Dufour was a Maoist militant with the Proletarian Left. Occasionally, it happened that he yielded to ritual to obtain the required diplomas, but on condition that it did not take too much of the time he devoted to the "cause of the people," which could not suffer.

When he began the DEA in philosophy in 1971, he "established" himself in a factory, as did a certain number of Maoist militants of his generation. Not far from Nancy, he was hired as a worker at the Vittel mineral water plant. "I worked at night in a state of total exhaustion. I didn't see or understand a thing, since everyone I worked with was Portuguese."[18] Dufour was treated harshly by the workers in his shop, as his state of fatigue did not allow him to follow the infernal pace. When, two weeks after his arrival at the plant, a major sit-in strike broke out, he took the mike and became the natural spokesman of the movement. Everyone then believed that this stray had been the leftist instigator of the permanent disorder that would henceforth reign in the plant. Groups of young people even committed acts of sabotage, and that confirmed the suspicions of management with regard to this "dangerous leftist," who was condemned by default to a strict sentence of eighteen months in prison. Dany "the Red" made an appeal in Paris a year later and the sentence was reduced to four months. "So I stayed in prison four months, and it did me a lot of good."[19]

Paradoxically, it was in prison that Dufour learned to read something other than the classics of Marxism-Leninism. So he spent the summer of 1973 behind bars, as did a certain number of Maoist militants, and he considers this time essential to his intellectual maturation. One of his professors from the university provided him with books: Hegel, Sartre, Foucault—what impressed him the most was his reading of *Anti-Oedipus* by Deleuze [and Guattari]. Leaving prison life with more solid philosophical baggage, Dufour was appointed assistant in psychology at Algiers, where he remained for three years, from 1973 to 1976. He pursued his reading and notably took in the structuralist works that then dominated the publishing scene. He began a thesis on the confrontation between the discourse of development and its effects of repression on a certain number of symbolic practices in Algeria: the vernacular languages of the Algerians, dialectal Arabic, Kabyle, the Berber languages, the ecstatic religions, and an entire series of microknowledges that organized social life according to networks with complex ramifications.

This thesis enabled him to return to Paris for a teaching post at Paris VIII-Vincennes, and primarily for a post as an engineering researcher at the Conservatoire National des Arts et Métiers. "I was bored to death there."[20] Subject to the rhythm of the office, eight hours a day, Dufour was nostalgic for prison life and shut himself inside to spend most of his time reading. He broadened his reading to literature with Artaud, Beckett, and Kafka. "The discovery of Beckett was an event for me. I don't think I'm done with it yet."[21]

In the early eighties, he began work on a *thèse d'État,* "La Parole, le Silence et l'Écriture," whose object was a set of language and symbolic practices. "For five years, until 1984, it was a work in the course of which I progressively cut myself off from the known world that surrounds us. I shut myself in my office, turned off the phone, and was submerged in texts without knowing where I was going."[22] This crisis, which he terms a "graphomania," ended with a monument of twelve hundred pages in which there are questions of the personal bond, of

the social bond in and through language, and of the critique of structuralism. He defended his thesis in 1985 in a still somewhat hypnotic
state, without really knowing what underlay its enormous amount of
work, but conscious of having passed through a language experience
that continued to work within him. "Strangely, it was only after my
thesis that I knew what it was about."[23]

In 1988, he published his first book, *Le Bégaiement des maîtres*,[24]
which is essentially a virulent critique of the structuralist theses, of
their binarity that at once makes audible and represses the unary figure.[25] On this occasion he met Marcel Gauchet, who wrote him to
convey his enthusiasm. Gauchet deemed that Dufour had put his fin-
ger on something essential and invited him to write an article on this
theme for *Le Débat*.[26] He asked Dufour if he thought intellectuals
were condemned to stammer eternally. "I was beginning to work on
the trinitary form, and somewhat by chance I threw out the idea that
we aren't condemned to stammering as long as we can get back to the
mystery of the Trinity."[27] This work on the ternary figure would give
way to a work of rare richness, published by Gauchet with Gallimard
in 1990.[28]

## Political History Gets a New Skin

Historians could not remain on the sidelines of this renewed interest in
the political. For the most part they had contributed, in the wake of the
*Annales* school, to discrediting this dimension, tossed in the trash of a
definitely bygone contestatory history. Of course, this political history
that was taking on a new vigor had never really disappeared from the
landscape of the historians. But it found itself confined to a restricted
space between the Institut d'Études Politiques and the University of
Paris X-Nanterre, dominated by the tutelary figure of René Rémond.
The new political history, metamorphosed by its strict relations with
the social sciences, found for itself a new and particularly dynamic
place, the IHTP,[29] which was created through the initiative of the
CNRS in 1978 to take over for the Committee on the History of World
War II. The "true leaven," as Jean-François Sirinelli terms it, of the history of the present time is political history, in a new sense of the term.

The birth of this institute in 1978 is indicative of a major change
of direction in historiography. In the late sixties, the reading of World
War II, of Vichy, changed radically, as Henry Rousso has shown.[30] The
heroic discourses of the Resistance were left behind, the bodies were

unearthed, and among the accomplices to crimes against humanity the French were discovered. "At that time, the idea was to rethink the relation to the Second World War in a wider perspective, by reinserting it into the present time."[31] Grasped in this case are the first signs of history's being turned over to memory, based on the idea that the event continues in duration through collective memory. This creation owes a lot, as Michel Trebitsch has shown,[32] to the social Christianity embodied in the 1950s by René Rémond and later by François Bédarida. The impact of the wars in Indochina and even more in Algeria had allowed the continuation of a tradition of the historian of the present time, directly confronted with the political dimension.[33]

Michel Trebitsch does not belong to that tradition. He comes from Marxism. His itinerary is atypical, and he did not join the IHTP until 1988. First he chose as the subject of his thesis a great figure of critical Marxism, Henri Lefebvre, whose "intellectual youth" he had undertaken to study, under the direction of Madeleine Rebérioux. What attracted him about the 1920s and 1930s was the notion of the avant-garde. Arriving at the IHTP in 1988, when Jean-François Sirinelli was leaving for Lille, Trebitsch assumed the direction, with Nicole Racine, of the research group in the history of intellectuals. What he discovered in Lefebvre was the latter's proximity, in his denunciation of the various forms of alienation, to the personalist current, in the broad sense, to the point where Lefebvre had almost converted to Christianity. "Henri Lefebvre studied Saint Augustine as much as Hegel or Nietzsche."[34]

Trebitsch was attracted by concepts in Lefebvre that were less "clear-cut" than those Althusser used. Notably, the notion of the possible is to be found, "on the limit of the poetic and the philosophical,"[35] with a refusal to reduce the real to a narrow definition. Lefebvre is opposed to the "reification of the factual."[36] His position may be compared to the Christian conception, Augustinian in part, of human time. What holds Trebitsch, and what has inspired his work at the IHTP, is that a fact is not reducible to what has happened. Access to the total event, which must remain the ambition of the historian, is in a certain way impossible. Historical evolution, conceived as a succession of actualized possibilities, allows its entire dynamic to be restored to the history of the present time. Political history, in the broad sense, is not conceived as the reopening of a supplementary drawer, but as a place of focalization, of crystallization of the spirit of the time.

# Part II

## The "American" Detour

The Francocentrism of the structural period, reinforced by a respectable anti-Americanism at the time of the Cold War, presented an obstacle for the entry of the Anglo-Saxon debates into France. This is no longer the case today: one of the characteristics of the new intellectual conjuncture is the more systematic accounting for the American contributions. The increase in translations and the intensity of the debates over the theses of the academics from across the Atlantic are there to attest to the increasingly evident phenomenon of importation of philosophy of an "analytic" inspiration, which comes to join—or to break with—the "Continental" tradition.

In a certain way, this American "detour" marks a return to the old countries of Jewish thinkers in central Europe who fled Nazism and became assimilated on American soil. This opening of the borders to a more international intellectual space also profits from the rediscovery of other traditions than the French sociological one. In this way the lineage of comprehensive sociology of Dilthey, Simmel, and Weber, introduced in France by Raymond Aron, but until very recently broadly ignored, is actively revisited or rediscovered today in the social sciences in France.[1]

## Five

# Ethnomethodology

As we saw in the preceding chapter, it was through the impetus of Louis Quéré that a group of sociologists strongly contributed to making ethnomethodology known in France in the early 1980s, through seminars and publications of the Center for the Study of Social Movements at the EHESS. Quéré was then plunged into studies of Habermas and Gadamer. He located himself in the dual perspective of communicative pragmatics and hermeneutics, when by chance in his readings he discovered a text by Aaron V. Cicourel that had not yet been translated into French, on the problematic of the meaning given to actions that were situated by the social actors. At the same moment, he became interested in the Austrian scholar Alfred Schutz, who had given the decisive impulse to the idea of a sociological or social phenomenology.[1] "I occupied this area to see what it would yield, and very quickly I proposed to colleagues a group reading of these texts."[2]

On this occasion, a small group of sociologists formed, as we have already mentioned. Thanks to its work in translation and interpretation, the texts of ethnomethodology were brought bit by bit onto the horizon of sociological knowledge so as to understand how cognition of the social is deployed. They constituted a rupture with the considering of the social actor as a "cultural idiot," as was the habit in the French epistemological tradition, because of the radical break between scholarly knowledge and common sense. Garfinkel had been the first, beginning in the 1950s, to glimpse the possibilities of a new type of sociological analysis whose object was constituted by the very operations of cognition. Indeed, he acknowledged, in the course of observing jurors' deliberations in 1954, that they were able to put to work quite remarkable capacities for evaluating elements of cases, without having the least benefit of a legal background. From this Garfinkel deduced the full importance of this common knowledge, of the common sense hitherto ignored by the sociological tradition in the name of the competence solely reserved for scholarly knowledge. He would be followed by a certain number of disciples in the United States, among them Cicourel and Sacks.

On the French side, the small research group around Louis Quéré quickly perceived the relations of proximity among the ethnomethodologists, Wittgenstein's theses, the phenomenology of Maurice Merleau-Ponty, and Schutz's theses. In this perspective, Durkheimian methodology, dominant in the French sociological tradition, was put to the test, revisited by those who had systematically explored ordinary language and the theories of social practice. "It was actually the discovery of America for me, with American pragmatism. For me, it was George Herbert Mead."[3] More recently, Quéré has been interested in the theses of Charles Taylor, the Canadian philosopher, at the intersection of the American and Continental traditions.[4] As a disciple of Merleau-Ponty, Quéré defends a program of phenomenological hermeneutics quite close to that of Paul Ricoeur.

Among this group of sociologists involved in the discovery of ethnomethodology was Patrick Pharo, for whom, we have seen, "one of the clicks"[5] would be learning of a little book published by the Presses Universitaires de France in 1973, whose objective was to take stock of American sociology.[6] Nicolas Herpin, the author of the panorama, notably emphasized how the work of Goffman could be seen as innovative, as a break with dominant sociology.[7] In the conclusion of this book, Goffman explained that he had sought to cast the foundations of a "dramaturgical" analysis of social facts, distinct from the research done in culturalist and functionalist terms: he thus gave birth to the current of symbolic interactionism.[8] Goffman's foundational book takes recourse to three registers of language: theatrical dramaturgy, sociology, and finally everyday language. The objective is to account for a "process of individualization through expressivity."[9] Interaction places individuals in relation with one another not in their singularity, but in their representation of a role. Now, when consensus is impossible, a process of exclusion is engaged, posing the problem of deviancy.

A professor at the University of California at Los Angeles, Harold Garfinkel for his part studied the conditions necessary for social interaction.[10] He used game theory in order better to bring to light the mechanism of actualization of the perceptive system of the social actors in a situation of interaction. Nonetheless, Garfinkel was not taken in by the idea that the situation of a game with a set of rules like chess can simply be transposed to explain phenomena of everyday life, much more complex and less subject to norms. Garfinkel then shaped an innovative current, that of ethnomethodology,[11] conceived as an empirical science whose methods enable the understanding of how individuals give meaning to their everyday actions.

After reading Herpin's book, Pharo began an examination of ethnomethodological research and returned to Garfinkel's phenomenological route by integrating Schutz, Berger, and Luckmann within his horizon of research.[12] For Pharo, this collective discovery of American ethnomethodology represented a very promising connection with the area of sociological research. For him, as for his entire generation, this was also the delayed discovery of America, with the unhinging, for "old anti-imperialists,"[13] of a series of firmly anchored stereotypes. In the late 1980s, Pharo perfected his evolution by crossing the Atlantic. Indeed, he had the opportunity to teach for a semester in the Department of Political Science at a small university in New York State, near the Great Lakes, Syracuse. "I then discovered the American academic universe with great interest."[14] He especially appreciated the intensity of intellectual debate, the shared taste for sophisticated conceptualization, the sense of dialogue. Of course, he did not for all that idealize what he had earlier caricatured. He was not unaware of the compartmentalizations, the struggles over interest, the presence of cliques fraught with exclusion on both sides of the ocean; but he discovered "clear argumentation,"[15] to which the systematic use of parables and the opacity of speaking most often insisted on in the French debates had not accustomed him. Furthermore, in France there was the point of view in which the debater was more prepared to bait than debate.

The American detour was just as essential for Bernard Conein, who was also invited to teach for a time at Syracuse University on Pharo's recommendation. In the mid-1980s, he met Aaron V. Cicourel there. Cicourel had broken with Garfinkel and was seeking a link between ethnomethodology and cognitive science.[16] Conein returned to the United States in 1988, to the University of California, San Diego, in the Department of Cognitive Science. "That's where I noticed that certain impasses in ethnomethodology, in particular regarding the social, were surmountable if one brought in categories of cognitive science."[17] In the American universe, he discovered a whole series of disciplines reconceived through cognitive science, which enabled reflection on the social in a new way: ethology, primatology, the theory of social cognition, and so on.

Conein had already concentrated his attention on the problem of social categories, thanks to ethnomethodology and Harvey Sacks's theory of conversation. The idea that the social categories were the resources to describe the social world, and that they were indeed categories of common sense, was already familiar to him. But he tried then to establish a connection with the way in which cognitive science apprehends the categorizations as a progressive acquisition of concepts. From there, he became interested in the idea of social cognition in a particular sense, that of "general cognitive aptitudes, proper to the species and concerning the social, and not only of the cultural aptitudes proper to a society."[18]

## The Laboratories

The anthropology of science was also born from the detour through America. We have already seen that Bruno Latour spent 1975 to 1977 in California, where he completed his first lab study at the Salk Institute in San Diego. He discovered a passionate atmosphere there, where the researchers defined themselves as scholars, without the pretension of inventing a new vision of the world every morning. In San Diego, Latour conceived an anthropology of science in a context where a new area of research was developing, that of "science studies" (sciences, technologies, and societies), which involved American as well as English and German scholars. At the moment Latour was studying the "construction of scientific facts" with Steve Woolgar,[19] a true international research community was forming with Harry M. Collins, Karin Knorr, and Andrew Pickering, among others. Latour, like his entire generation, was enthusiastically discovering the sense of true dialogue, the fact of working in a milieu of careful, benevolent researchers, who did not allow just anything to be said.

This mode of working—more collective, less spectacular—rapidly allowed the assimilation of foreigners, the constitution of a community of scholars in which there was little need to "kill one's colleague."[20] This system meanwhile had its inconveniences, its obstacles: the inconvenience "of constant peer review, which can promote stagnation. When there is no more grist for the mill, it becomes very conventional."[21] Without fully adhering to the ethnomethodological theses, as he was skeptical about their formalism, Latour was immediately sensitive to their respect for the position of the actors. Indeed, he recognized it thanks to Woolgar, who had been trained in that school. "I've learned a lot from ethnomethodology, even if I've never really believed in it as a method of inquiry."[22] His first work, which he wrote with Woolgar, *Laboratory Life,* meanwhile bears the mark of ethnomethodology. The central idea is not to trust discourses that scholars maintain about themselves, as they habitually adopt an overarching position, and to transform what they say through a laboratory ethnography that views them as informers "whom one doubts."[23] Ethnomethodology is also suggestive in its capacity to react to all the forms of metalanguage that take over the discourses and narratives of the social actors: "Ethnomethodology will rid sociology of its metalanguage and take the participant, with his practice, as the only competent sociologist."[24]

At the same moment, dissatisfied with the models at his disposal for studying technological creation, Michel Callon decided to take a detour through the analysis of science. Now, a field was beginning to form autonomously around the sociology of science and technology, while taking account of contents in the inner sense. This current was also Anglo-Saxon, essentially British, taking shape around the studies of the Edinburgh school.[25] "I remember very well when I read Barnes's and Collins's first articles, both of them British sociologists who were in their own way starting a new sociology of science, no longer as interested in the institutions as in the content of the sciences."[26]

In 1974, the British sociologists, who were considering questions previously relevant to the domain reserved for epistemologists, quickly founded a new journal, *Science Studies,* which became *Social Studies of Science.* Reading his British colleagues would direct Callon to the innovation "in the process of being made" and enable the breaking of the partition that had artificially separated a sociology of science condemned to the institutional realm alone from a philosophy of science cut off from the social. But Callon remained isolated in France in defending his point of view, before he met Latour: "The journal *Science Studies* was for me a puff of oxygen that made it possible to survive."[27] For Callon, the three books that enabled the creation of the anthropology of science were Latour and Woolgar's *Laboratory Life,* Karin Knorr's *The Manufacture of Knowledge,*[28] and Michael Lynch's, published later,[29] but based on a field study undertaken the same year as Latour's, in 1975.

## American Civic-Mindedness

In their evolution from "Bourdieusianism" to pragmatism, the passage across the Atlantic also counted greatly for Luc Boltanski and Laurent Thévenot—not so much in the way of a particular source of new inspiration as in the way of the discovery of a quite other and more open intellectual climate. They both began with a short stay of two or three months at Harvard, in the early 1980s, in the Department of Political Science. Thévenot did not learn much about American political science, but it contributed to his acceptance of America, "which changed everything."[30]

The resulting change in perspective came not only from seeing France from the outside, from leaving its provincialism; more profoundly, it was the encounter with "American civic-mindedness"[31] that would play on two levels. On the one hand, Thévenot discovered rules of professional conduct that were very different from those he had known in the Bourdieusian milieu. The requirements of critical discussion, the necessity of making explicit the argument of every demonstration, offered a serious contrast with the "battles of insinuation through footnotes."[32] In the United States, this type of practice reflects a moral flaw: it is "monstrous,"[33] for what is sought is a dynamic of adjustment to others. Thévenot quickly understood that it was a way of taking his interlocutors seriously, and that it would have a great heuristic value for him in his approach to the resources of "common sense." On the other hand, American individualism made it impossible to avoid the level of the person. Without in that respect necessarily limiting him to the individual level, the American experience would strongly contribute to his departure from a holistic procedure.[34]

*Six*

# Analytic Philosophy

Paul Ricoeur was, along with a few others such as Jules Vuillemin, Gilles-Gaston Granger, Maurice Clavelin, and Jacques Bouveresse, one of the forerunners of the acceptance of analytic philosophy in France. In the early 1960s at Nanterre, he made known the theses of J. L. Austin very early on, whereas the structuralist linguists, wishing to ignore the dimension of the subject, firmly remained at a distance from any pragmatic dimension. In the middle of the anti-American wave, Ricoeur was already teaching at Chicago, and immersed himself in the Anglo-Saxon studies that he attentively discussed after closely following the trajectory of this current. For Ricoeur, the Anglo-Saxon "linguistic turn" had the advantage of not barring the dimension of the subject, which had been removed by the structuralist paradigm. A whole generation would follow this intellectual course that passed through America, but much later than he did. In this way, a missing link in the history of thought would, for contingent reasons having to do with World War II and the emigration of the intellectuals from central Europe to the Anglo-Saxon countries, be assimilated little by little in a France that then had to pass through America. This movement would accompany the reevaluation of the notions of singularity, contextuality, and contingency.

## Communicative Action

Jean-Marc Ferry also passed through the pragmatic detour and the "linguistic turn." Just before defending his thesis, Ferry sent his work to Jürgen Habermas, whom he had had the opportunity to meet on the occasion of the German philosopher's visit to Paris in 1983 at the invitation of the Collège de France. "I was much surprised and very moved to get a phone call: 'This is Habermas.' He asked me to come to see him."[1] So Ferry hurried to the rue de l'Université, where a small room had been reserved for the distinguished guest, and began a very speculative discussion on the way in which he understood the evolution of "architectonics" in Habermas's work.

Ferry indeed distinguished several moments in the work of Habermas. In the first, knowledge is considered as a theory of society, with the main idea the interests of knowledge.[2] The second is the theory of communicative activity, in which there is an interest in the differentiation of registers of enunciation; it brings the relations with the world into correspondence with these differentiated levels, with variable degrees of validity. There is, finally, a third moment in the Habermasian system, with the integration of phenomenological concepts of the "world of life," which Habermas wanted to translate into concepts of the formal pragmatics of discourse, a task he began to deploy in his *Theory of Communicative Action.*[3] The detour through Habermas quite naturally led Ferry onto the paths to Germany. After defending his thesis, he won a scholarship from the Humboldt Foundation, thanks to the firm support of Ricoeur and Habermas, to pursue postdoctoral studies at the Goethe University in Frankfurt, where he remained for two years. He adjusted quite well when Habermas welcomed him, inviting him to his *Colloquium* (the equivalent of a seminar, with meetings every Monday). Paradoxically, it was in Germany, where he went to pursue his work on German idealism, that Ferry discovered analytic philosophy. "Every week, we discussed books in philosophy that had just come out, and mainly Anglo-Saxon philosophy."[4] There, for the first time, he heard of Richard Rorty, Donald Davidson, Hilary Putnam, Alasdair MacIntyre, and others. These American philosophers were very seriously dissected and discussed. After this preparatory stage, the German university invited the Anglo-Saxon philosophers, and that allowed them to explain their positions in public sessions before a packed exchange and a small private seminar. "It was a real experience, no waste of time."[5]

This study in Germany enabled Ferry to work on his big book, *Les Puissances de l'expérience,*[6] which drew the axes of a philosophical anthropology. After this detour through Germany, Ferry found his ground of choice in Belgium. He took a job as professor of philosophy at the Free University of Brussels, where he was a colleague of Isabelle Stengers. He also teaches at the University of Louvain-la-Neuve, and, in 1994, launched a new series in philosophy, "Humanités," for the Cerf publishing house. The aim of this low-priced series is to make known and accessible important texts from contemporary philosophy and the social sciences. It thus enables active participation in international public debate, and that poses the possibility of an awareness of the problematics developed abroad. Once again, the departure from French provincialism is claimed as an imperious necessity. "Over our heads a very international discussion unfolded between the Germans and the Anglo-Saxons. We must take part in it, and it is not chauvinism to say so."[7]

## Paris-Stanford

The most "American" institution in the social sciences is incontestably the CREA. The itinerary of a philosopher such as Joëlle Proust is in this respect emblematic of the connection.[8] Jean-Pierre Dupuy, director of the CREA, organized a conference on self-organization with René Girard at Stanford in 1981. Since that date, he has divided his teaching time between Paris and California. So his American detour is more than passing; it has become second nature, and has been the source of much inspiration for him. As he is very attracted to paradoxical figures, he has in addition enjoyed putting the two traditions in tension to the limits of their possibilities. For more than ten years, from 1979 to 1991, he examined the tradition of Anglo-Saxon moral and political philosophy; he contributed to the introduction in France of the American debate between the liberal theses of Friedrich August von Hayek, which are hostile to all social constructivism and apologetic for the laws of the market, the more social-democratic theses of John Rawls,[9] and the libertarianism of Robert Nozick—that is, the array of liberal thought on justice. Within this current, he brought into consideration the other to the figure of the market, regulated by reciprocity, the ever-near presence of an inner demon, panic, an omnipresent threat, most often denied but at work on the inner structure.[10] Dupuy found in Rawls a figure who reconciles the transcendental Kantian philosophy and Humean utilitarianism,[11] for the subject is precisely Anglo-Saxon, motivated by interests. "An American could thus say that Rawls's Kantianism was a Kantianism with a Humean face."[12]

Dupuy appreciates the conception of a "modest" subject in the Anglo-Saxon tradition, which contrasts with the way in which the continentals alternate between the deification of a subject disengaged from the empirical, from interest, and its pure and simple dissolution. That explains the proximity between social and economic philosophy in the United States. Thus, Rawls had a solid early background in economics, and Davidson began by working on the theory of rational choice: "Not economics in the sense of the study of inflation or unemployment . . . , but really the model of *homo economicus.*"[13] Torn today between France and America, Dupuy conducts a dual task of bringing to light the oxymorons of thought in the social sciences.[14] On the one hand, he is undertaking a philosophical critique of the rationalist paradigm in the social sciences and cognitive science. His intention is to bring out the paradoxes of rationality. On the other hand, as a French philosopher teaching in the United States, he is asked to present the "deconstructionist" works: Michel Foucault, Jacques Lacan, Jacques Derrida, who are "divinities"[15] over there. He then tries to demonstrate across the Atlantic that the adherents of relativism, of the irrational, are in fact motivated by figures of rationality. From there, he breaks through the "logics of irrationalism,"[16] such as that at work in Lacan's seminar on "The Purloined Letter," which is strongly influenced by the cybernetic paradigm.

## Social Cognition

Bernard Conein also took the path to America; in the United States, thanks to a colleague in mathematics, he discovered a technique of conceptual analysis that he considered appropriate for the social sciences, which came from analytic philosophy. "I didn't find this technique of language analysis in the French sociological tradition."[17] Getting interested in social cognition at San Diego, he read a book that he considers essential, *How Monkeys See the World*.[18] If he found no direct interlocutors in the framework of his interest in social cognition, he still met Donald A. Norman and his group, which was working on problems of artifact[19] and distributed cognition.[20]

Norman's studies had the aim of researching, in the sphere of objects implicated by action, the set of resources that enable the cognitive tasks, allotted to the human actors, to be lightened. In this work site, Conein was able to take up his interest in objects and his search for a theory that could account at once for the manipulation of objects and for their role on the cognitive level. Now, Norman had published a work in which he presented a cognitive theory of artifacts.[21] Objects play a major role in it, that of lightening what Norman calls the burden of reason in action. This means that an action without an object is much heavier on the mental plane than an action with an artifact. His objective, therefore, is to see how an object, when an action is mediated by an artifact, is capable of facilitating human intervention and thus the cognitive burden. So the object then plays the role of the agent. Thus, the piloting of an aircraft is conducted by a pilot and copilot, but also by a plethora of artifacts that structure the task of piloting by an ever more sophisticated technology.

Participating in the CREA brought Laurent Thévenot to return to the United States, to Madison, Wisconsin, then to Stanford, where Dupuy was teaching. He then took all the interest he could in an analytic philosophy that certainly led to the reverse of his own procedure, because it began with the individual; but he glimpsed the possibility of bringing the two logics together. His intention to get back to the collective on the individual level in fact intersected the efforts of certain adherents of analytic philosophy who attempted to move from the individual to a more collective plane. In this framework, he especially saw convergences with the analyses of Michael E. Bratman.[22]

Pascal Engel, a philosopher at the CREA, also had his American visit, in 1978–79. In that period, he took courses from Austin's disciple, John Searle. Then, at the French lycée in London, he spent a year in which he became familiar with the works of the Oxford school, and that enabled him to become the presenter-translator of Davidson and Dennett in France.[23]

## The "Linguistic Turn"

This encounter with analytic philosophy places Wittgenstein at the center of the references of the new thought in France. Already in the early 1970s, Jacques Bouveresse had become the solitary presenter of the original work of Wittgenstein.[24] It is mainly the later Wittgenstein who has become a source of inspiration, less the Wittgenstein of the *Tractatus Logico-philosophicus* than the one of the *Philosophical Investigations*.[25] He is above all used as the philosopher of language games who relativizes logic by relating it to systems of conventions, giving philosophy the ambition of breaking with the bad habits of its tradition that have led it to proceed with an abusive critique of ordinary language. On the contrary, Wittgenstein holds that ordinary language functions well when it is freed from the artificial obscurities with which it has been weighted down. The task of the philosopher, according to Wittgenstein, is therefore to wage war on these opacities and restore the meaning of words.

The current pragmatic and descriptive turn in the social sciences therefore finds in Wittgenstein a philosophy in resonance with its own orientations, because it denounces the fascination that science exercises over philosophy: "Philosophers constantly see the method of science before their eyes, and are irresistibly tempted to ask and answer questions in the way science does. This tendency is the real source of metaphysics, and leads the philosopher into complete darkness. . . . Philosophy really *is* 'purely descriptive.' "[26] All the "Anglo-Saxon" adherents of the "linguistic turn," of pragmatism, were thus discovered late by the French social sciences.

Charles Sanders Peirce, considered the founder of semiotics and of a new philosophy, pragmatism, defined thought as a sign.[27] According to Peirce, thought is deployed on the basis of a semiotic triangle (sign-object-interpretant) that refers to an indefinite dialogic between interpretants. Gottlob Frege is also presented as the "father of the linguistic turn because of his extreme focus on the difference between *Gedanken* and *Vorstellungen,* between thoughts and representations."[28]

One of the current figures of American pragmatism, Richard Rorty, has elsewhere paved the way in the opposite direction by building bridges with "Continental" philosophy, notably by appropriating Derridean deconstruction. Language has for him become the very core of contemporary philosophy: "*All* awareness . . . is a linguistic affair."[29] Rorty attempts a rehabilitation of common sense and grasps every truth as the result of a "conversation between persons."[30] In this perspective, he reexamines the entire Cartesian and Kantian tradition, of the formulation of philosophical problems in terms of representations of a real conceived as exterior to discourse and structured by specific laws.

Rorty's pragmatism is radical and purely contextualist: "If one claims that a theory that presents the truth as what is effective is more effective than any other of the current theories, one is saying that it is more effective in relation to our ends and our particular situation in intellectual history."[31] On the horizon of this perspective, Rorty does not really see an interdisciplinarity, but rather a possibility of "dedisciplinizing" a philosophy that would, properly speaking, no longer be a discipline. Contemporary pragmatism has enabled the renewal of three fields of knowledge: literary theory—especially with Arthur Danto—the history of science, and political philosophy.[32]

Very diverse directions—those of Hilary Putnam, Donald Davidson, and Richard Rorty—nonetheless have in common the search for a position that avoids, in varying degrees, any form of skepticism. Putnam advocates distinguishing between an externalist approach that is, he says, dependent on a metaphysical realism in which truth is found in a relation between words and things, on the basis of a single theory, and an internalist approach, reduced to the sole internal coherence between beliefs and experiences.[33] What results from this position is that a heavy emphasis is placed on the concept of a "performative contradiction" that prohibits coherence itself, the condition of communication, of mutual understanding. Putnam meanwhile does not go as far as Rorty with contextualism, and he reproaches the latter for a relativism that may lead to an attitude of indifference. Against Rorty, Putnam maintains the necessity of a restrained realism. He recognizes a fecundity in Kant's pure practical reason,[34] and he wonders, "What has to happen for there to be judgments of value that are true?"[35] Between the objectivist and the relativist attitude, Putnam defends a more hermeneutic attitude, close to that of Peter Winch.[36] It implies the fact that "to understand a language game is to share in a form of life."[37]

## The Pragmatic Age

The penetration of the pragmatic theses and their assimilation into the French debate occurred late, but they have since found avid presenters. Besides the work of Paul Ricoeur, who has for a long time discussed the Anglo-Saxon theses, there are more and more specialists in this area of thought: Pierre Jacob in the field of the philosophy of science, François Récanati in linguistics, Jacques Bouveresse, Gilles-Gaston Granger, and Christiane Chauviré as interpreters of Wittgenstein, or Jacques Poulain, who critically examines phenomenological reason.[38]

Joëlle Proust also speaks of her "analytic detour."[39] After publishing *Questions of Form: Logic and the Analytic Proposition from Kant to Carnap* in 1986, she turned to a new field of investigation in the philosophy of artificial intelligence and of cognition. She found two sites of debate to assimilate the orientations of analytic philosophy. The "Friday group" presented and discussed the theses of the philosophy of language as well as the relations between philosophy and psychology. Among its members were Dan Sperber, Pierre Jacob, François Récanati, Dick Carter, and Gilles Fauconnier. The second place was the seminar that Pascal Engel was conducting on the philosophy of cognition. This task of elaboration, especially around the "frame problem," led Proust to form the research group at the CREA on cognitive science in 1989.

## Keynes Revisited

For economists, the American detour is something quite different, for modern, formalized economic science is, for all practical purposes, totally dominated by the Anglo-Saxons. The sources of inspiration of the economics of convention are also for the most part found outside France. Thus, Olivier Favereau for the first time encountered the notion of convention in Keynes. The latter was indeed interested in the way people were capable of anticipating and formulating forecasts for a financial market. Keynes used a theory according to which there would be a "sort of convention when one had no reason to think that things were going to change."[40] Favereau was then interested in logic and philosophical debates, and discovered the work of the logician Saul Kripke. "I started engaging in an admirer's philosophy, very close to analytic philosophy, very Anglo-Saxon."[41] In this search for modal logics,[42] he noticed in the bibliographies the repeated reference to a work by David K. Lewis, *Convention*,[43] which he must have been the first French economist to read. Favereau then grasped what he considered a possible means of surpassing the aporia on which Keynes had stumbled and proposing, following Lewis, a "semantic of possible worlds."[44] At the same time, he read Doeringer and Piore,[45] who worked out a description of what happens in modern corporations on the level of personnel management. They acknowledge the permanent use of notions of rule, norm, and custom, as substitutes for the functioning of the markets, thanks to their power to harmonize behaviors. "I told myself that here there was an extremely rich theoretical area in which people from the most diverse horizons would come together around the notions of possibilities."[46] On this basis Favereau undertook to work from the inside of this vast theoretical area, in the confines of analytic philosophy.

# Seven

# The Philosophy of Science

The other aspect of the "American detour" may be found in the discussion of the theses of the philosophy of science, of epistemology. In this area, the Anglo-Saxon tradition has broken with positivism. A whole current has registered a crisis of confidence in Reason, which goes back to the beginning of the century with the theory of relativity and quantum mechanics. The formulation of Gödel's theorem in 1931[1] enabled a link, over incompleteness, to a questioning of determinism. This scientific crisis posed the problem of the limits of any foundational enterprise and imposed a new philosophical problematization of scientific discoveries. Scientific truth became a "deferred error." A whole program in the epistemology of science would be fertilized by this crisis of confidence.

Thomas Kuhn proposed the notion of paradigm to distinguish the state of "normal science" and valorize the sociological and historical constituents of scientific revolutions. Crises would then find their resolution through the appearance of a new paradigm within a historical evolution that has lost its linearity.[2] The paradigm no longer defines a truth in itself, atemporal with regard to science, the activity that is legitimate within the domain of scientific activity that the paradigm governs. Meanwhile, the appearance of unsolved enigmas and anomalies provokes repeated crises that are amplified until a rival paradigm presents itself as an alternative, through its capacity to resolve the problems posed. At that moment, it is adopted by the scientific community; this passing of the baton characterizes a scientific revolution, according to Kuhn.

Paul Feyerabend goes even further in the way of relativism, thanks to his famous consideration according to which "anything goes."[3] He wages war on the idea that science is organized according to fixed, universal rules. Feyerabend considers this belief negative with regard to the way in which scientific discoveries proceed. The latter are most often the results of transgressions with respect to tradition, ingenious intuitions off the beaten path. The intensity of this reflection on the history of science has crossed the Atlantic. "What immediately nourished me from the United States was the new history of science."[4]

## Karl Popper

In a break with Kuhn, the major reference in the philosophy of science very quickly became the work of Karl Popper.[5] It allowed the question of the scientific status of a theory to be posed frontally, and it found the answer in the aspect of its falsifiability. Popper challenges the thesis of the members of the Vienna Circle according to which one opposes science and pseudoscience in the name of the empirical criterion of an ineluctably inductive scientific method. Popper also breaks with the epistemological tradition and pleads for a certain form of indeterminism,[6] without for all that renouncing the ideal of truth. "The adherence to indeterminism and to the thesis of the conjectural character of our knowledge does not lead to an encouragement of relativism and skepticism."[7] In passing through America, according to Daniel Andler, one also escapes the consideration of the history of science as a succession of geniuses. "What Berkeley offered me was the idea of a continuum throughout the ages, and the fact that there is not one unique, self-generating species of developmental modality of the manifestation of the genius."[8]

For his part, Alain Boyer, a philosopher who also works at the CREA, finds his great inspiration in Popper;[9] this has not kept him from having other influences, such as that of the German tradition around the work of Weber. In the 1980s, he deemed that there were two major authors who treated the epistemological problems on which he worked: Jon Elster,[10] an American philosopher of Norwegian origin, and Philippe van Parijs,[11] a Belgian philosopher. Boyer draws on Popper and his antipositivism. This Popperian position implies a certain number of corollaries. In the first place, and contrary to a very widespread misunderstanding that comes from the way in which German publishers have presented the quarrel among Adorno, Habermas, and Popper as a quarrel over positivism,[12] Popper's work does not in the least involve positivism; quite the opposite. His antipositivism may be translated as the recognition that what is not scientific may nonetheless be endowed with meaning. In the second place—and this is important for the social sciences—contrary to positivism, Popper "does not refuse hidden entities."[13] In the third place, Popper criticizes the inductive method of positivism, that is, the accumulation of data preceding the generalizing hypothesis. "On the contrary, the Popperian hypothesis is the primacy of theory over experience."[14] The latter maintains a privileged status, as a means of testing the reliability of hypotheses, a way of proving them. Where Popper most picks up the pragmatist theses and analytic philosophy is in the attention he accords to the scientific institution as the framework of a debate, of a collective necessary to science, of a site of intersubjective argumentation—all the while preserving the idea of a unified scientific method. Now, the French tradition, in its contestation of positivism, had obliterated this dimension of subjectivity, of intentionality. Therefore, the reintroduction of this dimension, with diverse linguistic or logical variants, definitely passes through a series of resources, from Continental philosophy to the Anglo-Saxon school.

*Eight*

# The Chicago School, Elias, and Weber

In the realm of the writing of historical studies, too, the sources of inspiration have diversified and opened onto the foreign. The scientistic phase of the new history—which purported to have found historical truth in the output of a computer, thanks to a serial and quantitative history—is done with. The study of the present time and the encounter with oral sources constrained historians to ask themselves new questions. These questions necessitated in turn a certain number of detours that involved the increase of international exchanges and the opening of the field to sociology: "In France, oral history came in through sociology."[1] Daniel Bertaux has analyzed the link between the massive use of oral sources and the discourses of revolt of the generation of 1968.[2] And for his part, Michaël Pollak has shown that oral history has been carried along atypical trajectories by a whole new generation of "beginning" scholars, who little by little took positions of power in the 1980s.[3] This new generation has found the essentials of its inspiration in American sociology.

## Oral History

In 1948, a Center for Oral History was formed under the direction of Allan Nevins at Columbia University. This first establishment and its success immediately served as a model for the creation of other centers, the culmination of which happened on the federal level, when, in 1967, Nevins created the American Oral History Association; in

1973, the Association founded its journal, *Oral History Review*. But the model of oral history at Columbia, "privileging the study of the elite and not the excluded,"[4] underwent a strong contestation during the 1960s. A whole critical trend, fed by the radical minority movements, then developed oral history from a militant point of view and revisited the tradition and orientations of the Chicago school.[5]

The formation of a department of sociology at Chicago dates from the late nineteenth century, in 1892. It was distinguished by the personality of Albion W. Small, the director of the department for thirty years. One of his students, William Thomas, returned to teach there from 1897 to 1918. It was he who demonstrated the richness of this school through his greatly renowned study of the "Polish peasant," which he published in 1918 with Florian Znaniecki. It represented an impressive amount of work in five volumes, the fruit of the collection of thousands of letters by immigrants, life stories, on the comparison between the old and the new countries.[6] Later, and under the influence of the pragmatist theses of Charles Sanders Peirce and John Dewey, sociologists took their distance from the speculative tradition of the grand theoretical systems and turned to empirical studies. Research was oriented toward the study of the modalities of social change and the problems it engenders. At the time, in the 1930s, American sociology was dominated by empiricism. "Nonetheless, far from rejecting every theoretical orientation, it was rather characterized by its defiance with regard to a hypothetico-deductive procedure on the basis of a systematized set of postulates, preferring a study of each particular social phenomenon in the framework of problematics constructed according to specific 'rationalities.'"[7]

In this context, the Chicago school developed a series of research projects on "urban ecology," termed Urban Area Projects. What formed the unity of these projects was the consideration of the city as a privileged laboratory for the study of problems of marginality, segregation, and violence. These sociological investigations would permit the widespread acceptance of the very pragmatic concern of concentrating the sociologist's attention on the reciprocal actions of individuals and their environment. One of the major promoters of this school, dominant in the United States in the 1920s, was R. E. Park; a former student of Wilhelm Windelband and Georg Simmel, he arrived in Chicago in 1915. Deracination was one of the major elements explaining the forms of "urban pathology," according to the Chicago school. Historian Gérard Noiriel, who has written a history of immigration in France in the nineteenth and twentieth centuries,[8] would revisit this tradition. "There has certainly been an American detour, through sociology, through the Chicago school."[9]

History thus takes its inspiration from sociology in order better to master the reduction of the number of its sources. It further recognizes the competency particular to yesterday's witnesses, their capacities to describe and hence to explain the events as the latter affected them. This introduction of oral history has fomented a number of controversies and adaptations regarding its use in the field of investigation of present-day history. Danièle Voldman, whose object of research is also the city, very quickly disqualified the addition of a new area termed "oral history" alongside manuscript history. She finds, on the contrary, that oral sources and archives are an integral part of general history. And she concludes that the militant positioning of a critical oral history in relation to the dominant power/knowledge belongs to the "historiographical period between 1950 and 1980."[10] If historians have not had a true, direct knowledge of analytic philosophy, one may affirm with Roger Chartier, on the other hand, that "they have been doing pragmatism without knowing it."[11] Pragmatism becomes familiar to them the more they take their distance from analysis in terms of the long period. Further, it allows them to favor a reorientation toward the study of individual interactions in the framework of contextualized rules. It causes relations to prevail over structures, situations over positions, and thus converges with a tendency that belongs to the ensemble of the social sciences in France.

## The Rhine: A Link

In these new investigations, two major references stand out as accompanying the current paradigm shift: Norbert Elias and Max Weber— that is, a direct connection to Germany. For more than ten years, Roger Chartier has been introducing the complete work of Elias, undertaking the publication of all of his writings in French. Elias enables us to surpass the false alternative of subject and structure, and to avoid the reduction of the notion of situation to the set of relations perceived, known, and consciously used by social actors, as in the interactionist paradigm. "The interest of such thinking as that of Elias to me seems to be located in the operation of interdependencies at a much greater distance, not necessarily perceptible or manipulable by individuals, and nevertheless causing them to be what they are."[12] Chartier has recently elaborated the reasons that the rediscovery of Elias is attracting a major interest.[13]

Chartier met Elias in 1979, at a dialogue organized by Elias's German colleague Adolf von Thadden in Göttingen. Elias realized on this occasion that the reception of his work in France, in the mid-1970s, had been fundamentally biased and reductive. In France, we had essentially isolated from his work the elements that described behaviors, manners, mores—a historical anthropology of everyday life in the West from the sixteenth to the eighteenth century, corresponding to the vogue of the history of mentalities at the time. Now, this 1979 meeting brought about the appearance of an opus of quite another range, and it was the opportunity, "at least for me, for a moment of truly reading Elias."[14] The reason for the late and biased reception of the work of Elias is based, as with analytic philosophy, in extreme French provincialism. Of course, *The Civilizing Process* appeared only in 1939, but the French university system in its rigidity did not allow the refugees of Central Europe to move to France in the 1930s. Elias, fleeing Nazism in 1933, stopped in Paris. Isolated, without a real response from a particularly rigid university system, he continued on his way toward the Anglo-Saxon world, even though his field of study was the history of France: "In 1933, with Hitler's coming to power, I first went to France to take refuge. But the French university system had no place for me. In Great Britain I had better luck."[15]

We therefore had to wait for his arrival in Paris in the early 1980s, when he was invited successively by the EHESS and the Collège de France, to take stock of the importance of his work. His central concept of configuration allows the appearance of the processes of complex recomposition of preceding elements. It allows one to be opposed to both the illusion of transhistorical invariants and the enigmatic eruption of discontinuous events. Elias makes it possible to think at once in terms of continuities and indissociable discontinuities. In addition, he allows one to understand the dialectic of individuals' incorporation of constraints, the mode of individuation of a single specific configuration that engages all the levels of the historical situation:

> The reference to an oeuvre like that of Elias has two functions. The first is that it proposes more dynamic, less fixed models of intelligibility. The second function of the reference to Elias is to propose a perhaps questionable schema of evolution of Western societies from

the Middle Ages to the twentieth century that would be centered on the construction of the state and the transformation of the psychic categories.[16]

The reintroduction of the field of multiple possibilities offered by social configurations, therefore, allows one to avoid the alternative between the postulate of an absolute freedom of man and that of a strict causal determination. One may then consider a conception of the social link, individual liberty, on the basis of chains of interdependence that connect the individual to his or her fellows. The dissatisfaction with a "history in bits and pieces" and the current concern with re-globalizing, as well as the renewed investigations into the political realm, may find solutions in Elias that are on not so much the factual as the methodological level, thanks to the globalizing and dynamic aspect of his approach to power, to the role of the state in the social.

We may thereby understand how this opus has been suggestive for Noiriel the historian, whose object is also the study of the mechanisms at work in the construction of a national identity. Beginning the project of casting the foundations of a social history of the French nation, Noiriel writes, "Although the French university system rejected Norbert Elias in 1933, it is to his credit that most of his intellectual life was devoted to elucidating the mechanisms of French national construction."[17] The analysis of the phenomena of assimilation, the contributions of a comparatist method, in the work of Elias, inscribed in duration, are so many precious orientations for Noiriel; Noiriel can make his own the affirmation that "the individual is both coin and die at the same time,"[18] meaning that each human being bears the indelible mark of the social.

## The Weberian Horizon

Max Weber is also enjoying a renewed interest today in the social sciences that is so spectacular that Jean-Pierre Olivier de Sardan has recently spoken of a Weberian sphere in the social sciences.[19] Noiriel's direction is just as symptomatic of this recent rediscovery. "When I began to read Weber closely—we didn't read him when I was young— I realized that he defined comprehensive sociology as a science whose object is the elementary atom known as the individual."[20] Certainly, the true introduction of Weberian ideas goes back to the eve of World War II. Indeed, it dates from the publication of Raymond Aron's thesis.[21] After that, Julien Freund took over the effort to introduce the Weberian theses in France.[22]

If it has taken so long to recognize and discuss Weber, it is certainly not because of a misunderstanding of his work by the guardians of French sociology. In this area, the factual demonstration according to which there have always been ties between French and German sociologists is convincing.[23] Meanwhile, the thesis that Laurent Muchielli defends, which holds that the Franco-German rupture caused by the influence of Durkheim is a myth, is hardly tenable. There was contact, but the relationship of the two sociological traditions finished with the complete success of Durkheimianism in France, which confirmed and extended its hegemony with the triumph of structuralism in the 1960s. The entire tradition of Weber, Simmel, and Dilthey found itself delegitimated. The divorce of the two traditions was then evident and, as Monique Hirschhorn shows,[24] the references to Weber in French were rare, in contrast to the abundant Anglo-Saxon bibliography.[25] Certainly, with regard to this delay one may raise commercial factors concerning the rights held by the Plon publishing house, which had the monopoly beginning in 1955;[26] but if Plon was not particularly motivated to market Weber, it was because he did not have the audience that was commercially necessary for the multiple printings of his books.

This situation reflects the voluntary ignorance of an orientation of antinomical sociology in relation to the Durkheimian-Marxist current that was dominant at the time. As a result, there were two opposing trends: the positivistic, Comptian filiation, whose heuristic model was mechanical physics, and the filiation of comprehensive sociology, for which the sciences of the mind were dissociated from the sciences of nature. The rupture between the critical philosophy of history of Simmel, Dilthey, and Weber and the positivist tradition, which reproached the former with psychologizing the historical sciences, was therefore complete.[27] The lack of appreciation for the current of German comprehensive sociology that resulted from this confrontation is presently dissipating in France. When Jean-Claude Passeron recently defined what he meant by "sociological reasoning,"[28] he opposed a Popperian sphere, that of the experimental sciences, to the non-Popperian sphere of the historical sciences, which cannot be "proven false" in the strict sense. Thus, he took as his own, by defining what he calls the historical sciences (sociology, anthropology, history), the Weberian distinction between the autonomy of these sciences and the necessity of defining the limits of their objectivity. The social sciences, according to this schema, do not belong to the domain of the nomological sciences.[29] They are submitted, says Passeron, to deictic constraints that refer every association to its proper sphere of enunciation.[30] This characteristic corresponds to the importance of another borrowing from Weber, that of the ideal type constructed by sociological reasoning. "These are not the *logical* ties that bind what is essential in knowledge, but the *typological ties*, as such indissociable from the semirigid distinctions and the endlessly rectified distinctions on which the types are *indexed*."[31]

To show the logical, semiproper noun status of historical, sociological, or anthropological concepts, Passeron takes the example of a descriptive concept, that of the attitude of "white trash," who are very close to the disenfranchised masses and who valorize what still separates them from the latter's condition: "When we use it to bring to light a type of social relation in a historical situation other than that of the 'white trash' of the southern United States, the concept introduces a *comparative intelligibility*."[32] In another situation, the concept used takes an analogical form. Thus, it is extracted from its original context, and at the same time its economy cannot be established. "Neither full common nouns (susceptible to a 'definite description') nor simple proper nouns (identifying a unique *deixis*), sociohistorical concepts are *logical mixtures* whose typological nature commands common semantic effects in the discourses of history and of sociology."[33]

The other great borrowing from Weber is the comparative horizon of the historical sciences, which must place contexts in equivalence according to the typology that links them together. "Two or more historical contexts can be distinguished as different, or brought together as equivalent, only through a comparative reasoning."[34] This operation eliminates from the theoretical sphere of the social sciences the illusion of a capacity to postulate formalizable invariants detached from natural language and their context. Quite to the contrary, the concepts incorporate reference. These "hybrids," half conceptual and half referential, which Passeron qualifies as semiproper nouns, are in fact the equivalent of what Weber termed the ideal type.

So France in the 1990s seems to have decided to open the borders resolutely. It should be able to make up for its delay thanks to the meetings with the United States and Germany, even as it maintains its capacity to construct a specific paradigm that is not the mere translation of foreign resources.

# Part III

*The Social Bond*

The return of ethnologists to Western society has modified views in the social sciences. It has strongly contributed to a departure from the discourse of denunciation, which made no sense in the ethnographic description of cultural difference. In this sense, the anthropological vogue of the 1960s in a certain way continues to irrigate research re-centered on the metropolis. The ethnological experience has allowed for a new attention to the basis of the social bond by considering it as constitutive of the symbolic.

The dual crisis in the conception of the social in terms of pure cen-trality, whether originating with the invisible hand of the market or with the omnipresence of the state, has otherwise facilitated this atten-tion to the basis of the social bond, to the microbonds. Of course, this interrogation has always animated sociological reflection; but we wit-ness displacements in the angle of analysis and in the choice of more restricted scales to reinstate the various logics at work in interaction, in the micromilieus of sociality, in the introduction of objects in the study of the social, in the questioning of the great traditional divisions. On the horizon of this innovative research the stake is eminently politi-cal, because it aims to revitalize a (lost) sociality that would allow for the opening of public space to the deliberation of the great problems posed by modernity. The very perpetuation of the democratic adven-ture assumes the transformation of a culture of experts that would be open to active participation in the great social decisions made by users who have become citizens.[1]

The attention to the social bond, to its basis, can be considered differently if it is conceived as a mutual self-engendering. It allows one to avoid the false alternative between holism and methodologi-cal individualism or the now classic opposition between the social and the individual. The double impasse encountered by both the utilitarian model and that in which the reproduction of structures prevails invites a shift of viewpoint toward what constitutes the very heart of the social. This in-between is not all that easy to distinguish, because of its hybrid and complex character. "The social bond is a highly enigmatic object that is neither a given of nature, as postu-lated by an entire sociology that is organicist without knowing it, nor a construct, as is believed by the liberals and an entire somewhat naive school of legal thought."[2] Until recently holding the status of unproblemetized evidence, today the social bond occupies the place of the Sphinx who questions man about his own being, posing a riddle that puts him to work; for knowledge in the social sciences is still very poorly armed to approach this central question, which has always remained the unsaid, the implicit of every analysis of the social.

# Nine

# A New Triad: Nature/Society/Discourse

The new anthropology of science that was born, as we have seen, at the Center for the Sociology of Innovation (CSI), around Michel Callon and Bruno Latour, took as its object of study the processes emerging from scientific and technical innovation. These are conceived as a "total social fact."[1] The discoveries that allow a disturbance of the social bonds themselves result from multiple effects of the networks, and at once involve laboratories, public policies, private finances, relations with potential consumers, and so on.

Such an anthropology implies the combination of various disciplines, an all-terrain attention and competency for the study of the great controversies that have accompanied innovation, the inner workings of laboratories, and the ways in which these workings are brought to the public. All these lines of research involve an accounting for the contents of innovations, but also for the networks mobilized to bring about their socialization. This anthropology, whose privileged object is scientific or technical discovery, brings a primary attention to crises at the expense of static situations. In all its examinations, the content and context are always studied in concert. The essential rupture with classical sociology, realized by this anthropology, lies in constructing the "social sciences at the risk of the object."[2] This anthropology holds that science is social, through and through. Calling into question the naturalization of objects that is generally practiced by the disciplines in the social sciences, as well as the sociologism that consists of considering these objects as the mere setting of the social, the CSI maintains that "objects are at the center of sociology."[3] Along with objects, the nature and foundation of the social bond, as well as its capacity to endure over time, are examined. "Technical objects become a particular way of assuring a durability of the social bond when they incorporate nonhumans in the interaction of humans. To study them is to extend sociology by other means."[4] This attention to the social bond, to its basis in the realm of practices, places, and objects, enables this approach to surpass the "old opposition between actor and system, agent and structure."[5]

## The Networks Resonate

One of the central notions of this anthropology of science is the notion of networks, in a novel and very broad sense of the term: "The networks are *simultaneously real, like nature, narrated, like discourse, and collective, like society.*"[6] In opposition to its usual meaning, the use of the term *networks* in the anthropology of science coincides with the desire to employ a notion that allows one to avoid any territorialized view of society. It thus demarcates notions of field, subfield, institution, and so on, that presuppose homogeneous sets defined by types of actions, particular rules of the game. The second characteristic of these networks is the mix they imply between humans and nonhumans, subjects and objects. They are sociotechnical networks that involve "flows of instruments, competencies, literature, money, which tie and connect laboratories, enterprises, or administrations."[7] Networks are thus marked by a strong heterogeneity. Accounting for them allows for the emphasis on the importance of what previously seemed to be in a situation exterior to science. Considering the scientific fact as the expression of a network enables one to test the solidity and relative novelty of the latter. The notion of networks enables the understanding of the effects of size, of the effects of scale.

Sociotechnical networks, which are more or less proliferative, shift chains of delegation, redeploy the device of spokespersons. "This work of seaming, sewing, relating, evaluating, can take a fair amount of time."[8] Now, there is no solution of continuity between one particular point in the network and another. Thus, the effect of the size of the network is in general inherent in its dynamic. Entire networks may even be transformed into "black boxes, and manipulated as such, without the need to go into the contents of the black box."[9] It is from

this perspective that Michel Callon analyzes the "agony of a laboratory"[10]—the latter begun in the early sixties—on the theme of the
conversion of energies by means of fuel cells in the setting of the Beau-
regard Laboratory. He shows to what point the construction of scientific facts on the inside of a laboratory is indissociable from the actor-
networks and from the strategies of the laboratory at the heart of the
networks it manages. All of these characteristics of the notion of networks have allowed it to become "our Bible, in a way."[11]

Bruno Latour considers the notion of networks to be a war machine against the idea of structure and against interactionism. "Face-
to-face interaction exists among baboons, but not among humans."[12]
So it is a very powerful operator. It nonetheless has certain drawbacks,
essentially because it implies a certain void on the level of content,
which leads to an impoverished vision of the world in which we live.
"Interactions are reduced to undefined associations."[13]

Of course, this device remains separate from all content in order
to acquire new elements; the concern is with avoiding a preconception
of the actors, the controversies, and the most diverse configurations,
so as to follow them better. But today there is the question of "classifying the different registers of interaction."[14] It is in this way that
Latour has proposed introducing the notion of the regime of enunciation; and Callon, in even closer relation to economists, uses the notion
of the modality of coordination, which falls within the perspective of
the economists of conventions. This perspective does not do away
with the notion of networks; the notion is maintained, as each modality of coordination has points and segments—and that allows one to
give substance to the graphs.

This relationship with economics brings Callon to offer another
definition for the notion of networks. Economists hold that coordination occurs either through the market or through hierarchy. Meanwhile, they present another modality of coordination made up of personal relations of confidence. They then term this third informal
modality a network, and in certain cases term networks the whole—
the assemblage of the market, the hierarchy, and confidence. Callon
borrows this definition from the economists and classifies what coincides with every form of assemblage of the modalities of coordination
as a network.

Even within the CSI, two apparently heterogeneous domains coexist. Jean-Pierre Vignolle began a research program on the entertainment

industry, and he recruited Antoine Hennion for its completion.[15] Since 1976–77, they have developed an inquiry of an ethnological bent into the fabrication of a "hit." Hennion wished to surpass the traditional approach of critical sociology, which in this domain has a tendency to practice the systematic avoidance of aesthetic examination. Critical sociology tends from the outset to consider popular successes as the expression of the zero degree of musical quality. It therefore attributes these successes to the simple effect of economic and social mechanisms of public manipulation. Taking the players themselves seriously, Hennion, for his part, brought in all the mediating factors in the production of entertainment. Around the pop stars, he brings back into the picture the know-how of the producer, the recording engineer, the arranger, the music critic, the radio programmer, and others, and it is by way of these multiple tests of qualification that the "hit" is constructed. The understanding of success or failure is then clarified at the end of this long chain. Eventually, this program, somewhat atypical in a center more oriented to scientific innovation, appears as a participant in similar research. The study of the manufacturing process on the basis of heterogeneous elements—which, once it has linked these elements together, appears in the aftermath of its commencement as pure and naturalized—allows one to understand how effects of truth and beauty are produced. Along these lines, Hennion has pursued his sociological study of musical taste on the basis of its multiple mediations, objects, and controversies.[16]

The sources of this convergence on the theoretical level, which have enabled the formation of the program of the anthropology of innovation, are many. Relativism, if not skepticism, in the face of every transhistorical value has had the consequence that "we are described as somewhat Nietzschean."[17] Bruno Latour certainly recognizes that he is more in the tradition of Epicurus, Spinoza, and Nietzsche than in the lineage of the philosophers of consciousness, Descartes, Kant, and Husserl. Among the contemporary philosophers, two play a major role, he says, even if they are only somewhat useful in defining a program of inquiry in the social sciences: they are Michel Serres and Gilles Deleuze. It may be said that the notion of networks is quite close to the model of the rhizome in Deleuze. "The little book called *Rhizome* is an absolute masterpiece."[18] Nonetheless, the Deleuzian notion is not entirely similar to that of networks used by the anthropology of science. For the latter, the first intention, contrary to that of the Deleuzian notion, is to reterritorialize. In the second place, the notion of rhizome is too fluid, without stopping points, and it is therefore not very well adapted to the mechanisms put in place with the intersection of science, technology, and the market. In such cases, if there is no territory, one may nevertheless control, at a single point, the set of networks. "IBM is not a territory but rather constitutes networks that can gather at one point under the gaze of the chief executive officer."[19] *Finally, a truth...*

## Starting with Mediations

We have already evoked the importance of the notion of translation, so essential to Michel Serres, for this new anthropology of science. And the visibility of the scientific fact for Callon and Latour is tied to the chain of translation along multiple displacements; this connection enables the deduction of the initial heterogeneity of discourses, laboratories, and mobilized resources. This proximity to Serres has in addition been recently concretized by the publication of a collective work.[20] Above all, this anthropology of science identifies itself as breaking with the modern project of separation, of placing a great distance between the natural world and objects, on the one hand, and subjects, on the other. It is with Kantianism that the modern project takes shape. "Things-in-themselves become inaccessible while, symmetrically, the transcendental subject becomes infinitely remote from the world."[21] Once the break is complete, the attempts to surmount it will turn out to be impasses. In this way, the Hegelian dialectic, according to Latour, expands the abyss between the poles of subject and object that it aims to fill. The phenomenological project is deployed over an "insurmountable"[22] tension between the object and the subject.

The semiotic turn, marked by the structuralist moment in France and especially by the work of Algirdas Julien Greimas, offers greater freedom to maneuver, according to Latour. It allows one to say that the construction of a subject, a time, and a space is indeed the expression of a choice within a range of possibilities. But this discursive, linguistic moment also led him to an impasse because the proponents of semiotics "have themselves limited their enterprise to discourse alone."[23] Now, quasi objects are at once "real, discursive, and social,"[24] according to the foundational postulate of the anthropology of science.

Therefore, Latour advocates reversing the customary formula of the moderns, according to which one had to start with a process of purification to divide what comes from the subject from what is extracted from the object, and in a second phase to multiply the intermediaries in order to arrive at an explanation situated at the point of contact between two extremes. In opposition to this procedure, Latour proposes transforming the point of division/contact into a starting point for research that leads toward the extremes of subject and object. "This explanatory model allows us instead to integrate the work of purification as a particular case of mediation."[25] After all the talk about each paradigm shift in the Copernican-Galilean revolutions, Latour proposes terming this new orientation a "Copernican counter-revolution."[26]

The second great shift in the anthropology of science, in the tradition of David Bloor's work,[27] is the principle of the symmetry of explanations in scientific development. This symmetrization of treatment between the arguments of the winners and those of the losers of scientific history breaks with the French epistemological tradition. In this tradition, science must detach itself from its ideological shell; the task of epistemology is to perform this surgical act, after which "objects alone will remain, excised from the entire network that gave them meaning."[28] Dispensing with the teleological facility of putting the losers aside has the effect of suggesting a "slimming treatment for the explanations."[29]

Latour and Callon do not, nonetheless, assume Bloor's notion without modification. They radicalize and generalize it in a Kuhnian relativist perspective. In this respect, Thomas Kuhn has had a decisive role in initiating a sociological bent in the history of knowledge. Limited to an equality of treatment between the winners and the losers, the notion of symmetry enters the anthropology of science with a similar equalization of the elements of nature and those of society. This principle of generalized symmetry implies strict logical requirements. First of all, in renouncing the postulation of a distinction between truth and error, it limits recourse to all overarching metalanguage. In addition, the anthropologist is proscribed from passing from one register of explanation to another, a passage that is customary in the explanation of external reality by society or society by external reality. One of the principles of generalized symmetry is, on the contrary, to start with the need for a simultaneous explanation of both nature and society—whereas there is the habit of placing all the weight of explanation on society, which amounts to remaining in an asymmetrical schema. This mode of reasoning is therefore in radical rupture with the French epistemological tradition, which privileges an entire hierarchy of determinations in the context of a metalanguage. "Symmetrization, as well as the system of explanation it implies, is perhaps a methodological translation of realism."[30] Latour does not give up the search for causal explanations, but on condition of paying the price they entail. They are situated along a chain of narratives, mediators, and mediations in the course of a true transfer of forces and equivalences.

This orientation leads Latour and Callon to question anew the "great divisions": that between society and nature, constitutive of modernity, as much as that which opposes social processes to scientific discoveries. To these artificial oppositions, they prefer a vast, joint movement of expression of the spokespersons of society and nature. The anthropology of science then becomes a "sociology of representatives, of spokespersons, and of witnesses who appear in the chain of translation through which the scientific utterance or technical innovation takes shape."[31] The privileged place of revealing this chain of translation is the laboratory. There the researcher makes nature speak. Now, electrons, enzymes, and other manipulated elements have no more existence in themselves than the category of managers or that of proletarians. They only exist according to a narrative, a discursive placement, what Paul Ricoeur calls a "narrative identity." They are "what their spokespersons say they are."[32] Technical operators then become active operators of the social bond in the same way as human operators in the setting of a generalized symmetrization.

## The Parliament of Things

This anthropology leads to the project of revitalizing the mediations and mediators indispensable to the social bond, thanks to the image of the "Parliament of Things."[33] The latter implies a renewed questioning of the great division of the constitution of modernity and its program of purification. On the horizon of the revitalized debate on public place, among the various representatives and spokespersons, the political can take shape. This parliament is already there, in the heart of the many networks, and at the same time it is not yet recognized. In this way, it functions as a fiction and a vector of becoming. It has the "virtues of humor."[34] The participants in this parliament of things are no longer defined on the basis of convictions derived from the world of things; they are, on the contrary, representatives of problems in relation to which they are situated.

The dialogic at work in the heart of this parliament of things is therefore fundamentally new. It may be articulated with a model (which we will consider below)—that of the Cities, put forth by Luc Boltanski and Laurent Thévenot—insofar as this parliament puts mediators and spokespersons in conference with plural logics, with partial and often incommensurable knowledges. Such a dynamization of what one could term a situated social bond occurs by way of the transformation of the modern, serialized citizen, outside the field of competency of the arbitrations reserved for the experts, into a citizen capable of gaining access to the debates that enable a recovery of the great stakes in play and to the processes of decision making. "It is not a question here of 'making' the citizen vote, but of inventing the set-ups such that these citizens the experts speak of may be effectively present, capable of asking questions to which their interest makes them sensitive, of requiring explanations, of setting conditions, of suggesting modalities; in short, of participating in invention."[35]

In this way, Isabelle Stengers has taken account of an experiment of this type in Holland involving *junkiebonders*. In this experiment, addicts were able to validate their points of view on drug use. The problem, reformulated as such, until now reserved for the experts alone, has enabled the invention of innovative solutions. The addicts, considered as "citizens just like the others,"[36] were not placed at a distance and simply treated as sick people to be cured or offenders to be punished. This parliament of things invites not a utopian transparency of intersubjectivity, but a generalized dialogic implicating all concerned spokespersons. The social bond is then reanimated, thanks to the multiple mediators needed to make possible the emergence of public debate. This renaissance implies another relation to the political and the scientific, until now presented as two incommensurable dimensions that mutually contaminated each other. To rethink the political in new terms implies conceiving of how the "notion of emancipation is linked to science and reciprocally . . . , [of] what becomes of politics, of freedom's task of representation, if we so radically change our position on the sciences."[37]

This parliament of things that Latour envisages is not the parliament of suffering whales; it is that of the spokespersons in the fashion of the scientist who comes to testify to the United States Congress that the forests are dying from acid rain. This new manner of apprehending problems contributes to the birth of a different democracy that multiplies its principals, its spokespersons. In this regard, Latour advocates adding a seventh city to Boltanski and Thévenot's model, that of ecology, which is not resolvable into the six other existing ones. "The city of ecology simply says that we do not know what forms the common humanity of man; and that even perhaps without the elephants of Amboseli, without the divagating water of the Drôme, without the bears of the Pyrénées, without the doves of the Lot, without the water table of Beauce, there would not be any humans."[38]

Prudential judgment is indispensable within this new city, for it requires that one take into account the views of multiple principals in uncertain relations on the chain of transformation of problems—problems as concrete as the politics of recycling waste, the question of clean water, or of whether the Amazon forest is encroaching on the savanna, and so on. Besides, this parliament of things is already a potentiality in the current controversies among politicians, technocrats, and scientists. The parliamentary device it is inaugurating is in fact a hybrid of politics, science, and administration. "This parliament resembles a laboratory much more than it does the Chambre des Députés, but this laboratory resembles a forum or the Paris Stock Exchange much more than it does the temple of truth."[39]

*Ten*

# A Great Innovation:
# The Introduction of Objects

The major index of the change of paradigm, of the renewed questioning of the old divisions, was the introduction of objects very much within the field of investigation in the social sciences. "That changed a good part of the social sciences, which were previously sciences without objects."[1] The true innovation is essentially located there, and it does not fail to pose important problems of a philosophical order. The anthropology of science of the CSI went the farthest in the direction of introducing objects, nonhumans, into its field of observation. There resulted from this a certain number of shifts that necessitated a redefinition of science, society, and what was destined to link the two: discourse. In classical scientific theory, the object is already there, a given of nature that is transformed by history. Now, the anthropology of science directs its gaze toward objects in the process of being constituted, "hot objects."[2]

A greater and greater attention was mobilizing at once the anthropology of science, the economics of convention, and certain cognitivists around objects. There were more and more seminars in the new field of study. This revealed a common evolution of breaking with the structuralist period, during which objects were of course studied, but as mere props for signs. Meanwhile, among the various currents, the differences remain great and the debate open concerning the place to attribute to objects, to nonhumans in relation to humans.

## Humans and Nonhumans

The anthropology of science of Callon and Latour goes the farthest in insisting on the lack of distinction between the two. The consideration of quasi objects, hybrids that increase in number, favors the requirement of total symmetrization between the two poles. "What we're trying to do, with Bruno, is to have an interest in all the somewhat extreme situations in which the attribution of the status of humanness is negotiated, discussed, debated, questioned."[3] It is then fitting to follow the chain of objects very closely. Now, they change status according to the points where they are located in the chain of translation that they follow. They reconstruct the whole in the framework of a complex process.

Callon has carried out this tracking of the object by applying it to waste ("You take a can of peas and you follow what happens to it"),[4] in order to arrive at the conclusion that there is no true source that begins the action. The latter is continual along the chain of transformations in which there is an assembly of each of the entities, which intervene by adding something to the previous action, thus becoming new sources enabling the action to keep moving.[5]

Recently, Philippe Pignarre has followed this chain of transformation with regard to medications. Tracking the route that leads to the approval of a medication after many tests clearly shows that "the medication consumed has a 'social life'; it takes two years, on the average, for it to be 'constituted' as a medication and to obtain the administrative authorization for it to be sold."[6] One of the major tests that leads, in modern medicine, to the approval or rejection of a medication is its comparison to a placebo. Now, in this area, the statistical studies undertaken remain unsatisfactory and do not allow an answer to the question posed by the important rate of cure obtained through the effect of placebos, that is, through suggestion.

Pignarre, in order to show to what point a medication does not derive from its chemical substance alone, compares two chemically similar substances that have closely equivalent effects: methadone, which has been a medication since late 1994, and heroin, classified as a drug. He asked the question of what happens "on the level of the consumers."[7] The dependence of the substance on the semantic social chain of which it is an integral part is in this special case quite spectacular. The "same" product classified as a drug, heroin, refers to marginality, the risk of HIV infection, anxiety, and a mental state nearing psychosis, termed "borderline," whereas methadone, classified as a medication, has the aim of social reintegration, protection against infections, relief of anxiety, and psychic and emotional stabilization. Of course, for Pignarre it is not a matter of denying the characteristics of the molecule in question and making the medication a pure semantic product, dependent on its administrative classification; but "these chemical characteristics are not the 'truth' of the medication."[8] What stands out in this comparison is the necessity of reconstituting all the steps in the chain of production, appropriation, and distribution of the object in the social fabric from which it is inseparable.

When he participated in an expedition in the Amazon forest at Boa Vista to see if the forest was advancing or shrinking there, Latour was not really interested in the social context; but he closely followed a curious orange box, the Topofil, a measuring device indispensable to the pedologist. The Ariadne's thread of the scientific experiment in progress, the Topofil enabled the transformation of a segment of virgin forest into a laboratory, and offered the possibility of diagramming it. The object was raised, within the narrative of this expedition, to the status of a true hero of the experimentation so as to demonstrate that "the phenomena are not found at the meeting point between the things and the forms of the human mind, but spread along the reversible chain of transformation where, at each stage, they lose certain properties and gain others that make them compatible with the calculation centers already in place."[9] Not all those who have reintroduced objects share, for all that, this position regarding the symmetry between humans and nonhumans.

The researchers at the CREA maintain asymmetry and accord a privilege to the organizing capacity of action, to intentionality, which they situate on the side of the human being. As intentional actions presuppose a programming, an argumentation, a capacity to connect situations in the medium of a discursive framework, all these competencies can be placed only on the side of the human being. In the case of intentionality, the observer may introduce the relation to objects, but only in the form of an instrumentalization of things. A second relation to the object is at work, notably with Luc Boltanski and Laurent Thévenot, that of justification. It proceeds by the classification of objects according to their capacity to fit into the world that the subject constructs. There is a third type of action, involving the accommodation or adjustment of objects, mere adaptation, placement in compatibility, yet without the intervention of justification or intention. It is still another register of the use of objects, which are then defined by their material properties in a privileged relation to the body of the subject.

Each of these conceptions has its own analytics, but what they have in common is the will to introduce the world of objects into the domain of the social sciences. It happens that they coexist in one undertaking. This is the case for the international seminar on objects that took place for two academic years, from 1991 to 1993, at the International Institute at La Défense, in the context of the activities of the EHESS and of the research program of the Institute on the "conventions and coordination of action." This collective project was directed by Bernard Conein, Nicolas Dodier, and Laurent Thévenot.[10] It ended by recentering the object at the very heart of action, whereas the object had the tendency to oscillate between the position of a rigid, natural constraint and that of a sign of common beliefs. The procedure came down to very precisely considering the interaction between the human actor and his or her environment and getting to the prevalence of the notion of "situated cognition."

In this regard, the works of Donald Norman are particularly suggestive when he demonstrates that the objects implicated in action can be so many resources enabling the actor to lighten his or her cognitive tasks.[11] Conein got to know Don Norman and Phil Agre at the University of California, San Diego. At issue was a whole current that came from artificial intelligence and in which there was an interest in situated action, for the purpose of finding computational models termed reactive, that is, interactive. Norman applied himself to the study of the cognitive artifacts omnipresent in our everyday activities. "Certain artifacts make us stronger or faster; others protect us from the elements or from predators; still others feed and clothe us."[12] The cognitive artifact thus plays the role of a support for human activity and may contribute to an improved understanding of human cognition. Conein is particularly interested in Rodney Brooks's research in robotics. Brooks finds that, from the moment the manufacture of autonomous creatures begins, they may be used as a heuristic frame so as to know better the mode of inscription of human intelligence. Brooks has thus focused on small creatures, artificial insects endowed with a perceptual system that move to avoid obstacles. "Brooks's idea is to get back to the fundamental inspiration of artificial intelligence, which was not limited to the sole framework of 'AI,' but rather presented the functioning of intelligence from the point of view of the foundation of cognitive science."[13] In placing himself at the junction between theories of action and cognitive science, Phil Agre has invented a reactive system called Pengi.[14] It is a video game programmed and founded on the principles of reactive intelligence.

## Situated Cognition

The project of situated cognition is not merely speculative. On the contrary, it aspires to find extensions in industrial enterprise. On the basis of a study of objects and thanks to the increase of the various levels of analysis (cognitive, interactive, functional), it is possible to draw lessons on their concrete use in the world of work, with what this may limit through constraints but also with contributions to effective aid. The artifact is conceived as a possible cognitive alleviation. Any space may become a place of observation of these interactions.

Bernard Conein and Eric Jacopin have thus also taken home cooking, a classical site of everyday functionality, and the preparation of a short pastry to "grasp how the placement of objects is susceptible of generating planes of action in various ways."[15] The elucidation of a microscale of interaction between the stabilized universe of the disposition of objects and the practical use of this recipe allows the close dependency of the plane of action in relation to the degree of stabilization of the environment to be brought to light. The objects play an active role here, insofar as they may serve as an instrument of the evaluation, of the channeling of the action. In the framework of such a problematic, the links between action and objects "cannot, as Mead and Gibson suggest, be reduced to a control of the execution."[16] Of course, the deduction of this study on cooking seems to depend on evidence; but it can be measured to what extent a similar attention to the spatial disposition of the cognitive prostheses constituted by objects in a factory may lead to fertile observations on production.

To remain at the stage of ordinary objects, we may follow Laurent Thévenot's observations on the stroller and the many tests to which it is submitted before becoming operational. It must in fact be able to bear going up and down stairs, cross over pebbly ground, roll in the mud or sand without damage—all the while providing security for the baby in it. To do this, the technicians must leave their lab to stage the situation of the potential user of the ordinary object. "Inspired by methods in the social sciences, [they] will include instruments of investigation that treat humans in the function of actor."[17] The need to account for the actor makes it impossible to reduce the object to mere intangible properties. The testing of the object even follows the contours of an integrative "emplotment" of the user.

On the horizon of these very concrete studies on the deployment of action, there is a new way of apprehending the social bond as closely as possible to the way in which it emerges and inscribes itself in the lived world. Such a perspective can only excite the interest of the economists of convention, Thévenot's in particular. The latter also recognizes his debt in this area to the studies of Michel Callon and Bruno Latour. "The sociologists and anthropologists of science have opened our eyes to the poor treatment of things. They have brought into evidence the interwoven links between humans and nonhumans in the networks that confer their consistency to scientific and technical objects."[18] Meanwhile, it is on the other side—not that of networks in formation, but that of humans—that Thévenot situates himself, in order to recapture the way they treat the environment on the basis of organizing schemas of action. Thévenot especially directs attention, with Luc Boltanski, to the place of objects in the modalities of justification of the social actors and thus puts the "social bond to the test of things."[19]

In this regard, Boltanski and Thévenot are inspired by Latour's principle of symmetry, according to which attention to the links between the reasons evoked and the objects engaged allows one not to bring the weight of the coordination of conduct exclusively to bear on the systems of rules and beliefs alone; this has the effect of placing "all the potentialities of order alongside the regularity of things."[20] It is fitting, on the contrary, to recognize the site that returns to things within the constraints of realist judgment. It is then a matter of examining and problematizing the reality test by wondering how the actors come to terms with what will have the status of reality. This orientation breaks with the constructivism generally adopted by the social sciences, which have had a tendency to reduce the social dimension to an unproblematized level of reality. These two planes are examined in order to "know how humans get along in their environment, including the human one."[21] Now, the economic and the social are combined in the world of things, and the procedures of qualifying the latter are so many occasions for stakes, for quarrels between varied and contra-dictory logics.[22]

## A Technodemocracy

Contrary to the Heideggerian positions concerning the critique of technical modernity, certain scholars today show that the new technologies can be a good means of strengthening democracy and citizen participation, and effective supports for the revitalization of the social bond. In this way Pierre Lévy makes the plea for a "technodemocracy."[23] He has especially studied the place hypertext may occupy and the configuration that may result. Digital support opens a field of possibilities in which the interpretive, reflexive dimension is particularly appealed to. Hypertext[24] is in fact an essential instrument to aid interpretation and commentary. "On the technological level, the golden age of hermeneutics is before us."[25] The object is not an in-itself separable from its conditions of emergence and social extensions; it determines nothing by itself, but contributes to creating new possibilities in the order of communication. The latter involves two axes: the first one is temporal, that of interpretation, of giving meaning, and the other is spatial, that of the transfer of information from one point to another. At the conjunction of these two poles, techno-science is "hermeneutic through and through."[26] It is therefore absurd to oppose the interpretive to the technological dimension; they are less and less separable in hybrid realities where the human and the non-human are mixed. "For science and technology, the effect of laicization that Machiavelli achieved in politics remains to be done. This work is already advanced, thanks to the efforts of the new school of the anthropology of science."[27]

The approach to communication in terms of interpretation is opposed, on the other hand, to the conception in terms of mere transmission, and in this sense it is the reality of the social bond that becomes the major stake. From the moment that communication is conceived as a process strongly linked to the contextuality of the relations among messages, it becomes an essential moment in the understanding of social acting that should be recaptured in a globality always open to the other and to new interpretive attempts. So communication passes through a multiform process of elements that enter into a synergy with one another.

On the basis of such a conception in terms of an emergent process,

Lévy intends to locate the moments of blockage in communication and elaborate a project of maximum democracy that would use collective intelligence. Every individual and group knowingly situated in the communicative process would have the opportunity to negotiate its positions, at any moment to propose new interpretations. Within this process of constant subjectification, the social bond is constructed as endlessly redefined emergence. The technical object, in this case hypertext, is neither impugned as an oppressive machine nor praised as a demiurge; it is rather the simple redeployment of the configuration of possibilities. It is not so much a matter of postulating a mastery of the technology on the basis of a distancing from it as it is of bringing its potentialities into play in the sense of a project that enables the creation of the bases of a technodemocracy. "The full integration of technical choices into the process of democratic decision would be a key element in the necessary transformation of the political."[28]

It is this attempt at articulating new technological means with the desire to recover a concrete human solidarity that directs the project of Lévy and Michel Authier involving the focus on trees of knowledge.[29] The project consists of adapting democracy to the era of communication and of allowing everyone to take part in speaking and collective decision making. Whereas earlier society essentially located itself in rural space, and then occupied industrial space, today's society finds its identity within the space of knowledge. This still poorly stabilized identity is in crisis, for it has not yet found the means of collective location in this new space. It is a system that would enable the readability and visibility of this space of knowledge that the project of the trees of knowledge would attempt to define.

This system is founded on a dynamic that belongs to communities of knowing. It aims to articulate individual and collective knowledge. "The setup of the trees of knowledge does not obey a (statistical) logic of sampling or of the average, but a dynamic of singularities."[30] The dynamic of the trees of knowledge, their capacity to visualize the process of the collective acquisition of knowledge, allows for a reversal of the relation of transmission; it begins with the demand for a better correspondence to the particularity of needs according to a real time evaluated for the set of actors that constitutes the community of knowledge. "The proposed setup gives rise to a social bond that could be the beginning of a new form of citizenship."[31]

The system rests on the combination of three types of image: that of individuals, which is symbolized by an evolving blazon, according to the acquisition of knowledge; that of knowledges, represented by certificates granted to individuals after passing tests; and finally, the image of the community, identified with the tree of knowledge that organizes and articulates the community's set of certificates. Thus, the cognitive life of the community itself, and not some hierarchical classification preliminary to the knowledges, provides the shape of the tree. This setup notably has the effect of favoring a democracy of free exchange in relation to knowledge and a self-organization of individuals. The modes of appropriation of knowledge in this setup are characterized by their plasticity and their constantly evolving character.

*Eleven*

# Civility

*...the generation of May '68
discovered this virtue
rather late...*

The feeling of a loss, that of the traditional social bond—of a disaffiliation, as Robert Castel calls it[1]—or the orphan status of "fifty-four million individuals who do not belong," as Gérard Mendel put it in 1983,[2] has reinitiated reflection on what society meant in seventeenth-century terms: mutual understanding among persons, civility. This semantic shift allows a recentering of the early investigation of the social sciences, which concerned a broad social domain, toward what precisely specifies "being together." "The etymology of the word civility brings out four dimensions: the art of 'being together,' voluntarily restrained force, a respectful familiarity with one's fellows, and finally a virtue, as a nonobjectifiable truth, the hidden source of the first three qualities."[3] Problematizing this dimension induces a "tacit" reevaluation of the invisible yet major bonds that enable social relations to be woven.

The attention to what this bond covers passes through an entire notional project, in which empirical study and the conceptual dimension link up so as to elucidate the different inflections of the interpersonal relation. Understanding these nuances enables one to be situated at the heart of human relations. "This notional project can for itself be conducted much more directly, as it has explanatory virtues."[4] This research workshop aims to construct a theory of the mode of social constitution of the subject, by a conceptual rather than a genetic socialization. It will enable the analytic categories of latent meaning to be reinvigorated, to be made explicit. This is the case when one finds the very content of acting, of ressentiment, of the various forms of social connections. Thus, the difference between vengeance and punishment will be seen by placing in evidence a higher justificatory agency than mere feeling in the case of punishment, thanks to the existence of an absent third in the notion of vengeance. One may apply this procedure to all sorts of interactions, and ask what praise is—or flattery, invitation, or a relation of love or friendship.[5]

The detour through the way in which individuals represent to themselves the social bond that they weave with their environment is therefore essential, even if it does not imply the postulation of a clear consciousness, some mastery on the part of the actors over what they are doing. It is a whole culture, woven by the past and the conventions the past has engendered, that must be reexamined in its complexity. This comes down to asking what society is, not on the plane of great entities, great abstractions, but on the level of its everyday microreality. The concrete operations and operators that provoke the constant changes in the social bond are today becoming the object of a more vigilant attention. The term *civility* also refers to a broader dimension, which is that of the City. It enables the recovery of the political horizon of the social. "What as a last resort gives meaning to the political is not that it is the unique, central place, but rather that it is the place through which maintenance of the social bond is effected at the deepest level. Through the political dimension, we are sure of being members of the same world."[6]

## The Civil Bond

The examination of the mutual understanding at work in human relations also connects the sociology of the civil bond to a theory of knowledge and a phenomenology. This implies that one will treat social facts "as significations, that is, as singular events attached to and comprehensible by conceptual universals available in our common sense."[7] The problem of civility thus presents an invitation to revisit the phenomenological tradition in order to accept the richness of the experience of the social world as an intimate experience of what is lived: "The concept of civility is precisely that of the place of the intimate in the social."[8]

By the dissociation and articulation between the levels of the social and the intimate, sociology as Pharo understands it is a somewhat less ambitious project. It no longer claims to get at some presupposed totality, but, on the contrary, it scrupulously defines the autonomy of its field in relation to other levels of intelligibility—the structures of the mind and those of biology. No longer starting with the amalgam or the recovery of the human by the social, this "reduced" sociology thereby limits the "claims of social explanation."[9] Max Weber already linked the notions of meaning and legitimacy. Pursuing this exploratory avenue, Pharo proposes to systematize it by examining the relations of interdependence between the meaning of personal and intimate actions and their justification as legitimate in the civil world. Without an analytic tool on the plane of individual engagement, sociology has most often passed over its object. It must recover it, says Pharo, by revisiting the phenomenological tradition, in which the experience of the social world is in the first place an intimate experience. This phenomenological inspiration will allow a submission of every singular experience to the test of common sense.

The attention to the ordinary and the everyday may also be found in the positions of Simmel, when he put sociology on guard against its propensity to study only the great institutions. Rather, he engaged the field in considering reciprocal actions and "banal" relations among people.[10]

This shift must nevertheless not lead to turning one's back on the historical dimension that models the social bond on the basis of symbolic institutions. In the tradition of Claude Lefort, Marcel Gauchet and Louis Quéré both hold that the way power, knowledge, and law are figured in a society gives its members the certainty of "belonging to a common space and at the same time defines a certain possibility of relations among them."[11] Political democracy, for example, allows entry into a relationship by preserving a degree of anonymity, and therefore by respecting a certain lack of knowledge of the person, an indeterminacy, according to Claude Lefort.[12] The horizon of historicity is essential for situating this mode of articulation and the configuration of civil bonds. Historicization notably allows the emergence of the discrepancies and discordances as Norbert Elias analyzed them[13] between the consciousness individuals have of the nature of these bonds and their objective situation. In the society Elias studied, individuals situated the major site of the social bonds on the level of kinship at the very moment when the national state was consolidating. Today, on the contrary, the feeling of belonging is increasingly identified with the nation, whereas the latter is losing its substance to the advantage of larger entities. There are three levels of analysis that one must manage to correlate: that of the objectifiable data of the social, that of the analyst with her or his conceptual categories, and between the two the work of interpretation on the part of the actors themselves. These three views may enable access to that infrapolitical civil order, indispensable to the political order, of civility.

Nevertheless, Pharo deems that on the basis of this new attention there are still two pitfalls to avoid. The first is that of a strategic and utilitarian theory of action, which has a tendency to reduce civility to a search for personal profit on the basis of a preliminary rationalization of one's own interests. The other pitfall is the use of a conventionalist theory according to which civility is only the reflection of conventions deep-rooted in social practices; in these practices, individual behavior would merely be molded. Now, according to Pharo, these two orientations pass over the two dimensions proper to civility: its noninstrumental character and its inventiveness. In this regard, ethnomethodology serves as a good tool against these tendencies, because it advocates a constant attention to the contingent and perpetually mobile character of civil "commerce." "It seems more heuristic to look in the endogenous characters of the civil bond for the conditions that assure it the possibility of guarding itself against evil and the state of rage that flows from it."[14]

## Panic

The search for the basis of this "being together," this infrapolitical civility, is also at the center of the analyses of Jean-Pierre Dupuy. Dupuy has tried to surmount the impasses inherent in the binary opposition of individual and society by giving particular attention to emergent systems and to the disorders that create orders and by valorizing the notion of autonomy.

Among the first figures that Dupuy used for his heuristic power was that of mimetic desire, which he borrowed from René Girard. The matrix of the social was thus found in imitation based on a model furnished by others in the framework of a triangular relation between the subject, its alter ego, and the object. In the heart of civility, therefore, there is a conflict, a situation of competition that engenders violence. Societies then secreted antidotes to curb and regulate this violence. The appearance of the social, of "being together," is the corollary of an initial and foundational sacrifice.[15] Girardian anthropology has mainly interested Dupuy as a morphogenesis, in that it permits a restoration of radical indeterminacy to the constitution of the social bond through a break with the mechanical and determinist approaches to the social. The logic of the social is then translated by its capacity for self-organization. It renders null and void both the sociological reduction that grasps individuals as mere reflections of a first social reality and a methodological individualism for which the social is reduced to the sum of individual energies. "Instead of opposing the individual and the social, we must conceive them together, as mutually creating each other, defining and containing each other."[16]

How do we understand this bond that seems to escape reductionist enterprises and that nonetheless allows the essential question to be asked of how a society holds together? Dupuy invites us to read the symptoms when he seeks to account for the social bond on the way to dissolution on the basis of a particular collective phenomenon, panic. "If the social bond is invisible, it is when it is undone that we have the greatest chance of perceiving its effects, in a loosening of some sort."[17] In this regard, Dupuy evokes studies in the social sciences in the area explored especially by political economy (on stock market panics) and mass psychology, in order to show that the two approaches lead to the same inability to account for the phenomenon of panic.

Although the most extreme individualization that panic incites, the withdrawal into self-preservation, should make the analysis in terms of methodological individualism adequate, one of the founders of this current, John William Nevil Watkins, excludes all phenomena of panic from his field of application, considering them irrational phenomena.[18] For its part, political economy fails in its attempt at rationalizing a financial crash that may strike after a period of speculative fever. Explanation as a manifestation of the irrational, proper to mass psychology, fails just as much to delimit what happens.

Dupuy, on the contrary, sees in Keynesian analysis certain essential intuitions, such as that according to which the good speculator is the one who guesses better than the crowd what the crowd is going to do. Thus, Keynes introduced analysis in terms of specular logic, as a mirror effect. "In a situation of radical uncertainty, the only rational behavior, according to Keynes, is to imitate others."[19] Dupuy's analysis links up with the positions of a socioeconomics as defined by American sociologist Mark Granovetter, who has also searched for a third

way between the desocialized conception of the actor that the economist sketches and the oversocialization of the same actor that the sociologist insists on. Behavior takes place within social microstructures
that are so many levels of mediation for the actor. Granovetter wrote
his thesis on the process induced by looking for a job. He cited as evidence the fact that information about a job comes to the individual
along chains of relations among groups of people, in the manner of
mathematical chains. He thus shows the strength of weak bonds, of
those that derive from networks of friendship, proximity, collegial relations, or membership in the same association. This group brings into
circulation the information necessary to find a job more so than the
group of strong bonds woven by familial relations.[20]

Attention to thresholds, to mediations, to the singularity of situations thus allows one to approach the phenomenon of panic as relevant to a possible analysis by social sciences located between rationality and irrationality. "By explaining paradoxical outcomes as the
result of aggregation processes, threshold models take the 'strangeness' often associated with collective behavior out of the heads of actors and put it into the dynamics of situations."[21]

On the very basis of the individual, according to Dupuy, the researcher may have access to the signification of behavior, and therefore to the nature of the civil bond. From methodological individualism, defined on the epistemological level by Karl Popper, Dupuy
retains the basic principle according to which "in no case should one
attribute to collective beings the qualities of a subject: wills, intentions, conscience . . ."[22] He does not for all that adopt all the positions
of methodological individualism. As we have already seen, for him
individuals are not self-sufficient, but, on the contrary, they construct
themselves in specularity according to René Girard's mimetic model.
In this way, the speculative bubbles that generate movements of panic
are no longer considered the exception, but the rule, that of the chain
of speculations of the actors on the desire of the others. The coherence
of the social world is thus held together only by a tenuous thread, the
almost magical one of shared illusions. If in the end the thread that
enables the social bond comes undone, everything is ruined. The
crowd is then carried away by panic and the market becomes chaos.
"Crowd, contract, and market all have the function of 'containing,' in
both senses of the term, the violence that wells up everywhere and
threatens to explode at any moment."[23]

## Self-Deception

What remains to be introduced is the temporal dimension, absent from game theory, which exclusively privileges instantaneousness. The articulation of individual psychology and collective phenomena is broadly assumed by the philosophy of mind in which there is an interest in, among other things, so-called irrational beliefs. Pascal Engel and Jean-Pierre Dupuy share the same interest in what the Anglo-Saxons call self-deception—that is, taking one's desires for reality and so voluntarily blinding oneself. "There is no reason not to think that this type of irrational belief can't also have collective dimensions."[24] In this area of investigation, contacts are made to mobilize different disciplines, in order to explore the paradoxical behavior of self-deception. On this point, Engel has thus begun a dialogue with Pierre Fédida, the psychoanalyst, that allows a departure from the abstract considerations of the philosophy of mind.

This desire to depart from abstractions may more generally be found in Bernard Conein's research program in social cognition; for Conein, it is an issue of constructing a theory of social relations, in particular around the question of reciprocity, cooperation, altruism, and empathy. On this level, the ethologists' work of observation may be useful in finding out what happens when there is an alliance between individuals, and what that implies in the area of required aptitudes: "An understanding of relation is needed for this."[25] The social ritualization destined to repress violence is thus at the heart of the examinations of the construction of the social bond.

The social rituals' function of pacification may be observed at many minute levels of relations of civility. As Edmond Marc and Dominique Picard have brought to notice,[26] the stakes of communication may be apprehended by observing the social rituals whose purpose is to pacify. Thus, in the course of a conversation, the speakers not only exchange information, but respond to the desire to individuate themselves. So they give a value to their personal identity at the same time as they show their will to integrate into the group. "These needs direct the strategies of identification that each pursues in his social relations."[27] The prescriptions and proscriptions of savoir-vivre respond to a logic, which is of course variable according to place and time but permanent in its purpose of maintaining civility around notions of sociality, reciprocity, deference, and discretion.[28]

## Taming the Drives

Denis Duclos advocates civility as a remedy for and choice of the properly human dimension.[29] Civility alone can tame the desire for power and serve as a counterweight to hatred, moderate the iconic transports, whether they have to do with identity or simple technicist utopias. Putting back to back the hubris of the hypertrophy of identity and that of the dissolution of the subject, Duclos sees in civility the possible reinscription of responsibility "within the limits of a negotiated use."[30] It avoids the still possible unbalancing of heroes with two faces: humans and animals, humans and machines, represented by Dr. Jekyll and Mr. Hyde, Frankenstein, or Bioman.[31] In the face of these risks of overflow, civility is vigilant and discreetly maintains the humanity of mankind. "If civility exists, it does so in spite of the great homeostatic schemas."[32] Civility—by its plasticity, its informal character—enables one to depart from the frameworks of binary analysis to bring into prevalence a logic with multiple criteria, which refers to the singularity of situations. In this regard, it serves to redefine the emergence of the political according to new and more pragmatic lines of force in which often contradictory logics come into consideration, as well as solutions that can only account for complexity. "How will the surveyor respect the interests of the farmers in a regrouping of lands, without doing harm to the interests of the residents of the village?"[33]

Civility thus brings on a detour through the human, thanks to intersubjectivity, to find solutions to problems of a political order, whether on the micro or macro scale. It contributes to the consideration of possible solutions in terms of a dialogic between social actors, rather than on the basis of a priori categorical postulates. Through the reactivation of relations of civility, the intensity of the social bonds may be recovered. A whole new continent remains to be explored that leads the scholar to track down the discrete manifestations of civility apart from the obvious aspects of the social, in the interstices, in the mediations that retie the bonds between traditions and institutions.

In this regard, the quest for civility is an area of the future. It appears as a beyond in relation to the sector of traditional employment in agriculture and industry. It is open to the entire relational domain. Now, this last refuge of sociality is not easily automated, as Jacques Chaban-Delmas, a presidential candidate in 1974, can clearly and bit-

terly remember; Chaban-Delmas inopportunely advocated the re-
placement of the teaching staff by video. He misunderstood that the
function of the school, as for many institutions, is above all relational:

> When I arrived at the University of Paris VIII, they introduced a
> charming young woman to me as the pillar of the department. She
> was the secretary and occupied a central place—not because she had
> and processed information, but because she was always there and so
> formed the bond among everyone, teachers and students. Without
> her, everything would fall apart.[34] *No, you'd get another secretary.*

The progressive deconstruction of institutions' capacity for integration makes more and more manifest the role of the social bond, the
desire to "be together" in a collectivity; in this regard, the social sciences can play a major role: "If there is a science to invent, it's how to
form a social bond."[35]

A whole new sector may open in this way, in which attention
would be given to the process of making commonality, of the emergence of the collective, of the connection among individuals sharing
their competencies, knowledges, resources, and projects. Henceforth,
the social bond no longer has a single, topical, and assignable foundation, whether territory, tradition, the social contract, or communication. It is in some ways all of these, but it does not allow itself to be reduced to a single dimension. On the contrary, the social bond finds in
the notion of a network—with its nodes and indeterminate routes—its
current possible expression.

The civil bond may, we have seen, be realized in the parliament of
things in which the notion of a minority is not opposed to that of a
majority. In this perspective, there are only minorities that can add up,
without acceding to a discourse of general scope and majoritarian vocation. "If the parliament of things exists, it is in an aesthetic of the
plus one."[36] This utopia of a new civil bond may function as a booster
project, may put in motion, learn to resist, and thus contribute to a social problematic of the active production of self-organizing minorities.
It may therefore have concrete effects.

In the scientific realm, the operational model is that of laboratory
purification of the social elements, of the ethical dimensions, considered as so many parasites in relation to the properly scientific dimension. On the basis of this culture reduced to its expression of expertise,
the scientist refuses to engage in another terrain than that of his or her

rational experimentation. Thus, the director of Généthon,[37] Daniel Cohen, does not answer when he is questioned about the risks (which he knows well) of possible manipulation of the genetic map. He hides behind the answers society must give and places himself outside his own scientific position. "In this case, rational practices cease, and we enter the domain of the decisions by which society will be constituted in the future."[38] There is another possibility: that of a collective culture of joint expertise all along the process that leads from the lab to the decisions, which attempts to incite the broadest debate in society, to engage controversies where the plurality of approaches to the problem at hand might be found, thereby associating all the concerned minorities.

# Twelve

# Gift and Countergift

The search for the basis of "being together," of the social bond, has for a long time been the objective of Alain Caillé and the journal he directs, *La Revue du MAUSS*. He achieved a founding break through his radical critique of generalized utilitarianism. In this way, he began taking his distance from a sociology of unveiling backed up by a philosophy of suspicion. Caillé enabled a shift in the view of what acting means by giving weight to the heuristic value of the gift. This idea was transformed from a tutelary reference to Marcel Mauss to a genuine paradigm with the capacity to shed light on human behavior. The figure of the gift would enable the avoidance and denunciation, in the lineage of Maussian anthropology, of all forms of economic reductionism. Caillé succeeded in reconciling the tradition left by Mauss and the new interactionist research by proposing a third way, that of the logic of the gift, between interest and disinterest, between the state and the market.

## Antiutilitarianism

This attention to the gift was born from a break with the utilitarian paradigm that was dominant in the social sciences during the 1960s and 1970s. Utilitarianism postulates that only the rational, calculating, interested behavior of social actors is comprehensible to the social sciences.[1] It is backed up by the model of *homo economicus* and has been much used in economic science to elucidate the laws of the market. On the basis of this position of strength, it has been extended into other areas of human behavior. In this way, it has been adopted more or less explicitly by a sociology traversed by numerous currents, but that recognizes a common paradigm in this explanatory model.

With the market, "we have finally found the ultimate cause of action: interest."[2] The paradigm of interest has the merit of having all the signs of scientificity, that of mathematical formalization and that of causality from mechanical physics. It also bears a vision of human historicity as a struggle against scarcity and the progressive emergence of the rules of the market. Of course, this model, which has inspired methodological individualism and the theory of rational choice, has undergone several recent adaptations. In general, the rustic representation of the calculation of interests has been abandoned in favor of substituting, for the calculating subjects, more socialized and contextualized subjects; the latter react on the spot with successive and precarious arrangements. The axiomatic of interest is thereby complexified.

There is another tradition of utilitarianism, an Anglo-Saxon, analytic utilitarianism, which is a normative, ethical version. "This utilitarianism is ordered around a simple criterion by which what is just is what contributes to maximizing the happiness of the greatest number."[3] This philosophy belongs to a perspective that seems to be an alternative to that of interest, because up to a point it postulates that it is desirable to sacrifice one's own happiness to that of the greatest number. Utilitarianism thus puts in motion two seemingly antithetical theories, one resting on calculated egoism and the other on altruism. Caillé advocates rejoining these two poles, which have been dissociated to the point of becoming contradictory.

To overcome this disjunction, one must pass through an accounting for the multiple states of the subject. This implies that "human action does not proceed from just one focus, but rather from several."[4] The principles of action are irreducible to each other, as Max Weber already saw when he formulated four ideal types of action.[5] Between the poles of egoism and altruism, the paradigm of the gift presents itself as a third way between the subject enclosed in his ego, too folded in on himself to be open to the gift, and the subject who is too free of all social contingency to integrate herself into an interactionist perspective. Under a secondary sociality marked by functions and institutions, whose efficiency is undeniable, one may reach the understanding of a primary sociality that organizes relations among persons.

Thanks to this tilting toward the heart, toward the matrix of inter-action centered on the obligation of giving/receiving/returning, one may surpass the traditional dichotomies and think, as Jacques Godbout writes, that "in the gift, the kind circulates in the service of the bind."[6]

This third site, that of the order of human interactions itself, of intersubjectivity, escapes both pure constraint and pure interest, all the while undergoing the one and the other. The social sciences substi-tute, for the exclusive attention to relations of verticality, a new inter-est in instituted relations among individuals, on a horizontal plane. The fertility of such a scale is obvious, as we have seen, in the notion of the network as Michel Callon and Bruno Latour define it.

## The Third Way

This recent theorization has brought about the appearance of a third way that, even though not infinitesimal, is still not a macroreality. Modernity has had a tendency to separate primary from secondary so-ciality, to the point of making the latter into a plane of abstract rela-tions, cut off from their referent, from the content of what they imply in the interrelation between persons. This is the case for those entities that have become objectifiable, such as the market, the state, or sci-ence. "Now, there exist relations between person and person that function according to laws other than the abstract laws of abstract economics—other than the equalizing law of the market or the law of objective reason."[7] This opening allows access, through interaction, to the core that is common to all civilizations. It is this core that is what it is a question of bringing to emerge, without being limited to a microscopic scale of human relations. All this implies taking account of a vertical dimension, which transcends the relations between per-son and person and opens the political dimension, that of collective "being together," to societal existence.

Thanks to this political perspective, Caillé has returned to Hannah Arendt and Claude Lefort for their concern with thinking of the politi-cal not as a subsystem, but as an all-encompassing reality, symbolic and transverse. Now, the great political theories have hitherto been polarized over the question of who in the state or the market brings in the political as a solution to societal problems. Hence, they have "purely and simply forgotten the essential, which is the properly so-cial relation among individuals and groups, that which is not struc-tured on either economic interest or power. It is nonetheless this, the social relation, this nebulous protean form of microcosms, families, communities, work, networks, or associations of all kinds, that constitutes the true end of the overall process."[8]

A political horizon that integrates the question of the gift, of exchange, of the social relation as a third way between the logic of the state and that of the market is sketched in the current projects of the social sciences. The recent work of Godbout and Caillé[9] shows that the gift does not belong strictly to primitive societies, but also to our modern world. It is among us, so omnipresent as to become imperceptible. Marcel Mauss already characterized the gift as a universal category proper to archaic societies.[10] If we consider the gift more broadly as what is irreducible to relations of economic interest or of power, we must notice that it still defines many social relations at the very heart of modernity. "One must first of all surpass the early timidity of Marcel Mauss and formulate the hypothesis that the gift does not concern only archaic societies."[11]

Thus Godbout and Caillé went looking for the gift beneath exchange, thereby inverting the usual proposition concerning modernity. The market continues to occupy an eminent and indispensable place. It is most often a relation that is preferable to that of the gift in the case of relations among strangers: "Utilitarianism is the only possible morality common to two strangers."[12] Society cannot, nonetheless, construct itself solely on the basis of the relation of distancing, of the "weak bonds" that Granovetter has studied.

## Giving/Receiving/Returning

In order to grasp the gift in its relational function constitutive of the social bond, it is necessary to avoid two forms of reduction: that of simple "giving" that refers back to altruistic disinterest, and that of "returning" that reveals market exchange. Only in a triangular form, that of the "strange loop"[13] of giving/receiving/returning as an indivisible entity, may one hope to seize the nature of the gift. A total social phenomenon, as Marcel Mauss viewed it, that undecidable which the gift then is, is pulled between its at once spontaneous and obligatory character in a tension that makes it a paradoxical figure. The gift is an undecidable that causes a crisis of both the determinism of the mechanisms of causality that reduce all liberty to an illusion and the conception of a rational and calculating actor motivated solely by the maximization of his interests. Even as something free, the gift does not have the mechanicity of calculation. A strange attractor without a fixed point, the gift "is truly understood only through recourse to metaphor."[14]

Starting with a restricted definition of the gift—"Let us term a gift every benefit of goods or effected service, without guarantee of return, in view of creating, nurturing, or re-creating the social bond between persons"[15]—Jacques Godbout and Alain Caillé nonetheless have a tendency to cover all social reality with the unique view of their conception of a gift that becomes, at the end of their work, a source of life, of universal energy, and an apprenticeship to death.

To avoid this encompassing and excessive centrality of the gift, one may, with Luc Boltanski, situate it in a place that does not make it an undecidable All but rather a particular sphere of the economies of magnanimity, that of the inspired City. The gift is then an aspect of a social behavior moved more by other motivations, other magnanimities. The gift, for Boltanski,[16] refers to *agapē*,[17] which reveals that there is something preceding justice, Aristotle's *philia,* which is defined by a logic of equivalence, of reciprocity; but it also precedes *eros,* the love that implies a will to hold, to possess, to covet. Boltanski does not for all that advocate a disembodied approach to *agapē,* and the gift is only one magnanimity among others whose meaning is easy to find. When he evokes the controversy between Claude Lévi-Strauss and Claude Lefort, Boltanski takes as his own Lefort's criticism of the structuralist position because it passes alongside the "meaning of exchange through gifts."[18] He relies on the sociology of action that Lefort represents for him, for which men who give confirm to themselves "that none of them are things,"[19] against a sociology of Durkheimian tradition founded on the critique of experience.

The value of Boltanski's approach to the gift is that it begins with a pluralization of the diverse modes of identification. He thus avoids any form of individualistic or holistic reductionism by placing himself in the center of acting in a perspective that also goes back to the possibilities that Paul Ricoeur developed in 1950, in his thesis, when he differentiated having, being able, and valuing.[20] Only this pluralization of the various levels of acting allowed an escape from the risk of transforming the figure of the gift, repressed in the past, into an ahistorical invariant that would preserve a holistic approach to the social, into a disembodied figure, a simple and purely ethereal relationship, but that would nonetheless have the claim of making the social understandable.

The gift as a totality refers back to the disappearance of the gift, and it is this very erasure that interested Jacques Derrida when he used the figure of the gift to extend his work of deconstruction, begun in the 1960s. For Derrida, "If [the donee] recognizes [the gift] *as* gift, if the gift *appears to him as such* . . . , this simple recognition suffices to annul the gift."[21] The gift is the limit point, the impossible. Devoted to *dissemination,* it is an undecidable in the same way as *différance,* the hymen, the pharmacon, and the supplement in the economy of Derridean discourse—that is, an instrument of deconstruction that erases the opposition of inside/outside, of truth/error, all the forms of deployment of the logos.

The gift, then, is an evanescence alien to calculation, a simple simulacrum that organizes the carnivalesque order of reason. It contributes to the unsealing that radicalizes the structuralist program of the evacuation of the signified and of the search for corporeality in writing. Derrida thus empties the gift of one of its dimensions, that of interest, which, he says, is by nature alien to its function. "The gift suppresses the object (of the gift). It denies it as such. . . . One must give without knowing, without knowledge or recognition, without *thanks*: without anything, or at least without any object."[22] A figure of the impossible, the gift here breaks with the trilogy that constitutes it, that of giving/receiving/returning; it then loses all meaning other than the poetic.

## The Ternary Figure

The social bond is at the center of Dany-Robert Dufour's investigations. "What makes it hold? What makes it be a social bond that is sometimes undone in a brutal fashion?"[23] At the start of his project, there were especially a certain number of literary texts that had a common questioning, a suspension of a certain number of great referents. Samuel Beckett, notably, would play an important role, insofar as he radically suspended the spatial, temporal, and egological markers that organized the relation of the subject to its discourse: I/Here/Now. The first sentence of Beckett's *The Unnamable* questions these self-referential operators, these foundational deictics: "Where now? Who now? When now? Unquestioning. I, say I. Unbelieving. Questions, hypotheses, call them that."[24] The questioning, the suspension of these indicators led Dufour to a vigorous critique of the structuralist paradigm and the prevalence the latter accords to the binary figure.[25] He opposes another figure to it, a unary one, which inverts before and after, here and there, self and other.

This inversion could lead to madness if it did not somewhat fortuitously encounter another figure of order, as its object is at first to demonstrate the effectiveness, among the operators of language, of the unary operator, its audible character, repressed by the structuralist masters in favor of binarity alone. Following the publication of this work on the binary, Dufour undertook an exploration of all the continents of knowledge to realize an archaeology of the ternary that led him to discover a trinitary reason in debate/combat with binary reason for more than twenty-five hundred years, which today is taking over the former: "Trinitary man is disappearing."[26] The triumph of the categories of binarity, imposing various actualizations such as dualism, the dialectic, and causality, poses the problem of the human in its relation with the other, with the absent, and with death. Whereas the binary human being aspires to eternity and wishes to eradicate death by removing it from all sociality, the ternary figure allows a symbolization of absence. Beginning here, Dufour examines the way in which absence as a symbolic category governs a category of a different nature, of an organic nature, that of death. In this realm he discovers two conflictual modes of this governance, the binary and the ternary.

The social stake of this symbolic confrontation is great, because Dufour sees in the repression of ternarity a source of discontent in our civilization. "The triumph of binarity has considerable implications: the specific discontent of our century, the current discontent of human beings and of civilization to me seem to be conceivable by way of the major event of the enclosure of trinity by binarity."[27]

The development of the technosciences, of cybernetics, of systemic and structuralist theory reveals the spectacular character of the triumph of the binary conception. Now, this triumph represses the very naturality of the language that implies the ternary a priori. Enunciation, as Émile Benveniste showed in the 1960s, implies the existence of a pragmatic triangle: "In sum, the trinity represents the essence of the social bond, because without it there would be no interlocutory relation, there would be no human culture."[28] It is this escheat of the personal bond, of the social bond left fallow by the exclusive domination of Two-thinking, that should be reexamined by revisiting the tradition and the ensemble of the social sciences on the basis of the ternary figure, with the will to "make sense,"[29] after making a sign.

He sees this quest in the later work of Jacques Lacan, on topological models, notably on the Borromean knot that brings to pass the trinitary principle. "The Borromean knot is the topological occurrence of the trinity."[30] The repression of the symbolization of absence in a black box or an empty space, implicit in the structuralist program, has grave consequences. It goes as far as the destruction of the other, to fratricidal wars, to the proliferation of conflicts in which "each subject can basically negotiate the question of absence in the disappearance of the other. So there is a return of those paranoid wars in which one's neighbor is the worst enemy, and, when the paranoid has suppressed the other and in a certain way encountered the Law—that is, death—things go better."[31]

The social relation, the humanity of humanity, is therefore of a trinitary type: "*I, you, he* represent *the minimal social bond,* an *archisociality.*"[32] In different registers, one cannot not make a connection between the positions of Alain Caillé and those of Dufour, even if their respective efforts have been deployed in perspectives apparently alien to each other. Besides, Caillé explicitly recognizes this proximity and perceives an analogy between what Dufour defines as binarism and what he himself designates in speaking of utilitarianism, as well as one between the trinitary dimension and the logic engaged by the gift.[33]

# Part IV

*At the Risk of Acting*

*Thirteen*

# The Paradigm Shift

The thought of action imposes itself today in favor of what Marcel Gauchet has defined, as we have seen, as a "change of paradigm in the social sciences."[1] He has explained the meaning he gave to the term *paradigm:*[2] for him, this notion especially has the interest of being more cautious than the other more imperialist and more totalizing terms, such as *epistēmē*. The relative fuzziness of the notion allows a relativization of the influence of a model of explanation in the social sciences, which is not necessarily uniform or used by all in a univocal manner.

The dominant paradigm between 1950 and 1975 is the one whose history I have retraced, the structuralist paradigm.[3] Gauchet defines it as a "critical paradigm"[4] and characterizes it as an assembly constituted by a model discipline, linguistics, two reigning disciplines, sociology and ethnology, and two doctrines of reference, Marxism and psychoanalysis. This configuration of the social sciences had its philosophical expression in the thought of suspicion, the strategies of unveiling, with the idea that scientific truth is accessible but hidden, veiled. What characterized this paradigm was the deployment of a "thought of decentering."[5] The social sciences exalted during this period were those that had the greatest capacity to expropriate presence, the attestation of self, and in the first place everything that proceeded from action, from the act of language, all the occasions to conduct signifying operations. In this framework, structuralism allowed the combination of the effects of the theoretical sketch of the destitution of the subject with the ambition of an objectifying grasp with a scientific character.

## The Reflected Role of Action

During the 1980s, there was apparently a falling into a new paradigm marked by quite another intellectual organization, in which the theme of historicity was substituted for that of structure. This new period is especially marked by the "rehabilitation of the explicit and reflected role of action."[6] It is not for all that a matter of a mere return of the subject, as was once envisaged, in the plenitude and transparency of its postulated sovereignty. Research has, of course, shifted to the study of consciousness, but a consciousness problematized thanks to a series of projects concerning pragmatism, cognitivism, or the models of rational choice.

The schema of unveiling consisted of bypassing, moving behind the conscious stratum to go directly to the unconscious motivations. The new paradigm reverses this perspective and makes the unconscious an end point and no longer a starting point: "Explaining why people are deceived is not the same thing as showing why they are mystified."[7] Therefore, the procedure consists of saving the phenomena, the actions, what appears to be a signifier, in order to explain the consciousness of the actors, "quite obviously beyond and independent of what is present to this consciousness."[8]

This research program is above all not reductionist, and Marcel Gauchet gives, as an illustration of what this new dialectization of the conscious and the unconscious may be, the enigmatic case of witchcraft: "We will understand the phenomenon of witchcraft the day we are able to explain why that crazy theory, that crazy idea of a plot of witches, forms the inverse of the doctrines of political sovereignty. These phenomena are contemporary; there is a link between them."[9] To establish it, one must apply these theories to the functioning of the courts of the period, to the reconfiguration of the relations between church and state justice. It is a matter therefore of finding the contemporaneities that may offer meaning, thanks to a placement in evidence of systems of relations. The actors themselves were not aware of this connection, and it is the historian who allows it to come to the surface, without proceeding "with some reductive operation that would consist of saying that Jean Bodin's treatises on demonomania would enable an explanation of his theory of sovereignty."[10] It is a matter of understanding how this coexistence can occur in the same individual. This explicit and reflected role of action, brought back to the first level, has the effect of placing historical identity at the center of examinations, in the framework of a threefold object privileged for the historian: a renewed political, conceptual, and symbolic history.

This shift to the explicit and reflected role of action is particularly noticeable in the new sociology. Analyzing the bases of this paradigm shift, Luc Boltanski sees in it the disappearance of the implicit philosophy of history at work at the time of the critical paradigm, and the current incapacity to project into the future, which began at a point of rupture that one may situate around "1978, Khomeini, Cambodia."[11] The second vector of crisis of the old paradigm is situated in the crisis of the nation-state that was at the origin of theoretical systematizations on society. What resulted was an incapacity to globalize around the great tableaux of the nation. On another level, connected to the crisis of the idea of the nation, the complementary bond that allowed sociologists, jurists, and politicians to work together became more and more evanescent. "The sociologist explored the state of normativity in society; he let the jurist know about it; the jurist transformed it into law, and law governed the action of the politicians. This worked in the sixties, but today this accord is completely broken."[12] Now, the belle époque of classical sociology corresponds to the postwar years, those of national reconstruction and the modernization of the state, subtended by an emancipating project of society, with an aim of unveiling the hidden and of rapid change.

This paradigm has had its social effectiveness, but the new sociology holds that many of the old postulates must be reexamined, insofar as the paradigm avoids accounting for social action. In the first place, the radical break effected by the critical paradigm between scientific and common competency has the effect of not taking seriously the claims and competencies of ordinary people, whose words are referred back to the expression of an ideological illusion. In the second place, the critical paradigm was driven by an implicit pessimist anthropology that made interest the one and only motive of action: "Interest was an important agent in comprehending the unification that took place in the seventies."[13] Interest notably played the role of lever in all the projects of unveiling, of denouncing the claims of the actors. In the third place, the critical paradigm was offered as a global reading code of the social, capable of making the behavior of all individuals in every situation understandable: "The central proof consisted in showing that the same person would reproduce behaviors of the same type, whatever the situation."[14] In the fourth place, the paradigm did not function very coherently, because it claimed to be critical, denouncing the normative character of the positions of the actors, their illusions, their beliefs, without for all that unveiling their own normative foundations. Finally, the unifying element of the social sciences in the 1960s around the critical paradigm was the unconscious: "It constituted, in quite different senses, the cornerstone of linguistics, ethnology, sociology, and, in a certain way, history, as the latter developed in the *Annales* school."[15]

## A Grammar of Justification

The paradigm shift in progress makes reference to these criticisms in order to reformulate a research program that might better account for the constitutive elements of action. When Luc Boltanski and Laurent Thévenot conducted their study of disputes, of "affairs," they gathered an important, diverse body of work, which we have already considered.[16] The problem, from a sociological perspective, was to understand what conditions a public denunciation had to meet in order to be admissible. This work necessitated a renewed interrogation of one of the great divisions of the critical paradigm, that which opposes the order of the singular to that of the general. "Far from accepting the a priori split between the individual, which would henceforth be an affair for psychology, and the collective, which would thereby derive from her discipline, the sociologist must treat the singular or collective qualification of the affair as the product of the very activity of the actors."[17]

To grasp the process of generalization that is being realized presupposes that one take what the actors say seriously, recognize that they have a competence suited to analyze their situation. This was determinative in the rupture with the critical paradigm, because it was necessary to renounce the denunciatory posture and start listening to the actors. The new sociology was thus led to renew the interrogation, as Bruno Latour and Michel Callon did, of the great division between scientific knowledge and normativity, between the judgment of fact and the judgment of value. "The task consisted of shifting breaks and overcoming separations,"[18] and so of adopting a procedure that placed the researcher and the actor in symmetry. Ordinary knowledge, common sense, is then recognized as a repository of knowledges and savoir faire.

Ethnomethodology has usefully contributed to this shift, which consists of looking for the similitudes between scientific explanations and those furnished by the actors themselves. This approach has enabled a decisive reversal by which criticism itself has become an object of sociology. The old paradigm could not take the critical operations as an object, insofar as, relying on a radical break between facts and values, it sheltered the sociologist from any critical undertaking, on an "islet of positivity on which the ambition of a radical unveiling is based."[19]

## Attention to the Discourse of Action

The test of the new paradigm is situated in the search for terrain, on the empirical level. But the renewed interrogation of the great breaks also enables a retying of the pacified links between philosophy and the social sciences. What is postulated is the complementarity between these two levels: the social sciences are viewed as the continuation of philosophy by other means; and they contribute to the realization of the philosophical task of constituting a grammar of the orders of justification of the social actors. This new orientation implies that one take seriously the "linguistic turn" and give great attention to the discourses on action, to narration, to the "emplotment" of actions, as Ricoeur calls it, without for all that becoming enclosed in discursivity. The researcher then must compel himself "to follow the interpretive work of the actors as closely as possible. . . . He will take their arguments seriously, as well as the proofs they bring to them, without seeking to reduce or disqualify them by opposing them with a more forceful interpretation."[20]

To complete this task, to avoid any stabilized form of interpretation, the new sociology must complete a certain number of detours, of investments in the area of analytic philosophy, of pragmatics, of cognitivism, of political philosophy, as many connected domains, crossed paths that contribute to the emergence of a feeling of unity in the reversal that is taking place. The latter may be termed an interpretive paradigm insofar as it aims to bring into evidence the place of interpretation in the structuration of action by revisiting the entire conceptual network, all the semantic categories that belong to action:

intentions, wills, desires, motives, sentiments, and so on. Hence, the object of sociology passes from the instituted to the instituting and reinvests the objects of the everyday as well as the scattered and various forms of sociality.

Defining the minimal requirements of knowledge in the social sciences, Alain Caillé recalls the four methodological imperatives that they must satisfy: "The first requirement is to *describe,* the second to *explain,* the third to *understand,* and the fourth to *normalize* or evaluate."[21] Of course, these four levels are inextricably linked. Ricoeur has shown well how the explanation is internal to descriptive deployment and induces an interpretation. But these requirements must constitute the horizon of the scholar who cannot neglect a single one. Among these four levels of analysis, there is one, within the others, that seems to impose itself as more eminent, in a matrix position, the normative level: it is the "intimate moment of structuration of the three others."[22]

Behind this primacy, we find the act of interpretation, Ricoeur's paradigm of reading, and the necessity to return to what has been lost. This detour through tradition and interpretive subjectivity is indeed indispensable to the act of judgment, to the conditions of a possible normative dimension. The social sciences are really constituted on the basis of a foundational break that releases them from the normative level in order to produce judgments of fact, excluding judgments of value. Whether this is through Weber, earlier, or more recently through Hilary Putnam, the pertinence of this distinction is contested, and Putnam even extends his notion of restricted realism to judgments of value.[23] Recognizing their normative dimension, and thus explicitly returning to their moral and political ambition, may allow the social sciences to reclaim a major place in the choices of the City.

*Fourteen*

# A Philosophy of Acting: Paul Ricoeur

The shift of attention, previously concentrated on the conditions of action, to action itself in its signifying procedures gives a central place to the French philosopher who, since his thesis on the will, has continually asked the question of the meaning of human action, Paul Ricoeur.[1] In spite of an ongoing dialogue with the social sciences—whether semiology, the structural anthropology of Lévi-Strauss, or Freudian psychoanalysis[2]—for a long time Ricoeur remained unknown to the practitioners of these social sciences during the period of structuralism's triumph.

It is quite a different story today and, even if a few warnings persist with regard to the positions on hermeneutics that he incarnates, he has become a major reference in many studies in the social sciences. What has changed and finally permitted the beginning of this fertile dialogue is intellectual conjunction and the connection it enables to the fact that the previously dominant, great unitary paradigms are now exhausted. Contrary to the majority of the philosophers taken with the structuralist vogue, Ricoeur was able to resist the latter even as he took account of certain contributions of the illuminating disciplines of the period. This resistance today allows the relaunching, the redeployment, of the problematizations of the social sciences in a new relation with philosophy. Ricoeur could resist the illusions of the period, through which he passed without deviating from his initial orientations, thanks to a very intense relation with the German hermeneutic tradition that begins with Friedrich Schleiermacher. This tradition also includes Wilhelm Dilthey's science of mind and Edmund Husserl's phenomenology, the reflections of Martin Heidegger on historiality and those of Hans-Georg Gadamer on tradition, and also other major influences such as existentialism—that of Karl Jaspers and Gabriel Marcel—or the personalism of Emmanuel Mounier. Now, "we have with Dilthey, and differently with Husserl, two means of very strongly resisting the objectivism that one may find in Marxism, positivism, and structuralism."[3]

## Between Explanation and Understanding

The guiding line of Ricoeur's work consists of his situating himself at the heart of the tension between explanation and understanding, most often presented as exclusive alternatives. With a dialogic concern, Ricoeur explores all the potentialities of these two poles by avoiding a presentation of them as the expression of an insurmountable dichotomy between what would fall in the area of the sciences of nature (explanation) and what would suit the sciences of the mind (understanding). If this great division is questioned by Ricoeur, he no less takes up the initial orientation of Dilthey and Husserl that must begin with lived subjective experience, with its placement in discourse, and with its horizontal deployment in the intersubjective universe proper to communication. The lived world and the various procedures of possible subjectification and socialization are therefore at the base of a task that could only encounter the social sciences when the latter examine acting—that is, the meaning to be given to social practice.

The other great reason for the centrality that Ricoeur's work has acquired is its exceptional location at a crossing of paths. Faithful to its epistemological orientations, this work is in a dialogic position between Continental and analytic philosophy; Ricoeur has discussed the latter for a long time. While the social sciences today are engaging with the Anglo-Saxon world, they are discovering in Ricoeur an introducer, a meticulous reader who preceded everyone in the detour through America. Walter Benjamin said that philosophy must ally rigor (Kant) and depth (Hegel), and that it should be systematic: "I find that Ricoeur exemplifies this very precious alliance between rigor and depth."[4] From the beginning, Ricoeur's project has been to construct a phenomenology of action, all the while increasing the necessary detours that led him to a second moment, marked by the hermeneutic graft, necessary to the phenomenological program.

This twofold horizon situates Ricoeur between the lived and the concept. He can thus avoid giving in to the "reductions of the concept, of the thought of the outside in France,"[5] and at the same time avoid the exaltation without mediation of the transcendental ego. This in-between corresponds quite well with the third way that some of the social sciences today seek in the quest for the basis of the social. Ricoeur is situated in an intermediate space between common sense—whose competencies are being reevaluated, even though they were once rejected in the *illusio* that belongs to *doxa*—and an epistemological dimension that has lost its overarching position. The concept is no longer opposed to the lived in order to disqualify it, and Ricoeur has undertaken a quest for meaning on the basis of "imperfect mediations" in an "incomplete dialogue" always open to new meaning. This connection with temporality, on the generational chain inscribed in the web of historicity, is opposed to the absolutization of the notion of the epistemological break that is proper to the structuralist paradigm.

## The Hermeneutic "Graft"

To the scientist and objectivist claim of structuralism, Ricoeur opposes the more patient and modest route of a "hermeneutics of historical consciousness."[6] The hermeneutic graft onto the phenomenological project presupposes a threefold detour, a threefold mediation that causes the eidetic quest[7] to pass through signs, symbols, and texts: "Mediation by *signs*: that is to say, it is *language* that is the primary condition of all human experience."[8] Ricoeur has effected the mediation through symbols at two different times, as Olivier Mongin has shown.[9] It is present in *The Symbolism of Evil*, where Ricoeur deploys the explanation of a second and hidden meaning of ambivalent expressions. He then goes in search of the signification of primary symbols, showing that the symbol is more than a sign, insofar as it manifests a double intentionality in its scope. Symbols lead all the more to thinking that they offer not only a first, literal meaning, but that beyond this there is a second meaning that must be attained, on condition that one find the first meaning. So Ricoeur follows, for example, the notion of the stain in sin, and that of sin in guilt. The symbolism of sin takes something from the stain, and the gap of meaning between the two is "'phenomenological' rather than 'historical.'"[10]

In the sixties, Ricoeur valorized the polemical dimension of the conflict of interpretations that stemmed from this plurivocity of meaning. But this time, the plurality of the latter founded the ineluctable, irreducible character of conflict, and even of the tragic, staging the confrontation among interpretations that have their proper legitimacy but are nonetheless incompatible, as in the case of the opposition between Creon and Antigone. With the ineluctability of the plurality of points of view, Ricoeur then reinvigorated the hermeneutic project by situating it at the heart of a true war of hermeneutics,[11] in a tension between a legitimate strategy of unveiling, led by the masters of suspicion (Marx, Freud, Nietzsche), and a no less legitimate recollection of a higher meaning.

But the third mediation, textual mediation, would occupy a still more important place in the work of Ricoeur. The attention to discursive formations does not mean anything like shutting oneself, in the structuralist manner, within the closure of the text. With Ricoeur, it is accompanied by an overcoming of the Saussurean alternative between language and speech, by relying on Benveniste's theory of enunciation and the notion of reference as defined by Frege, so that the question of meaning may be reformulated.[12] With the threefold autonomy that discourse acquires thanks to writing—with regard to the intention of the speaker, the reception by the reader, and the context of its production—the hermeneutic project puts "an end . . . once and for all to the Cartesian and Fichtean—and to an extent Husserlian—ideal of the subject's transparency to itself."[13]

## Convergences

This particularly demanding and rigorous course could not leave indifferent the scholars in the social sciences who were concerned with departing from mechanical causalities and deterministic schemata. The sociologist Louis Quéré read *The Conflict of Interpretations* on its publication in 1969, but what would count for him came later: the discovery, during a trip to Canada in the early 1980s, of a text by Ricoeur in English that went back to 1971.[14] Then the publication of *Time and Narrative* between 1983 and 1985 enabled Quéré to understand the "shifts that hermeneutics effected on the question of action, of intentionality, of signification, in particular on the status of the subject of action."[15] The latter shift is decisive, as the hermeneutics of Ricoeur, like that of Gadamer, allows one to surpass the aporias that comprehensive sociology runs up against with its ambition of piercing the intentions of the author. Ricoeur indeed shows that the understanding of a text comes from the relationship of the text with a reader who returns to herself through this meeting. The paradigm of reading thus presents itself to Ricoeur as a solution to the methodological paradox of the social sciences, and a possible response to Dilthey's dichotomy between explaining and understanding, whose correlation constitutes the "hermeneutic circle": "I found a lever there and seized it to reflect on the possible transposition of strong intuitions in the area of the semantics of action."[16]

This point of convergence would be at the origin of a meeting that took place in 1985 between, on the one hand, the Center for the Sociology of Ethics and the Center for the Study of Social Movements and, on the other, Paul Ricoeur. In the letter of invitation, Paul Ladrière, Quéré, and Pascale Gruson—Claude Gruson's daughter—were interested in placing sociological research in the vicinity of hermeneutic philosophy; they held that the sociological hypotheses did not allow access to the meaning that the social actors entrusted to their action. In the hermeneutic procedure, the sociologists recognized the merit of reopening the question of meaning and of having shown the importance of language games in social interactions. In his presentation, Ricoeur situated himself more toward Max Weber than toward Wilhelm Dilthey, in order to overcome the opposition between explanation and interpretation. In this regard, he recalled the Weberian expression of "explanatory understanding."[17]

With the sociologists, Ricoeur agrees with the idea that the theory of action encompasses semiotics—in any case, one of its branches, that of the theory of language acts. Now, this area of action does not adapt to the idea of mechanical causality, which is only an external relation of sequence, as Hume showed. On the contrary, in the area of action, "there exists a law of implication between a reason, a motive, a reason to act, and an action."[18] No physicalist reduction is then possible, and this irreducibility is the basis of an always complementary approach between explaining and understanding: "To explain more is to understand better."[19]

Ricoeur also encounters an echo among the sociologists concerned with reevaluating the competencies of the social actors and their capacity to describe the social world, and so to give an explanation. It is such for Luc Boltanski and Laurent Thévenot. Boltanski only discovered Ricoeur's work in 1981, a significant fact in French intellectual evolution: "In 1981, during the summer, I brought along *The Conflict of Interpretations* and I was extremely impressed by the opposition Ricoeur made between the interpretation of suspicion and interpretation as the recollection of meaning.[20] That was absolutely central to our taking up denunciation.[21] It was one of those readings that makes you leap from one state to another."[22]

## Causes and/or Reasons

The discovery of Ricoeur's work was facilitated by the influence exerted on French sociologists henceforth by phenomenology, pragmatism, and ethnomethodology. Now, Ricoeur is situated at the crossroads of these currents so as to confront their positions on action, notably posing anew the question of intentionality, which has been particularly argued over between analytic philosophy and phenomenology. At the intersection of text and action, he discusses the positions inspired by Wittgenstein and expressed by G. E. M. Anscombe[23] essentially by opposing them to the arguments of Husserlian phenomenology. This testing of the semantics of action passes through the formulation of the "tie between action and its agent."[24]

These two entities belong to the same conceptual horizon that covers many notions: those of circumstance, intentions, motives, deliberations, voluntary or involuntary motions, and so on. The Wittgensteinian position of Anscombe, who distinguishes language games and attempts to mark off various registers, differentiating causality and motivation in action, is nonetheless termed by Ricoeur a "conceptual impressionism."[25] Anscombe takes up the central concept of phenomenology, intention, but not in the Husserlian sense of consciousness transcending itself. Leaving aside the perspective of the inside, of interiority, she allows no discriminating criteria but those of observable public linguistic space. She distinguishes two different language games: that of the register of action in which motive and project are linked, and that of the register of causality that translates a purely logical distinction. There would be an order of causality and an order of motivation.

For Ricoeur, this dichotomy is artificial. Of course, it has the merit of aiming to defuse a problem, but it ends up making it volatile: "This seemingly conciliating position is in fact untenable."[26] The refusal of this *distinguo,* which duplicates the refusal of the dichotomy of explanation and understanding, allows Ricoeur to bring the paradigms of textuality and action into convergence. "Human action is in many respects a quasi text. It is externalized in a manner comparable to the fixation characteristic of writing. In separating itself from its agent, action acquires an autonomy similar to the semantic autonomy of a text; it leaves a trace, a mark."[27] The descriptive restriction that analytic philosophy imposes on itself, differently from the phenomenological orientation, cuts itself off from the question "Who?" and thus occludes the "problematic of attestation."[28] Now, attestation escapes vision, and so also the exclusively descriptive paradigm. Thus, Anscombe avoids accounting for the use of intentionality as understood by Brentano, then Husserl, in the sense of an "intention of . . ." Now, this phenomenology of the experience of acting has inspired numerous studies in the social sciences concerned with accounting for a semantics of action.

We are thus already far from that time in the 1970s when, according to Michel Callon, "independently of the fact that philosophy was considered to be the plague, it would have occurred to no one to use Ricoeur as a resource."[29] Today, Ricoeur is a part of Callon's theoretical horizon, for whom "*Oneself as Another* allows a reflection on a whole series of categories that were considered self-evident."[30]

The adherence to the orientations of Ricoeur is nonetheless not unanimous among the innovators in the social sciences, notably in the current of the anthropology of the sciences marked by Nietzscheanism. For Bruno Latour, Ricoeur is only concerned with one side of the system, that of the relation of the subject to the world, of intentionality, and totally neglects the other side, that of objects: "This is the entire problem with hermeneutics: there is no possible repertory to speak of objects."[31] According to Latour, hermeneutics is an obstacle that reserves for itself a separate, solid area, that of philosophy, preserved against the invasion of the sciences, and in which one may speak of the subject, persons, faces: "By magnifying the importance of that, they lead us to believe that the other side is objectifying, outside the lived."[32]

## Historians and Narrative

The publication of the magisterial trilogy *Time and Narrative* between 1983 and 1985 could not for long leave a group of historians indifferent, a group nonetheless self-satisfied at the time, in the comfort of the public triumph of the *Annales* school. The group was rebaptized the "new history," and its natural tendency was to the rejection of all dialogue, in the very name of the trade of historian, with philosophy. A few historians, meanwhile, very quickly took stock of the importance of Ricoeur's intervention in the field of history and discussed his theses. Eric Vigne and Roger Chartier thus actively participated, in June of 1987, in the conference devoted to Ricoeur, whose proceedings were published in a special issue of *Esprit*.[33]

Vigne recorded the central place of mediation occupied by the plot that takes form between the event and history in Ricoeur. The poetics of narrative elaborates a third time, historical time, itself a mediation between lived time and cosmic time. "In this sense, history quite belongs to the hermeneutics of human experience in its temporal dimension."[34] As for Roger Chartier, if he tries to affirm his distance, the strangeness he feels as a historian, he still does not consider Ricoeur's *Time and Narrative* any less than "the most important book published on history over the last ten years."[35] The primary merit of Ricoeur, says Chartier, is to break with what historians impugn, the interventions of philosophies of history, outside the practice of history: "He seizes bodily a certain number of historical works."[36] Ricoeur, contrary to the customary interventions of philosophers into the field of history, has passed through the historical works, those of Braudel, Duby, Furet, and others, and he is in this regard one of the rare philosophers who is not content with the metanarratives on history. He thus assimilates the genuine labor of historical inquiry.

Ricoeur's second merit, in Chartier's view, is that he does not have the ambition of proposing a philosophy of history, but of "understanding how the discourse of history is organized and what may be the truth status, the epistemological dimension of history."[37] Ricoeur demonstrates that the historian's discourse belongs to the class of narratives: in this regard, he situates himself in a particularly close relation with fiction, and it is impossible for him, contrary to what the *Annales* school believed for a long time, to break with narrative to constitute a purely formalizable, nomological discourse. If history is narrative, it is nevertheless not just any type of narrative. Indeed, Ricoeur discusses, without adopting them, the theses of the American narrativists who have attempted to abolish all distinction between the writing of history and that of fiction. He maintains the tension within historical writing, which shares with fiction the same rhetorical figures, but which also aims to be, above all, a discourse of truth, of the representation of a real, of a past referent. In this regard, "Ricoeur will have, I believe, a place for all the attempts aiming to articulate historical explanation on narrative comprehension."[38]

Chartier, like the sociologists, is also very interested in a second meeting point with Ricoeur, the centrality of reading. Erected as a paradigm, this theory of reading is at the heart of Ricoeur's hermeneutic project, notably developed in *From Text to Action*. "The concept he holds central, that of appropriation,"[39] may be the source of a decisive inspiration for the historians, so that they may grasp how the experience of time can be reconfigured. With reading, one touches on the conditions of historical consciousness. On this point, Chartier takes a path different from Ricoeur's. According to him, to ask the question of the historicization of this meeting between the world of the text and the world of the reader requires that one "break that species of textual idealism that functions in Ricoeur and that curiously associates him on this point with the currents of structural semiotics."[40] As a historian, Chartier holds that this world of texts does not sufficiently refer to forms of inscription, to supports productive of meaning. Besides, the reader must be historicized and not presented as the incarnation of an abstract universal, of an ahistorical invariant. A sociological and historical differentiation of readers is necessary to delimit their different competencies and conventions. "In the universal subject of hermeneutics, I have always wondered if there wasn't an undue projection of the position of the hermeneutic philosopher."[41]

This very Bourdieusian critique, in which we find Chartier's warning with regard to philosophy repeated, takes nothing away from the merit of his leading a true dialogue with the work of Ricoeur. But his final critique on the absence of historicization in Ricoeur mostly has to do with a difference of register between what is represented by the sociological and historical differentiation of readers in the historian Roger Chartier and narrative historicity in the philosopher Paul Ricoeur—who has never, on the contrary, invalidated the specificity of the historian's procedure in the name of philosophy. The "forms of inscription" and "productive supports" in Chartier are intellectual technologies and symbolic goods distributed unequally in time and social space. The historical analysis of this distribution is never impugned by Ricoeur. Quite simply, it is not his point; rather, he concentrates on the construction of narrative identity. Ricoeur's object of analysis is historical narrative itself in its various configurations, as a place of effectuation of narrative identity, a mediated source of self-knowledge: "Narrative mediation underscores the remarkable character of knowledge of oneself to be an interpretation of oneself."[42] The imperfect mediation represented by historical narrative, according to Ricoeur, is, to be sure, unsuitable to making action and time transparent, but it enables the reintroduction of the interrogation of acting, an acting and suffering rooted in tradition, bearers of a debt and always open to a project, a telos, or at least a horizon of expectation.

*Fifteen*

# The Descriptive Turn

One of the major aspects of the reorientation toward action that is taking place is an accounting for practical consciousness, which was ousted by the structuralist paradigm. This amounts to bringing attention back to what seems to be a matter of the order of evidence, of everydayness. To be sure, the critical paradigm had already founded its inquiries on a critique of the evidence of the everyday. But the mode of unveiling was fundamentally different because, in the case of the critical paradigm, it was a question of a denunciatory unveiling, whereas in the current orientations it is a matter of an understanding, of a recovery of the latent meaning that fills the everyday. The familiar, describable world, which participates in our environment, must then become problematic, an object of questioning, no longer a starting point but an end point of analysis. It must be treated not as a given, but as a construction found at the end of an activity whose corollary it becomes.

The shift from the conception by which the place of truth is to be sought in the strata of the unconscious to an attention to the explicit role of action involves according more importance to the descriptive scheme, and thereby reducing the ambition to explain. Whereas the facts had to be viewed in the framework of a causal, deterministic fatality, which seemed to distinguish the properly scientific procedure, "scholars in sociology have come to attenuate their claims to explaining social phenomena causally."[1] On the basis of this crisis in causal explanation and of the "slimming treatment" that it necessitates, description, terrain, and the empirical have appeared with a new freshness as a base of possible retreat. In his debate with the historians, Michel Foucault already lauded, at a roundtable on May 20, 1978, this reduction of the causal apparatus by substituting for it a procedure of "evenementalization":[2] "Alleviating the causal weight will therefore consist of building, around the singular event analyzed as process, a 'polygon' or rather a 'polyhedron of intelligibility,' the number of aspects of which is not defined in advance, and may never be considered as fully finished."[3]

## Ethnomethodology and Interpretation

This revalorization of the descriptive paradigm has been affected by the assimilation of the major theses of ethnomethodology, which have acclimated the methods of the study of primitive societies to Western societies. Indeed, Harold Garfinkel and Aaron Cicourel practiced an ethnographic procedure of simple or participatory observation of the acts of everyday life, in order to perceive and reveal the procedures at work, without for all that advancing hypotheses that would be preliminary to field study.

The ethnomethodologists have placed the accent on three main properties of social practices when the latter have been involved in language practices. In the first place, there is their *indexicality*: this necessitates a particular attention to the data of the situation, because any expression refers back to a singular context that becomes a source of such and such a "token" of typical words, whose meaning refers in its turn to the particular circumstances of each exchange. Therefore, indexicality does not correspond only to what the linguists term deictics—that is, indicators of person, time, and place—but to all the expressions of ordinary language whose meaning is not reducible to the "objective" signification of the words of the expression. "On this basis, there occurs a slippage of the notion of indexicality of expressions to that of the indexicality of actions."[4] Each time the pragmatic context changes, the signification of its expression is modified. So the notion of context is central to the definition of indexicality.

In the second place, *reflexivity*, a notion borrowed from the philosophy of language, allows one to describe everything while constructing a meaning. In this regard, Harold Garfinkel distinguishes his positions from those of Alfred Schutz, who inspired him, when he deems that giving meaning is not limited to completed action, but is extended to actions in the course of their completion. Here ethnomethodologists break with tradition and "begin, indeed for the first time, the practice in the process of being completed as the *irreducible* foundation of the social order."[5] The context is no longer external to the action or the description of which it is a constitutive element—as in the anthropology of science practiced by Michel Callon and Bruno Latour. Social facts are here considered as practical accomplishments. In the third place, *describability* completes an analysis according to which the description elaborated by common sense in fact refers to constructed practices and so to a proper competency.

This principally descriptivist orientation of ethnomethodology may be explained through various reasons:[6] among the first of them is the crisis of the great unitary paradigms; but there is also the concern with better knowledge of social diversity, which has been poorly apprehended by the great typologies constructed on the basis of statistical means. Ethnomethodology has thus been able to present itself as a possible alternative to the hypothetical and deductive procedures current in sociology until recently—which, by their reifying tendency, had the tendency to "pass over the effective dynamic of social processes, of the actors' creativity, and of the role of significations in the structuration of the social world."[7] Careful to respect the dynamic proper to social phenomena, ethnomethodologists are proposing a procedure that is more inductive than deductive, refusing to postulate a priori the nature of observed phenomena. Besides, attention to the explicit role of action has driven this current to privilege the context, the singularity of the situation in the narrative emplotment of actions, and therefore in the understanding of their meaning.

We have already emphasized that Louis Quéré and his group played an important role in the introduction in France of the ethnomethodological theses; notably, they organized important sessions in December of 1984 on the theme of description, at the end of a series of seminars in the epistemology of sociology that had begun in the fall of 1981.[8] In 1985, the group published texts by Harold Garfinkel and Harvey Sacks, attempting to situate this current in relation to the sociology of understanding from which it derived.

One of the central notions of ethnomethodology is that of *member*: "The notion of *member* is the heart of the matter. We do not use the term to refer to a person. It refers instead to mastery of natural language."[9] This knowledge, induced by natural language, refers to a structure of activity, and so to the action engaged in processes of structuration: "Knowledge has nothing to do with what is in our heads in a sort of hidden place. . . . Knowledge resides, as Aaron Cicourel has shown, in the capacity to generate recognizable sentences."[10] Ethnomethodological analysis is situated at the intersection of a formal theory of practical activities and a theory of natural language. The link between the two is the notion of indexicality: "Garfinkel and Sacks seem to have integrated into their arguments two essential revolutions in the philosophy of language: the Fregian theory of the precedence of meaning over reference, and the Wittgensteinian theory of the plurality of modes of signification."[11]

## An Attention to Everydayness

This descriptive analysis must bring into view what, though perceived, never holds attention. It responds to the concern for how the social order is produced and maintained. For the determinisms exogenous to the structures, there is an effort to substitute, in the framework of ethnomethodology, a particular attention to the operations and procedures of the agents. These are unconscious insofar as they receive no particular attention; this does not mean that they are to be sought in a buried and repressed structure. They have a particular status of visibility, according to Garfinkel.[12] The fact that the social world is describable—"accountable," in Garfinkel's terms—does not mean that it derives from a given, but from a true production, from an accomplishment of the actors. It is this intermediate stratum that ethnomethodology must restore as mediation between order and social action. For the "member" to be able to describe, interpret, explain, and recount the social world, "he must be available in one way or another, that is, intelligible, describable, analyzable, observable, recountable—in short, accountable."[13]

Among the characteristics of accountability[14] is, in the first place, its reflexivity, which refers to the singularity of circumstances constitutive of activity; this means that the actors arrange their actions according to the circumstances of the latter, thus enabling others to recognize action for what it is by referring to its circumstances. In the second place, accountability is characterized by its rationality: the latter designates a methodical production in a situation; in its situation, the production is intelligible, and this allows it to be restored through description. In the third place, accountability is marked by its normative aspect.

Garfinkel borrows from the phenomenology of Maurice Merleau-Ponty his problematic of "interlacing" (things are not given as in themselves in an outside—the latter would give them an identity that the subject would only have to appropriate). According to Garfinkel, this "interlacing" "is socially occluded: the objectivity of the object, its observability, its describability, and its analyzability are implicitly posited as existing-in-themselves, whereas they are practical achievements."[15] Accountability for Garfinkel is above all a heuristic means that has the objective of gaining access to the modes of structuration of ordinary activities, to the ordinary competencies of the "members," these competencies deriving from a capacity for configuration. Savoir faire, then, is coextensive with the mastery of natural language.

The terminology used by ethnomethodology may appear formal and theoretical, but it has the objective of accounting for concrete cases. Its field of investigation is made up of empirical cases. This is what Quéré accounts for when he takes up the lessons of the fifth chapter of Garfinkel's study,[16] the one devoted to the case of Agnes. This is the matter of a young man who has decided to change his sex, to affirm his right to be recognized as a woman with the customary attributes of femininity. Having undergone a sex-change operation, it remains for Agnes to acquire the cultural attributes of a "normal" woman: "She has to produce here being-woman as a known practical achievement, ordered from within, perfectly proportional to circumstances and occasions."[17] As she cannot rely on the routine exercise of feminine reflexes, she must constantly control her reactions. Hence, she reveals to herself, as to Garfinkel, the procedures of construction by which a "normal" sexuality is conceived in everyday life. "How does Agnes here view herself as practically achieving the accountability of her being-woman?"[18] In this precise case, with the routine avenue impossible, a self-control is required to effect the cultural being-woman that can give the appearance of naturalness.

This descriptive turn is strongly anchored in the phenomenological project of the "return to the things," of the "consciousness of. . . ." This descriptive program stops asking the question "why," because what Garfinkel characterizes as "radical phenomena" are sequential assemblages that one may notice and describe: "As they are not matters of depth, but of the surface, they do not need to be exhumed. We must simply succeed in apprehending them in their proper phenome-nality."[19] The other reason for this renunciation of "why" bears on the fact that these procedures are devoid of intersubjective content; they derive from a grammar that conditions meaning and usage, as Wittgenstein understands it. Thus—and we will return to this—the ethnomethodologists have found, notably with Sacks, a preferred ob-ject to test their ability to analyze conversations. The horizon there-fore shifts from "why" to "how," and the scale of analysis passes from the general level to that of the study of micropractices. Rational-ity is available to be read in action, in the doing that transports mean-ing and that may be restored.

Garfinkel's program is different from that of the sociology of under-standing from which he inherits, for rigorous, formal description leaves interpretation in the background, to limit itself to the restitu-tion of formal structures of action. Shifting the sociological object up-stream, ethnomethodological inquiry is therefore, according to Quéré, "of a protosociological nature."[20] It would then be a useful means of giving a singularity to practices, but would represent only a first level of sociological analysis, which would not stop with overly local eluci-dations. On this point, Quéré remains skeptical with regard to the to-talizing dimension of the ethnomethodological project: "I cannot help continuing to think that in any society there exist procedures of pro-duction of accountability that derive from a macrosocial machinery."[21]

This descriptivist program, in spite of its limits, nevertheless has a twofold merit. It breaks, in the first place, with the nomological ap-proach of a sociology considered as a social physics, beginning with ideal types to approach field studies. The second rupture questions anew the overarching posture of the sociologist, who gives meaning to behavior thanks to interpretive work. One may still ask, with Patrick Pharo, if it is conceivable to envision an ethnomethodological descrip-tivism independent of an interpretive procedure.

The theory of description as Quéré conceives it also owes a great deal to Wittgenstein's idea of grammatical description: "For some time, I have been sensitive to the following slogan from Wittgenstein: at a point we must simply pass from explanation to description."[22] Wittgenstein thus took the example of the tourist obsessed by the question "why" and who would be happy to read his guide conscien-tiously in front of the monument he is visiting, without even raising an eye, without even seeing it! But Quéré also places himself, and even more so, in an interpretive, hermeneutic perspective: "I have been sensitive to the emphasis that Gadamer[23] places on the constitution of reality in language."[24]

## Configuring Practices

On the basis of this twofold theoretical requirement, Quéré distinguishes two levels of practice. The first concerns the standard practices of our everyday universe. They cannot be reduced to physical processes, for they are recognizable only on the basis of the "symbolic mediations" Paul Ricoeur speaks of, which provide the means of identifying the matter at hand. This type of practice can easily be appropriated or rejected by the actors who can account for them, justify themselves, recount.

Besides, "configuring practices" are constitutive/instituting activities, at this point mastered and no longer holding attention. These practices, therefore, do not dispose of a language in which to be expressed. The language of action, which refers to intentions, reasons, ends, and motives, is not fit to account for something. The sociologist must then dispose of a specific language to describe them, to make them accessible to view, to "equip" them, and thus to compensate for the lack of symbolic mediation. On this level, the descriptive paradigm would have its pertinence.[25]

Quéré has explored this specific field, on the model of conversational analyses. Harvey Sacks, representing an undercurrent of ethnomethodology, established the bases of the "analysis of conversation," a privileged field of investigation insofar as language is, according to this current, at once an instrument of construction of the social order and an object of analysis of this process. The detailed study of microphenomena such as conversation provides a privileged support for the descriptive method. In fact, Sacks chose his object somewhat by chance, especially for its capacity to be recorded, retranscribed, listened to again, and hence to be studied attentively: "Thus, it is not a particular conversation, as object, that really interests me. Rather, what I am after is to succeed in transforming, in a sense I conceive as almost literal, physical, our vision of what has happened in a particular interaction."[26]

Telephone conversations could easily be recorded and so constituted an easy body of work to assemble. But they required bypassing an analysis in terms of illustration; they necessitated that categories of analysis suited to the assembled material be found, in order to account for the observed action as something in progress. Quéré therefore conducted an empirical study in the area with Michel de Fornel, asking seven or eight households to record their phone conversations for one to two months. On the basis of this material, Quéré did a study on the notion of invitation, concretely describing how the interlocutors spontaneously put in place a structure of activity without having expressed it verbally. The case of invitations offers a fine example of a "problematic of self-organization."[27] The latter brought Quéré to see to what point people are engaged in different plots, imbricated with one another, that they manage at the same time. "This goes back to what Paul Ricoeur says about the fact that people are permanently tangled up in plots."[28]

## The Cities

A magnificent example of the inherent fertility in this descriptive turn, in this construction of a grammar of action, even if it is nourished by sources other than ethnomethodology alone, was recently given in the previously cited work by Luc Boltanski and Laurent Thévenot, *De la justification*,[29] with their construction of "Cities" as individuals' models of greatness. The manifest breakthrough that they achieve is above all located in their capacity to pluralize the social world and hence to leave behind the constant dilemma between holism and individualism; they show that social reality is not one but plural, and that on the basis of this plurality of worlds of action, the processes of subjectification are articulated.

At the outset, we have seen, it was an empirical study on the case of disputes and a desire to construct a sociology of dispute. In this perspective, Boltanski reexamines the cases of affairs of complaint and denunciation that he came to know while he was studying management. The sociological problem that Boltanski and Thévenot faced was that of knowing what condition a public denunciation of injustice must satisfy in order to be admissible. The study remains quite sociological insofar as there is no question of discriminating among the recriminations by their pathology, but rather of constructing a grammar constituting a certain number of intangible rules that will belong to the register of "normality," whatever the motive of the complaint examined.

To establish this grammar of protest, the study disposed of two principle axes: the traditional axis was that of the opposition of the individual and the collective, which had the function of reducing the diversity of the affairs and thus arriving at ideal types. The first shift consisted of substituting for it another axis of codification, the particular and the general, which allowed the treatment of the whole of the body of research. "It was the opposition between the state of persons when they are in personal relations and the public state of these relations. . . . The scandal being the existence of bonds, whatever they were, under generality. Hence, the mayor, representing the common good, the collective, who sold or bought land for his cousin by using his public position."[30]

Confronted with the justifications given by the actors, Boltanski and Thévenot had to take seriously the actors' explicit intentions, their motivations. Thanks to this study, they broke with the philosophy of suspicion and the posture of unveiling bad faith from critical sociology; this break was augmented by the account of the real capacity of the actors when they argued before the law. Boltanski and Thévenot had to proceed to a symmetrization, to a shift in the field of competencies—until then the exclusive domain of the sociologist—to the actor, to the one subject to justice. Precisely following the argumentation of the plaintiffs enabled a break with the monist schema by which everything would begin with a state of domination that would hold only through the power of the strong in the face of the weak. Without ignoring the phenomena of violence and domination, "we take issue with the claim to account for all situations by violence or routine."[31] There resulted an analysis attentive to the performing activities of the social actors, which came close to the currents of comprehensive, phenomenological sociology. When agreement was difficult to obtain, the actors had to demonstrate that their case did not derive from a singular situation but participated in a more general case.

What was then engaged was a whole process of elevating a particular case to generalization; the process could be followed thanks to the restoration of the mode of argumentation of justification. This acknowledgment is the source of a new, essential axis of analysis, according to which "persons must become great in order to gain access to the public sphere."[32] The axis of great and small therefore configures an entire "economy of greatness." On this basis, the authors of the study would achieve the decisive rupture by acknowledging that types of "greatness" are not the same for everyone, that there are several of different natures; this invalidates any analysis in holistic terms founded on unique oppositions. The project was then articulated around two combined axes, the particular/general axis and the plurality of types of greatness. The disputes examined for their concern with gaining access to the public sphere indeed need to refer to superior principles of justice, to a scale of shared, legitimated values. This ambition to universality is the basis of the distinction between the greatness oriented toward still more universality and the values that may keep a local and particular dimension. The types of greatness are incommensurable among themselves, and each defines a common world of equivalences, a common humanity.

From there, the problem was to define what these greatnesses or "Cities" were:

> At the time, we had civic greatness, domestic greatness, and inspired greatness. But I ran into an objection that came from Latour's work. The fact of being great stems less from scientific credit than from the fact of being recognized as great by others. I was happy the day I was able to endogenize this form of greatness in the model by making it one greatness among others, the greatness of renown.[33]

A code of reading the world was then elaborated on the basis of topics represented by different "Cities," each founded on its own principles of equivalence. The basis of legitimacy of each type of greatness is its capacity to respect a certain number of constraints in construction. These criteria or axioms are those of the feeling of "common humanity" that founds a collective identity, but also of an order established on the basis of this common humanity. This order answers an economic formula according to which access to a higher level has a cost, and requires a sacrifice for arriving at the stage of greatness in the world at issue. It also requires an equivalence between the happiness to which one gains access in elevating oneself and the positive fallout on the whole of the City. Also, among the axioms of analysis, there exists a principle of uncertainty according to which persons are always in power in all the types of greatness in the available world. Therefore, what would be determining in situating the concrete cases in this model of the Cities would be testing the types of greatness.

To Boltanski's four initial Cities, Thévenot would add two others: "He told me—and I must admit I hadn't thought of it—that there are two other greatnesses: mercantile greatness and industrial greatness."[34]

The modelization of these Cities was sought by way of the works of political philosophy that had served as carrier myths for each of the Cities. Hence, Saint Augustine and his *City of God* enabled the modelization of the inspired City, in which greatness is acquired through access to a state of grace that forms an immediate relationship with the superior principle. Bossuet and his *Politics Drawn from the Very Words of Holy Scripture* furnished the model of the domestic City, in which greatness corresponds to a place in a hierarchized order. Hobbes and his *Leviathan* constituted the City of renown or of opinion, in which the greatness of a person depends entirely on the opinion of others. Rousseau and his *Social Contract* illustrated the civic City, in which the bonds between persons are mediated by the general will. Adam Smith and *The Wealth of Nations* conveyed the mercantile City, in which the bonds between persons are assured by rare goods circulating freely; its greatness depends on the acquisition of wealth. Finally, the work of Saint-Simon revealed the industrial City, where greatness depends on efficiency and determines professional capacities.

Philosophical systems of thought therefore form so many heuristic instruments for the construction of this "grammar" of justification—not out of concern with calling on philosophical knowledge to illuminate the social at a second level, but as a metaphorization of the social, as political metaphysics necessary for the deployment of practical reason (and because of this, these systems play a role similar to that of cosmogonies in primitive societies). These models are to be articulated with field study, in the course of which theory remains connected to the empirical task of observation: "The detour through political philosophy has therefore served to advance the understanding of the capacities the actors deploy when they have to justify their actions or criticisms."[35] An essential point in common with the work of Erving Goffman may be found here—the importance accorded to the notion of situation, which puts the social bond to the test and defines the orders of greatness: "We took up something we found in Goffman."[36]

At the same moment, and without a relation of direct influence, one finds a similar desire for pluralization in the American philosopher Michael Walzer.[37] As soon as he had established the model of the economies of greatness, Boltanski discovered Walzer's theses, on the advice of Hirschman. "This pluralism brings our position into contact with the one Michael Walzer has developed, and leads to an interest in a theory of justice that would account for the variety of the ways of defining the common good."[38] But this accounting for the theories of justice and the American debate between liberals (Rawls) and communitarians (Walzer) only occurred late with respect to the study Boltanski and Thévenot completed.

## A Pragmatics of Reflection

The first motivation, for Boltanski as well as for Thévenot—both trained in the school of Bourdieu—was above all to relativize the construction of the habitus. They do not deny that the actors have interiorized a way of being, habits resulting from their early education. But what they contest is that the model is valid in every situation. In such a case, "the social world would quite simply be impossible because no agreement could be found among people who did not have the same habitus."[39] The attention to the singularity of the situation and the construction of the plurality of common humanities has brought on much distancing from Bourdieu's model.

In effect, the descriptive procedure they adopt requires a suspension of judgment, of criticism, so that one may better identify with the economy of greatness implicated by the action described in the precise situation in which it came into being. This procedure also implies a metaphysician's competency among the actors, as they need to know and to recognize in themselves a common good, in order to be in agreement. "This capacity is not required by the reductionist or behaviorist theories, for which behaviors are determined by outside forces or are mechanical responses to stimuli."[40] The situation plays the major role in the determination of behavior and the adjustment of the procedures of justification.

Quite obviously, in the concrete of the social bond, the six Cities are interactive. They are present in each of the various levels, and the qualities of such a world may be valid in another world. The reduction of possible justifications, most of them hybrid, then allows a contribution "to stabilize, to *clear the way for* compromise."[41] Hence, the principles of authority or responsibility can define the relationship of father and child in the domestic city just as well as that of superior and subordinate in the industrial world.

The model of the Cities allows for measuring the tacit or explicit arrangements among the various parties. On this level is the real test of the various worlds. So we find, in Boltanski and Thévenot's study, the conjunction of an analysis that is at once descriptive, interpretive, and pragmatic. In addition, the study ends with an opening in the form of a program, "Toward a Pragmatics of Reflection."[42] Thus, they privilege the reflective return of action onto itself, the movement of interpretation of the actor with regard to what is taking place. This movement is grasped in a privileged moment, that of the hatching of crises, a paradoxical moment in which the "sense of reality is lacking."[43] In these crises, the privileged object of attention is not a chaos, even an organizing one, but the search for coordination among partners in order to establish this problematic reality.

In this destabilized framework, the principle of uncertainty takes place. The dynamic model, articulated for an intelligibility of action, allows one to avoid the pitfall of the introspection of implicit intentions as well as that of mechanistic objectification, which has a tendency to reduce action to systemic causalities.

## The Limits of the Model of the Cities

Nonetheless, two tensions that are not really surmounted remain in this model of the analysis of action. The first is that of temporality. The valorization of notions of situation, of moment, implies short sequences, instants without true temporal thickness. In this sense, the model is well inscribed in the lineage of interactionist and ethnomethodological studies for which historicity does not really count. In the desire to break with the institutional schemata and the determinations in terms of long-term interiorization of the habitus, Boltanski and Thévenot's model valorizes, on this point, the plasticity of the actors; it has a tendency to enclose it in a surface temporality, that of the horizon of action adequate to apparent motives, leaving aside deep temporality.

In the model of the Cities, the attention given to the least inflection of the justifications of the actors and to all the tiny modifications of situations leads Boltanski and Thévenot to privilege short sequences, in the course of which the decisive proofs of the model unfold. The aporia of the procedure is then revealed in the fact that the proofs cannot be permanent. "The problem that is absolutely not resolved by the model is that of on what basis and when one may deem that the proof has a validity or that it must be repeated."[44]

A second source of tension belongs to this descriptive model. It stems from the fact that people pass from one situation to another, from one form of justice to another, from one city to another. The description that results from this corresponds well to what happens on the empirical level; but that poses the unresolved problem of responsibility and so implies a retotalization of the personality. Unless one manages to justify extreme situations, such as that of the "concentration camp directors who spoke of doing their work in the camp, where they responded to an imperative of productivity—while they were excellent family men at home."[45]

Boltanski and Thévenot are also conscious, on this level, of a lack in their pluralist model, as there exist moments of totalization that they have not been able to integrate. "It's what Ricoeur provides in *Oneself as Another*. We see very well that there is a problem involving the totalization of the person that isn't resolved."[46] We find, in this case, the necessary reglobalization through the political, which may be the unifying scheme of the plural configuration of the Cities. But such a perspective would necessitate a rearticulation of the Cities with a level considered central, though not one of a reductive causal determinism. Not yet complete, this global renewal of meaning may result from a potentially fertile connection with the area of research that finds the most global level of intelligibility in the political.

Jean-Marc Ferry sees, in the uncoupling of several worlds, a rooting much deeper than that of a surface temporality. In this regard, he regrets not having been able to compare his theses with those of the sociologists, which command all his interest. He considers this plurality to be the expression of a grammar situated well beyond mere social or political contingency. He finds the same implicit code in Kant, Weber, the young Hegel, and Habermas. "When I approach a theory of society, my temptation is to propose a typology of the different complexes and subsystems that have an architectonic pertinence of the same type as that which characterizes the world of life, and I take them as heuristic hypotheses."[47] Thus, the declension of three grammatical moods refers, according to Ferry, to different worlds. In the first place, the indicative mood corresponds to constative, descriptive utterances, and so answers the question of the objective world, that of science and technology. In the second place, the gerundive and imperative mood corresponds to normative and prescriptive utterances, and so to the world of legitimacy, the social world; here one finds Weber's sphere of the values of law and ethics. In the third place, the subjunctive, optative mood is connected to a subjective world and to the world of art and culture.

The description of the moods allows for the discovery of constants in the relation with the lived world, of plural worlds. The juxtaposition of Weber's three systems seems therefore to derive from an anthropological invariant that remains to be articulated and to be connected with the plurality of Boltanski and Thévenot's cities.

## Sixteen

# The Hermeneutic Horizon

In order to avoid the physicalist as well as the psychologistic pitfall, the analysis of action henceforth accords the greatest importance to interpretation. The latter is not seen exogenously; it is internal, present in action itself, constitutive of its objectivity. It is a matter of a semantic or conceptual order: "Action is never a brute fact."[1] So the analysis of action mobilizes an entire tradition encompassing phenomenology, comprehensive sociology, and hermeneutics. It is the endeavor of the new sociology.

Patrick Pharo, notably, tries to reconcile all these approaches and assume all these associations. An introducer of ethnomethodological theses, he nonetheless criticizes their formal aspect, found in certain currents where there is an attempt to efface their interpretive dimension. He thus distinguishes, in the ethnomethodological program, a "strong" version, which he impugns, and an "open" version, "of a hermeneutic character,"[2] which he favors; he makes it necessary to renew the links between ethnomethodology, the comprehensive sociology of Max Weber, and, more broadly, the entire hermeneutic tradition.

In large measure, the ethnomethodological program has resulted from this association, and notably from the work of Alfred Schutz, which has inspired it greatly. In it, there is a suspension of judgment similar to the phenomenological *epochē* (suspension).[3] This principle is radicalized by the "strong" version of ethnomethodology so as to be free of an interpretation and find in description a solution to the complex problems posed by the interpretive requirement. "A common feature of the perspectives is an avowed concern to make sense of the object. In making sense of it each may be said to pose the problems of understanding it consists of, and to produce as solutions a 'description' of the object."[4] In this radical version of ethnomethodology, with its intention of practicing a "literal description," derived from circumstances, is to be found an ambition to gain access to the stage of the formal sciences similar to that of the structuralist program.

To this procedure, Pharo opposes the inevitable character of the accord of the intersubjective community to validate the utterances and analyses proposed. This dimension invalidates the idea of a naturality of described phenomena, which are a matter "of what Gadamer calls a 'fore-project'[5] of meaning—in short, an anticipation."[6] Without for all that assimilating the positions of Weber's comprehensive sociology to those of Garfinkel, Pharo brings them together in their common concern with constructing a sociological project whose objective is to understand social activity through interpretation. On the other hand, even within the ethnomethodological project, he opposes Garfinkel's project to that of Sacks. The latter is situated, according to Pharo, in a break with the interpretive procedure of Weberian sociology and with the Husserlian phenomenological perspective according to which "everything objective demands to be understood."[7]

## Intimate Consciousness

Pharo wishes to orient the analysis of practical reason, on the side of consciousness, of the subject in its passage through a social experience that has of course its public part, but also an intimate, private, passional part. "One can't conceive of the social relation without accounting for what one says to oneself in an interaction."[8] Such an approach is not only valid in the sphere of private activities. It is applicable to all the domains of experience, including the most public, political practice. Thus, the observation of politicians as war machines allows for a grasp of the moments during which they reveal something other than the basis of their political identity. The denunciation of the cynicism of political professionals is thus a somewhat shorter vision. "If one doesn't grant the agents the moral capacity that one doesn't hesitate to accord oneself, one risks misunderstanding a certain number of things."[9] The ethical dimension of social action must be taken into consideration: it is constitutive of it and refers to the principle of personal responsibility.

On this point, the defense of the phenomenological program is radical in Pharo's work; he has difficulty positioning himself with respect to the work of Ricoeur. Indeed, he holds that Ricoeur is too critical with regard to the Cartesian tradition of the philosophy of consciousness. The hermeneutic graft onto the phenomenological program seems to shift the understanding of action too much toward reconfiguration, and so toward the task of reconstructing the narrative, relegating action itself to a mere preliminary stage of prefiguration: "There is something that escapes the task of reconfiguration."[10] The primacy accorded to the recovery of meaning in the aftermath risks, according to Pharo, allowing the escape of the evenemental meaning of the action itself. This meaning presupposes a sociology attentive to the reality of experience, to its effective scope, and to the physical and ideal environment that brings on the state that Weber terms "semiconsciousness."

We can relate Pharo's acute sensitivity to evenementality to the intensity with which he lived May 1968, an unexpected moment of breakage that may be recognized only with difficulty in the reconstructions after the fact. He does not for all that reject Ricoeur's contribution to sociology: "Ricoeur's perspective is very rich. Understood in the perspective of narrativity, it shifts the notion of event by making it a broader concept."[11] What he does not adhere to, notably in explaining the event of May 1968, is the perspective of critical sociology with its causalist explanations, such as those that enclose the event in a set of statistical curves describing the demographic explosion and the mutations of French society. Not that these explanations are false; but they fail to restore the sense of the event, which is more to be sought "in the reasons stated and incarnated by the action itself as well as its discourse."[12]

This recovered association is what Pharo explicitly claims. In this regard, he establishes a pertinent relation between the quest for meaning in the movement of 1968 and the development of social field studies in the 1970s, as well as with the turn to the theses and methods of comprehensive sociology, which enables a deepening of the theory of the meaning of action. "Such a sociology does not deny the influence of cultural habits on human behaviors, but rather seeks the conditions in which an action may exercise its own structuring power over these influences."[13] So the meaning of action is twofold, at once present in the event itself and in its description. Contrary to Ricoeur, Pharo considers in a positive and complementary manner the analytic theory of action, as G. E. M. Anscombe expounds it, and the theses of comprehensive sociology. He thus establishes a parallel between the distinction that Anscombe sets up between causes of and reasons for action[14] and the two Weberian paradigms for understanding the meaning of action: that of rational reason and that of time, the latter subtended by the immediate manifestations of what is to be understood in trying to grasp the motives, the significant reasons for behavior.[15]

## The Completed Act

In Weber, the central problem is that of recovering the assumed and the real meaning of action. We find its equivalent in the interrogations of an analytic philosophy on the description of intentional contexts, and in phenomenology with its attempt at elucidating the relations between consciousness and things. These three perspectives have the same object of explaining the motives of action, and allow a reconciliation of the two imperatives of explaining and understanding action. In this regard, Weber established a distinction between immediate understanding, which refers to a contemporaneity with the action and its comprehension, and an explanatory understanding, which refers to the motives and significant ramifications of the action.

In this sense, explanation is nothing else than the consideration of the motives for action, the reasons for the latter. Pharo insists on the fact that this connection between explainability and understandability of action in Weber is possible only thanks to a shift. The latter leads from the problematic of the means and ends of action, grasped on the scale of the actor herself, to that of the causes and consequences of this very action on the basis of outside observation and after the fact. It is an essential point of the demonstration that Weber never stops repeating in various forms, such as this one: "It is not necessary to repeat that in all these studies it is possible to invert 'cause to effect' relations to 'means to end' relations each time the *result* in question is indicated in a sufficiently univocal manner."[16]

Schutz enables this project, revisited with a tie to the Husserlian phenomenological program, to gain access to the exploration of the unvarying semantic structures of the social world.[17] Schutz reproaches Weber for not sufficiently distinguishing between the act being completed and the past act, as well as between the significance of the point of view of one's own action and the significance of that of the other. Amid these criticisms, Schutz targets the fact that it is convenient to make an interpretive act autonomous with respect to the object interpreted. "According to Schutz, the central point is that the access to meaning in all cases assumes, whether it is a question of others or ourselves, an act of interpretation, essentially distinct from what is to be interpreted. Hence the notion of typification, which plays an increasingly important role in the development of his work."[18] The twofold relation—to temporality and to differentiation between self and other—conditions the act of interpretation. "*Meaning is a certain way of directing one's gaze at an item of one's own experience.* This item is thus 'selected out' and rendered discrete by a reflexive Act."[19]

Even if Schutz's critique does not resolve the difficulties encountered by Weber's program of comprehensive sociology to gain access to the endogenous meaning of social action, it attracts attention to the necessary phenomenological detour around the central notion of intentionality. It alone makes possible, thanks to the *epochē* itself, the revelation of the object as aim or phenomenon. This inclusion of the world in consciousness, we have seen, is on the horizon of Husserl's eidetic quest. Consciousness then covers two levels: the pole of the *I* of intentionality (noesis) and the pole of the *that* (noema), the latter designating the manner in which the object aimed at by consciousness is "intended." The object toward which the act of consciousness is directed is otherwise distinct from the act of consciousness itself. Because, according to Husserl's expression, all consciousness is consciousness of something, these two poles, endogenous and inextricably linked, both refer to the same intentionality and the same necessity to describe how and by what procedure the meaning of the object's being is constituted.

The phenomenological program may also be introduced in the empirical field work of the social sciences. It is situated upstream, as an eidetic logic. In addition, we find it downstream, as though resumed in the results of the experimentation in order to grasp its significance, its meaning. It is only at the end of this double moment of framing experience that phenomenology aspires to a true scientific objectivity.

## Charles Taylor's "Clarification"

With analytic philosophy and its particular attention to the discourse of action, we complete the internalization of the relations between intention and action. This is notably defended by Charles Taylor, an anglophone Québécois philosopher, who has been inspired by both

Wittgenstein and Merleau-Ponty. He achieves the link between analytic philosophy and phenomenology in the area of the sociology of action. Taylor takes up G. E. M. Anscombe's main idea, according to which human action is not assimilable to a thing because action and the discourse on action are indissociable. Thus, the concepts of analytic philosophy that refer to "characters of desirability" (criteria, range of judgments, desires) are at the basis of every description of actions. This basis therefore implies using criteria in a manner similar to that of the actor in the course of his action. This presupposes according more attention to the very utterance of the action, to its justifications, to the discourse by which it is recounted. To call an individual generous in such and such a circumstance, it is necessary to have an idea of what generosity or generous action is.

On the basis of this observation incorporating discourse and action, Taylor develops the idea of paradigmatic action, which results from a model in which action takes on meaning, when the actor does something without constraint. Taylor qualifies this example as a happy action, and it is the vector that pushes each person to action. From these inextricable links between language and the reality of action, a thesis Wittgenstein already developed, Taylor draws a certain number of consequences. In the first place, he formulated a distinction between the function of the intersubjective validation of actions in the natural sciences and its function in the social sciences. These do not presuppose an agreement on the meaning of the technical terms used, or an institutionalized hierarchization of the characters of desirability. Taylor here aims for functionalism, which fails to account for what belongs to action.

Must the social sciences, before these obstacles, renounce access to a scientific horizon? For Taylor, this horizon is necessary and is located on the plane of intercultural understanding. At the basis of the horizon of labor of the social sciences is a work of "clarification." With this concept, Taylor intends to surpass the opposition between explaining and understanding in the traditional conflict of methods. The concept of "clarification" refers to action itself. It also links up with the task that Wittgenstein assigned to philosophy itself as an enterprise of elucidation of common sense, of ambivalent expressions. This "clarification," according to Taylor, is necessarily normative, because human actions incorporate a self-definition of the self and a qualification of others. Taylor places himself in an interpretive perspective and assigns the social sciences a twofold task, both prescriptive and descriptive; this third way impugns the illusion of a neutral language, on the model of the natural sciences, just as much as that of the total empathy on whose basis one may say nothing more about the culture of others. The reformulations and descriptions of the social sciences have, according to Taylor, an effect of returning to our understanding of ourselves.

We understand to what point this thematic is close to that of Ricoeur, who adheres to Taylor's formula according to which man is a "self-interpreting animal."[20] This detour through the other in interpretive work on oneself is the very axis of Ricoeur's hermeneutic procedure, at the heart of action, of practice. "Our concept of the self is greatly enriched by this relation between interpretation of the text of action and self-interpretation."[21] This position involves the epistemological distinction defended by both Taylor and Ricoeur. "This means that the search for adequation between our life ideals and our decisions, themselves vital ones, is not open to the sort of verification expected in the sciences of observation."[22] The correlation established between intentionality and the narrative laws is common to both Taylor and Ricoeur; Ricoeur takes up Taylor's idea whereby classifying an action as intentional is deciding to what type of law it owes its explanation. "This means that the condition of the event's occurring is that a state of affairs obtain such that it will bring about the end in question, or such that this event is required to bring about that end."[23] The semantics of action must then establish the link between the form of law internal to teleological explanation and the descriptive traits of action. In *Time and Narrative*, Ricoeur has meticulously analyzed this aspect, which belongs to historical discourse.[24]

## The Public Sphere

As intentionality is revealed in the language of action, its elucidation necessarily implies a detour through textuality, which is in the area of the hermeneutic approach. It is appropriate to avoid two pitfalls with regard to the relations between the language of action and action itself. First, there is a tendency to attribute a status of representation to the language of action, hence to postulate an independence of the real processes with respect to their placement in discourse. This position is conveyed "by what Ricoeur calls the concern with true description, or the correspondence of utterances with the real state of the world."[25]

The second pitfall consists of practicing the closure of the language of action on itself and deeming that the intentional structure is entirely discernible at the very heart of the grammatical structure.

A third possible position involves recognizing the function of the structuration of the practical field by the language of action. Discursive explanation then remains open to the plane of its temporality and clarifies something that has been configured and made possible: "It gives it 'the traits of its own determinacy' (Gadamer)."[26] Now, the natural place of intentionality is the public sphere in which concrete action occurs. Taylor particularly insists on the importance of this incarnation of action in the public sphere, the privileged place of expression of practical intersubjectivity. Such a conception is opposed to the dualist approach, insofar as action is not the exteriorization of an already present interiority to which it would suffice to give form. Interiority is constituted through reappropriation, through the internalization of public expression. Such a conception introduces necessary mediations to proceed to a renewal of interpretation, whereas there has been the custom of describing the process of subjectification in a postulated transparency. The major task for a sociology of action is to be able to envisage the "language of action for what it is, a method and technique of construction of the objectivity of action and of the subjectivity of the agent."[27]

These are the two imperatives that Nicolas Dodier addresses with regard to a specific case in the sociology of labor.[28] He adopts a hermeneutic perspective and admits two sacrifices inherent in the procedure of analysis: first, he does not postulate a model agent that would enable him to develop a critical examination of actions and discourses in terms of that principal model; and then he adopts the same principle for objects. For Dodier, "hermeneutics therefore abandons the search for a transparency of action."[29]

In this way, Dodier has studied how the contemporary forms of expression of the imperative of security have erupted as technologies of risk in the tools of governmentality and the administration of society.[30] These techniques are productive of regulations that define the legal boundaries of risk and of the agents, the workplace inspectors, whose role is to effect the continual work of the accommodation of regulation. This work of adaptation is effected on the basis of concrete tests, which mobilize all resources, in part resistant to the attempts at standardization. The workplace inspectors thus create a space between the stated law and the concrete cases to be resolved. "Beyond the question of the interpretation of texts, the inspectors must know how to compose from or decide among several ways of constituting the generality of the cases they treat."[31] The workplace inspectors must produce three forms of accommodation: the problematization of the legitimacy of the regulations, the integration of resistance, and finally the personalization of acts. In this sense, Dodier judges as secondary the classical sociological description that opposes the general rules to the particular cases. "The problem of the inspectors is above all to juggle with opposing modes of constructing their legitimacy."[32] The workplace inspectors, agents, like all those confronted with two projects of rationalization, demonstrate through their savoir faire the existence of a competency linked to the person and claimed as such.

## Enunciation

In the area of linguistics, the interest in Émile Benveniste's studies of enunciation, in the early 1970s, allowed a new attention to the precise circumstances of the speech act, to the sites and meanings of speaking for the speaker. A disciple of Benveniste and an active participant in the Paris school of semiotics, Jean-Claude Coquet would have preferred to see the school and its most eminent representative at the time, Algirdas Julien Greimas, follow the tradition of Viggo Brondal rather than that of his evil twin Louis Hjelmslev, as was the case in the 1960s. The adopted perspective consisted of normalizing and objectifying the text and therefore of eliminating everything connected to a subject or dialogue. "Precisely everything that interested Austin, Ricoeur, and Benveniste was eliminated."[33]

Conversely, the reintegration of the positional field of the subject and notably the triad that constitutes Benveniste's framework of analysis (I, here, now), the basis of every use of speech and of every discursive utterance, allows linguistics to intervene in the elucidation of action. This evolution also passes, for Coquet, through the phenomenological program of Maurice Merleau-Ponty, around the central notion of "one's own body"—an antipredicative act by which the individual affirms her singularity, an indispensable preliminary moment for the subject to take on what she says. Here there is a first relation with the lived world, an appropriation of the latter, the sketch of a reflection that Merleau-Ponty noted on the basis of his reading of Husserl. "It's something particularly fruitful insofar as it is a period of genesis during which the distinction between subject and object is not yet made."[34]

## Hypertext

The most modern communication technologies, such as hypertext, also prompt a departure from causalist schemas and an assurance of an essentially hermeneutic becoming of communication. The very operation of giving sense that interpretive activity is, essentially consisting of linking texts among themselves, may be figured, as we have already noted, by the constitution of a hypertext. "The main object of a hermeneutic theory of communication is therefore neither the message, nor the sender, nor the receiver, but hypertext, which is like an ecological niche, the ever mobile system of relations of meaning in which the preceding ones are involved."[35]

Technoscience itself is, according to Pierre Lévy, hermeneutic through and through. One cannot arbitrarily separate subject and object, the world of technology and the world of consciousness, the human and the nonhuman. What best defines technology is the "teeming hermeneutic activity of innumerable collectives."[36] We again find the thematic of networks of Michel Callon and Bruno Latour's new anthropology of science, and their demonstration according to which scientific utterances are objects of controversy, uncertain and interpretive.

## The Interpretive Turn of the Historians

If modern technologies refer to a hermeneutic perspective, one may say so with still more certainty of the old practice of the historian. For having forgotten this, the *Annales* school got lost in the meanderings of a neopositivist, quantitativist illusion of history as problem, which was a definite break with history as narrative.[37] Only recently have certain members of that school begun to question anew their nomological ambitions and taken into consideration the interpretive role of the historian's discourse. It is a question of a true turn, a critical turn in the interrelation of history and the other social sciences, but especially self-critical with regard to the scientist past of the 1970s. "Much material was gathered and analyzed in this way. But the very development of research, the accumulation of data, has gotten a step ahead of ambition and at times even the concern for interpretation."[38] The prevalence accorded to the long period, to great, immobile bases, relegated evenementality and especially human action to the rank of epiphenomena. Social acting also recovers its place when one emphasizes the complexity of the social processes and the fact that they refer "to a multitude of existential, individual, and irreducible experiences."[39]

Marcel Gauchet has always expressed this concern for interpretation in his work. In this regard, he shows very well, in *La Pratique de l'esprit humain*,[40] the tension the historian comes across when he must enter mental categories that are no longer those of his present and in so doing must have an impartiality, as necessary as it is difficult, in the task of inquiry; but he must also maintain the posture of interpreting the configuration of the other. This tension impels its dialectic of interiority and exteriority in the analysis of the confinement of the mad in the modern age. This demonstration would therefore encounter the one that Michel Foucault developed in *Madness and Civilization*:[41] whereas Foucault denounced the confinement that accompanied the consolidation of Western modernity, Gauchet and Gladys Swain for their part show that if madness is a problem, if it indeed undergoes confinement in an asylum, it is not by some mechanism of rejection, but on the contrary thanks to the consideration of the mad person as an alter ego, as a fellow creature whom society must take charge of. It is also at this level, that of normalizing integration, that the real danger is situated, and not in the practice of exclusion. Interpretation is on this account the key concept of *La Pratique de l'esprit humain*— "interpretation, and precisely not explanation. In interpretation, there is the infinite and there is suspension. I think that is an effect of the hermeneutic condition of the historian."[42]

Archival analysis, as Jacques Guilhaumou conceives it, participates in a hermeneutic perspective bearing on the manifestation of meaning. A specialist in the French Revolution, Guilhaumou is interested less in the search for a hidden meaning than in "manifesting the meaning of the archive through a configurational procedure."[43] Attentive to the archive in its authenticity, he sees in it first and foremost a form of attestation in which descriptive elements and reflexive data join up. In its materiality, the archive offers itself for reading as a configuring emplotment of the event, in Paul Ricoeur's term.

This hermeneutic reading of the archive is the result of several influences—in the first place, that of Guilhaumou's background in linguistics, which complements a specialization in the history of the French Revolution. Early on, he discovered the linguistics of enunciation promoted by Benveniste, and the early commentary the latter gave the work of Austin, in which he introduced pragmatism and the study of performative utterances. From this linguistic turn, which was a break with the first phase of structuralism, Benveniste essentially maintained that the relation of act and event is self-referential: "A performative utterance has no reality except as it is authenticated as an *act. . . .* This leads us to recognize in the performative a particular quality, that of being *self-referential,* of referring to a reality that it itself constitutes."[44] This contribution was decisive, as it shifted the traditional opposition that the historian generally sets up between text and context.

In the second place, Guilhaumou discovered ethnomethodology in the mid-1980s, thanks to the previously discussed work of the group of sociologists at the Center for the Study of Social Movements directed by Alain Cottereau, Louis Quéré, Patrick Pharo, and especially Bernard Conein; the latter was at the time working on the same period as Guilhaumou, defending a thesis on the massacres of September 1792. Thanks to ethnomethodology, he takes account of the reflexive role of social descriptions and so holds, with Quéré, that "social facts are not positive data, but 'practical accomplishments.'"[45] That allows him to envisage a new categorization of the event on the basis of the archive and to gauge the limits of any attempt at the closure of its description. There results a necessary "stretching out" of the description of the archive, so that literalness may be recovered and the field of its multiple possibilities reopened.

## Phenomenology Revisited

In a somewhat different perspective, the theme of intentionality, of interpretation, is very present in the philosophy of mind, especially the cognitivist project. In this way Francisco Varela aligns his cognitive research with the tradition of the work of Merleau-Ponty: "We like to consider our journey in this book as a modern continuation of a program of research founded over a generation ago by the French philosopher, Maurice Merleau-Ponty."[46] Varela does not wish to betray the initial project of phenomenology, that of the originary or intentional giving of meaning, which refers to an experiential giving. Merleau-Ponty had a similar objective, that of understanding subjectivity as inherent in the world. "The essential point is clearly to grasp the project towards the world that we are. What we have said above about the world's being inseparable from our views of the world would here help us to understand subjectivity conceived as inherence in the world."[47] The meeting point, central today in cognitive science, between the examination of lived experience and neuroscience was already formulated as a project early on by Merleau-Ponty.[48]

The Husserlian attempt to have access to the structure of the experience itself thanks to the *epochē* of the empirical world cannot succeed, according to Varela, insofar as Husserl, prisoner of a Cartesian phenomenology, fails to take the step that follows the one he had the merit of exploring. This block comes from the fact that he began with the Cartesian principle of the mind as subjective consciousness, and "took the structure he was seeking to be entirely mental and accessible to consciousness in an act of abstract philosophical introspection."[49] In addition, according to Varela, Husserl's all too theoretical project lacked the pragmatic dimension, and because of this it could not overcome the division between science and experience.

At the intersection of these two, Varela situates his central concept of enaction, which for him constitutes a naturalized intentionality. Enaction effectively takes up Merleau-Ponty's intuition that we must study the organism and the environment in their reciprocal determinations. With the term *embodied,* Varela emphasizes that cognition depends on experiences and that individual sensorimotor capacities are also placed in a larger context that is at once biological, psychological, and cultural. With the term *action,* "we mean to emphasize once again that sensory and motor processes, perception and action, are fundamentally inseparable in lived cognition."[50]

This program presupposes a relinking with common sense through an inversion of the traditional perspective that consists of conceiving it as a representation of the world as it already is. Common sense is then grasped as the essence of creative cognition. Again on this point, "the philosophical source for this attitude is to be found largely in recent Continental philosophy, especially in the school of philosophical hermeneutics."[51] Interpretation is therefore, on this level, at the very heart of the inquiry into enaction, the emergence of signification on the basis of intersubjectivity and mutual understanding. What Varela defines as "embodied understanding"[52] represents only one current, otherwise marginal, in cognitive science; the latter for the most part remains more attracted to objectivism.

This orientation presupposes an accounting, which links up with the hermeneutic type of analysis, of historicity, as it implies that capacities are rooted in a bodiliness that is at once biological and cultural, and therefore historical: "These embodied patterns do not remain private or peculiar to the person who experiences them. Our community helps us interpret and codify many of our felt patterns."[53] So this implies a reevaluation of the place of common sense, of the explicit role of consciousness, an orientation that may be found in the set of renewals taking place in the social sciences. Cognitive science participates in this reevaluation through its respect of the mechanisms focused on action, which constitute the equipment of every human being. The failure of artificial intelligence in the modelization of certain simple functions "has brought this respect to the tools of common sense. In this sense, there is a rehabilitation of common sense."[54] This otherwise poses a basic problem for the social sciences in general, as the reevaluation of common sense may extend, in certain extreme cases, to purely and simply taking up the arguments of popular psychology.

In the face of the physicalist version of cognitivism, which holds that there is really no longer a need for a "philosophy of mind," but only for a neurophilosophy,[55] an "interpretationist" current has developed in cognitive science. It is defined as a materialism that impugns any form of reductionism that would consist of boiling mental properties down to physical properties. This current is represented notably by the work of Donald Davidson, Daniel Dennett, and, in France, Pascal Engel.

## The Maximization of Animal Competency

Dennett has the objective of integrating the interpretive component in a more general framework, that of intentionality. He gives a particularly broad definition of intentionality that goes beyond the narrowly semantic and logical conception. He includes not only intentions, desires, and beliefs, but also expectations, ideas, and fears—"broadly speaking, all the mental orientations toward the external world."[56] With another broadening of the intentional phenomenon, Dennett refuses the limitation of his field of application to the human species: he extends intentionality to animals and even objects. Even if we know quite well that objects do not have mental states, to attribute these to them plays a heuristic role in Dennett's demonstrations. "Thus defined, intentional systems are not limited to persons. We attribute beliefs and desires to dogs and fish and in this way we explain their behavior."[57]

Contrary to the classical procedure of ethology, Dennett maximizes the level of the competency of the animal whose behavior is to be explained, even if it is then necessary to minimize its capacities when confronted with the empirical realm. "Dennett allows that these normative principles of interpretation may be broken, and even are most of the time. In this case, we 'reduce' the initial attributions."[58] This concern with confronting the empirical has led Dennett to do research in Kenya so as to familiarize himself with the studies of Dorothy Cheney and Robert Seyfarth on green monkeys.[59]

Even if the concern with avoiding any form of reductionism is common to both the interpretive stance of hermeneutic theory and Dennett's approach, Dennett impugns a point of view on action that would be "interpretationist." "What mainly interests him is the objectification and objectivity of intentional phenomena."[60] His perspective is that of a naturalization of intentionality, and in this respect it is a form of the manifestation of common sense. For Bernard Conein, the reading Dennett offers of the role of intentionality in the explanation of action is particularly stimulating and notably allows the avoidance of the famous dilemma of "the Weberian dualism between the sciences of the mind and the natural sciences."[61] Conein's interest in Dennett has to do with the latter's proximity to hermeneutics. This has come to Dennett from the necessity he feels to "integrate an interpretive component into cognitive science"[62]—but on condition that this dimension is not the means to separate two epistemologies, that of the natural sciences and that of the social sciences.

For Pascal Engel, Dennett illustrates the current mentalist turn, which follows the linguistic turn. There exists another, quite similar interpretationist approach, that of analytic philosopher Donald Davidson, who works in the tradition of Quine, whose courses he took at Harvard in the early 1940s. In the same way as Dennett when he maximizes intentionality, Davidson maximizes convention:[63] "The interpreter must assign to the interpretee as many true beliefs as he himself assumes."[64] At the center of Davidson's inquiries is the question of acting, of its interpretation, for him weighted with an ethical dimension. He marks a dissociation to be made between the reasons for the acts of individuals as they represent them to themselves, and the causes that make us act but remain in opacity.[65]

## Avoiding Reductionism

The duality belonging to all action makes impossible any reductionist enterprise that would boil psychic processes down to neuronal phenomena, even if this position postulates a materialist monism: "The position we must adopt, to my mind, is naturalist with regard to ontology but antireductionist with regard to explanation."[66] Basing his theory of signification on the principle of "taking as true" the discourse of the actor, Davidson has valorized the study of the functioning of the interpretive process, impugning the split between mind and matter. For him, interpretation remains fundamentally indeterminate even if it is framed by the constraints of normative rationality. "That is why one may call his conception of interpretation 'rationalizing,'"[67] a matter of the truth conditions of the attributions of mental contents.

Rejecting the Cartesian dualism of body and mind, Davidson defines himself as a monist, in the manner of Spinoza.[68] The two levels, mental and physical, do not refer to two different orders of reality, but to two ways of conceiving the same things. Davidson impugns any ambition psychology might have of one day becoming a natural science for three essential reasons, which are so many factors of resistance to reductionist enterprises. In the first place, concepts of psychological origin such as that of intentional action are ineluctably normative concepts. In the second place, intentional action must be incited by cognitive states that are then placed in a causal position. In the third place, one must postulate, to understand their behavior, that human agents act according to criteria comparable to those of the observer, whereas to study the functioning of genes, such a condition is not necessary. Davidson situates his position as close to Gadamer's, "whose hermeneutic approach to language is related to my treatment of 'radical' interpretation."[69]

## Attestation

But the tradition of Davidson's work, like that of Dennett's, is associated with that of analytic philosophy, which has enabled the reflection of cognitive science on action, through a return to the "things themselves." Between the interpretation of action as Ricoeur understands it and Davidson's "radical" interpretation, there exist important differences in perspective. Ricoeur, in his ongoing dialogue with analytic philosophy, has extensively discussed Davidson's theses.[70] First of all, he hails the "remarkable rigor"[71] with which Davidson achieves a twofold, logical and ontological, reduction, which leads him to see in action a subclass of events dependent on an ontology of the impersonal event.[72] So causal explanation has the function of integrating actions in an ontology that sets up the notion of event on the same level as that of substance. Davidson's 1963 demonstration[73] consists of showing that explanation that invokes reasons is related to causal explanation; this does not necessarily refer to a nomological conception. This internal relation of description and explanation that governs singular events also links up with the positions Ricoeur develops in the first volume of *Time and Narrative*. But Davidson misses the phenomenological dimension of the conscious orientation of an agent capable of viewing herself as responsible for her acts. He attenuates both the temporal status of intentionality and the reference to the agent. The major criticism that Ricoeur addresses to Davidson is that he "conceal[s] the ascription of the action to its agent, to the extent that it is not relevant to the notion of event, whether it be produced or brought about by persons or by things."[74]

In the correction he undertook fifteen years later, in 1978, in his more recent essay on action,[75] Davidson recognizes that he neglected some of the essential dimensions of intentionality: orientation toward the future, delay of completion, and the implication of the agent. Meanwhile, he does not for all that revise his conception of causal explanation. The notion of the person remains barely pertinent. "Neither ascription nor its attestation can have a place in a semantics of action that has been doomed by its strategy to remain an agentless semantics of action."[76]

There are two different perspectives to be found in France stemming from the positions of Pascal Engel, philosopher at the CREA. Engel affirms a great admiration for Ricoeur and notably for the dialogue Ricoeur conducted alone for years with analytic philosophy; but he does not for all that share Ricoeur's hermeneutic perspective: "My position on the problem of truth is not a hermeneutic position, but rather what I have called an 'interpretation without hermeneutics.'"[77] In this article, he opposes the German hermeneutic tradition to the theory of interpretation according to Quine and Davidson, deeming that the Continental tradition remains too post-Kantian (this judgment may also be found in the United States, in authors such as Strawson).[78]

Engel, impugning reductive attempts in the area of explanation, adopts a naturalist position, similar to Davidson's, with regard to ontology. One must therefore be particularly attentive to the various levels of explanation. Philosophy has passed, he says, from a Kantian horizon to a Humean and naturalist problematic "centered on the question, What conception of reality may creatures like ourselves have, who are endowed with natural capacities?"[79] Engel considers contemporary philosophy to be too enclosed in textualism and the idea that the truth can be found within the text. His reaction against an overly hermeneutic, historicizing, and textual attitude does not mean that he gives up on reaching a form of objectivity. The latter would be the result "of the intersubjective effects that allow philosophical work to progress."[80] This position introduces us to a necessary pragmatic dimension of the theory of action.

## Seventeen

# The Social Sciences: Pragmatic Sciences

The reorientation of the social sciences to social action invites us to revisit the pragmatic tradition, of which Peirce appears as a founder.[1] Peirce constructed an entire semiotics, encompassing linguistics, and he placed language under the dominance of communication. Meaning, then, is revealed in its practical function. This perspective is an early prefiguration of analytic philosophy. He was one of the rare philosophers who took action as an object and posited a difference, of a metaphysical order, between physical (dyadic) action and human (triadic) action. According to Peirce, only the triadic principle organizes human relations.

This philosophy of action, centered on pragmatism, nonetheless has precedents, and Peirce admits to borrowing the very term *pragmatism* from Kant. In *Anthropology from a Pragmatic Point of View,*[2] Kant develops this theme, barely touched on in the *Critique of Pure Reason.* What pertains to pragmatism is "the belief or hypothesis on which one bases the decision of what means to use in action."[3] In his anthropology, Kant defines a pragmatic level, that of praxis and its understanding. Pragmatism then takes on a sense similar to that of its Latin variant,[4] which is to address all that pertains to political and judiciary affairs. This acceptation refers us back to the reevaluation of common sense, of the procedures of justification of the actors, with particular attention to their discourses, in order to achieve a pragmatic program.

By what route is this dimension grasped? The path Dilthey and Husserl advocated, which takes lived subjective experience as the starting point, comes down to seeing how this experience occurs horizontally in communication, in interaction, and hence to grasping the stabilization of what Dilthey defines as the universal experience of life.[5] In fact, it is a matter of a collective experience proper to a given social community that is expressed "in the form of sayings, adages, maxims, of a shared cautious knowledge, a sort of common sense, shall we say, today."[6] On this basis, in Dilthey's schema, a process of objectification is at work that belongs to the social sciences: the movement of autonomization that begins with the lived is objectified in the form of a common sense stabilized on the intersubjective plane. Today, this route is reversed to become a new dialectic. "We first have a public sphere that more or less models public opinion, which reacts on common sense."[7] The other great reversal consists of no longer conceiving the world as physical but, with Peirce, as fundamentally semiotic. Such a reorientation implies that semiosis itself results from a succession of traces left by the chain of interpretants that is constitutive of a lived world, from a background reference necessary for the idea of sharing a world and communicating in it.

This shift from the physical to the lived world has been achieved by Husserl and Dilthey, and as a whole by the phenomenological program: "It is a completely different vision from that of the ontological problematic, as we have individuals who attempt to understand one another."[8] What this understanding is elaborated on is rooted in the resources of meaning that are in the background of the lived world, and that can be actualized by the intersubjectivity acknowledged in the processes of communication. "Hence the importance accorded to the different registers of discourse, which may be narrative, interpretive, argumentative, or reconstructive, depending on the case."[9] From the type of discursive mode employed, there may result different modes of understanding the world.

This turn with a dual origin (phenomenological and semiotic) enables the deployment of the pragmatic and communicational program of analysis. The importance of the register of discourse in the form of identity has been brought into evidence especially by Paul Ricoeur, with his notion of narrative identity and his distinction between sameness and selfhood:[10] "The genuine nature of narrative identity discloses itself, in my opinion, only in the dialectic of selfhood and sameness."[11]

Jean-Marc Ferry shares with Ricoeur the idea of a very strong link between the register of discourse and the form of identity. But he holds that Ricoeur has overly privileged two registers of discourse, the narrative and the interpretive, at the expense of other modalities; in this regard, Ferry proposes a register specific to our own time, that of "reconstructive" discourse. The latter requires the reexamination, in a new light, of the theories of argumentation, so as better to understand that the paradigm shift corresponds to a tipping of the modern era toward a new era. The reconstructive mode revisits and reappropriates the tradition, "but not in the fashion of a traditional hermeneutics, not exegetically or apologetically."[12] Ferry defines it as first and foremost an intersubjective process, at once cooperative and conflictual, destined to thematize repressions committed, such as genocide, the situations of a colonial yoke, and so on, and hence doing justice to situations of domination or repression, bequeathed by the past in prior communications: "Communication itself is thematized in reconstructive discourse."[13]

## Pragmatic Interaction

The thematic of communicational rationality is Habermasian par excellence. Ferry began his career as a philosopher, as we have seen, very close to the work of Habermas. Here he found the very tight link that unites rationality and argumentation. Habermas maintains the transcendental questioning of the conditions of possibility of the social order produced by intersubjectivity, and so aligns himself with the project of a universal pragmatism. He situates rationality on the level of the speech exchanged in an interaction. So rationality reveals itself in interlocutory practice, through the mediation of communicative reason.[14] Habermas's pragmatism with universal application questions the truth claim of language acts. Communicative rationality passes, with Habermas, from a position as an attribute of action to the status of a "foundation of an interpersonal relation, as a means of organization of interaction."[15]

The thematic of pragmatic interaction does not originate with Habermas, but it was particularly developed by him. It signifies the struggle for recognition, less tragically than the Hegelian register of the struggle to the death. It is played out on the communicational register. We find three levels, three worlds conceived not as resources of particular objects, but as correlates of basic attitudes: the relation of the knowing subject with her environment, which defines a rationality with respect to the technical rules in the dimension of work; the relation of the moral subject acting in the social world of legitimate norms; and that of the subject with respect to her own subjectivity and that of others. These ternary topics, constitutive of Kant's architectonics as well as those of Weber and Habermas, "have a very deep pragmatic anchoring in the socialized activities of work, memory, and language, and the struggle for recognition."[16]

Meanwhile, holding that we are prisoners of these trichotomies, Ferry advocates envisioning a fourth dimension, reflexive with respect to the others: that of discourse, not reducible to language or interaction. The discursive dimension is constituted by a grammar of a natural order, deeper than what is enclosed in language. This fourth dimension is situated on a level and in different contents of ethicocommunicational rationality. It is, at a more fundamental level, that of a grammatical ontology.[17]

Ferry's project is therefore to show the profound meaning of this grammar, with an eye to what Fichte called the "pragmatic history of the human mind." The hard core of communicational identity, what enables exchange, translation, is therefore found in a grammar whose anchoring is deeper than its linguistic and cultural variants. This grammatical ontology allows mutual understanding in the lived world. On this plane, we find the positions that Wittgenstein expresses when he sees in grammar the configuring activity par excellence: "Grammar tells what kind of object anything is."[18] Now, it is on the plane of acting that grammar may situate such and such an occurrence and discriminate what is within the area of an action and what is not. This "natural semantics of action," as Ricoeur defines it, specifies a language of action. "This passage from the factual to the grammatical has been much discussed in sociology for around fifty years."[19] This perspective imposes a pragmatic problematic that bears on the processes constitutive of intersubjectivity and of "operating praxes."

The linguistic turn, after its binary phase dominated by structuralism, leads to the pragmatic triangle. These pragmatic markers have been the privileged object of analytic philosophy (Austin and Searle) taken over by French specialists in the study of language (Oswald Ducrot, François Récanati, and others). Breaking with the Saussurean *distinguo* between the object constituted by language, proper to linguistic science, and speech, rejected as contingent and unscientific, they have shown that speaking is acting—that is, communicating a meaning. They situated the importance of context so as to understand and make intelligible the phrases emitted. From this twofold reevaluation of speech as contextualized act is born the concept of the performative, which defines a fundamental register of language acts. Benveniste also clearly perceived this pragmatic dimension, with his distinction between the utterance and an enunciation in a situation of prevalence: "In the last analysis, human experience inscribed in language always refers to the speech act in the process of exchange."[20]

## Dialogic Polyphony

This dialectic of enunciation located in the heart of the utterance has been developed particularly by Mikhail Bakhtin, with his concept of the dialogic, which covers the polyphony of voices carried by discourse. Bakhtin compares the work to a link in verbal exchange, in dialogue. As Bakhtin conceives it, "dialogic relationships are a much broader phenomenon than mere rejoinders in a dialogue, laid out compositionally in the text; they are an almost universal phenomenon, permeating all human speech and all relationships and manifestations of human life."[21] In this way, the meaning carried by textuality and history is dialogically linked between successive generations: hence it assumes a new configuration, marked by a contextual decentering, which amounts to analyzing the text in a context no longer its own. So there is no meaning in itself, a priori, to be sought; meaning is given in response to a question asked, contemporary, and situated: "This meaning (in the unfinalized context) cannot be peaceful and cozy (one cannot curl up comfortably and die with it)."[22]

In the area of philosophy, Francis Jacques has developed this theme of the dialogic, which he sees as a possible surpassing of the traditional alternative between consensus and dissensus.[23] The solution that is sought may also be found on the pragmatic plane of a new analysis of communication: this is thanks to a conception of dialogism defined as coextensive with all discourse, as an internal structure of discourse, and functioning transitively between two enunciating agencies. The world is implicated in the pragmatic relationship of interlocution: "In the final analysis, the everyday world we all share . . . [is] derived from a relation of knowledge between *I* and *you*. . . . It is the task of communicational activity to engender the ordinary world of our coreferences."[24]

## The Topics of Suffering

Luc Boltanski has recently offered a fine example of a pragmatic study with his *La Souffrance à distance*. One remains in this area on the plane of acting: "All moral requirements in the face of suffering indeed converge toward a single imperative: action."[25] Boltanski wonders under what conditions speech on suffering may be considered active; he begins with a very current thematic, that of the presentation of suffering in the media. The argument developed involves showing that the problem is not, contrary to what is generally said, that there is media dramatization. The emergence of the public sphere and the singularity of the suffering body around the principle of equivalence emitted by the unifying dimension of the political dates from the eighteenth century. "A politics of pity must face two requirements. As a politics, it aims for generality. . . . But in its reference to pity, it cannot completely free itself from the presentation of particular cases. Generality does not inspire pity."[26]

Therefore, to address this question, the problem is posed of the distancing necessary for the apprehension of pity by the political. Boltanski shows that the incongruous spectacle of suffering on our screens at dinnertime is not so new. The argument he develops, in part a response to the charge of ahistoricism directed at his earlier work, *De la justification,* is an attempt to find the traces, over time, of three topics put in place since the eighteenth century.

During the Enlightenment, a first topic is born, which until today has structured the political space between right and left: the topic of denunciation. It develops in the twofold form of an affair and an inquiry, so as to support the indignation that subtends it. Denunciation implies the individualization of the impostor or persecutor one intends to deliver to public condemnation or judicial proceedings. "In the topic of denunciation, attention to the spectator is not held up by the sufferer. It shifts from the place of the sufferer who inspires pity to that of the persecutor one is accusing."[27] Emotion will then be mastered, and directed toward an argumentative rationalization supported by a file, pieces of evidence gathered during an inquest. The paradigmatic model of this topic is Voltaire, who transforms the emotional into a meticulous investigation in order to give an objective basis to the innocence of the case defended, as Élisabeth Claverie has shown in her study on the affair of the Chevalier de La Barre.[28] This topic leads to public deliberation and so to justice, after containing one's indignation, so as better to accuse the persecutor.

The second topic is that of sentiment. Contrary to the first, here one lingers over the unhappy victim, whose tragedy one shares, and who dedicates to his benefactor the greatest gratitude. It is a matter of another register, no longer that of confrontation or trial, but that of the interiorization of suffering, of sharing. To illustrate this topic, Boltanski takes the example of one of the major English writers of the second half of the eighteenth century, Samuel Richardson, an initiator of the modern novel: Richardson's heroines, Pamela and Clarissa, are tearful victims, young women who are ever virtuous in the face of adversity. The deployment of sentimental discourse in this case implies, contrary to denunciation, avoiding the pursuit of the wicked persecutors, the demon-lovers (the Count of Belfont and the libertine Lovelace), so as to "shift attention to the gentle emotions that stir the sufferer and move the spectator."[29]

In a third period, the nineteenth century, these two topics are the object of a virulent criticism. That of denunciation is disqualified with the argument according to which aid to the unhappy that is transformed into a legal case and into revenge will lead to the creation of more unhappy people. The topic of sentiment is considered to be the expression of the shift of the unhappy person apparently in question to the one who expresses pity and gives himself over to debauchery of personal sentiments and to an unavowed erotic pleasure. On the basis of this twofold criticism, a third topic is born, whose paradigmatic traits Boltanski sees in Baudelaire's portrait of the dandy: "The dandy's magnificent character especially consists of the cold quality that comes from the unchangeable resolution not to be moved."[30] The dandy illustrates what Boltanski calls the aesthetic topic. Following Pierre Pachet's demonstration,[31] he brings Baudelaire and Sade together in the same denunciation of the desire for revenge as an illusion one plays before oneself and of sentimentalism as a hypocritical expression. "If you take away the benefactor and the persecutor, you see the unhappy one naked, you see the horror."[32] So the impassiveness of the dandy who looks suffering in the face, with no way out, characterizes this third attitude in the face of suffering.

The intertwining of these three topics has extensions in the area of politics. It inspires such and such a position on the political scene, as its placement in the public sphere is at the heart of the question of suffering and its treatment. In addition, Boltanski's study is more broadly aligned with the concern "with producing a pragmatism of the spectator."[33]

## The Power-Act

We find this pragmatic concern in the original work of Gérard Mendel, at the intersection of psychoanalysis and sociology, in the attempt at constituting a "sociopsychoanalysis." The search for a connection between these two universes has always left Mendel skeptical with regard to strategies of unveiling; rather, he is attentive to the human act in its concrete, manifest deployment, to the explicit role of acting that is most often disqualified, notably in psychoanalysis. In this regard, he recalls, with just cause, the limits, the borders necessary for each of the practices, and places back to back the "social aporia of psychoanalysis"[34] and the "aporia of the social psychology of the subject."[35]

At the heart of this new field of investigation that he attempts to deploy, that of a sociopsychoanalysis, is a reflection on social acting— what Mendel qualifies as a "power-act," defined as an individual's appropriation of her position in social interrelation. Indeed, he notes the existence of a "spontaneous psychic motion,"[36] in general unconscious, by which the author of an act tends to try to appropriate a power over the act. Mendel is aware that this spontaneous propensity may be transformed into immoderation and one's own power over others or others' power over one; so it is important to grasp this blind spot, the "power relation of the subject with his 'doing,' his act, his action."[37] As a psychoanalyst, he ironically notes that the "failed act" has occupied a choice position in Freudian theory, whereas the "successful act" has been forgotten by psychology.

On the basis of this dead angle of analysis, Mendel has developed a sociopsychoanalytic intervention since 1971, in the framework of a collective practice, that of the "Desgenettes group"—in corporations, schools, institutes of health; the intervention is in the content as well as the structure of organization of labor. Taking the act as a privileged object again brings us back to the pragmatic nature of the social sciences.

# Part V

*Representations*

# Eighteen

# Mental Representations
## The Cognitivist Orientation

During the time of the structuralist paradigm, it was thought that the perceptive abilities of the human being were to be sought exclusively in the cultural sphere. That is why linguistics at the time served as a pilot science: in language abilities the discriminating factor was found that separated the human from the rest of the world, the animal, and the vegetable. The explanations of the variants and invariants of human behavior were found therefore to derive from an essential dimension, to the exclusion of organic considerations. The current shift is on this spectacular point with the development of cognitive science, to the degree that, for some, it constitutes a potential science of human nature.

This science is far from a homogeneous whole; it is rather a constellation of disciplines. What they have in common is considering human representations to be the result of constant interpretive work that the brain executes and stores. Taking this element into consideration provides a basis for representations that do not exist in themselves. Their understanding therefore passes through the detour of the processing system from which they have issued, and that is found in the physical, biological nature of the mental system. In the aim of reducing human thought to its biological foundations, the risk of reification is great. It is no less the case that the social sciences can only respond to the many discoveries of cognitive science that remind us that man is a "bio-anthropo-socio-logical" being.[1] The adoption of a procedure that privileges complexity and autonomy is here more necessary than in other areas, in order to avoid all forms of reductionism.

## At the Origins of Cognitivism

Cognition is an autonomous field of study of mental representations that emerged little by little from cybernetics in the 1940s and 1950s. Generally, the 1943 publication of the article by Warren McCulloch and Walter Pitts is considered essential for the definition of the cybernetic era.[2] The ideas the authors developed in it would be at the basis of the future invention of digital computers. McCulloch and Pitts held that mental activity could be rendered intelligible with the help of logic, insofar as the brain is a mechanism that functions logically by nature, thanks to its components, neurons.[3] "Such simple neurons could then be connected to one another, their interconnections performing the role of logical operations."[4]

The second major moment in the emergence of the cognitivist program took place in 1956 during two notable meetings, first at Cambridge and then at Dartmouth, in which Herbert Simon, Noam Chomsky, Marvin Minsky, and John McCarthy defined a project that corresponded with what today is cognitive science. On this occasion, they spoke of artificial intelligence; the fate of cognition as an extension of the modelization made possible by information processing was sealed. Somewhat later, John von Neumann defined a program in the science of biological intelligence.[5] A constellation of disciplines began to grow around this project. Besides Chomskyan linguistics, around the notions of competency and performance were found psychologists and computer scientists who were evidently at the core of the project, but also philosophers, for whom "the study of language and communication directs philosophical reflection to intentionality."[6] Symbols, hitherto viewed only in their cultural dimension, were then examined in their dual physical and semantic nature. At the first stage, the model was the computer—a mechanical, logical model of thought. With this postulate as a starting point, at Harvard in 1960 a Center for Cognitive Studies was formed, and there was a questioning of the "classical behaviorism of the psychological studies, [and a proposal] to substitute a cybernetic approach."[7] This initial configuration, in which cognition was strongly influential on the AI (artificial intelligence) model, would evolve in the 1970s toward a more neuronal, biological orientation of cognitivism. This first paradigm of cognitivism was defined by three principal propositions, according to which the mind-brain complex was describable on two levels, material on the one hand, and informational on the other, independent of each other. The first proposition "defines functionalism in the strict sense, as a nonreductionist monism."[8] The two other propositions characterized the "computo-representational" character of the theory.

## A Constellation of Disciplines

Nonetheless, today there is no longer a truly unifying paradigm, but a constellation of disciplines partially engaged in common programs of research. There are six disciplines, or groups of disciplines, that are the "official constituent members":[9] neuroscience, psychology, linguistics, philosophy, anthropology, and computer science. This configuration presses for investigations on frontiers that separate the disciplines, on their specificity, their historicity, their object. It leads to reexamining the old dualisms, such as those traditionally opposing body and mind, to find new articulations between these two poles. The convergences are located in a common rupture with behaviorism, and so with the schema of behavioral explanation based on the simple pairing of stimulus and appropriate response. In this in-between, in this interval, cognitivism's program of investigation is defined. Cognitive explanation therefore covers mental activity considered to be the linking of regulated transformations of representations. It also postulates the neutrality of information in relation to its support. "This schema is often called 'functionalism,' sometimes with the qualifier 'computational.'"[10]

The hard core of this program is constituted by neuroscience, which in its turn covers a heterogeneous set of disciplines—neurophysiology, neurobiology, neurolinguistics, neuropsychology, and neuropsychiatry—all of which take the brain as an object of study. It is a realm in which the recent discoveries are most spectacular. One may now distinguish in the brain three distinct realms, each of which governs one part of human activity. To the reptile brain, the core in which are found the primary drives, a second envelope is added, that of the limbic brain that commands the gregarious instinct, and a third set, the neocortex, which appears only with the human species and directs symbolic thought.[11] Quite evidently, these three sets are connected, acting together on human behavior.

Neuroscience explores the cognitive functions of perception, memory, and action, in an attempt to gauge the role of the cerebral structures in their functioning. Now, the complexity of the human brain is a true challenge to human intelligence. A century ago, in 1891, Wilhelm Waldeyer identified the cells of the brain, which he named neurons. We have learned since then, thanks to the projects of neuroscience, that the brain is constituted of several hundred billion neurons that establish among themselves around one quadrillion connections. These neurons are organized in modules and rings. "This modular organization permits a recognition of cerebral localizations."[12]

## The Neurological Model

The first model of intelligibility, whose purpose is to account for the sophisticated instrument that the brain is, has been that of an interconnected electric circuit, traversed by a current, that of the nervous influx. This was during the era of the cybernetic model—the moment when the brain was considered to be a supercomputer and neurons likened to microprocessors. In a second stage, neuroendocrinology revealed evidence of the relations between the nervous and the hormonal systems. One could gauge neurotransmitters, chemical modules that ensured, on the level of the synapses, the nervous influx from one neuron to another. We have passed from the vision of an electric circuit-brain to that of a gland-brain secreting chemical molecules that control human passions.[13]

In addition, today there is agreement to question anew the automaticity of the link that MacLean introduced between the cerebral localization of the nervous centers and mental functions. In the third place, a temporal element is intervening, on the basis of studies on memory, on the "memory traces" left in the brain. Indeed, Gérard Edelman has formulated an encompassing theory of memory on the basis of a selection of the connections between neurons.[14] Among the infinity of possibilities, the subject in interaction with his environment incites and stimulates certain networks at the expense of others.

This model, which seems to be "one of the most fashionable today among theoreticians of neuroscience,"[15] is inevitably tied to the social dimension, to historicity, and nullifies any mechanical reduction of thought to a biological substratum. So we are witness to what Jean-Pierre Changeux has termed the "neurological revolution,"[16] insofar as neuroscience penetrates the "black box" of the brain, whose genesis, architecture, evolution, and structure we are beginning to explain.

But the epigenetic traces of selective stabilization of the synapses raise the necessity of a theory of complexity and the notion of autonomy, of the singularity of each of the brains.

Consequently, the reduction to a notion of immutable human nature is, strictly speaking, impossible, for biological reasons that stem from the fact that the brain interacts with its environment thanks to its self-organizing properties. Such a characteristic requires the neuronal sciences to associate with the social sciences, in order to avoid the pitfall of a reductionism and to gauge the founding interactions of human behavior: "What I question is the notion of a biologically determined human nature."[17]

## Connectionism

Neuroscience is at the origin of a new paradigm that is often presented as an alternative to classical cognitivism, a possible surmounting of the impasses that the AI model has met: connectionism. It borrows from the mode of neuronal functioning to construct abstract networks of formal neurons. This model offers the advantage of a constantly evolving evolution in relation to the environment, whereas classical cognitivism was founded on a preliminary and intangible programming, in the manner of computers. This capacity for adaptation and adjustment to the environment borrows from the "theory of dynamic systems."[18] For its part, connectionism constitutes a new approach to cognitive modelization, inspired by biology. This orientation has been defined as an alternative to the classical model since 1982.[19] It offers the advantage of a possible convergence between "computer science and psychological modelization on the one hand, and neuroscience on the other."[20] Connectionism is accompanied by a partial return to behaviorism, as well as to cybernetics, insofar as the heuristic model is constituted by the machine of the network of neurons. So the connectionist program seeks to be as close as possible to neurophysiological reality.

According to Daniel Andler, connectionism "should be more sympathetic to scholars in the social sciences,"[21] as it gives more room to context. Meanwhile, connectionism has not until now succeeded in endowing itself with concepts having a workability for the social sciences.

Cognitive science, nevertheless, has already profoundly modified the horizon of the social sciences, in a somewhat different way for each discipline. On the one hand, psychology and linguistics occupy a central place and are broadly involved with this perspective, even if several sectors of these disciplines hold that certain functions of language and the psyche escape the competency of cognitive science. On the other hand, for the social sciences with a principally social dimension—such as sociology, economics, social psychology, and legal and historical science—"there is no doubt that their discipline is by definition irreducible to cognitive science."[22] So the instituted relation between the social sciences and cognitive science is more tenuous and cannot in any case be viewed in terms of absorption or fusion, but is rather a simple alliance of reason. In this regard, cognitive science may constitute a highly fruitful repository of knowledge for defining the bases of rational action, decision-making procedures, and risk taking; it may illuminate the notions of the rules and conventions on which economists, sociologists, anthropologists, and historians reflect.

## The CREA

One of the high places of the internal interactions in the constellation of the different disciplines in the cognitivist galaxy is the CREA. The inclusion of the "cognitive science" group in the CREA rests on the bet of a fertile synergy between cognitive science and the social sciences. From this contribution there has resulted a bipolar structure, with one division of the team given to "cognitive approaches to the social" and the other termed the "research group on cognition." The one corresponds to the initial vocation of the CREA, which is analytic philosophy and cognitive psychology, and the other has been grafted onto the initial project in the purely cognitive perspective, with neuroscience, artificial intelligence, the physics of disordered systems, the study of complex networks, and neoconnectionism. This eruption of cognitive science began in 1986, the date of publication of an issue of *Cahiers du CREA* devoted to the theme "Cognition and Complexity" that announced the following: "The integrated research area of the CNRS devoted to 'communication science' has assigned the CREA a study on the relations between cognitive science and the social sciences."[23] This new research orientation makes strong reference to the most recent work by Dan Sperber and Deirdre Wilson.[24] The earlier Girardian orientation has since faded to the advantage of this sector, which contains the "cognitive science" team integrated in 1987.

Meanwhile, in 1990, Jean-Pierre Dupuy, director of the CREA, feared a potential explosion. The spectacular passion for cognitive science poses the risk of forgetting the CREA's vocation of shedding light on the interactions with the social sciences. So Dupuy advocated fusing the two research groups in order to return a principal role to the philosophical project of mutual nourishment between the social sciences and cognitive science. Philosophy then presents itself as the only possible cement in a coexistence that is by definition heterogeneous.

One of the main problems lies in the manner in which the institutionalization of cognitive science has taken place in France around neuroscience, and so essentially around Jean-Pierre Changeux, whose concern is not really with the connection to the social sciences: "Changeux even has the greatest contempt for the sciences of man, as is evident in *Neuronal Man.*"[25]

## The Fertility of the Social Sciences

The connections between cognitivism and the social sciences are nonetheless already quite advanced, and in certain areas the fertility of these relations is manifest and even spectacular. In artificial intelligence, which early on enabled a modelization in the cognitivist paradigm, the advances, as much theoretical as technical, are among the most amazing. Notably, there has been a focus on expert systems, which necessitates that one "analyze the reasoning of a human expert on the field considered with a view to coding this reasoning in logical and informational terms."[26] Modelization of this type of reasoning on three distinct levels (structural, conceptual, and cognitive) also enables the reevaluation of the reasoning of "common sense"; in the latter are imbricated general knowledge and the program destined to use the data and heuristics of the basis of knowledge. We have already seen to what point this reevaluation links up with a general evolution of the social sciences toward the recognition of the descriptive capacity of the agents.[27]

Another major advance made possible by artificial intelligence, robotics, has opened an area with greater and greater efficiency, and has profoundly shaken the world of labor in the industrial sector. First, industry obtained robots capable of prerecorded serial motion; today, robots have an autonomy of action with regard to the types of tasks they are given.

The third field of application, which has astonishing effects, is that of image processing. In this area, the last decade has seen the birth of a focus on a remarkable means of analysis that allows a better understanding of neurological illnesses. At the basis of this progress, one may invoke the role played by the development of sophisticated techniques of imaging and the focus on a highly effective means of analysis, defined as positron emission tomography (PET); this process allows a gauging of the cerebral structures active during the execution of a cognitive task.

We have seen to what point neuroscience has been radically transformed by the model of information processing from cognitivism. Psychology is also to be found in the cognitivist paradigm since the renewed questioning of the behaviorist procedure that has long dominated experimental psychology. It is especially on this level that a reevaluation of the "long-suppressed" heuristic capacity of common sense is reappearing.[28] The field of investigation of cognitive psychology is made up of the various mental activities: perception, apprenticeship, memorization, and reasoning.[29] Here again we find the importance of action, already emphasized in the general reorientations of the social sciences today. Hence, the perceptive and motor capacities allow the appearance of invariances, a certain stability of perceptive representations. Perception appears to be both constructed by the organism under the influence of the information processing due to the environment and constrained by mechanisms belonging to the perceptive system itself. Invariant properties of motor performance have also appeared. The distinction between reflexive and voluntary motor action, which poses the problem of their articulation, leads to the thesis of the reorganization of the elements of reflexive motor action as a function of voluntary—intentional—motor action.[30]

Representations are analyzed on the basis of the distinction of three levels: the infrasemantic level, the semantic level of the identification of physical or symbolic objects, and the semantic level of the processing of meanings in view of actions. In the same way, the study of memory processes leads to distinguishing the encoding or storing of data, the retention and reactivation of these data. Above all, memory is no longer perceived as a simple passive appendage of knowledge, but rather as "an integral part of this knowledge itself, and perhaps the form of all knowledge."[31]

## The Unconscious Revisited

The relations between cognitivism and psychoanalysis are particularly ambivalent, as there has been quite a shift of attention from the unconscious to the conscious, and so a relativization of the mechanisms revealed by psychoanalysis. Meanwhile, as Hubert Dreyfus has shown, Freud always adopted a procedure related to cognitivism in demonstrating that all behavior is mediated by representation. The interactions between cognitive science and psychoanalysis have led to a rediscovery of the unconscious. This is the object of study that Marcel Gauchet has recently taken up.[32] He shows that next to the unconscious of the philosophers, two other forms of unconscious appeared during the nineteenth century, in an exaltation of nature against the thematics of the Enlightenment during the Romantic period:[33] the hereditary unconscious, which transferred the theory of evolution to the level of the human psyche and urged a look at the past; and more so the neurological unconscious, which imposed the idea of an automatic functioning of the brain, of a reflexive type—the source of somnambulism and hysterical manifestations, but which was also seen in a normal situation in the individual who did not totally control her own behavior. This conception, at first called "unconscious cerebration," "has quite effectively sapped the bases of the classical representation of the subject and its voluntary power."[34]

The discovery of a role of automaticity in the functioning of the brain indeed begins a questioning of the traditional equation of the psyche and consciousness. This comes back to the notion of the *member,* from ethnomethodology, which designates an infrasubject: "The member is a set of competencies, of knowledges, of masteries of a certain type of operation to be undertaken, and not a subject."[35] The valorization of this radical turn in the conception of the subject is aligned, for Gauchet, with a vast project, which is to show that at the turn of the century, around 1900, there was a decisive point of inflection: "The change of course in the representation of subjectivity marked by the rise of the unconscious is inseparable from a change of the same extent in the representation of the political and social order."[36]

In the relations between the cognitive unconscious and the psychoanalytic one, the differences today appear notable. Daniel Widlöcher insists on carefully distinguishing the two perspectives.[37] He holds that the representations that are the object of the psychoanalytic cure have the unique features of being complex, deriving from the declarative memory, and being the object of an active repression. "These are the phantasms, which could enter into consciousness if defensive measures did not hinder access to a verbal or preverbal representation."[38] Nonetheless, some scholars plead for a "cognitivization" of psychoanalytic notions.[39] Incontestably, several perspectives are being sketched, in a fertile dialogue between the realms claimed by the two parties.

Even if psychoanalysts are more reticent—as they take into account the risks of neuronal reduction in the approach to the unconscious—some of them are more open to an exchange between the two avenues of approach to the unconscious. Thus, psychoanalyst André Bourguignon holds that "psychoanalysis may propose fertile hypotheses to neuroscience, and the latter may impose limits on psychoanalytic speculations."[40] Marie Bonnafé goes in the same direction when she writes, "If there is no place for a direct application to psychoanalysis of the schemata of the exact sciences, in his procedure the psychoanalyst cannot neglect to refer to models and attempt to gauge determinisms at work in his practice. If this is not done scientifically by the analyst, it risks being overlooked."[41] Psychoanalyst Pierre Fédida is also open to dialogue with cognitive science and regrets that the debate has not yet taken place. Judging that twenty years of research in analytic philosophy have not enabled the establishment of the existence of possible bridges between the brain and thought, he remarks that "we must know if the reformulations may serve as transactional paths between psychoanalysis and neurobiology."[42] The current enforcement of the heterogeneity of the models may permit a dialogue, on condition that the cognitivist positions are not presented as denying psychoanalysis in their description of the singularity of mental states. Fédida notably is interested, as a psychoanalyst, in everything the philosophy of mind says about belief.

## Language

Insofar as the object of cognitive science is the functioning of human intelligence in its observable dimensions, we understand how language and linguistics are a particularly important realm for it. Of course, linguistics no longer occupies the position of pilot science that it had during the structuralist era, but many of its advances over the course of this period are taken up again at the heart of the cognitivist configuration. It is thus allowed that our cognitive universe is a universe of signs. The cognitive grammars developed in the most recent period are applied to describing the elementary mental operations at work in all language, with a pursuit of the search for the levels of competency in a Chomskyan fashion. "The status of language is first of all 'cognitive,' in two senses: as a medium and site of operation of everyday labor on our states of knowledge, and as a dynamic productive system."[43]

Social demand is particularly important in the realm of the automatic processing of language. Electronic hypertext allows all possible interconnections, as Pierre Lévy shows.[44] Computer science intervenes in cognitive ecology, but also in the processes of individual and collective subjectification. This dimension enables the envisioning of a pragmatic approach to electronic communication. For example, there is the case of the set of programs conceived by Terry Winograd and Fernando Flores.[45] Their network of conversation does not merely transfer information, "but, truly, *speech acts* that involve those who enact them to themselves and others."[46] They have in effect proposed an approach to organization as a network of conversations in which the offers and the promises, the consultations and the decisions intersect, and in which the promises must be kept, in the framework of a true conversational community. Thus, the use of hypertext opens up many possibilities of interactivity.

Linguistic pragmatism is also being reconsidered according to the new cognitive orientations. This reinflection has general consequences, because the current paradigm shift in all the social sciences may be qualified as a pragmatic turn. A paradox, as François Récanati points out,[47] is at the heart of this evolution because, at the outset, the attention to the pragmatic dimension of language was opposed to the cognitivist point of view. Impugning the reduction of communication to a mere affair of coding and encoding, and placing the accent on the notion of the context of the "illocutionary act," of the language act, the linguists of the pragmatic current kept their distance from cognitive analyses. It is otherwise today. According to Fodor's theory of "modularity,"[48] the human mind is constituted by two types of systems of information processing. On the one hand, the "peripheral" systems are specialized for the processing of a particular type of signal. Thus, there is a "module" whose task is to decode the linguistic signals, another has the task of recognizing faces, another melodies, and so on. On the other hand, the "central" systems are assigned the task of centralizing the information collected by the various peripheral systems, of processing them, and of exploiting them. This theory of "modularity" permits a connection of the pragmatic and the cognitive analyses:

"This reinterpretation gives pragmatism an important role to play in cognitive studies."[49]

All of these advances enable a better outlining of the phenomenon of representation and a surpassing of the old reductive dualisms; but it remains essential to reflect on the necessary articulation between the social sciences and cognitive science.

# Nineteen

# The Neuronal Temptation
# and Its Limits

Georges Canguilhem reacted strongly to the criticisms of Michel
Foucault's structuralist program, the latter announced with the publication of *The Order of Things*. He ridiculed the hearts of the mourn-
ers who defended the rights of man against the one who, in the name
of a philosophy of the concept, proclaimed the recent birth and the
future death of man. He then ironized, "Humanists of the world,
unite!"[1] Nonetheless, this was the same Georges Canguilhem who, at
a 1980 conference on the brain and thought, attacked the limitless
ambitions of cybernetics and computer science, and reductionism in
general, to defend a threatened "I," whose last defense would defini-
tively be philosophy. In the face of this defense, one can only subscribe
to Daniel Andler's position, that "one does not defend a mystery, at
least not against science";[2] meanwhile, he adds, rightfully, that cognitive science only addresses a part of the real. One is forced to note
that, behind the spectacular progress achieved by neuroscience, there
is still a risk of triumphalism, which through its power of attraction is
in danger of broadly leading the social sciences toward illusory
heights, toward new reductionist traps.

## The Risks of a Neurophilosophy

Jean-Pierre Dupuy, who brought together the two research teams at
the CREA in 1990 so as to maximize synergies and avoid centrifugal
forces, in 1994 deemed it necessary to distinguish once again two

noticeably different perspectives. Without reinstating the two separate groups, Dupuy thought it enough to define two axes of research, "an axis of cognitive philosophy and an axis of practical philosophy."[3] In the face of the temptation for the disciplines to withdraw into themselves, which was connected to the delicacy of research in France, there was the possibility of filling the void with cognitive science. It is therefore important today to preserve the inquiry belonging to the social sciences and philosophy. "Cognitive science is a very important thing, even fundamental. I'm happy that it has its place at the CREA, but on condition that it isn't everything. Now, cognitive science has a tendency to invade everything, including the theory of action, the philosophy of action, and the normative."[4] The success of cognitive science effectively poses the danger of pulling everything along behind it in the blindness of a naturalization of the normative. Its ambitions are manifest, as is shown in the recent publication of a collective work on ethics edited by Jean-Pierre Changeux.[5] The objective of finding a biological causality in the brain that would allow the explanation of all forms of human behavior is defended by a current that sees itself as resolutely materialist. It represents a fundamentally reductionist position. Some, such as the neurobiologist Jean-Didier Vincent, assume a dual position. Reductionist on the level of scientific inquiry, when it comes to understanding how the memory functions ("When you see a hormone capable of triggering a natural behavior, you cannot help being reductionist"),[6] Vincent nevertheless impugns a generalization or organic reduction: "I am against a certain neuronal imperialism, a neuronal order that would substitute itself for the moral order, in which everything is determined, everything's hooked up, in which man is a prisoner of his determinisms."[7]

This epistemological tension leads to a dual position, which the philosopher Pascal Engel, a member of the CREA, also defends. Impugning a simplistic causal mode, he aligns himself with the center of the mentalist turn in cognitive science, as a philosopher of mind: "The position we must adopt, to my mind, is naturalist with regard to ontology but antireductionist with regard to explanation."[8] For Engel, the divorce of philosophy and psychology is at once foundational for contemporary philosophy and already outmoded. Frege and Husserl both rejected the psychologization of logic when psychologism was characterized by introspection alone. At the present moment, psychology, no longer behaviorist but rather "cognitive," "does not have much to do with the introspective psychology attacked by Frege and Husserl."[9]

The philosophy of mind, a new discipline going back to the 1950s, is deployed within the horizon of reconciliation between philosophy and psychology on the basis of materialist and naturalist assumptions. But its disciplinary duality keeps it from succumbing to the reductionist sirens. In such a perspective, it is a question of defending at once the autonomy of mental states, of representations, of beliefs, and the existence of the constraints weighing on them. This is the case of the conception that Hilary Putnam defended beginning in the 1960s. He gave more "plasticity" to the then-current theory on the identity between mental states and properties of the nervous system. Putnam proposed a functionalist schema to make possible a gauging of the variation of mental states. The tension within materialism around a permanent dilemma "between its 'eliminativist' and 'nonreductionist' versions"[10] is also found in the philosophy of mind, between a physicalist ontology and a defense of the autonomy of the mental.

On the one hand, some would like to pull philosophy into the neuronal wake and build a neuronal theory of thought. Patricia Smith Churchland defends this position when she proposes a neurophilosophy that advocates a purely reductionist route.[11] On the other, the current that has Engel's "sympathy" is represented by "interpretationist" theses, favorable to a nonreductionist materialism. These positions have been developed by Davidson and Dennett.[12]

In the Humean, naturalist tradition, it is then fitting to surpass the tension in this research on mental states by distinguishing the various levels of explanation on which the different properties intervene. This is what Hilary Putnam defines as a proper conflict between a metaphysical or transcendent realism induced by a naturalist conception, in which the world exists independently of the subject, and an internal realism in which the same world is interwoven with knowledge, representations, and human practices.[13]

## The Philosophy of Mind

The philosophy of mind is located in the tradition of analytic philosophy, which has had the merit—contrary to structuralism—of not denying the problem of reference. But, under the influence of the naturalist and Humean turn in American philosophy, notably in Quine, it has attempted to develop the consequences of a position by which philosophy can no longer have a second position of transcendental discourse over the other disciplines.

The philosophy of mind, assuming its naturalist position on the ontological level, had to begin with the idea that humanity is a natural being that produces representations, among other natural beings. In this perspective, it has introduced a whole set of concepts: that of the "multiple realizability" of mental states, which Putnam introduced in the 1960s, according to which the same mental state may be realized in physical states that are different in each individual. Another concept with a heuristic function that emanates from the philosophy of mind is that of "taking place," which intervenes when the content of a mental state is determined by the environment—that is, by an extrinsic, relational framework, placed outside individual psychology. On the basis of this placement, broad mental contents have no causal power.

The concept of "posture or intentional strategy" also belongs to Daniel Dennett's philosophy of mind. The interpretation of behaviors postulates a priori that these behaviors obey certain optimal conditions of rationality. This imputation of rationality must be applied not only to humans but also to animals and machines with artificial intelligence. This is an area that permits the unexpected reconciliation of beliefs, of popular psychology, with contemporary philosophical analysis.

Whereas analytic philosophy supported its studies in the realm of language, the philosophy of mind assures the mentalist turn that connects it with cognitive science without for all that resulting in a total naturalization of the mental. This turn was already prepared by Chomsky, who placed his study of generative grammar under a naturalist register according to which the truth is found in the human mind, as linguistic science can establish.

In the manner of Davidson, Pascal Engel thinks that the way we represent the world and the theory of knowledge are necessarily the product of a certain causal interaction between humanity and the latter's surroundings. But, at the same time, he impugns all forms of reductionism. To avoid them, he preserves the epistemological dualism that separates the social and the natural sciences. "I don't think the social sciences can ever be sciences in the same way as physics or biology."[14] In this regard, the naturalist program suits Engel as a limit program enabling an understanding of the foundation of this epistemological distinction—without for all that postulating it, but by demonstrating it anew, with new conceptual tools. What is interesting is exactly his position in tension that takes into consideration the two sides of mental phenomena. Engel finally finds the position of the philosopher investigating a "theory of the conditions of possibility of the forms of discourse."[15] The borders that can be traced between the social and natural sciences are to be historicized in a strict relation with the evolution of scientific knowledges.

This approach leads the CREA to return to a certain number of classical problems in philosophy around notions of intention, action, and will. It takes up Dupuy's suggestion to constitute an axis of practical philosophy insofar as it is appropriate to revisit "the chapter in philosophical psychology that has been considered old hat."[16] Thus, the notions of conventions imply the postulation of an intention of individuals to follow certain regularities in their action. The reference to the notion of intentionality does not for all that mean, for the naturalist current, an adherence to phenomenology. "Husserl is interested in intentionality. But at no moment does he see that it may furnish a theory in naturalist terms. I myself take it seriously, even if it is definitely a trap."[17]

The phenomenological approach commits, according to Engel, the error of deeming that the natural world is to be situated alongside illusion. Without in the least supporting a biological conception of the social sciences, Engel finds it necessary to maintain the hypothesis by which certain types of behavior have biological determinants. On this basis, he holds that Searle much too quickly separates philosophy and cognitive science when the latter states that intentionality refers to subjectivity, to consciousness. The fact of positing a consciousness of the subject is situated sooner as an end point of analysis than as one of its conditions in Engel's naturalist perspective. Engel refuses to postulate any primacy of consciousness: "That distinguishes me from the phenomenologists."[18]

## Enaction

In the area of the natural sciences, Francisco Varela, a biologist and member of the CREA, also defends an antireductionist position. Strongly inspired by phenomenology, he starts with the indissociable character of perception and action in every cognitive act and in this regard proposes the concept of *enaction,* of incarnated action. Cognitive science must, therefore, according to Varela, bring into evidence this circular interaction between the organism and its environment, which remain strictly autonomous with respect to each other. The cognitive phenomenon contributes doubly to the sensorimotor capacities of the body, and these capacities are themselves inscribed in a broader biological, psychological, and cultural context.

To illustrate this circularity, Varela gives the example of the perception of colors, which has a paradigmatic value.[19] This phenomenon illustrates quite well the fact that cognition is not the mere reflection of a world already there, independent of individual perceptive capacities, and that it is also not the mere product of representations. The "objectivist" thesis, the most common in neurobiology—that the perception of colors would be only the reflection in the brain of the colors of nature corresponding to specific wavelengths—runs up against a certain number of aporias. Experiments indeed show that a wavelength may be interpreted differently depending on the context. There is thus an overall reinterpretation of information that invalidates the "objectivist" thesis. The "subjectivist" position is just as unsatisfying when it presents the vision of colors as the mere expression of "mental categories" belonging to the human species. "Color provides a paradigmatic domain in which our twin concerns of science and human experience mutually intersect."[20]

Cognitive processes therefore contribute to the construction of reality and not only to its passive representation. And Varela takes into consideration the dilemma of cognitive science, in the form of the circle between itself and experience. The axis of this circularity is represented by the bodiliness of experience, as Merleau-Ponty understands it, and encompasses the body as a lived structure and the body as the context of cognitive mechanisms. This refusal of "objectivism" has led Varela to broaden the perspective of cognitive science to the necessity of an ethical dimension, at the intersection of the sharpest discoveries of Western science and Buddhist meditation.

Varela remains in the lineage that has belonged to the CREA since its creation, by insisting on *enaction* and the notions of autonomy that it implies. He continues to recognize himself as within the initial epistemological project of the Center, which today he considers to be the "golden age of the CREA."[21] He is, on the other hand, more skeptical with regard to the current situation, which he perceives as a dogmatic closing due to the very success, to the too-great visibility of this research institution: "Today the CREA is better known as a center of analytic philosophy, and the consequence is that it's no longer a center of interdisciplinary research."[22]

## The Epidemiology of Representations

Dan Sperber, another member of the CREA, an anthropologist who came out of structuralism and then Chomskyanism, adheres to an exclusively materialist position in the area of cognitive science. He holds that the naturalist model may be extended to social, communicational, and cultural phenomena. He defines this ambition in his research program around the notion of the "epidemiology of representations,"[23] whose object is not representations but rather their diffusion, with progress in the causal explanation of sociocultural phenomena as an aim.

Sperber has taken his distance from the heuristic capacity of semiological models, and for them he has substituted a cognitive model of communication founded on the notions of pertinence and inference.[24] With Deirdre Wilson, he proposes a model of communication that accords a central place to the inferential processes and that is therefore integrated into cognitive science. In the tradition of the Lévi-Straussian ambition of seeing anthropology one day wake up among the natural sciences, Sperber has always defended a monistic, naturalistic position. The becoming of the social sciences does not occur through broadening the realm of the natural sciences as they are, but rather in qualitatively modifying their nature and quantitatively modifying their dimensions. "The day biology was combined with physics, the natural sciences were no longer the same. If some of the undertakings in the social sciences become naturalist, the natural sciences will thereby be modified."[25]

In order to realize this transformation, Sperber holds firmly to maintaining a strong notion of causality in the social sciences, which he perceives as potentially hard sciences, on the condition that one weigh a certain number of constraints on the way of thinking of social objects. First, he postulates the absence of an epistemological dichotomy between the natural and the social sciences: "There are no causes other than natural ones. There are no exceptions to the laws of physics. In the social, we are confronted with the same material."[26] The first postulate of a scientific procedure, says Sperber, is therefore constituted by the naturalist and causalist hypothesis. The second assumes the most explicit possible generalizing theory, which would be testable and falsifiable in the Popperian sense.

Quite obviously, not all the social sciences can answer all these draconian constraints. Only a small, hard core can eventually extract itself from contingency, from the descriptive. Thus, Sperber, already in 1968, defended the naturalist part of Lévi-Strauss's program, detached from its ethnographic, descriptive, and fictional "gangue."[27] Starting from a materialist ontology, from a monism of principle, Sperber in fact agrees with Jean-Pierre Changeux's reductionist positions when he states that collaboration between cognitive science and neuroscience allows for the vision of a "continuous field. So we are seeing a peaceful diminishing of the boundary between the science of man and society on the one hand, and the sciences of nature on the other."[28]

This continuum leads Sperber to redefine the notion of representation on the basis of neuronal modelization and to envision a research program on the question of the diffusion, the contagion of these representations: "Such an explanation derives from a sort of epidemiology of representations,"[29] in which social structure is only an extension of mental structure. The site of causal explanation is designated: "It is the material interactions between the brain and its environments that explain the distribution of representations."[30] Symbolicity, in this framework of analysis, is not a property of phenomena and their perception, but rather a property of the conceptual representations produced by the mind: "Contrary to structuralist rationalism, Sperberian cognitivist rationalism sees in symbolism the action of a specialized apparatus of the intellect, not that of general operations of the mind."[31] So Sperber removes the project of the social sciences, in any case of its hard core, from any hermeneutic perspective: "A culture is not a text, and the relations among the elements that compose it are ecological rather than logical relations."[32]

The affirmation that anthropology has the possibility, thanks to cognitive science, of becoming a science in its own right, the equal of the natural sciences, sparks debate at the very heart of the CREA. Lucien Scubla, an anthropologist and an original member of the CREA's team at the time when the orientation was centered on autonomy, Girardian inspiration, and complexity, impugns Sperber's blatant optimism.[33] He does not think that a reduction of anthropology to an epidemiology of representations is possible. He denounces it as a reductionist enterprise. "For him, studying a ritual is always studying the causal chains of representations, and studying causal chains of representations is, in the last analysis, studying physicochemical interactions."[34] Scubla does not deny the necessity of linking anthropology to biology or that of perceiving technology as a cultural phenomenon indissociable from life. In this regard, he also notes an incoherency in Sperber, who tries to confine himself to representations by according them an exorbitant privilege, from which the study of human actions and behaviors, as well as that of technical objects, risks suffering. Now, if the manufacture and use of instruments requires cognitive capacities, the conditions in which this diffusion is deployed are broadly independent of the required cognitive capacities. It is the same for most social activities, and a fortiori for the institutional logics that take place over time.

What Scubla disputes is not Sperber's materialist postulate; rather, he cautions against mental atomism: "To believe that one can restore entire institutions and cultures by starting from representations or, better yet, from cerebral micromechanisms that correspond to them, seems as reckless as trying to use an electron microscope or even an optical microscope to describe the structure of the solar system or the anatomy of a vertebrate."[35]

According to Daniel Andler, this controversy stems essentially from a misunderstanding. On the one hand, Scubla accuses Sperber of deifying matter by postulating a radical materialism, and in this demonstration he can show at leisure that philosophers and physicists do not always know so well what falls in the area of matter. On the other, this is not really Sperber's main problem; as a cognitive anthropologist, Sperber does not need to instill more ontology than in the physicist's practice. For Andler, Sperber has the merit of proposing a program in the production of knowledges, of going as far as possible in the direction he has defined. Meanwhile, the direction this research program assumes is fundamentally reductionist.

This ambivalent situation incites Andler to a position split between passion for the spectacular progress achieved by cognitive science and the conviction that the problematics of the social sciences and philosophy will be shifted only slightly a century from now. Still at issue is the dialectic of the respective places attributed to freedom and to constraint: "The great advances consist of noticing that a certain number of behaviors that didn't seem in the least constrained, that seemed totally free, are not."[36] Of course, linguistics already brought into definitive evidence a certain number of invariants, but in cognitive science these were perceived as a pure cultural accumulation, pertaining only to the historical order. Cognitive science unveils other constraints, and the possible meeting point for evaluating the latter could be in asking once again the famous question of the innate and the acquired. This renewed investigation, into what weighs on the exercise of thought and action, also has the effect of modifying the "way we think of the relations between the individual and the collective."[37]

## Cognitive Psychology and the Economics of Convention

This possible rearticulation brings us back to the studies of the economists of convention. "We've always been interested in judgment and therefore in a cognitive activity submitted to the constraint of a collective orientation."[38] In *De la justification*,[39] one may easily perceive the differences in the qualification of things, but it is suitable to inquire into the basis of these values, to wonder why an object is treated as a sign whereas otherwise it has nothing to do with any functional treatment.

After a reconstruction of the great social artifacts that define a collective perspective, the test in the realm of reality necessitated a return down to the level of individual justification. "At that time, it seemed perfectly normal that we were concerned with what was being done in cognitive psychology,"[40] even if that encounter was not fully satisfying—the point of view examined was that of the adjustment of the world, which implied a dynamic approach to human activity. It was not for all that a matter of a simple recourse to the studies of cognitive psychology, as what prevailed was still the situation of interaction between the individual and collective levels. Laurent Thévenot was at once assured of the fertility of the relations with cognitive science and aware of their potential danger. "Cognitive science advances like neoclassical economics. It's the same model. I don't believe, though, that the answer is ignorance."[41]

The economics of convention is therefore involved with the effort to illuminate the obscure zones of the standard model of orthodox economists. Thus, there is the question of whether "calculating rationality is as strong as the most traditional microeconomics says it is."[42] If, on the contrary, one notices that the agents have limited capacities of memorization, calculation, and analysis, one must reconsider the manner in which they make decisions and manage uncertainty. "If you accept this question, the whole field of cognitive science becomes pertinent to the economist."[43] Of course, Herbert Simon was already asking these questions in the 1950s,[44] but they were barely perceived in the thirty glorious years of postwar France. Today, on the contrary, the crisis in cognitive science, on the one hand, and its progress, on the other, limit one to the renewed interrogation of the model of optimization that the economists found particularly operational and reliable. The notion of limited rationality, which is offered to the economist and others in the disciplines of the social sciences, thus has the effect of defatalizing the explanations and asking the question of the new modes of causality. It opens a systematic investigation of the field of representations. In the area of economics, the connection with cognitive science is situated on the plane of cognitive phenomena linked to collectives, and therefore on a very tangential level in relation to neuroscience. The criteria of optimization and of the maximum efficiency hoped for are thus reexamined by the cognitive experiments and discoveries that allow responses to be brought to the recent introduction of incompleteness and uncertainty.[45] Game theory has also enabled the discovery, on the cognitive plane, of behavioral logics, as Jean-Pierre Dupuy has shown, using the dilemma of prisoners in the framework of his demonstrations.

Olivier Favereau is interested in a second axis of fertility of the relations between cognition and economics, the whole emerging area of social cognition linked to phenomena of organization. Indeed, we are seeing the beginning of an opening to the social, to the collective, in cognitive science. "We are especially beginning to speak of actor-systems that we describe on the basis of simulations of interactions between the agents whose cognitive capacities we have specified, and we are examining the evolution of the whole of the system."[46]

## Sociality

The elaboration of a social cognition is one of the objectives of the sociologist Bernard Conein, who sees in the new hypotheses—results of observations of cognitive ethology or of the psychology of development—the possibility of constituting a new area, that of social cognition. The discoveries in this sector enable a demonstration that social categorization does not always stem from the cultural sphere, as is shown by the observation of behavioral attitudes in the sociality of green monkeys.[47] One ends up with conclusions similar to those resulting from the observation done in the studies of developmental psychology.[48]

Thus, Conein uses the hypothesis of "Machiavellian intelligence," which he borrows from the ethologists. This consists of attempting to isolate a certain number of mechanisms belonging to the social and that stem from cognitive phenomena. "Cognitive science has in general underestimated this idea. People don't have only perceptual aptitudes, aptitudes for natural cognition, but also social aptitudes."[49] There is therefore a possible basis of elaboration of a social cognition; and if Conein immediately places himself within the cognitivist paradigm, it is above all because he does not think there is an autonomy of the social sciences. The latter must conceive of themselves as compatible with biology, psychology, ethology, and so on.

Barkow has recently defended this thesis: "I set the requirement that any sociological explanation of ethics be compatible with the psychological theses of ethics, and that the latter be compatible with both neuroscience and evolutionary biology."[50] He advocates not an interdisciplinarity founded on biology, but rather making the sociological hypotheses compatible with what is otherwise known about the functioning of the other sciences. "The way in which the social sciences isolate themselves is indefensible. That doesn't mean one must be reductionist; one must just be compatible."[51]

## Nonhuman Humans

Conein, we have already seen, works with Thévenot to introduce objects as central elements of social analysis.[52] This new interest in objects is in fact a subject of disagreement and controversy between the CSI, which sees in it the great innovation that is enabling a revolution in the social sciences, and the CREA, which is much more reserved—even if Thévenot, a member of the CREA, actively participates in this introduction. Behind this controversy there remain, in a somewhat new way, old debates on what specifies human nature, from the ontological point of view, and on the possible relations between humans and nonhumans.

On this point, the director of the CREA, Jean-Pierre Dupuy, best grasps what separates him from the anthropology of science of Michel Callon and Bruno Latour when they "attribute the predicate of subjectivity, in some way—in any case speech, action—to things. When I hear that, I say to myself that we have to return to Marx and denounce what to me appears to be a fetishism, if not of merchandise, at least of objects."⁵³ Of course, Dupuy admits that relations among human beings are possible only in the framework of common worlds, of positioned objects constitutive of human relations: "And it was Hannah Arendt who made me understand that."⁵⁴ To go from there and attribute an intention to objects is a step that Dupuy refuses to take. The differences hinge on the question of the competencies one requires of the agents to introduce an order into the world they construct.

Callon and Latour, for their part, reproach the CREA for underestimating the role of nonhumans in the construction of order and in giving a form to interaction. "For someone like Jean-Pierre Dupuy, the problem is to construct a totality that is in return imposed on individuals, but constructed by those individuals. It is a somewhat sophisticated methodological individualism."⁵⁵ Callon says that Dupuy holds a much more astute view than the one in which individuals would be capable of assimilating, through their rationality alone, all possible interactions, rules, and conventions. It is more workable to think that individuals do not blindly follow rules without interpreting them. But the avoidance of these two pitfalls, that of overly rational actors and that of actors much too determined by outside rules, is not for all that satisfying with regard to the requirements of the new anthropology of science. "One notices that these are means that require relatively naked individuals."⁵⁶ On the contrary, the anthropology of science views phenomena of interaction by introducing a particular and consequential role for objects, nonhumans, quasi humans, at the very heart of interaction.

Latour is particularly polemical when he qualifies the CREA. Of course, he concedes, the latter is a research center where one professionalizes, where there exists a sort of ethos of professional relations. In addition, he recognizes a certain community of mind that comes from the fact that many of the researchers at the CSI and the CREA have come out of the *grandes écoles* for engineers. But, for Latour, a first major difference results from the fact that the anthropology of science works toward the exportation of problematics, whereas the CREA "is for importation. Basically, like the entire American tradition in which it is imbued, it's totally scientistic."⁵⁷ Otherwise, he regrets that the CREA is artificially giving a second life to epistemology, which had lost all vitality. But the major disagreement is found especially on the question of field study, of objects, and of the relation with empirical study: "We're interested in the field. We have rich objects that cause a stir—whereas questions of soul and body and of what cognitive corridor you open when the cat is on the mat don't hold much interest."[58]

These utterances clearly reveal that the search for a new paradigm in the social sciences is far from taking place consensually. Besides the institutional stakes, which are not negligible, there also remain cleavages on the level of theoretical positions that oppose scholars to one another. Nevertheless, these positionings must not occlude a certain underlying community in the mode of questioning and in the current repositioning of the social sciences toward experiential frameworks of action.

# Twenty

# Collective Representations
## Leaving the History of Mentalities

The notion of representation is, of course, not really new in the historian's practice. It was used broadly in the 1970s as a connecting notion, stimulating a history of mentalities in full sway. Meanwhile, today it has taken a new meaning, at a moment when the discipline of history seems to be, after its hour of glory, the poor relative of the cognitive team. Some send history back to its contingent dimension, to its incapacity to transform into a true science. Others fully intend to participate actively in the current paradigm shift by demonstrating that, next to individual mental representations, collective representations must necessarily be historicized and even constitute the strongest rampart against any reductionist temptation.

Also at stake with this increasingly insistent reference to the world of representations are a redefinition of and a certain critical distance from the manner in which the *Annales* school treated mentalities in the 1960s. In the framework of this distancing, Alain Corbin has spoken of the "subversion by the history of representations."[1] Roger Chartier defined this shift in a programmatic article in an issue of the *Annales* devoted to the "critical turn."[2] He recalls that the third level,[3] that of mentalities, offered the opportunity to open history to new objects, but through already tested methods in demographic and economic history. This conjunction of serial, quantitative methods, effectively applied to objects hitherto more frequented by anthropologists and philosophers—such as fear, sexuality, death, and so on—has assured a strong success for the discipline of history.

Meanwhile, the history of mentalities was in fact content to transpose the methods used in another field of investigation around a deliberately fuzzy, catchall notion, such as that of mentality. What resulted was a vision that accorded priority to the long period, to socio-professional division, to a dichotomy postulated between a popular culture of great number and an elite culture, and to an absolute confidence in the disconnected numbers and series of the interpretive schemes. This serialization was a source of explosion in a history that becomes more and more crumbled.[4]

## The Various Modes of Appropriation

Roger Chartier records three shifts that have recently marked the historian's practice. First, there has been the progressive renunciation of a project of total history articulated around agencies of determination. This abandonment has increased the number of attempts at entry into the past by way of more particularized objects, such as a singular event or life story, "through deeming that neither practice nor structure is produced by the contradicted and challenged representations by which individuals and groups give meaning to the world that is their own."[5] The second shift comes from no longer considering territorial singularities as the only possible partition in research and substituting for them the valorization of regularities of an anthropological nature. Third, the transposition of socioprofessional divisions to the level of mentalities has been questioned anew by recent research in this area showing that "it is impossible to qualify motives, objects, or cultural practices with immediately sociological terms."[6]

These shifts invite further attention to the process of the construction of meaning that turns out to be the consequence of a meeting point between the "world of the text" and the "world of the reader." Chartier borrows these notions from Paul Ricoeur, but in a perspective specific to the historian involving the restoration of the practices, supports, and concrete modalities of the act of reading and writing.

Chartier situates the new area of research at the intersection of a history of socially differentiated practices and a history of representations; this crossing has the objective of accounting for the various forms of appropriation. The pluralization of cultural constructions questions the "fundamentally dualist division of dominator and dominated,"[7] used until now as a way of bringing coherency to descriptions that burst forth within the socioprofessional hierarchy. "Things appeared more complex from the moment we directed our gaze to the circulation of objects, beliefs, and practices that cut across the social divisions."[8] The renewed interrogation of the organizing capacity of this reading code gives a central position to the question of the forms of appropriation.

The rediscovery of Norbert Elias[9] has strongly contributed to reinforcing this direction of research in history concerning the various modalities of appropriation. In the conception Chartier provides of it, the history of appropriations does not correspond to the sense that Michel Foucault gave to the concept of the "social appropriation of discourses" as a procedure of subjection and confiscation of discourses.[10] It is also not the equivalent, we have already seen, of the meaning that hermeneutics gives it. "Appropriation, as we understand it, aims for a social history of uses and interpretations, brought back to their fundamental determinations and inscribed in the specific practices that produce them."[11] Chartier intends in this way to give a place to textuality, to reading, but more broadly to all the sense-bearing processes, without forgetting that the latter are never disembodied, that they always have material support that conditions their historical effectiveness:

> It is also on the basis of the divisions set up by power (for example, from the sixteenth to the eighteenth century, that between the state reason and moral conscience, between state control and the freedom of the heart) that we must appreciate the emergence of an autonomous literary sphere as the constitution of a market of symbolic goods and intellectuals or aesthetic judgments.[12]

This orientation owes a lot to Michel de Certeau, who studied everyday practices of appropriation that were characteristically ephemeral, unstable, without a place.[13]

Even while demarcating his own positions from those of Foucault, Chartier nonetheless traverses Foucault's interrogations, notably from *Discipline and Punish*,[14] when he asks the question of how to account, through discourse, for nondiscursive practices. "Here is one of the extreme challenges that historians who work on this point are confronted with,"[15] that of the almost automatic functioning of the nondiscursive practices uniquely accessible through the texts that describe them, impose norms on them, forbid them, prescribe them, or proscribe them. The notion of appropriation and its autonomization in relation to social categorization must nonetheless not end up, says Chartier, as a "sort of generalized equivalence of all appropriations."[16]

Leaving the schema of reflection in terms of positions of domination must not cause one to forget that the power to produce, impose, and name representations is unequally distributed; and this implies linking phenomena of appropriation to practices. In this regard, sociocultural history articulated exclusively according to socioprofessional classifications "has for too long depended on a mutilated conception of the social."[17] It has not given a place to other distinctions that are just as pertinent, such as sexual, generational, religious, and territorial membership. There results an attention to networks that links up with that of other disciplines like sociology or anthropology, and that has a paradigmatic value: "Whence the necessity of a second shift, directing attention to the networks of practices that organize the historically and socially differentiated modes of relation to texts,"[18] of inverting the social history of culture into the cultural history of the social.

This notion of network especially enables one not to forget that there are perceivable historical variations, social hierarchies, and industrial cultures, without for all that reducing the consumer of culture to a sort of ectoplasm, totally submitted to these powers. "After a phase in which, by reaction, we had especially to insist on notions such as practice versus discourse and appropriation versus imposition, I think now it's possible to try to rearticulate these forms with one another."[19] Chartier advocates a return to the notion, put forth by Marcel Mauss and Émile Durkheim, of "collective representation"; when viewed as a matrix of practices constructing the social, it allows the articulation of three modalities of relation to the social world: "First, the task of classification and separation that produces the many intellectual configurations by which reality is contradictorily constructed by the different groups composing society; next, the practices aiming to bring a social identity into recognition. . . . Finally, the institutionalized and objectified forms."[20]

Thus, one may restore the dynamic of the struggle of representations, the stakes of symbolic strategies in confrontation. In this spirit, the concept of representation can be fertile, on condition that it be conceived on the basis of its capacity to articulate the space of possibilities within which productions, decisions, and explicit intentions are inscribed. In general, it was said of a whole series of constraints that they determined, commanded, and bridled action by establishing among themselves a mechanical relation of causality, whereas it would be preferable to use the term of social inscriptions unknown by their agents.

## The Effectiveness of Symbols

At the heart of the current paradigm shift in the discipline of history, as Marcel Gauchet analyzes it, is the necessity for the historian to understand how symbolism acts in society. The historian must decode this new field of investigation on the basis of the split effected between the explicit and unconscious roles of representations. This implies a new view, for the historian is then confronted with "new problems with regard to which we are at the stage of preliminary exploration."[21]

Breaking with the radical historicism of the period of the history of mentalities, the reactivation of classical questions from the new angle of the history of representations leads to the postulation of "very deep structurations of experience that also make history possible."[22] Deeming that one has access to the past implies thinking that there are, beyond the variations, changes, and ruptures between the culture of today and that of yesterday, something that allows a possible communication between them. This would be a "common humanity," what Joëlle Proust calls the "comparative topic," which allows us to recover, for example, the sense of the beautiful in Plato or any other cultural value of a society that is no longer our own. This postulate, then, is linked to the orientations of cognitive science.

Therefore, on the historical level, there is the question of the basis of this common humanity. Marcel Gauchet confronted this problem with *Le Désenchantement du monde*,[23] from the angle of the observation of religious beliefs. Gauchet's central thesis involves demonstrating that modern society, issuing from religion as the founding framework of sociality—and this very much represents an essential rupture—nonetheless reveals, behind this mutation, the continuum of a modernity endowed with equivalents that have substituted for the religious experience of earlier times by responding to the same needs. This history of the metamorphoses of the place of the religious therefore is intended to conjoin two approaches often presented as antinomic, "the unity of becoming and existence with its heart of radical discontinuities."[24]

This combination of continuities and discontinuities is at the basis of a possible intelligibility and understanding of the past, for a common human experience binds past and present. In Gauchet's demonstration, there is, therefore, an entire unconscious, collective lived experience of a modern society inscribed in the experiences that have a relation to the lived religious experience of the past. "The determination of the present is always effected under the sign of the invisible."[25] The eminent place accorded to science as well as aesthetics in modernity is a tangible sign of this postulate, whereby the site of truth is to be found at a deep level, at once invisible and present, in the things themselves. There is, then, an unveiling involved—but as an end point of the analysis, and in a perspective that is not denunciatory.

Gauchet's approach has the merit of departing from the twofold aporetic horizon of, on the one hand, historical continuism, evolutionism, and, on the other, the radical discontinuism in vogue during the period of structural breaks. His history of representations is deployed around a complex movement that combines variants and invariants. In this approach, many phenomena should be reread and revisited by the historians. "In this regard, the historiography of a particular realm, such as witchcraft, would be every evocative."[26]

Witchcraft is not a testimony from the inertia of the past, an archaic legacy opposed to scientific culture. On the contrary, it is a typical creation of the transition to modernity. The witch-hunts found their apogee at the moment of formation of the concept and personnel of the modern state. "What is important to gauge is the contemporaneity and the continuum that exist between diffuse and formed representation. From there, it is apt to demonstrate the mode of coherence that may exist between them."[27] In this way, one may succeed in understanding how the most irrational representations can coexist with sophisticated capacities of rational construction. Such is the case for Jean Bodin, promoter and conceiver of the modern state who is at the same time obsessed with demonology, even so without attempting to explain mechanically one type of representation by the other.

This reading of the past requires that we make the archives speak quite differently, by bringing a particularly meticulous attention to bear on their ambiguity, on their materiality, on the intention as well as the omissions of the composer of the document analyzed. This new requirement for the historian, which Gauchet defines—and which he compares with Arlette Farge's manner of situating the importance of the literalness of the archive[28]—brings the discipline of history into full participation in the current orientation of the social sciences, in their desire to recover as much as possible the experience of the actors, to go back down to the lowest level in order to interpret it.

This procedure favors a microscopic scale: "From this point of view, in a certain way, all history is to be redone."[29] Meanwhile, Gauchet does not opt for an exclusive level of analysis, which microscopic reading would be. Quite the contrary: the latter must be correlated with the macroscopic scale. This is what we find in Robert Bonnaud's efforts to construct a *système de l'histoire* supported by extremely precise dates, on a planetary scale.[30] "There is a renewed questioning of periods and scales in both directions. We must use the telescope and the microscope."[31]

## On the Borders of History

Such a perspective questions anew the usual temporal quadripartition of the institution of history and implies a broader conception of what constitutes the historian's archive. A historian such as Alain Corbin has made a specialty of exploring limit points, margins, borders, paroxysmal moments. It is nonetheless the same interrogation as Gauchet's: to understand unusual behaviors from the past in spite of the "common humanity" that binds them to us. After the history of the shore,[32] the limit point of a landscape, Corbin devoted himself to the Hautefaye affair, in the Dordogne, in which hundreds of peasants killed and burned a noble during a fair on August 16, 1870, in a particularly shocking horror show of the second half of the nineteenth century.[33] Here, there is another object that Corbin explores, that of limit violence—those moments on the brink of a gulf where the social bond dissolves and yields to the absolute horror that leads the historian to wonder how human beings were able to behave that way. The act of understanding, then, must examine the rationality of the players in the drama. One may, in this regard, mobilize the spectacular schema of René Girard, but one quickly runs into the undefinable. One may then have recourse to Gabriel Tarde and the old psychology of crowds, or to the anthropology of violence; or one may yet invoke the marginality of the place—but still the explanation remains insufficient. One is then at the edge of something that escapes explanation and that binds one to a descriptive detour, so as to be as close as possible to the behaviors analyzed. In this exposition of the unsayable, of horror, "the history of emotions most strongly puts to the test the pangs of the human condition."[34]

The history of emotions stands out against a certain history, especially that of the nineteenth century, that Corbin considers to be "mawkish, sweetened, linear, and full of good feelings."[35] The "common humanity" across the variations of time that interests Corbin is in the first place to be sought in the representations in effect in the past and through an accounting for their active role:

> The system of representations not only orders the system of appreciation; it also determines the modalities of observing the world and society in themselves. It organizes the description of affective life. In the last instance, it governs practices. Obviously, it would be absurd to conceive a history of sensibilities, of collective psychology, or, if one prefers, of mentalities that would not first of all be that of representations.[36]

The concern for restoring representations also necessitates a search for the mediations—the traces—to understand how the gaze of the other, differing over space and time, was structured, and to gauge the coincidences between the said and the experienced. The postulation of both a common humanity and historical variations contributes to a better understanding of the history of affects, passions, emotions, and human drives. Pain, for example, implies a judgment that the individual suffered as much in the Middle Ages as now, contrary to what is affirmed by certain hypotheses by which there was less suffering in the past than now. On the basis of this invariant of human suffering, one can gauge very well the variations in tolerance that the historian must restore to suffering, according to the place given to pain on the social level; and one may place pain in relation to the type of treatment considered bearable or unbearable at any given moment.

The history of sensibilities as Corbin conceives it is an integral part of the history of representations, which constitutes the preliminary to understanding the evolution of behavioral logics. The exploration of systems of representation necessitates a new procedure of bringing into coherency the "world of the text" and the "world of the reader," as Paul Ricoeur understands it: there must be a devotion to the construction of the archive, to the rhetorical procedures in question, to the silences, to the circumstances around the writing, to the audience, and so to the contextualization of interactions.

## A New Social History

The history of representations has great chances to renew social history, on condition that it not be considered a separate, supplementary area, simply adding to the economic, social, and political realms. Gérard Noiriel especially defends this reglobalizing perspective of social history nourished by the study of representations, proposing a reconciliation of the old quarrel between sociology and history.[37] Noiriel advocates a return to the epistemological model the Germans proposed early in the century, of which phenomenology is the heir. This model had the merit of "demonstrating the possibility of a historical science founded on the singular of lived experience."[38] In Lucien Febvre's notion of mental equipment, Noiriel sees a heuristic lever effective enough to offer access to an understanding of the strangeness that results from the temporal distance from the lived world of the past. "In hermeneutic logic, history is therefore above all a psychology. And Febvre's empirical work does not depart from this rule."[39] Noiriel accentuates the opposition in orientation that separates the two editors of the *Annales*—Marc Bloch in a Durkheimian tradition of objectivist sociology, and Febvre, who would be situated within the hermeneutic circle of circular interrelation between the individual and her age (hence the latter's interest in the area of biography). If this opposition is justified with respect to the comparison of the personal work of the two editors of the *Annales,* it is incongruous with regard to the way the *Annales* was positioned in the 1930s, firmly under Durkheim's influence.

Now, this hermeneutic logic of course had to guide the practice of history after the unparalleled success of the quantitative, scientistic Durkheimian tradition of the 1960s. It came down to situating history in the dependence on the past with respect to the questions the historian asks in the present, when confronted by the strangeness of temporal distance, seeking to reestablish a possible communication thanks to "common humanity." The reorientation of social history according to a consideration of the "subjectivist paradigm"[40] leads to an attention to intentionality, to a consideration of lived experience. The entire dimension of what is felt becomes the historian's object. Noiriel found the latter essential in his historically based studies of immigration.[41]

He especially shows here to what point an entire universe of symbolic signs may function in a community, but on condition of being adequate to the lived experience of individuals. Thus, the processions to the monuments to the dead organized by the Communist former members of the Resistance involved the entire generation of World War II, despite the collapse of influence of the Communist system. On the other hand, the new generation of young Communists, baby boomers, is turning away from this ritual, which does not respond to its lived experience. Representations are therefore strongly anchored in a lived experience that has been the central concept of comprehensive sociology and that is suitable for adaptation to the area of the historian, who will study how time deploys processes of subjectification, of the crystallization of the past in the present.

## Restricted Mentalities

The departure from the history of mentalities, as it was conceived in the sixties as a catchall concept, and the substitution of a more restricted conception of the history of mentalities were advocated by Alain Boureau.[42] This history of mentalities, a refuge of previously proscribed objects, has had the tendency to substantialize mentalities. "This substantialist drift contradicted the primary distributive function of the history of mentalities."[43] There remains a question unanswered by this writing of mental history: how does one proceed, through which mediations, from the historical collective to the individual? The solution generally proposed is to add contextual references to the description of affects. But there is great risk of an uncontrolled reductionism that would use relations of causality with a variable geometry.

The "restricted" reorientation leads to the main problem of the social sciences, the articulation of the individual and the collective. Boureau assigns to the collective "what restricts the possibilities of action and decision."[44] This in turn may lead to description, in the way Luc Boltanski and Laurent Thévenot have achieved it, as a "grammar of assent."[45]

This restricted history of mentalities belongs, according to Boureau, to the "description of discursive events," of the rare utterances Michel Foucault speaks of in *The Archaeology of Knowledge*.[46] But, differently from the deconstructive intention of Foucault, whose task is to explore spaces of dispersion, Boureau keeps a globalizing ambition in his desire to grasp the lived implication of global determinations. "It would be a matter of pulling apart the bundle of relations that link aggregates to historical agents and designating a border zone of intricacy where the same utterance simultaneously belongs to a determined social discourse and to individual utterances."[47]

The restricted history of mentalities is, then, that of appropriations in privileged moments of structuration—that is, in moments of emergence or autopoiesis. It then returns to the event, novelty, and it also presumes to take the actors seriously, to deem that they may act according to their representations. The latter are no longer perceived by the historian with an intention of unveiling the falsehood they reveal with respect to a postulated truth. They are also not conceived as mere instruments. The historian of representations assumes the task of grasping "differentiated use in tactics of appropriation and displacement."[48]

Faced with the phenomenon of collective beliefs, the historian may profitably take up the concept of "irreduction" from Bruno Latour[49] and that of the "competency" of the actors borrowed from Boltanski and Thévenot. Believing becomes an act in the recent historical studies on beliefs.[50] The enigmatic question is asked as to what the act of believing covers. That implies an entirely new reading of the archives on the basis of which the historian wonders how rituals act and hence produce concrete effects in people's heads. According to Marcel Gauchet, historians are led to bring to the level of the past the heuristic program that Claude Lévi-Strauss defines in his article on "the effectiveness of symbols."[51]

The cognitive imperative may contribute to providing some clarifications as to what this effectiveness of symbols really consists of, and thus surpass the simple descriptivism of the American ceremonialist school. This trend has been formed by the disciples of Ernst Kantorowicz,[52] who have developed a whole series of studies on civic rituals, notably in England, France, and Italy, unknown to most historians other than a few medievalists such as Bernard Guénée.

Belief is a very essential site of investigation, says Marcel Gauchet. It allows one to pose a particularly difficult problem, when one is not happy with reducing it to a mere mystified consciousness, but rather attempts a "laical description of what religion is."[53] Here the historian tries to grasp belief as the crucible of the social bond on the basis of its articulation with the coherency of the concerned collectivities.

## Italian Winds: Micro-*storia*

In this area the Italian historians of micro-*storia*—Carlo Ginzburg, Edoardo Grendi, Giovanni Levi, and Carlo Poni—play the role of precursors. Applying themselves to case studies, microcosms, valorizing the limit situations of crisis, they have turned a new attention to individual strategies, interactivity, the complexity of stakes, and the imbricated character of collective representations. The cases of rupture whose history they have retraced are not conceived as a quest for marginality, reversal, or the repressed, but as a way of revealing, at ground level, singularity as a problematic entity defined by the oxymoron of "the normal exception."[54]

The best-known case study is that of the Friulian miller Menocchio, exhumed by Carlo Ginzburg.[55] Menocchio, restored to his singular concreteness, is not an average or an exemplary individual but rather a singular identity. Here, there is a quest for common sense proceeding from the least ordinary. Even while studying microrealities, micro-storia does not renounce, but on the contrary searches for, the paths to generalization, globalization. "Very few historians would admit that their object of study has a local value."[56] Microhistory brings together a singular technique, the choice of a precise localization, and a vocation for more general elucidations. If this intention is common to all the studies of micro-storia, one can nevertheless distinguish two versions, two somewhat different ends.

Most of the studies in this current define new instruments, another scale of analysis, to respond to quite classical questions of social history. This is the case for the work of Giovanni Levi, among others, whose objective is to understand, in a well-determined chronological framework (the end of the seventeenth century and the beginning of the eighteenth) the relations between peasant communities and the modern state on the scale of a particular region (Piedmont). The concrete case that Levi treats is that of a village in Piedmont in the seventeenth century, Santena, in which a heretical priest is brought to trial for his activities as a healer-exorcist.[57] Levi's thread of analysis is nonetheless not the exoticism of marginal practices, but the cumulative failures of a village community in the face of various perils and the ineluctable rise of the Piedmont state.

This series of monographs may seemingly derive from the many studies in the sociography of the past carried out by the *Annales* school. One might think of Montaillou and Romans, of Emmanuel Le Roy Ladurie.[58] But in fact, the technique of analysis is otherwise, as it is especially applied to restoring individual, familial, ancestral, and clannish strategies within the system of norms.[59]

The other version of micro-*storia* is the one Ginzburg represents. The technique used is the same, but it is inscribed in a more anthropological finality of order. Ginzburg ties the method of micro-*storia* to a paradigm he defines as that of the screw. The latter enables him to break the crust that masked the great anthropological structures at a precise point and to bring on the advent of a landscape of very long duration, in the manner of the geologist.

Ginzburg's objective is, therefore, more to inscribe his investigation within a history of great invariants, of great historical regularities. Hence, the fissures, anomalies, and gaps are not objects to be valorized in themselves. They simply enable access to the observation of the underlying anthropological socle. This objective recently became explicit on the occasion of the reopening of the file on nocturnal battles, whose publication dates to 1966.[60] "A long time ago I seriously set myself the task of experimentally demonstrating, from an historical standpoint, the non-existence of human nature; twenty-five years later I find myself supporting a diametrically opposed theory."[61]

Having begun work on witchcraft with the idea of gauging the actors' practices by situating himself as closely as possible to these, Ginzburg wanted to historicize a phenomenon that was presented as recurrent. He discovered not a phantasmic projection of the Catholic church, as the historiography of witchcraft had it, but an autonomous, historically constituted culture, which staged battles involving good witches who left their bodies to combat bad witches. In 1966, Ginzburg evoked the possible comparison with shamanic practices. It is this cultural invariant that today is at the heart of the understanding of the phenomenon for Ginzburg. This invariant responds to the finitude of existence and to the construction—which it incites—of systems of relations with the beyond following various contextually determined modalities.

Boureau qualifies this invariant as a "transcendental form of a grasp of human finitude, which would be the basis of the invariance ('human nature') known by its variables alone, and in an intermittent fashion."[62] The historian's inquiry is then held in tension between the register of the proof, that of the contextual frame, and that which consists of gauging invariants, spatiotemporal transversalities belonging to "common humanity." This inevitable tension can be translated into terms of relations between belief as a competency that refers to a common culture and to its forms that vary according to the precise situation of social insertion, and according to the required scale.[63]

In these two variants, micro-*storia* has therefore restored a place to singularity, after a long phase of eclipse, during which the historian had above all to seek statistical averages, the regularities of a quantitative and serial history. It enables, in visibly shifting it, a redynamization of a genre believed to be on the way to extinction, that of biography. The biography defended by micro-*storia* is differentiated from a certain number of practiced approaches to renew a genre unanimously impugned in its traditional linear and purely factual form. It is distinguished from the biographies illustrating collective forms of behavior that Levi defines as "modal biography."[64] It is also distinguished from the biographies that are too strictly dependent on a fixed context that artificially provides the keys to intelligibility by transposing contextual coherence to the individual itinerary. It is also demarcated from a biographical approach in terms of limit cases as well as from interpretive anthropology.

The biography that Levi defends must allow one to examine the role of freedom of choice among many possibilities of a normative context that includes a number of incoherencies: "No normative system, really, is sufficiently structured to eliminate any possibility of conscious choice, of manipulation, or of interpretation of rules, of negotiation."[65] It leads one to examine the type of rationality put to work by the actors of history. This presupposes that one distance oneself from the schema from neoclassical economics of the maximization of interest and the postulation of a total rationality of the actors. This mode of biography leads one to define the bases of a limited and selective rationality and to reinterrogate the interrelation between the group and the individual. The conflicts of classification, distinction, and representation are as many means of dialecticizing cognitive procedures, by nature different when they apply to a group or to an individual.

We are measuring to what point these interrogations of micro-history extend onto the terrain of history a general paradigm shift in the social sciences when they reformulate, each in its own manner, the study of social acting and of its representations as modes of appropriation differentiated according to the intersubjective frame.

# Twenty-one

# The Memorial Moment

Another "exit" from mentalities is the one Pierre Nora advocates, an "exit" through memory. The main reason for this opening of memory comes from the recent dissociation of the incestuous couple of history and memory, which has always functioned, especially in France, in a mirroring relationship. National memory was fully taken charge of by a nation-state that bore a memory-history whose golden age was the Lavissian moment of the Third Republic. Declined differently in the Romantic and organicist model with a France that had become a person, exemplified in Michelet, or in the methodical model of a meticulous criticism of historical sources à la Langlois and Seignobos, the national scheme as a whole bore the historian's enterprise and its identity function.

The time of the *Annales* incontestably marked itself as a break with this schema, by pouring the historian's quest into other structuring molds, those of the social sciences. But the crumbling of the discourse of history, in spite of its fertility and its faculty to gauge new objects immediately on their establishment in the "historian's territory," could not for long be satisfying with regard to the identity function, on the collective level, of history. Besides, the time had come for "diminishing returns," in Pierre Chaunu's expression.

## A Need for Memory

In the mid-1970s, the memorial shock became spectacularly visible when Pierre Jakez Hélias's *The Horse of Pride* became a best-seller, going to a million copies. And Emmanuel Le Roy Ladurie, representative of a scholarly history, succeeded in reaching a broad public of several hundred thousand readers with his *Montaillou,* the French title of which, *Montaillou, village occitan,* some would call "*Mon caillou, village excitant* (my pebble, an exciting village)." It was then understood that a shift, a real sliding of terrain had just shaken the ground; its telluric force was related to the shock of 1789, to the point that sociologist Henri Mendras qualified it as the "second French Revolution," which took place in 1965, with cultural effects deferred until around 1975. The end of the France of the soil came to engender a France that was an orphan of this *world that we have lost.*[1] The social frames of memory had then disappeared: "We talk so much about memory only because we no longer have it."[2]

Other transformations came to dissociate history from memory. The crisis of revolutionary eschatologies at the same moment, right in the mid-1970s, came to obscure the horizon of expectation at the same time as it deconstructed the status of porter accorded to the present; the present was conceived only as a transitory place of passage between a past animated by a motor of history, the latter enabling a confident direction toward a predetermined future. This new opacity of the future strongly contributed to blurring the figure of a past at the heart of which one could no longer hierarchize what related to a potential and positive becoming. These tremors were at the origin of a twofold effect: on the one hand, memory, escaping history, could become its object, its problem. On the other hand, a new relation of past and present shifted in a constant instantaneous telescoping, in lived experience, to the everyday of a history that was increasingly globalized under the effects of mediatization.

Pierre Nora then began an immense project, which he had conceived in 1978–79 in his seminar at the EHESS. He completed it in 1993 with the publication of the last three of seven volumes devoted to the Republic, the Nation, and the different versions of France. This enterprise would correspond with a true return of the repressed to the house of France in the early 1980s, after President François Mitterrand became alarmed that the history of France was no longer taught. But Nora's enterprise was delayed with respect to the many publications on this theme, as he did not have the project of writing an updated Lavisse but of constructing another history, different, symbolic, in the second degree, in a novel and critical relationship between memory and history: "France is entirely in the area of symbolic reality; it has no sense, through the many meanderings of its history and of its forms of existence, other than symbolic."[3]

The transversal examinations in the social sciences of the question of representations and their successive metamorphoses over time are at the heart of this collective effort. In this regard, Nora takes up the manner in which Durkheimian sociologist Maurice Halbwachs explored the closely intertwined links between historical and collective memory.[4] Term for term, Halbwachs opposed these two notions, which he viewed in an antinomic manner. According to him, the time of collective memory is anchored in people's lives.

Memory is real, multiple, fluctuating, whereas the time of history is, on the contrary, abstract, arbitrary, conceptual, outside lived time. Ultimately, history begins only at the point where memory ends. For a collective memory to endure, it must have instituted frameworks, social groups to bear it, to frame it. Duration and place are therefore the necessary conditions for a crystallization, to borrow a Stendhalian notion, of representations, of memory. Halbwachs thus begins a pluralization of the memorial phenomenon as a function of its frameworks of existence.

From the beginning, Nora takes up Halbwachs's binary opposition to show effectively that the two notions of history and memory are not synonymous: "We realize that they are opposed in every way."[5] But this realization is recent, as history and memory have been more or less confounded until now around the myths of origin.[6] The crisis of holistic identity frameworks as well as the current pragmatic turn have reversed a relationship that consisted of passing from history to memory. The proliferation of lived narratives, tied to the progressive disappearance of places, of supports of remembrance, contributes to this reversal that leads from memory to history. What results is a fragmentation of the times and places of memory.

Memory then becomes the very problem of our modernity, a means of resuscitating experience to remedy the sense of historical exhaustion, the ambient skepticism before history.[7] These places of memory are just as much topographical marks of the traces of the past as symbolic forms of collective identification, as one can notice today with the commemorative vogue. The biblical commandment "Thou shalt not forget!" imposes itself, and memory makes its honey out of every heritage of the past.

## The Paradigm of the Trace

The historical writing induced by this new relation to memory is quite different. It even requires that the entire past be revisited from this angle. The central notion is that of the trace, at once ideal and material: it becomes the essential mainspring of Nora's fresco. The trace is the unsayable link that binds the past to a present. The present becomes a weighty category in the reconfiguration of time through the intermediary of its memory traces.

Nora sees here a new discontinuity in the writing of history "that we can only call *historiographic.*"[8] This break reorients views and involves the community of historians in revisiting differently the same objects on the basis of the traces left in the collective memory by the facts, the human beings, the symbols, and the emblems of the past. This undoing and redoing of the entire historical tradition through the memorial moment we are living opens the way to an entirely other history:

> No longer the determinants, but rather their effects; no longer the remembered or even commemorated actions, but rather the trace of these actions and the play of the commemorations; not the events for themselves, but rather their construction in time, the effacement and resurgence of their significations; not the past as it happened, but rather its permanent reuses, its uses and misuses, its pregnancy in successive presents; not the tradition, but rather the way it is constituted and transmitted.[9]

This vast work area enables, by its problematization of both the notion of historicity and that of memory, an exemplification of the intermediate time that Ricoeur defines as a bridge between lived and cosmic time.

## Demythologization

In the 1970s, Georges Duby undertook the task of the demythologization and historicization of memory.[10] In an especially traditional collection, "Thirty Days That Made France," Duby twice relativized the founding event of Bouvines by showing that the battle itself could be reduced to very little, and by resituating it in a longer temporality, that of the many variations of its remembrance. The problem is no longer so much what really happened on July 24, 1214—"no one has or ever will perceive in its total reality the whirl of a thousand tangled actions which on that day, in the plain of Bouvines between noon and five in the afternoon, came to be inextricably intertwined."[11]

Duby shifted the historian's view, then, so as better to scrutinize the various ways of thinking and acting. He also constructed a sociology of war on the threshold of the eighteenth century. But especially, he considered the event as at once an upsurge of the unexpected and an inscription, a trace in duration. The limits of Bouvines, then, are no longer those of an illustrious Sunday, but the sequence of its metamorphoses, of its fortunes and omissions in the collective memory. The historical object henceforth becomes the "fate of a memory in the midst of a changing set of mental representations."[12]

Also in the 1970s, Philippe Joutard became one of the precursors of a systematic investigation of memory when he noticed, in a project of examining the foundations of the persistent rancor between the Protestant and Catholic communities of the Cévennes, that this cleavage in fact dated only from the second half of the nineteenth century. Previously, historiography was unanimous in reproving the Camisard revolt. So official historical discourse did not succeed in erasing the wounds or in reuniting the regional community. Joutard then made the hypothesis, which he tested among the peasants of the Cévennes, of an underground oral memory, and he undertook the first true historico-ethnographic study in 1967. It established the existence of an oral tradition around the traumatic event of the Camisard revolt and its suppression, a repressed but deep-rooted memory. "I hope, with this study, to have shown that historiographic research cannot be separated from an examination of collective mentalities."[13]

Pluralized, fragmented memory today overflows all areas of the "historian's territory." A major tool of the social bond, of individual and collective identity, it is found at the heart of a real stake and often waits for the historian to give it, in the aftermath, its meaning, in the manner of the psychoanalyst. For a long time an instrument of manipulation, memory may be reinvested in an interpretive perspective open to the future, a source of collective reappropriation and not a mere museum study cut off from the present. The memory that supposes the presence of absence remains the contact point, essential between past and present, of this dialogue between the world of the dead and that of the living.

The studies thus multiply over the shadow zones of national history. When Henry Rousso addresses the Vichy regime, it is not to inventory what happened from 1940 to 1944. His historical object begins when Vichy is no longer an effective political regime. It is revealed as a survival of the fractures it engendered in the national consciousness. It is then that he may evoke the "future of the past."[14] His periodization explicitly uses the psychoanalytic categories, even if they are handled in a purely analogical manner. The mourning ritual of 1944–54 is followed by the time of repression, then by that of the return of the repressed, before the traumatic neurosis transforms into an obsessional phase.

For his part, Benjamin Stora would enter another shadow zone, that of the war in Algeria, studied by way of the mechanisms of fabrication of a true collective amnesia on both sides of the Mediterranean.[15] To the nameless war on the side of the colonial metropolis responds the faceless war of the Algerians.

The history of memory is particularly exposed to complexity by its central situation, at the very heart of the interrelation, problematic for all the social sciences, between the individual and the collective. This is what Michaël Pollak has shown very well concerning the collective memory of the deportees returning from the extermination camps. Inquiring among the survivors of Auschwitz-Birkenau, he demonstrates that silence is not forgetting. The buried sentiment of culpability is at the heart of the syndrome of the survivors gripped between the rage to transmit and the powerlessness to communicate.[16] Hence, the function of those who would frame their memories by keeping multiple associations alive. Their task is to grasp the fluctuating limits between the possibilities of the said and the unsaid, and thus to facilitate the mourning ritual of the individuals. Collective memories, like individual memories, are subject to multiple contradictions, tensions, and reconstructions. Hence, "silence—different from forgetting—may even be a necessary condition of communication."[17] At the heart of Pollak's work on memory, there is the quest for the "feeling of identity," in the words of Nathalie Heinich, who has worked with Pollak on the testimony of deportees.[18] A better understanding of this feeling was possible thanks to the refusal to dissociate the content of the testimonies from the conditions of their enunciation. That enabled Pollak to examine what was opaque in the phenomenon of speaking: "The probability of testimony is very small, and Michaël seized on its rare occurrences to try to understand its meaning, where the meaning of the enunciation was not reducible to the meaning of the utterance."[19]

Taking as an object the best example of framed memory, Communist memory, Marie-Claire Lavabre shows that it poorly masks, behind the official, wooden language, a more complex collective memory that remains plural, contradictory. Her inquiry demonstrates that the image of de Gaulle after his death remains negative among those who joined the French Communist Party during the Fifth Republic, whereas it was positive among the old militants who belonged to the party during the Resistance.[20]

In addition, the resurfacing of the intentions of former collaborationists and their young emulators, the deniers, calls the historian back to the task of memory, to the truth contract of the discipline to which he belongs. In this framework, Pierre Vidal-Naquet played a decisive role in a counteroffensive of historians in the face of the deniers' theses.[21] As for the survivors of that dark period, they feel the urgency, that of testifying, of delivering their memory to future generations by any means at their disposal.

## A Tyrannical Memory

The current memorial turn allows a better understanding of the factors in human behavior. In this sense it fully participates in the pragmatic turn in the social sciences as a whole, even as far as the least defined object it takes, at once material and ideal, fluctuating, always open to new metamorphoses and new twists of meaning. Its object "constantly eludes any simple and clear definition."[22] Far from being confined to the status of the illusory, mystified residue of manipulated actors, memory invites us to take the actors and their competencies seriously, and it reminds us that it often commands the making of history.

Held in another dialectic, that of *archē* and *telos,* the regime of historicity is thoroughly traversed by the tension between the sphere of experience and the horizon of expectation. In this regard, Ricoeur impugns the enclosure of the discourse of history in a purely memorial relationship of recovery of the past, cut off from a future that has suddenly been foreclosed. Pierre Nora also agrees that our memorial present is perhaps only a moment, an intellectual conjuncture when, in his concluding sentence to the seven divisions of *Les Lieux de mémoire,* he specifies that this tyranny of memory will perhaps last only for a time, "but it was ours."[23]

Beyond the current memorial conjuncture, symptomatic of the

crisis of one of the two metahistorical categories, the horizon of ex-pectation—our society's lack of an end—Ricoeur recalls the function of acting, of the ethical debt of history with regard to the past. The regime of history, always open to becoming, is of course no longer the projection of a fully conceived end, closed on itself. The very logic of action keeps the field of possibilities open. In this respect, Ricoeur de-fends the notion of utopia not as the support for a mad logic, but rather as a liberating function that "hinders the horizon of expecta-tion from fusing with the field of experience. This is what maintains the distance between expectation and tradition."[24] With the same firmness, he defends the duty, the debt of present generations with re-gard to the past, the source of the ethics of responsibility. The function of history therefore remains vivid. History is not an orphan, as is be-lieved, on the condition that it respond to the requirements of acting. Thus, mourning the teleological visions may become a chance to re-visit, from the point of view of the past, the many possibilities of the present, so as to conceive the world of tomorrow.

# Part VI

## *Conventions*
### *A Third Way?*

# Twenty-two

# From Regulation to Convention

At the crossroads of the examinations of the nature of the social bond, acting, and representations, there appears on the scene a current of economic thought, long closed off from the evolutions of the social sciences, the particularly innovative current of the economics of convention. We have already seen in the regulationist current an early departure from the standard theory of schemes based on mere production.[1] The regulation school (in which may be found, among others, Michel Aglietta, Hugues Bertrand, Robert Boyer, Benjamin Coriat, Alain Lipietz, Jacques Mistral, and Carlos Ominami) distanced itself from mechanistic determinisms in order better to reinstate the modalities of passage of the great economic transformations.[2] The necessary articulation of the logic of the state and that of the market has led the regulationists to valorize the role of intermediary, institutional relations.

This entrance, on the level of institutions, into macroeconomics allows an integration into the economic horizon of the plural rationalities of social groups. Partisans of a Marxist-structuralist program, the regulationists have enabled a dynamization of structure and a reintegration of economic agents, people who were previously viewed as mere supports of structural logic. Accounting for the institutional socle of mercantile phenomena has opened the regulationists to history.[3] Thus, Fernand Braudel and Immanuel Wallerstein have been used by the economists of regulation as historians of the uneven development of capitalism, who valorize the irreversibility of economic phenomena as well as new spatial logics of an intensity varying according to their location, at the center or the periphery of economic worlds.

Indeed, it is in the historical framework that the regulationists have been able to discern different moments of accumulation between the competitive mode of regulation of the nineteenth century, the Taylorism of the early twentieth, and the Fordism that occurred after the crisis of 1929 and enabled an economic rebound on the basis of a much more advanced rationalization of labor as well as a spectacular development of mass consumption.[4]

## Emergence

In the tradition of this heterodox current, what could already be called the school of convention was born. One of the economists of convention, Olivier Favereau, editor of the issue of the *Revue économique* devoted to this current, attended all the seminars of the CEPREMAP devoted to regulationist theory in the 1970s. "I witnessed the birth of all this. It was an extraordinarily invigorating and refreshing moment."[5] If there are a bond of affiliation and common enterprises between the two currents, the differences are more and more noticeable. The regulationists, having come from Marxism, remain attached to holistic positions. They had the merit, at a time when the theory of reflection was in effect, to complexify the relation between infra- and superstructure in order to give the latter all its weight. But the regulationists "don't want to cut the umbilical cord of Marxism, and so don't dare ask certain theoretical questions."[6]

They are still situated on the level of an encompassing system. As students of Keynesianism and Marxism, the regulationists start with holism, whereas the economists of convention claim a complex methodological individualism. But meeting points and areas of research appear in view of a privileged attention to the action of agents that is more and more present among the regulationists of today. For their part, the studies in terms of convention, based in the categories of limited rationality, open further to an accounting for the social, the context. "Hence, we may find we have many practical questions."[7]

The economists of convention, as methodological individualists, do not use collectives as pertinent categories of analysis. Meanwhile, breaking with orthodox economists, they deem that individuals have only a limited capacity for calculation, strongly constrained by the context. Finally, the use of limited rationality in methodological individualism enables the emergence of collective objects. "The collective isn't reducible to interindividual representations, in part because we are less rational than orthodox economic theory says."[8] Bypassing the limits of individual rationality leads the economists of convention to rely on a multiplicity of techniques, procedures, and collective objects.

So there is a possible zone of contact between the two currents, which also seem to have evolved jointly to meet on common fields of investigation opened by this in-between, this intermediate space between a hard and fast holism and methodological individualism. This potential convergence must not, however, mask the differences of position between the economists of convention and the regulationists. According to Laurent Thévenot, "There is a movement to break with regulation and the institutionalists in general."[9] Still, the economists of regulation and those of convention today seem to increase the common areas of work and publications, which bear witness to a mutual fertilization that creates a real dynamic behind theses that tend to approach each other.[10]

This paradigm of conventions was elaborated following a collective examination among a group of economists working in the 1970s at the INSEE on the notions of socioprofessional categories, on the borders of sociology. At the INSEE there have been relations among Alain Desrosières, Robert Salais, François Eymard-Duvernay, André Orléan, Laurent Thévenot, Olivier Favereau, and others.

## Categories

The problematic of conventions was born from a twofold examination—on the one hand economic, into categories, and on the other sociological, into the evaluation of people and things; hence, a hybrid socioeconomic paradigm that borrows from the INSEE its statistical resources, its tradition of coding, and its rich sources of information on organizations and enterprises.[11] It is also the extension of a collaborative study led by Laurent Thévenot and Luc Boltanski on the evaluative competencies of agents, on the passage from the particular to the general, which gives way, as we have already seen, to *De la justification*,[12] with its model of the Cities.

At the time of this socioeconomic work, Thévenot was working in the Employment Division of the INSEE. Robert Salais, in charge of this research unit, was quickly convinced of the heuristic value of these new tools of analysis. In the study of chains of unemployment, he found a field of application for these models.[13] The convergence of a certain number of studies pushed the research unit to take the initiative in organizing a joint roundtable between the CNRS and the INSEE on the topic "The Tools of Managing Labor," which took place in 1984. Placed under the responsibility of a preparation committee,[14] this meeting would "have quite a structuring effect."[15] This first grouping of interventions was still quite broad. It included sociologists outside the field of economics, such as Patrick Pharo, and regulationists, such as Robert Boyer. Published in 1986 under the direction of both Salais and Thévenot, the proceedings already bore in its subtitle a reference to "convention."[16]

In 1983, Thévenot had already carried his examinations to the cognitive character of material tools in a major article, "Les investissements de forme."[17] Not only was Thévenot innovative in his accounting for objects, but he also manifested his concern not to remain at a purely representational level, thanks to research on the possible articulations among mental categories and on tools. On that occasion, he advocated a broadened definition of the notion of investment that surpassed the opposition between material and immaterial goods. In this regard, he criticized the very secondary use of institutional objects in classical economic theory.

The term *form* in the very broad sense allows an answer to the wish to "treat the capacity to give an equivalency to beings that we wish to apprehend."[18] The major lesson of Thévenot's study comes down to viewing forms in relation with an investment. Thévenot especially brings into evidence the necessary cost of transformation in order to establish a capacity for equivalence.

## The Investments of Form

It is significant that the collection of articles in which "Les investissements de forme" appeared already in 1986 bore the title *Economic Conventions*. "The existence of a mixed area of sociology and economics is an original adventure, unique to France."[19] The proximity of the two disciplines is such that many people confound the two and think that the economics of greatness and that of convention are two ways of expressing the same thing: "I don't always clear up the ambiguity."[20]

In "Les investissements de forme," Thévenot demonstrates the centrality of the histories of trademarks, of the normalization of products. He directed the study in the realm of agriculture and nutrition of two researchers whose object was to show, in the area of cheese manufacture, the operation of two different models. The one derives from an industrial logic, centered on a mass production that corresponds to the manufacture of "normal" Camembert; the other responds to an entirely different logic, that of tradition, and it corresponds to the manufacture of "Norman" Camembert—top of the line, the product of an artisan's savoir faire.[21] With the restoration of manufacturing procedures such as the collection of milk in unrefrigerated cans, the use of unprocessed milk, of the ladle, and so on, one could thus show what an investment of form was. "That enabled a return to the tools of production and hence a link to one of the major themes of *De la justification,* which is the qualification of objects and the qualification of persons."[22]

The conventional forms allowed a better understanding, during the 1980s when necessary deregulations were discussed, of what a rule was, by comparing the fluidity of the market with the rigidities in the organization of production. This comparison led Thévenot to prefer the term *convention* to the term *rule,* which had too many strictly juridical connotations. The term *convention* has the advantage of covering a broader area through its ambivalence: "It can be used for an exchange of market services as well as to designate a technical norm, a customary use, the authority at a meeting, and so on."[23]

All this effervescence around convention would crystallize and expand with the preparation of a special issue of the *Revue économique* on this theme. Olivier Favereau was then a member of the editorial committee of that journal, canonical among economists, and he decided with Robert Salais and François Eymard-Duvernay to devote an issue to the convergence of studies in progress on rules and institutions.[24] For a year, a whole group prepared the issue in the perspective of a truly collective publication. In addition, Favereau refused to assume the sole responsibility for the issue, so as better to valorize the advent of a nascent school in the age of its public visibility. The issue appeared in 1989, and its introduction is a collective work. In this regard, the latter has the value of a manifesto and involves all the signatories.[25]

This manifesto-introduction offers a constitutive framework common to all the research in progress that converges around the idea of convention. It expresses the ambition of all the collaborators to surpass the opposition between holism and individualism: "Convention must be apprehended at once as the result of individual actions and as a framework constraining the subjects."[26] If the concept of convention refers to collective phenomena, it is nonetheless specified that the starting point of the analysis remains in the lineage of "methodological individualism."[27] With regard to what the constitutive framework of convention covers, the introduction allows diverse sensibilities to show. It is a paradigm for André Orléan, it derives from common sense for Jean-Pierre Dupuy, from a cognitive model according to Favereau, and a system of cognition for Salais. This issue was very favorably received. It obviously maximized the interactions among the various economists and beyond, because the enterprise of convention from the beginning was presented as pluridisciplinary. It was said to benefit from the "contribution of disciplines outside economics (sociology, psychology, anthropology, law)."[28] Besides, its network of distribution was the CREA, where, among the signatories of this issue of the *Revue économique,* Orléan, Thévenot, Favereau, and of course its director, Dupuy, were working.

## A Socioeconomics?

This convergence of disciplines was accompanied by a new passion for a socioeconomics in which is rediscovered—in the founding fathers of either economics or sociology—a similar desire not to reduce analyses to one or the other approach, but, on the contrary, a constant concern with conducting their economic and sociological studies in tandem. It is this way for Max Weber, Thorstein Veblen, Vilfredo Pareto, Joseph Schumpter, François Simiand, and others, all of whom impugn this mutilating split, as a certain number of recent publications attest.[29] In order to recover this founding inspiration, Alain Caillé even pleads for the creation of a new university discipline that would be a socioeconomics.[30] It would enable an escape from the current twofold process of the fragmentation of knowledge and the formalist reduction of a discipline of economics that is too centered on the analysis of the maximization of profit alone. Socioeconomics would make it possible to oppose to this state of things a true apprenticeship to complexity at the heart of a discipline with an encompassing aim.

*Twenty-three*

# Beyond the Opposition between Holism and Methodological Individualism

The major ambition of the economics of convention is to overcome the classical opposition between holism and methodological individualism. The introduction to the issue of the *Revue économique* devoted to the economics of convention essentially affirms the individualist tradition, but especially so as to insist on the rupture with Durkheimianism. With the notion of convention, these economists intend to pose the problem of the emergence of collective regulations subtended by dynamic processes of interaction. This notion therefore induces an overcoming of the false alternative that has long impoverished analyses in the social sciences. And by the centrality of the problems treated, it also enables one to envision a crossing of the strict boundaries of the discipline of economics. "The notion of convention and the very rich semantic space surrounding it of course do not properly belong to economic science. Because the notion has connotations of collectivity, commonality, it derives from other traditions, from sociology (social convention, custom) or, further back, from political philosophy (social contract, community of belonging) and, of course, from law."[1]

This notion of convention therefore allows a favoring of interdisciplinary confrontation. The latter is not conceived in the manner of the 1960s—during which the misappropriation of concepts from one discipline by another was de rigueur for one to take a position of knowledgeable legitimacy—but rather as a "codisciplinarity"[2] that permits a problematization of the boundaries of one's own discipline on the basis of transverse conceptual equipment. So the notion of convention may be a source of coming recompositions among disciplines through its paradigmatic value.

## Coordination

The question of coordination that the notion of convention carries with it, according to Laurent Thévenot, makes possible a new alliance between specialists of various horizons around the notion of judgment. The economics of convention, then, is nourished by a long tradition, that of comprehensive sociology that mobilizes the works of Weber, Schutz, Berger, Luckman, and Goffman, putting it to the test with a pragmatic procedure. The notion of convention is situated at the point of articulation between the interpretive-hermeneutic tradition and the pragmatic perspective. In this regard, it may especially allow a reconfiguration of the relations between economics and sociology, at a moment when the instrument that constituted the model of general equilibrium has been strongly questioned.

The reorientation in progress allows the problem of the basis of the social bond to be posed with a new centrality. We have already evoked a certain number of attempts at elucidation that move in this direction.[3] The economics of convention impugns the two models of traditional explanation involving the foundations of the social bond.

It once again takes up the question that has been asked since Adam Smith: what are the mechanisms of coordination among economic agents? It is located in this area in a break with the neoclassical theory according to which the exclusive form of coordination is the market, and the economic agent disposes of a rationality that enables her to maximize her interests in all circumstances. These are the two basic postulates of Standard Theory (ST). Now, "most forms of coordination are obviously not related to the standard model."[4] The coordination among agents passes through the mediation of rules, norms, and institutions. Meanwhile, the prevalence accorded to rigidified institutional structures of which the agents would be the mere supports is also not a good model of analysis. So the economics of convention does not consist of adding the missing institutional link to Standard Theory, but shifts the axis of analysis to finer entities, which are more central among those at the basis of the social bond.

This attempt at elucidation implies a shift of scale from macroeconomics to microeconomics; this does not in turn imply any enclosure on a microeconomic level, but rather paths from one to the other, thanks to the notions of contract, rule, convention, and coordination. In this area, the joint work of Boltanski and Thévenot has caused the appearance of a plurality of modes of coordination and justification with the model of the Cities, which enables one to complexify the traditional opposition between individual and collective interest and to "introduce a dialectic of the individual and the collective at the heart of economic analysis."[5]

This notion of convention borrows from a philosophical tradition, that of Hume, who exemplifies it with his famous case of oarsmen who, on a ship, without speaking, find a common rhythm, a conventional rhythm, an implicit, nonverbal agreement. Between the Smithian market and Humean convention, there is a common aspect, that of a sort of invisible hand, of tacit agreement. The main difference is located in the area of interests, of which the market expresses divergence, whereas convention depends on the various forms of coordination and social regulation.

Conflicts pass, then, to a second level: a limit of the model is reached, but the model is a good antidote in comparison with schemata of analysis that tended to be content with a binary opposition between a conflictual market and a regulating state, and hence lack the essential link of the effective social bond that is located in an in-between of the variable contours.

## Common Knowledge

The concept of convention was developed by an analytic philosopher, David Lewis, in 1969.[6] Lewis advocates criteria of differentiation between a contract, a convention, a rule, and a norm. Convention has no normative or moral character. Meanwhile, it acts as a norm insofar as it is a regularity "to which we believe we ought to conform."[7] Lewis introduced the notion, discussed today by Jean-Pierre Dupuy, of common knowledge.[8] For Lewis, convention responds to a problem of coordination and so implies a shared knowledge, what Dupuy defines as the infinite specularity of agents. From this point of view, Dupuy holds that common knowledge pushes methodological individualism to the extreme, because "the collective is made totally transparent to individuals."[9]

This notion leads therefore to an impasse, because the infinite specularity of the agents, instead of inducing a stabilization of social coordination, would come to an absolute undecidability. The opacity of the collective in fact limits the specular play of mutual identifications. So there really is a collective entity that exceeds the sum of individuals.

If Dupuy has strongly contributed to importing the notion of common knowledge, he presents it as a bearer of paradoxes, aporias. Lewis is the initiating figure for having made an epigraph of this notion of convention, but the school of convention is not for all that Lewisian, for "Lewis is radically nonsocial. He wants to achieve the most radical operation of reduction, which consists of bringing a coordination down to specifications of two individuals who coordinate with each other."[10] In this regard, the notion of common knowledge, which allows a link with pragmatism, becomes an operator of reduction of common representations into strictly individual representations. Only by accumulation, piled-up reflexivity, infinite specularity does one hope to reach the social. "In this relationship, no one supports common knowledge, and Jean-Pierre Dupuy is interested in it only insofar as it allows him to show its limits."[11]

Meanwhile, this notion offers the interest of being connected to a pragmatics of reflection whose initial use one may also situate. "The notion of common knowledge first appeared in a neighboring field, pragmatics—that is, the analysis of the context of verbal communication. In his pioneering 1957 article 'Meaning,' Paul Grice[12] showed that what makes communication possible is the capacity of the listener to recognize the intention of the speaker and inform him of something."[13] These notions of shared knowledge and specularity refer to the effectiveness of collective action.

The characteristics of common or shared knowledge are of several orders. First, it derives from a horizon of expectation that presumes a certain uniformity of relation. It is also incorporated within the very situation. And these two characteristics are in a relation of consubstantiality: "An expectation is imbedded in a situation, from which it arises."[14] In the second place, the beliefs put in motion exceed the propositional category and derive from a moral engagement; they are brought back to a normative framework. And especially, common knowledge is not of a theoretical order but rather corresponds to the vision of the world "from the point of view of the interests of members of the collectivity in the management of 'their practical affairs'

(Garfinkel). A properly pragmatic motive is thus inserted into the choice of conformity."[15]

For Lewis, convention presupposes the consciousness of several possible worlds, according to Robert Salais. One cannot therefore consider convention to be a mere routine or habit: "There is a plurality of conventions in relation to the situation."[16] Convention therefore does not intervene as an imposition external to the individual, because it has a choice among various possibilities and can appropriate one norm or another as a function of its action.

This postulate of a plurality of conceivable and accessible rationalities allows a better grasp of the extent to which there may be a complementarity between the use of convention in economics and Boltanski and Thévenot's sociological model of the Cities. Lewis's merit also consisted of redynamizing the theory of the invisible hand: "Obeying norms appears to be the unintentional product of the aggregation of individual behaviors guided by interest."[17]

## Contingency

In addition, the use of the notion of convention corresponds to a general "slimming treatment" of the schemata of causality, as we have already noted in Michel Callon and Bruno Latour's anthropology of science. For Lewis, convention derives from pure contingency. It therefore partakes of the register of description and not of causalist explanation. "Convention *proceeds* from circumstances (of time, place, persons, precedent, and so on); it does not *result* from them."[18] In this regard, the notion of convention in Lewis does not correspond to the usual use of norm, as it expresses the realization of a singular arrangement of stabilization of the contexts of interaction.

Between the apprehension of convention as a normative and social force and its apprehension in terms of pure interactive contingency, the range of possible uses is broad, and Louis Quéré finds that recourse to the notion of convention is still far from being stabilized. It still bears very diverse definitions among the theoreticians of this current in France: "They sometimes see convention as a 'theory,' a 'paradigm,' or a 'cognitive model,' and sometimes as a 'common sense,' a 'system of representation,' or a 'system of knowledge.'"[19]

Thus, in André Orléan's economic theory of financial convention, Quéré gauges quite variable uses of the notion of convention. Orléan insists on the importance of phenomena of representation and cognitive apprenticeship in the procedures of interaction of the agents, taking the example of bank crises as a privileged site of observation of this type of phenomenon. It is a matter of solving problems that are by nature uncertain with regard to their outcome. The propositions that Orléan puts forth "seek to establish that uncertainty is expressed within certain specific constraints, of a cognitive nature, which, in order to be managed, necessitate market forms different from the Walrasian market."[20] He gives his attention to movements of generalized mistrust pertaining to bank crises. In this way, he can show that mistrust is a cumulative process before which "market arbitrages are insufficient procedures."[21] Quéré underscores the originality of the path Orléan explores, in that it presupposes a common constitutive framework that enables coordination in action. This conventional framework indeed emerges from action itself.

Meanwhile, Quéré marks an internal tension between two heterogeneous dimensions with regard to the nature of economic convention. He in fact distinguishes a "procedural dimension, an a priori method of coordination of the intersecting anticipations of the agents," and "a more substantial dimension,"[22] which is at the origin of reified, objectified, exteriorized collective representations, finding in them an origin that is in nature foundational and thus guaranteeing their normative validity. For Orléan, this internal tension induces definitions, of variable geometry, of the problematic notion of convention.

## The Indeterminacy of Interaction

But one may say that these variations bear on the indeterminacy found in any situation of interaction characterized by the flexibility of conjectures and the unforeseeability of required information. Indeed, Quéré marks two distinct traditions, that of American analytic philosophy in the perspective of Lewis and that of the French theory of convention. On the basis of a common core on the procedural level, significant divergences appear in the area of the substantial dimension of convention, "because, on the one hand, we have regularities of behavior or belief, objects of a common knowledge, and, on the other, collective representations, cognitive devices, or even theories."[23]

On the strict plane of the economic tradition, Standard Theory has seen an evolution since the 1970s when, confronted with impasses, it had to take into consideration other variables than that of the individual that maximizes her interest on the scene of the market.

Standard Theory was then transformed into Extended Standard Theory (EST) by integrating under the term of organization a plurality of other dimensions, which cover heterogeneous phenomena "from the simple rules of individual behavior to the systems of rules constituted by collective institutions."[24]

Going back to Keynesian theory, Olivier Favereau distinguishes a tension in it, a hesitation between two projects. Keynesian construction "furnishes material for an impressive rapprochement with what has been called the philosophy of the second Wittgenstein."[25] The pragmatic project that Keynes finally adopted and the classical Keynesian tradition masked another ambition, that of a radical project that essentially rested on the notion of incompleteness. This second project could not be rooted in the base of the "Treatise on Probability" alone, but must be supported by the observation of mimetic, specular behavior.

This project caused a different Keynes to appear, a true initiator of the current project of the economics of convention. Conventions are indeed at the heart of his radical project as he succinctly expounded it in 1937.[26] The Keynesian intuitions according to which conventions, far from expressing a manifestation of irrationality, are, on the contrary, at the heart of the intelligibility of the social and allow a supplement to the failings of the market as a factor of explanation, have long remained a dead letter. Today, they may become especially fertile: "so, contrary to all expectations, the Keynesian revolution is not behind us, but ahead."[27] This radical project allows an entirely different appreciation of Keynes's theses.

Whereas they have hitherto been assimilated to an economic thought with the state as its basis, we notice, thanks to a reading of the symptoms of his theses, that Keynes's project accords a central place to productive anticipation and therefore to what incarnates it, enterprise. Hence, there appears, according to Favereau, the "hidden face of Keynesianism, an economic thought with enterprise as its basis."[28] Now, enterprise implies the existence of conventions through which a collectivity gets involved in a process of apprenticeship at a remove from the mechanisms of the market. In this regard, the economics of convention cannot be confined to questions of microeconomics. It takes as its field of investigation questions central to macroeconomics concerning the role of collective agents such as enterprises.

A particular attention is therefore brought to phenomena of collective apprenticeship, notably on the basis of a new problematic area under observation, that of the countries of Eastern Europe, which with difficulty are attempting to depart from state control by trying to dynamize the initiative of enterprise. The economists solicited to revive the market notice that there is nothing in economic theory that enables a response to the requests of the directors. This incapacity of the economic models of Standard Theory, even though it is exclusively based on the rules of the market, to confront concrete problems, those of the Eastern countries, forces a "return to the essential variables of market economics. These have to do with the manner in which a society produces cooperation, social bonds."[29]

This new interest in the processes of collective apprenticeship and the incapacity of Standard Theory to study them may favor fertile interactions between regulationists and conventionalists, between a "macroeconomics of reproduction" and a "macroeconomics of diversity." This potential common workspace may be the means of gauging the actors, networks, sizes (equivalencies), and objects on which they rely to define the rules and rhythms of limited cumulative dynamics, the states of equilibrium or disequilibrium, without neglecting the disturbances introduced by the effects of reflexivity and the "ecological" externalities produced or experienced.

In the same way, the study of phenomena of development by economists of convention offers a new terrain of experimentation for their orientations. The central notion is equally that of collective apprenticeship: "An organization is the fixed point of a process of collective apprenticeship."[30] This centrality accorded to collective apprenticeship implies a departure from the paradigm of Extended Standard Theory, whose basis is the decomposition of the enterprise into an architecture of contractual relationships. The contractual models of the rigidity of salaries—even the most unorthodox, those founded on the relationship of gift and countergift, such as those of Akerlof[31]— are also not workable, as they are too static. It is fitting to elaborate a theory of rules by means of a theory of organization, and not the reverse: "A rule is never a complete solution—it is, rather, always a heuristic device."[32] This detour through rules to understand market economics enables a demonstration of the effectiveness of certain social forms in the deployment of economic relations. Thus, "trust is an important lubricant of a social system. It is extremely efficient."[33]

The economists of convention therefore call on neither methodological individualism nor functionalist holism, as Hervé Defalvard suggests.[34] They are in fact at the heart of the current paradigm shift through their attempt to rethink the question of the collective by avoiding the aporias of structuralism.

The notion of the collective in the conventionalist model is that of one under construction—not of a given collective—of a subject acting under constraint whose action is exposed to a constant renewed questioning, and therefore to a precariousness that always allows an openness to new possibilities. By problematizing the individual through the study of his behaviors, the perspective of convention precisely allows a conception of the surpassing of the rift between the economic and the social, which was foundational in analyses in terms of methodological individualism on the one hand, and of holism on the other. The stake is of importance, for it is nothing less than the division of labor between economics and sociology that the research program of the economics of convention questions anew.

# Twenty-four

# A Historicized Interpretive Theory

Substituted for a naturalized conception of economy is an approach that takes account of the dimension of collective representations, and thereby enables one to accord a decisive place to intersubjective dynamics. *Homo economicus* then becomes a being endowed with beliefs, who weaves socialized relations in the framework of relations of exchange, production, or consumption. This new conception of economy opens onto a dimension that is both cognitive and interpretive. It is no longer the mere mechanical result of natural constraints, but implies a detour through the representation that economic agents have of the various economic interactions in which they are involved.

There results a spectacular reversal of the relationship between the economic and the social. "This new conception shows that the determination of economic values rests on a social choice, on an adherence to a certain convention."[1] We have passed from a conception that borrows from the natural sciences the idea of immutable laws to an economics of convention that privileges the sphere of action through the mediation of the notion of normativity, which has become the required route of this economics.

In this perspective, the economists of convention are going back to the hermeneutic tradition. "The hermeneutic tradition posed the problem of the tension between the objective—or in certain regards collective—trace and the singular character of the actor."[2] This tradition, nonexistent in economics, is, on the other hand, present in the sociology of understanding and requires a detour through philosophy. "Ricoeur has played an important role, in particular on the question of explaining and understanding, on the figures of action, and on the relationship to narration. . . . For us, hermeneutics is completely fundamental."[3] The relationship between understanding totality and restoring detail in its singularity is at the heart of hermeneutic reflection. It inspires the conventionalists in their aspiration to make the various configurations of social coordination intelligible: "When Ricoeur extends this tradition by passing from the interpretation of the text to that of action, he insists on traces, documents, 'monuments,' which are to action what the text is to speech."[4]

## The Cognitive Horizon

Besides the interpretive turn, there is also a cognitive turn that affects the analysis of action in economics. Herbert Simon enabled this reorientation by applying himself to the cognitive operations of the identification and selection of elements pertinent to action.[5] Simon's work has also become strategic in the connection between the economics of convention and cognitivism, thanks to his training in psychology, and because he allowed the notion, long problematic in economics, of limited rationality. "Simon plays an enormous role today. This is a fine example of tradition: Simon is tradition."[6] Simon had the merit of bringing all his attention to the nature of preliminary construction effected by the actor and to the criteria of pertinence of her selectivity with regard to the mass of mobilized information.

The cognitive orientation has been favored in France because of the affiliation of many economists of convention with the CREA. At the CREA, Thévenot met philosopher Pierre Livet, a specialist in the philosophy of language who is especially interested in the limits of interpretation, examining the categories of interpretation on the level of the individual.[7]

Livet elaborated his categories of analysis on an individual scale, impugning classical linguistic conventionalism, which consisted of placing acts of language within social conventions. He essentially began from Kripke's rereading of Wittgenstein[8] to complete the latter's skeptical argument on the aporetic character of the rule and private language by bringing it back to a community of reference. As a logician, Kripke demonstrated this aporia by designating those located outside the community as offenders marked as such, by default and afterward, by the community. "It's very interesting, because it isn't in terms of positivity, as with Durkheim, where the community defines the rule. Here the approach is in negative terms."[9] Livet took up this examination by shifting it to the relation between act and rule, and he asked the question of at what moment one might say that an act carries such and such a rule. The relation between the act and its intentionality would quickly become crucial for Livet in his definition of the collective, because one examines the other's intentions so as to infer from them things about the outcome of one's own acts. The truism that Livet brought to light, relying on Kripke's demonstration, consisted of arguing that "human beings are persuaded they can't control the positive reference of the rule, and are conscious of it."[10]

Livet thus arrived at considerations on the foundations of possible agreements, on the necessary suspension of suspicion, and so he brought the chain of the individual back to a more collective level. The notion of convention at which he arrived presupposed that there were no means to guarantee it. He had therefore reached an elaborate, complex formulation of a conventionalism that no longer had much in common with its usual sense of mutual agreement. "On the contrary, convention can rely on the certainty of the ever possible revival of frictions."[11]

By quite a different route, this conception links up with that of Boltanski and Thévenot in De la justification. It was at the starting point of a joint project with Thévenot, who, for his part, remained unsatisfied with his own elaboration of the different greatnesses and asked the question of what constituted them, what their basis was. With Livet, he then began a vast area of research to understand the dynamic by which social artifacts were constructed.

Their common field of investigation was located therefore in the area of the elucidation of cognitive questions and of a connection with ethics. They would thus examine what the categories of collective action covered.[12] The undecidability of the markers is associated with an approach to convention as a process of interpretation. The aporetic space of the rule is viewed as practicable on condition that three new approaches to the problem of coordination be opened. It is fitting, in the first place, to conceive coordination as an "interpretation-in-progress of action";[13] in the second place, to view the character of a cyclical dynamic between a definition that arrests judgment and a revival of the inquiry into objects that remain in a third position among the actors. In the third place, "this dynamic must take into account the actors' intersecting anticipations and representations, their attempts to verify the reciprocity of their points of view in the aim of a common judgment."[14] It is therefore a question of tracing the deployment of a fundamentally interpretive rationality. This rationality inevitably runs up against impasses of "pure" rationality that it recognizes as such.

## Emotions

Livet and Thévenot have pushed their investigations to the point of considering the place of the emotions in cognition in order better to assess the faculties of appreciation of the judgments of the actors.[15] Value judgment appears as an appeasement through its capacity to fix the emotions. There is, therefore, an intertwining of these two levels: that of emotion, which is related to affect, and that of judgment, which is located in the register of rationality.

The emotions carry in themselves evaluations according to a current that calls on a "cognitive-phenomenological" analysis of the emotions.[16] Livet and Thévenot look at the emotion excited by evaluation. Its origin is interaction. Insofar as we feel the bearing of the evaluation of others on us, we are able to evaluate our own conduct. It is, then, "undecidable as to whether it is through the evaluation I think is imposed on me that others evaluate me."[17] On the basis of this undecidability inherent in the process of social evaluation, Livet and Thévenot attempt a typology of the emotional field and its translation into collective terms of evaluation. They thus propose a differentiation of the movement of emotion along two axes: on the one hand, in terms of degree (affects, sentiments, emotions properly speaking, and passions), and on the other—thanks to a differentiation among various regimes or registers of justification of axiological judgment that essentially takes up the diverse orders of greatness—the Cities of belonging (domestic, mercantile, industrial, and so on). So they rely on plural emotional cores of coherence. Hence, the domestic regime is founded on the generalization of the judgment of confidence that begins with relations of familiarity. In the regime of opinion, the undecidability of self-evaluation is bypassed by the passion of collective communication. On the contrary, in the inspired City, emotional unleashing is purely private. As for the mercantile regime, it is deployed at a remove from familiarity and at a distance from emotion . . . These many correlations partake of a quest for individual categories that enable one to found a dynamic of regimes of collective coordination.

The economics of convention has until now been the bearer of a surface temporality through its exclusive attention to configurations that are too strictly situated in rapid sequences in the course of which coordinations in action are made and unmade. In the very first place, it was fitting to be opposed to the epistemological primacy of deep structures, which gave the past an overarching place with respect to the present. If the type of regime of historicity held by the economists of convention is indeed in rupture with the period of structuralism, it is no less open to history, but to a different history, centered on an understanding of acting, of actions that carry meaning.

## Temporalities

Already in 1989, Robert Boyer defined new possible alliances between economics and history.[18] Accounting for the multiplicity of logics and the necessary use of mediating categories may contribute to connections between the two areas; "in light of contemporary research, it doubtless becomes more and more difficult to pursue a research program that postulates the existence of a rationality whose principles and modalities are valuable in all times and places."[19] So it is fitting to perceive the variety of configurations of the social bond in the past and to notice the emergence of new alliances.

Boyer, as a regulationist, continues to see in Bourdieu's habitus a heuristic device that enables one to give a concrete content to the abstraction of economists, *homo economicus*. Moreover, he still considers the long period to be an "antidote to the economist's impatience."[20] He thereby manifests a somewhat dated sensibility in comparison to the economists of convention, who have the additional ambition of changing the relation with temporality. Two economists of convention who have become members of the editorial board of the *Annales*, André Orléan and Laurent Thévenot, have already undertaken such a project. In this area, as in that of the register of justifications, Thévenot opts for a pluralization of temporalities as so many constructions of the actors as a function of the requirements of social coordination. If time were an exterior given, there could be no test in action: "In domestic temporality, temporality isn't completely given. Otherwise, we couldn't do tests. If the tradition were the past, there would be no dynamic. So there would be no tradition."[21] For there to be a tradition, one must aim for a connection with the past, but, says Thévenot, this past cannot be determining. Contrary to domestic temporality, industrial temporality is quite different insofar as the permanence of tools, of instruments of production, allows a temporal regularity that opens the future to possible investments.

The attention to acting among the economists of convention has already had effects with certain historians in their new appreciation of the notion of time. Historian Bernard Lepetit, a member of the editorial board of the *Annales* and an initiator of the pragmatic turn of the journal in 1988–89,[22] accords a particular attention to society viewed as a category of social practice. Beginning with the principle of the economists of convention by which society produces its own references and should not be derived from some deep naturality, he accords a prevalence to the question of agreement.

The major effects of this redeployment on the actors for the historian is a reconfiguration of time with a revalorization of the short period, of situated action, of action in context, which were repressed by the Braudelian long period and the immobile history of Le Roy Ladurie. Still, it does not signify the disqualification of the long period. It is the point of view outside time that must be relativized. Such a position, guided by the notion of appropriation, "ends up placing in the present the center of gravity of the temporal. History is the present in motion."[23] This making present that takes place in the new historical discourse, which is awakening from its structural slumber, aims to take seriously the temporal models of action of the actors of the past by following the example of what the economists of convention do with respect to present society. Lepetit has made the pragmatic turn of the social sciences his own. He remarks on the "crystallization of a new paradigm"[24] and intends to bring in a history transformed and recentered on a problematization of the notion of agreement or convention. Lepetit prefers, to the idea of collective representations that is rigidifying in institutions, that of convention, which also refers to an anchoring in institutions or objects—the latter indissociable from their endowment of meaning, products of social interaction—and which permit one to confer on identities, deriving from variable forms and durations, the "utility and malleability of the categories of practice."[25]

The force of conventions seems to derive from their temporal thickness, from the heritage of a distant past, but, as Lepetit rightly points out, it also has to do with their capacity for actualization. On the level of their study, they therefore involve an endowment of meaning that varies according to context and a polysemic capacity. The historian, then, is no longer the one who recalls the weight of the constraints of the past, as Braudel saw him to be. He is no longer the mere purveyor of an antidote, as Boyer still defined him in 1989, because the past he retraces is a universe of actualizable resources.

In a spectacular and significant reversal of the new historical moment, Lepetit advocates an inversion of the Labroussian inspiration. Ernest Labrousse thought every society possessed the conjuncture of its structures, and one might inversely say that it "gives itself the temporal structures of its conjuncture."[26] Conventions then become a double school for the historian, as they contribute to changing the way of conceiving the real and procure her a heuristic tool capable of restoring the changes of configuration in the social field. Lepetit thus conceives society as a category of practice, and as such may once again become the historian's privileged object, on condition of being defined not as "one of the particular dimensions of the relations of production or of the representations of the world, but as the product of interaction, as a category of social practice."[27] The use of conventions thus becomes particularly pertinent in the framework of the current definition of a new social history, as it allows one to be situated within the crises of legitimation of the system that require successive rearrangements of the conventions emerging between the old and the new. "The days following the Revolution, and particularly the appearance of a new industrial order, offer the occasion."[28] Alain Coutereau has thus analyzed how society is made of reuses that are nonetheless different from the past on the basis of the concrete case of the appearance, at first as an experiment and then as a general framework, of the industrial tribunals in the early nineteenth century to regulate relations between workers and employers.[29] His analysis makes it possible to show concretely the precise modalities of the reestablishment of confidence in the economic sphere.

# Part VII

*Underdetermination*

*Twenty-five*

# The Unsayable, or the
# Crisis of Causalism

The division between the subject and the object, with the overarching position it implied, let it be understood that the social sciences could arrive at a situation of the closure of knowledge in which the subject could saturate the object by the envelope of its knowledge. Today, the principle of underdetermination, from Duhem,[1] has become the philosophical foundation of a growing number of studies in the social sciences. It reinvigorates questioning and renders vain any attempt at monocausal reduction. This principle is extended in Bruno Latour's work with his notion of irreduction.[2] Early and late, causalist enclosure refers to an aporia, as there are only singular proofs, no equivalencies, but translations, and also, at the other end of the chain, "nothing is, by itself, either knowable or unknowable, sayable or unsayable, near or far. Everything is translated."[3]

In addition, the evolution of the physical sciences toward an opening of the avenues of explanation on the micro and macro levels, with a variation of the causal relations from one to the other, contributes to the general opening of scientific procedures to an "indeterminacy as to what level has priority."[4] This leads to an accounting for a real viewed in its complexity, composed of several strata, without evident priority, held in interwoven hierarchies, giving a place to many possible descriptions.

The interpretive turn adopted in the current studies allows one not to be locked into the false alternative between, on the one hand, a scientificity that would refer to a monocausal organizing schema and, on the other, an aestheticizing drift. The shift is particularly spectacular in the discipline of history, which all through the sixties and seventies was nourished, under the impulse of the *Annales* school, by a scientistic ideal, that of finding the ultimate truth at the end of statistical curves and great immobile and quantified equilibriums.

Thanks to Paul Ricoeur's work on time, there is a rediscovery of the dual dimension of history that, under the same term in France, covers at once narration itself and narrated action. The historiographical operation, to take up Michel de Certeau's expression, is a complex, mixed operation, which renders null and void all objectivism; that does not mean that it breaks with its function, which has always involved the idea of a contract to reveal the truth. "It's a mix, science fiction, whose narrative has only the appearance of truth but is no less circumscribed by controls and possibilities of falsification."[5]

## Between Science and Fiction

Michel de Certeau, recapturing historical discourse in its tension between science and fiction, was particularly sensitive to the fact that this discourse is specific to a place of enunciation and hence mediated by the technique that makes it an institutionalized practice, referable to a community of scholars. "Before knowing what history says of society, we have to analyze how history functions within it."[6] The practice of history is therefore completely correlative to the structure of the society that sketches the conditions of an utterance that is neither legendary, nor atopic, nor stripped of pertinence. In 1975, Certeau emphasized the fact that history is also a writing on two levels: the performative, as is evoked by the very title of the trilogy edited by Pierre Nora and Jacques Le Goff in 1974, *Faire de l'histoire*—"making history"—and writing as a mirror of the real. The historian's writing plays the role of a funeral rite. An instrument of exorcising death, it introduces death into the very heart of its discourse and enables a society to situate itself symbolically by endowing itself with a language on the past.

The discourse of history speaks to us of the past in order to bury it. It has, according to Certeau, the function of a tomb, in the dual sense of honoring the dead and participating in their elimination from the scene of the living. Historical revisiting, then, has this function of opening in the present a space suited for marking the past so as to redistribute the space of possibilities. The practice of history is therefore in principle open to new interpretations, to a dialogue on the past that is open to the future, to the point that we speak more and more of a "future of the past." History, therefore, cannot remain enclosed in a self-contained objectification.

The attention to narrative, to writing in the discipline of history, was already broadly developed by Paul Veyne in 1971, in the midst of the quantitativist vogue.[7] He already disturbed the nomological claims of a history that he resolutely situated on the side of idiography. According to Veyne, history can be only a true novel, a truthful narrative. As for the causalities the historian introduces, they have no other value than that of literary artifice allowing the plot to unfold.

At the same moment, François Furet announced the end of narrative history and the advent of problem-oriented history, which had to allow the question to be asked of knowing "to what extent, by borrowing some of those advances and integrating them into its own practices, history has established a knowledge of the past that could qualify as scientific."[8] He expressed the ambitions of the *Annales* school, over whose destiny he presided at the EHESS and which was aiming to relegate narrative to the rank of antique oddity.

In 1979, a discordant note was heard. It came from across the Channel, from Lawrence Stone.[9] He opposed narrative history to structural history. The latter was incarnated in three forms of history termed scientific: the Marxist model, the French ecologico-demographic model (that of the *Annales*), and finally the American cliometric model. Now, they have in common a failing in their monocausalist ambitions. Stone opposed to them the necessity of a return to narration in order to explore what happened in the heads of people of other times. Such a quest induces a change of scale that today corresponds with the Italian orientations of micro-*storia*.

## A Mixed Epistemology

Paul Ricoeur had already shown, in the mid-1950s, that history involves a mixed epistemology, an interlacing of objectivity and subjectivity, of explanation and understanding. A dialectic of the self and the temporally distant other, a confrontation between contemporary language and a past situation, "historical language is necessarily *equivocal*."[10] Ricoeur, considering the necessary accounting for the evenemental, the contingent, as well as the structural, permanencies, defines the function of the historian, the justification of his enterprise, as being the exploration of what humanity involves. "This reminder sometimes rings as an awakening when the historian is tempted to repudiate his fundamental intention and yield to the *fascination for a false objectivity*—that of a history in which there would no longer be men and human values but only structures, forces, and institutions."[11]

In the mid-1980s, Ricoeur published his great trilogy on history.[12] Here he resumes, by broadening it, his reflection on the regimes of historicity conceived as a third time, a third discourse held in tension between the purely cosmological conception of temporal movement as it is deployed by Aristotle, then by Kant, and an intimate, interior approach to time that may be found in Saint Augustine and then Husserl. Between cosmic and intimate time is situated the time that the historian recounts. It allows a reconfiguration of time by means of specific connectors. So Ricoeur places historical discourse in a tension suited to it, between narrative identity and the ambition for truth. In this regard, and while recognizing their essential contribution to the reevaluation of narrative as a repository of knowledge, Ricoeur confronts the Anglo-Saxon narrativists: William Dray, Georg Henrik von Wright, Arthur Danto, Hayden White, and others. They have the sizable merit of showing that emplotment assures the transition between recounting and explaining, that explanation is internal to narrative.

Opposed to the narrativists, the attempt of the *Annales* to break with narrative is illusory and contradicts the historian's project. Of course, the *Annales* school, all the while allowing that the historian constructs, problematizes, and projects her subjectivity onto the object of research, seemed a priori to approach Ricoeur's position. But, in fact, this was not for the purpose of adopting the hermeneutic point of view of comprehensive explanation.

The essential target of the *Annales* was the methodological school, pejoratively called "historicizing history," that of Charles-Victor Langlois, Charles Seignobos, and Gabriel Monod. So it was, on the contrary, a question of removing oneself from the subject to break the historicizing narrative and bring to prevalence the scientificity of a historical discourse renovated by the social sciences. So as better to bring to light the epistemological break effected by the *Annales,* its initiators and disciples have pretended to wring the neck of what was designated by the pejorative term of historicizing history: the event and its narrative.

There have certainly been shifts of objects: a reevaluation of eco-

nomic phenomena in the 1930s and then a valorization of spatial logics in the 1950s. Fernand Braudel denounced the short period as a
species of the illusory in comparison to the permanencies of the great
socles of geohistory, the long period. Meanwhile, and Ricoeur showed
this well, the rules of the writing of history have hindered a foray into
sociology, because the long period remains a duration.

Braudel, as a historian, remained dependent on the rhetorical forms
proper to the discipline of history. Contrary to his thundering explanations, in his thesis he also pursued the realization of a narrative.
"The very notion of the history of a long period derives from the dra-
matic event . . . , in the sense of the emplotted event."[13] Of course, the
plot, whose subject is no longer Philip II but the Mediterranean Sea,
is of another type, but it remains no less a plot. The Mediterranean
figures as a quasi character that knows its last hour of glory in the sixteenth century, before we witness a shift to the Atlantic and America,
a moment during which the "Mediterranean steps outside the spot-
light of global history."[14]

Emplotment therefore imposes itself on every historian, even the
one who takes the most distance from the classical recitative of the political and diplomatic evenemental. So narration constitutes the indispensable mediation for making a historical work and thereby linking
the space of experience and the horizon of expectation of which
Koselleck speaks: "Our working hypothesis thus amounts to taking
narrative as a guardian of time, insofar as there can be no thought
about time without narrated time."[15] The configuration of time passes
through the historian's narration. Viewed in this way, it is displaced
between a space of experience that evokes the multiplicity of possible
trajectories and a horizon of expectation that defines a future made
present, not reducible to a mere derivative of present experience. "Thus,
the space of experience and the horizon of expectation do more than
stand in polar opposition, they mutually condition each other."[16]

The construction of this hermeneutics of historical time offers a
horizon that is no longer woven by scientific finality alone, but drawn
toward a human doing, a dialogue to be instituted between generations, an acting on the present. In this perspective, it is fitting to reopen the past, to revisit its potentialities.

By impugning the purely antiquarian relation to history, historical
hermeneutics aims to "make our expectations more determinate and
our experience less so."[17] The present reinvests the past on the basis of

a historical horizon detached from it. It transforms dead temporal distance into "a transmission that is generative of meaning."[18] The vector of historical reconstitution is then found at the heart of acting, of the making-present that defines narrative identity in the two forms of sameness (*idem*) and oneself (*ipséité*). The centrality of narrative relativizes the capacity of history to enclose its discourse in an explanation limited to mechanisms of causality. It does not allow either a return "to the claims of the constituting subject to master all meaning,"[19] or a renunciation of the idea of an encompassing power of history according to its "ethical and political implications."[20]

## Sciences of the Historical

The departure from the causalism borrowed from the experimental sciences is also manifested by the attempt to define a new space within the social sciences, that of sociology, history, and anthropology. The EHESS laboratory at Marseilles directed by Jean-Claude Passeron aligns itself with these three disciplines and defends an epistemology common to them. Thus, *Le Raisonnement sociologique*[21] figures as a delimiting manifesto of this common space, despite its falsely limiting title that simply recalls the academic specialization of its author, Passeron. These three disciplines derive from Weberian categories: their objects of study are characterized by the singularity of the historical configuration in which they are implicated. This phenomenality makes impossible the enterprise of nomological normalization that aimed to deindex the contexts. Deictics are indissociable from historical contextuality.

Weber opposed his ideal types to the illusions of objectivism and epistemological naturalism. These three disciplines (sociology, history, and anthropology) can produce only proper seminouns with a status that mixes their generalizing heuristic function and their capacity to translate a singular situation. Passeron is rightly guarded against the experimentalist illusions that have fed the nomological dream. All the more regrettable, then, is his unfounded denunciation, made for good measure, of "hermeneutic wandering,"[22] which he defines as mere interpretive delirium, through complete misrecognition of a tradition marked by the rigor of thought that Ricoeur illustrates in all realms.

The Weberian space that is defined and claimed belongs, moreover, to the hermeneutic tradition. It corresponds to an epistemological autonomy of the social sciences that have in common with the natural sciences a postulation of the existence of the real, with the empirical ambition of accounting for it. But this epistemology is autonomous with respect to the natural sciences because of its impossibility of treating social facts as things. Its space is defined by a "socle, which is historicity, and three pillars, which are typification, comparatism, and a horrible neologism, emicity."[23] Weber defined the socle of historicity as unreproducible, because marked by singular spatiotemporal coordinates. It is open to interpretive wagers that situate the social sciences in the register of plausibility. "Social actors endlessly produce meaning on their own actions, and this meaning itself becomes an element of the actions; performative effects are endlessly present."[24] As for the first pillar, typification, it is also borrowed from Weber's ideal types. It allows one to use artifacts that have the status of proper seminouns. The pitfall is in substantializing these typologies, which are in fact descriptive schemes borrowing from interpretation, because "every description is also an interpretation."[25] The second pillar is more traditional: it is comparatism, long used as a heuristic device in the social sciences. Finally, emicity represents the third pillar: "The emic consists of autochthonous indigenous representations."[26] It implies an incorporation in description of the analysis the actors make of it, and is thereby tied to the objective of Weberian understanding.

Once again we find ourselves, with the three social sciences of history, sociology, and anthropology, faced with what Anthony Giddens calls a double hermeneutic:[27] that is, the dual process of translation and interpretation. In the first place, the social sciences must take into consideration that actors' representations of actions carry a pertinent knowledge. In the second place, the social sciences are themselves interpretive disciplines. This double hermeneutic circle has a return effect in the actors' appropriations and the institutions of knowledge produced by the social sciences, thanks to the active and reactive capacity of the actors; Giddens calls this *agency*.

This competency for transformation opens a pragmatic horizon, proper to the human, common to history, sociology, and anthropology; for the latter three, "the performativity of representations is indissociable from the agency of the actors."[28] If the epistemological horizon is pragmatic, there can be no prejudging of what is to come. Prediction is only retrodiction. The social sciences are led to an oscillation between the why and the how, for "indeterminacy is inherent to this agency, which to me seems to be a particularity of the object of all the social sciences."[29]

## The Historical Exploration of the Sensible

This indeterminacy is exemplified by the work of a pioneering historian, as we have already evoked, in the exploration of the limit zones of the territory of his discipline: Alain Corbin. His procedure symbolizes the "uncertainty of the object."[30] The border zones and limit points Corbin revisits, at the heart of a historicized sensibility, square off with the usual taxonomies, the traditional and reified divisions of the discipline. The very complexity of these objects, at the limit of the sayable, between the perceived and the unperceived, makes the deployment of simple causalities impossible.

An innovator in France in the realm of the history of sensibilities, of emotions, fulfilling Lucien Febvre's old wish in this domain, Corbin, who felt constricted and unsatisfied in the framework of the retrospective sociography of Limousin imparted by his thesis adviser, Ernest Labrousse, took up the new object of the history of prostitution.[31] This research program led him to pursue further a study of the links between olfactory manifestations and social representations. "The likening of prostitution to dead meat, to the butcher shop,"[32] gave coherence to this original inquiry, the idea for which was suggested to Corbin by his reading of Jean-Noël Hallé, member of the Royal Society of Medicine and the first incumbent of the chair of public hygiene created in Paris in 1794. This maniac of deodorization conveys very well a collective hyperesthesia.[33]

In the confines of the history of literature, between the fantasies of authors such as Huysmans and Hallé's inquiry, Corbin asks the question, To what does this modulation of olfactory sensibility correspond? How does this sense that is habitually disqualified, considered as minor, suddenly crystallize collective discomfort? Corbin restores its complex configuration, which shifts between 1750 and 1880, in the climate of pre-Pasteurian mythologies, ignored by the teleological perspective of the classical history of science, which pushes the vagaries of knowledge outside its field.

Corbin reestablishes Latour's principle of symmetry in order to exhume the studies of putrid substances and pneumatic chemistry, as well as Latour's transference of the vital to the social. "Instinct, animality, and organic stench became traits of the masses. Repugnance to smell now focused on the poor man's hovel and latrines, the peasant's dung, the greasy and fetid sweat impregnating the worker's skin, rather than on the oppressive vapor of the putrid crowd in general."[34]

After restoring the links between the sense of smell and the social imaginary, Corbin took a new limit point, that of the shores toward which the West carried its desires beginning in the eighteenth century.[35] Corbin then sought after the perspectives that human beings of other times had on their environment as well as their emotions. Still further than with the discourse on actors, he plunged to the heart of sensibilities with the historian's concern with avoiding anachronism.

This rise of the desire for a shore "crosses all sorts of contributions, and the interest of such an object resides, precisely, in this interlacing."[36] This form of history, attentive to emergent processes, takes its distance from the Braudelian notion of the prison of the long period. On the contrary, it gauges discontinuities in the practices and discourses that attest to a new desire. So it leads to a particular attention to discursive practices. The renunciation of a causalist reconstitution involves an examination of the division of the said and the unsaid: "With regard to the coasts, I have chosen not to construct grids . . . for interpreting landscapes."[37]

Such a history of sensibilities cannot remain confined within the limits of the discipline of history. It ineluctably opens onto problems in the philosophy of language, so as to answer the question of whether one may liken the unspoken to the unproven when one gauges emergent phenomena. In addition, such a history implies an interrogation of the nature of the subject of which one speaks. In this regard, the philosophical reflexivity offered by Ricoeur's hermeneutic horizon[38]— and by the late Foucault (of *The Care of the Self*, of the governmentality of the self), with particular attention given to the body, to biopower—may inspire the historian's discourse. This horizon may become very suggestive in the framework of the construction of a new history of emotions or an "emotionology," as it is termed by American historians Peter N. Stearns and Carol Zisowitz-Stearns.[39]

## To the School of Defatalization

The appropriation of the sensible, and in general of representations, in the field of investigation of history, orients research toward objects that are more ideal, more symbolic than material. The processes studied do not have the linearity that permits an application of causal relations by which previous phenomena determine and engender later ones. Meanwhile, the historian may gauge emergences, coherencies, contemporaneities: "We observe the co-occurrence of phenomena we can understand. But this isn't a problematic of causality."[40]

The defatalization of historical processes is taking place with this placement in crisis of the postulated schemata of causality. Emergences are revisited, and no longer presupposed and subtended by a teleological vision for which they would be only the starting point of an already established direction. This reopening of the multiple field of the possibilities of the past leads to the notion of underdetermination. This does not for all that mean that anything is possible at any moment and that an indeterminacy translates a postulated lack of distinction. The notion of underdetermination designates at once the plurality of possibilities and the existence of constraints whose effect is that certain possibilities happen and others do not.

This dialectic of opening and closing is central to Roger Chartier's studies on the history of practices of reading. "There are bound spaces. Not every reading is possible for every reader at every moment. Every reader is a social being inhabited by norms, conventions, and competencies that are profoundly historical and social. At the same time, a whole space of appropriation may open up, understood as a set of differentiated possibilities."[41] The inscription of possibilities even within constraints has led Chartier to abandon the simple schema of opposition between scholarly and popular culture: "This book is first of all written against the now classic use of the very notion of popular culture."[42]

To this postulate based on the perfect adequacy between social and cultural splits, he opposes the deployment of shared practices, which are more fluid, more intertwined, and fundamentally hybrid. The greatest complexity of the historical object nevertheless does not imply, according to Chartier, a renunciation of all determination and a choice of the absolute aleatory. On the contrary: "We may employ the notion of weak determinations."[43] This notion is at the heart of the archaeology of reading practices Chartier has undertaken. It allows an understanding of the strategies at work as well as of the various procedures of operation.

This sphere of underdetermination is the very framework of analysis of Alain Caillé and *La Revue du MAUSS*. The gift, which for Caillé has a paradigmatic value, is possible and thinkable only on the basis of an indeterminacy within an intermediate area between utilitarianism, on the one hand, and institutional constraints, on the other: "The gift is the manifestation of the indeterminate and its openness to singularity."[44] The gift as a concrete operator in human relations allows one to affirm the power of the freedom of the actors; they thereby escape reduction to the mere sum of calculated interests. The greater attention to relations among persons, to their own competencies, allows a loosening of the grip of constraints without denying them, a valorization of the role of indeterminacy and therefore of the freedom of each. Even more than the relation among individuals, "the political is the direct, more general manifestation"[45] of this phenomenon. This idea places the being together of a society on the political level; the temporary, problematic unity of society is related to nothing but society itself. It cannot be reduced to a sum of interests: "It's the decided undecidable."[46]

# Twenty-six

# A Poetics of Knowledge

The indeterminacy proper to the discourse of history, held in tension between the literary humanities and scientific ambition, gives a particular importance to the very procedures by which the writing of history partakes of and at the same time removes itself from the literary. The "leafed-through" organization of the historian's discourse—as Michel de Certeau calls it, as it includes the materials on which it is based—leads to a necessary attention to the narrative procedures and rhetorical figures used. It opens onto the construction of a poetics of knowledge. The latter does not mean returning to the vagaries of the linguistic turn that marked the structuralist moment and implied a view of textuality as radically cut off from any referent.

The recent demonstration by the philosopher Jacques Rancière, inviting history to "reconcile itself with its own name,"[1] moves in the direction of constructing a historical discipline that can hold together three requirements: scientific, narrative, and political. Just as the historians of mentalities have taken their distance from the postulated adequacy between socioprofessional categories and forms of culture, Rancière, among whose privileged objects has always been a retracing of workers' speech, is no longer satisfied with a history of the latter in terms of an identification with social or cultural categories. The relation between the conditions of discourse and the order of discourse is not a simple one. It leaves an indeterminable fringe, an autonomized core of meaning, a singularized experience—what Rancière terms democratic heresy.

The progressive subjectification of speech makes it impossible to refer it to its compost, to identify it with a material home of which it would be only the expression. In the perspective of the reappropriation of the singularity of speech "from below," Rancière places back-to-back the old school of the royal or Republican chronicle and the *Annales* school. The latter nonetheless intended to exhume the speech of the mute, of the anonymous of history. "When Braudel speaks, in *The Mediterranean and the Mediterranean World,* of the Renaissance of the poor, whose precious paperwork encumbers the king's desk, he designates a figure of the masses that for him is negative: the multiplication of speakers that is a trait of the democratic age."[2] The history of the long period, of quantified series, of plurisecular permanencies, slides above the proliferation of speech. By rethinking the articulation of the three dimensions that belong to the discourse of history, the discipline of history may come back to the sensible material of its object, "time, words, and death."[3]

Arlette Farge, in her attention to the archive and her concern for restoring speech from below without destroying it, partakes of the same preoccupation as Rancière, with whom she shared the common adventure of one of the best journals of the 1970s, *Révoltes logiques.* Farge practices erasure so as better to give a place to the speaking beings that history occludes beneath its official narrative: "I do not need to do an inventory of what escapes here. What has escaped belongs to no one, not even the historian. It is there, untransmissible and secret, present and defunct."[4] Attention to the textual, narrative, and syntactic procedures by which history utters its regime of truth leads to reappropriating the gains of the studies of the whole narratological tradition, especially developed in the Anglo-Saxon world by Ricoeur.[5] The development of the narrativist theses has been nourished by the linguistic turn, by the critique of the nomological model, and by the treatment of narrative as a repository of knowledge, a deployment of resources of intelligibility.

## The Narrativists

The narrativists have thus brought to light how the mode of narrative has an explanatory value, even if only through the constant use of the subordinating conjunction *because,* which covers and conflates two distinct functions, consecution and consequence. Chronological and logical links are thus affirmed without being problematized. Now, it is fitting to untangle this password, the disparately used *because*.

Along these lines, William Dray showed, in the 1950s, that the idea of a cause must be distinct from the idea of a law.[6] He defended a causal system irreducible to a system of laws, criticizing at once those who practiced this reduction and those who excluded any form of explanation. A little later, Georg Henrik von Wright advocated a mixed model based on an explanation he called quasi-causal[7] as the most appropriate for history and for the social sciences in general. Causal relations are, according to von Wright, strictly relative to their context and to the action implicated by them. Taking inspiration from G. E. M. Anscombe's studies, he privileged the intrinsic relations between the reasons for action and the action itself. Von Wright then opposed the alogical, purely external causal connection, bearing on the states of the system, to the logical connection that is related to the intentions and takes a teleological form. The link between these two heterogeneous levels is located in the configuring traits of narrative. "For me, this guideline is plot, insofar as it is a synthesis of the heterogeneous."[8]

For his part, Arthur Danto revealed the various temporalities within historical narrative and questioned anew the illusion of a past as a fixed entity in relation to which only the viewpoint of the historian would be mobile. In contrast, he distinguished three temporal positions internal to narration.[9] The domain of the sentence already implies two different positions, that of the event described and that of the event in function of its being described. We must still add the level of the statement, which is located in another temporal position, that of the narrator. The epistemological consequence of such a temporal differentiation figures as a paradox of causality, because a later event may bring an earlier event to appear through a causal relation. In addition, Danto's demonstration comes down to considering explanation and description to be inseparable, history being of a piece, as he says.

Some, such as Hayden White, have gone even farther with the perspective of the construction of a poetics of history,[10] in presupposing that the register of the historian is not fundamentally different from that of fiction on the level of its narrative structure. History, therefore, would be first of all writing, literary artifice. White situates the transition between narrative and argument in the notion of emplotment.

Ricoeur is, then, very close to these theses. And he hails two of the narrativists' major achievements. In the first place, they demonstrate that "to narrate is already to explain. The *di' allēla*—the 'one because of the other' that, according to Aristotle, forms the logical connection of the plot—is henceforth the necessary starting point for any discussion of historical narration."[11] In the second place, to the diversification and hierarchization of explanatory models, the narrativists have opposed the richness of the explanatory resources internal to the narrative.

This proximity of fiction and history may also be at the origin of a historical writing that is other, metamorphosed by the fictional liberty that may enable history to endow itself with a discourse less closed in on itself, less saturated with meaning, more open to the polyphony of voices, the plurality of registers. This is what Régine Robin has accomplished in resorting to memory-fiction.[12]

Meanwhile, and despite the advances in the understanding of what a discourse of history is, Ricoeur does not subscribe to the most radical of the narrativists' theses when they postulate the lack of distinction between history and fiction. Despite their proximity, there subsists an epistemological break that is based on the regime of veridicality proper to the contract of the historian with respect to the past.

The attention to regimes of discourse implies an entry into this zone of indeterminacy in order to recapture how regimes of truth are made and what the status of error is, the character, incommensurable or not, of the various assertions presenting themselves as scientific. So Ricoeur does not follow the deconstructive attempt of Michel Foucault and Paul Veyne, which is inspired by Nietzsche and extols a mere genealogy of interpretations that would cover historical facts. Impugning both the positivist and the genealogical temptations, Ricoeur opposes to them an "analysis of historical reality that he places under the sign of 'representance' to emphasize its twofold status as reality and fiction."[13]

On this point, Ricoeur shares Roger Chartier's position: "The task of the historian is to provide an appropriate, controlled knowledge of this 'population of the dead'—personages, mentalities, prices—that is his object. To abandon this perhaps immoderate but foundational claim would be to leave the field open to all falsifications, to all the forgers."[14]

Of course, Hayden White has shown that the discourse of history is bound up with rhetorical figures, with the use of tropes similar to those of fiction. He has made possible a better distinction between the various possible registers of emplotment, the various argumentative procedures (contextualist, organicist, formalist, mechanist). But is the combination of these enough to postulate a lack of distinction between the discourses of history and of fiction? This is not Chartier's point of view. "For Hayden White, history's status of knowledge or its truthful intention, and what this involves on the level of the elaboration of working devices, of techniques of production of knowledge, has no importance and is even quite secondary. I think that's a completely untenable relativist position."[15]

Recalling the truth contract that has bound the historian to her object since Herodotus and Thucydides is of primary importance in opposing all forms of falsification and manipulation of the past. It is not in contradiction with being attentive to history as writing, as discursive practice. Paul-André Rosental's demonstration with regard to the use of metaphor in Braudel is a fine illustration of an epistemological strategy incarnated in a rhetorical figure.[16]

Braudel's major book is unanimously celebrated as an aesthetic monument. For its style, it is a work, in the literary sense. Now, Rosental shows that the constant recourse to metaphor in Braudel does not partake of a mere desire for ornamentation, but of a polemic, of a defense and illustration of the discourse on the method, that of the *Annales*. Metaphor has a twofold use: it personifies the new subject of history that for Braudel becomes nature, the Mediterranean Sea as a true hero whose setting becomes Philip II; at the same time, metaphor "transforms *The Mediterranean,* a work of history, into a work *on* history"[17] that aims to disqualify the adversaries of the *Annales*. Attention to the effectiveness of the rhetorical figures within the argumentative schemes offers many fields of investigation that surpass the mere field of the literary and appear as so many organizing principles of textuality in the social sciences, exploiting all the resources of the analogical.[18] This attention to textuality is doubled by the new interest in what surrounds the text: paratexts, footnotes, modalities of presentation.[19]

*Twenty-seven*

# A Horizon More Ethical
# than Epistemological

The recognition of indeterminacy or underdetermination in scientific matters has led to a judgment that the world is no longer susceptible to becoming the object of a nomological interpretation. As we have already seen, this crisis of causality allows the liberation of the reflexive moment, of a hermeneutics that is fruitfully pursued in a pragmatic, intersubjective moment. This evolution is quite fertile insofar as it enables the development of a model "in the direction of an ethic of discussion, of a theory of argumentation."[1] The unity of reason, then, is a possible horizon, no longer as an a priori of diverse experiences, but on the level of an a priori of argumentation. Whether on the scientific or ethical plane, the recourse "to this pragmatic procedure of argumentation is necessary to stabilize the claims to validity."[2]

The pairing of incompleteness and a renewed examination of the ethical is beginning to break through the tough armor of the social sciences constituted by economics. In a recent work, Amartya Sen distinguishes two origins of economics: ethics and mechanics.[3] Without rejecting the mechanist tradition in economics, Sen deems that it has become impoverished in being cut off from its other origin, ethics.

The utilitarianism of the theory of rational choice can never define anything but the minimal figure of "rational idiots." On the basis of the critique of the Walrasian mechanical model, a whole new microeconomics has been constituted.[4] It does not abandon analyses in terms of rationality, but these are reactivated and enriched by the notion of imperfect information.

Some economists are discovering, in the form of a lack, that they have removed all value judgment from their field of analysis. Even orthodox economists notice that, to conceive of cooperation, they cannot remain at the logic of individual rationality alone. Economists of convention, of course, are the most receptive to these problems. "There is a way to manage incompleteness rationally: it is, precisely, ethics."[5]

The completeness of contractual agreements, by which it is tacitly understood that all cases are settled a priori by the parties, is very rarely achieved. In general, contracts carry with them a margin of uncertainty, incompleteness. We may give two types of explanation for this phenomenon: on the one hand, we may valorize the cognitive impossibility of all prediction; on the other, we may deem that the actors can very well be exhaustive in their prediction, but that they still do not desire to complete a contingent contract. In both cases, the incompleteness undergone or wished for is a major element: "Incompleteness is not (necessarily) a lack, but (sometimes) an asset; it's not a 'less,' but a 'more.'"[6]

## Agreement

In this problematic Favereau goes back to Keynes's concepts to show that, far from making uncertainty a foundation of behaviors deriving from irrationality, Keynes establishes strong relations between incompleteness and behavioral rationality by making us attentive to the fact that in a situation of crisis or anticipation, when the risk depends on the behavior of others, the refusal of risk may aggravate this behavior. Ethics situates itself in an implicitly central position in the relation that arises between two contractors who know each other only slightly. Such a bond of cooperation may not be realized in total transparency and in the framework of a written contract. The signed agreement, by definition incomplete, presupposes that the two parties are seeking to fulfill their interest. The fact of agreeing to sign despite a large degree of uncertainty is the tangible sign accorded to the future partner that the signer agrees to cooperate on a long-term basis. "This agent, neither a madman nor a saint, also manifests all the symptoms of ordinary, selfish, and uncooperative rationality."[7]

What shifts in the case of this nonstandard *homo economicus,* whose rationality is limited at the moment he openly moves forward, is not really his desire for optimization but his relation with temporality. He renounces a short-term self-interest in favor of a longer-term rationality, opting for an "enlightened self-interest" or "weak altruism."[8]

Studies in the economics of convention allow an approach to the question of ethics on the social level. Ethics is not absent from the sociological tradition, including Durkheimianism. The will to reification did not out of principle exclude a place for the moral subject. But the essence of this tradition is inscribed in a nomological view of the world, exemplified by Kant. It opposes two heterogeneous realms to each other: that submitted to natural laws, in which social laws are inscribed, and that of a free subject that affirms itself as a moral subject in the face of natural determinism.

## The Normative Dimension

The sociological tradition has privileged the first level, leaving philosophy the concern of facing the ethical dimension. In this split, the freedom of the moral subject is removed from theoretical cognition: "In Kant, there is a concept without sensible intuition. It's a concept that enables us to act but doesn't enable us to have theoretical cognition."[9] The necessity of asking this question again on the basis of the junction of these two realms invites inspiration from the phenomenological tradition, better armed to allow the construction of a sociology of action that includes the ethical dimension of an empirical subject engaged in its natural and social reality; once again, we come back to the philosophy of Paul Ricoeur.

The fact that all cognition of the social is strongly normalized, saturated with value judgment, today becomes an essential dimension of knowledge. It is no longer to be rejected as an epiphenomenon in the name of the objective of scientificity.

The normative dimension therefore becomes a constitutive component of research. Bernard Conein, in the past reticent on this point and in disagreement with Patrick Pharo after working with him and Louis Quéré for a long time on ethnomethodology, has indeed come back to his initial positions. At the outset, the notion of norm for Conein was purely explanatory, allowing an establishment of the conditions of possibility of social relations, whereas Pharo gave it an interpretive dimension that made him consider the functioning of representations in terms of civility. Meanwhile, Conein evolved on this point, beginning with research on the question of categorization. He then noticed the necessity of reintroducing the question of morality and norms in the framework of an experimental epistemology. The observation led him to acknowledge that the categorization of natural species as recognitive categorization, a simple means of recognition (for example, of the natural species "dog"), no longer functions in the same way when one replaces a natural species with a human being. "It's no longer recognitive, but evaluative. Judgment intervenes here automatically."[10] So there is a strong intertwining of evaluation, the ethical aspect, and the activity of recognition, of social classification. One may not, therefore, practice a mere reduction of the problem of categories to their reference.

For its part, cognitive science is concerned with emergences, with the acquisition of moral categories. This aspect makes Jean-Pierre Dupuy "very aware"[11] of avoiding any reduction of ethical problems and practices to cognition. We have already seen that he envisioned a dissociation of these two axes of research within the CREA, and his examinations today bring him back to Sartrean philosophy as a philosophy of praxis. So the social sciences are more and more oriented to the question of judgment.

This evolution goes right along with the current interpretive turn. The epistemological naïveté of the sham of the author's lack of implication in what he says has become impossible. That is why more and more historians are returning to their past, so as better to situate their directions and choices on the basis of an equation that is quite personal to them and that tends to be recognized as an indispensable detour in order that the reader accept or reject their interpretive predispositions.[12] "All retrospection is normative."[13]

The problem shifts to the capacity to master this normativity so as to make it into a heuristic device, and not the mere expression of a pure subjectivism; hence the differentiation that Ricoeur makes between the investigative self and the pathetic self.[14] Guarding against the self of resentment recalls the necessary impartiality of the interpreter whose objective is to enter into the motivations of the actors whose itinerary she restores. But the mode of problematization, the type of questioning, is especially and above all the fact of a subjectivity steeped in values. "To study the French Revolution today, beyond everything that separates scholars, is to study the establishment of an object we believe in: democracy. It is to judge the normative event against the measure of this value that is ours and that gives meaning to the inquiry."[15]

## The New Scientific "Posture"

The ethical dimension is also not limited to the relation of the scholar in the social sciences with her object; it has become indispensable in the framework of the current pragmatic turn insofar as the truth is produced by the group, as Peirce said. "We must have confidence in the institution when we consider as true what the historians have considered as true."[16] The organizing discipline, the institution itself, is then conceived as both a place of elaboration of research and a practice of structuration of the milieu.

In any case, this is Gérard Noiriel's perspective, and it is strongly animated by a concern with the ethics of the professional milieu, which must remain in a situation of autonomy with respect to the state, on the basis of specific criteria of legitimation of a knowledge. "The ethical question is for me the bond with the collective practice of the discipline."[17] The sociology of the milieu then takes on a growing importance in the understanding of the evolution of a discipline's regime of truth, and this implies a place for relativism, uncertainty. On the basis of this acknowledgment of incompleteness, the scholar departs from the logic of denunciation, from the philosophy of suspicion, as Ricoeur has defined it. Greater attention to practices enables one to leave the dichotomy between civil society and the state and to realize to what point "we are held in institutionalized, administrated logics."[18]

The loss of the overarching position of a naturalized scientific truth may have the positive effect of an advancement in the direction of a democratization of the regime of validation of cognition by a collective subjectivity, as we have seen with Pierre Lévy's experiment with the trees of cognition. The choice adopted by the immanence of this validation linked to a specific practice has immediate ethical consequences because there is "no reason for me to put myself in a position of transcendence with regard to whomever."[19] Thus, the mode of communication, previously viewed as a mere system of diffusion, may first of all be transformed into a listening machine. But this presupposed that one begin with the question of the identity of the other and see him as a source of knowledge and a bearer of richness.

## Moral Philosophy

Evidently, the social sciences are not alone in reappropriating the ethical dimension. Philosophy is coming back to some of its most illustrious traditions, which for a moment were abandoned. During the structuralist hour, when philosophy wanted to be the social science of the social sciences, the supreme theory of practices, the mere mention of a moral dimension figured as a displaced archaism. Facing a pressing social demand by the state, which is installing ethical committees to resolve a growing number of social questions, philosophers are called on to use their conceptual equipment in order to enlighten the public debate.

Monique Canto-Sperber, who has been editing a new collection titled "Moral Philosophy" with Presses Universitaires de France, recalls that when she began her studies in philosophy in the 1970s, "moral philosophy, and in general all reflection on morality, was the object of suspicion and reprobation."[20] Nevertheless, moral philosophy was not absent from France. It was quite well represented by various currents: the personalism of Emmanuel Mounier, the Christian existentialism of Gabriel Marcel, the philosophy of values of Louis Lavelle and Louis Le Senne—to which may easily be added Sartrean philosophy and the reflexive tradition of Jean Nabert. Still, all these currents saw a long and radical eclipse during the sixties and seventies. Moral reflection was, of course, pursued, but outside France, particularly in the Anglo-Saxon world, where it animated a good number of the questions of analytic philosophy. In addition, in Germany it found a land of choice with Karl Jaspers and around the transcendental pragmatics of Habermas.

Is the current rediscovery of moral philosophy in France the symptom of a mere quivering withdrawal into the philosophical tradition, and does it announce a return of the moralism of long ago? It is not and does not, for here and elsewhere, returns do not exist. Moral philosophy goes back to and shifts the philosophical tradition essentially through the new examinations of analytic philosophy and phenomenology. In this regard, after personally undergoing the long eclipse of moral philosophy, Ricoeur is being justly rewarded with a spectacular increase in interest in his work; it places him in an all the more central position, as he is situated at the intersection of the Continental tradition, as an heir to the existentialism of Jaspers and Marcel, to the reflexive tradition of Nabert, to the phenomenology of Husserl, and to the Anglo-Saxon analytic tradition.

His philosophy, as a philosophy of acting, in fact constitutes the very object of this new moral philosophy in gestation, which concentrates its questioning on motivations, on the finalities of human action, and so on the forms of normativity it implies. It is, then, a matter of understanding "in what way an individual makes universal obligations her own."[21] This may allow an illumination of the current debates on medical ethics and many others, but the philosopher does not for all that intend to find a lost magister that would confer on him a mastering place of power thanks to its moral position. His objective remains modest; it is "to enlighten, sometimes to recommend, but in no case to prescribe."[22] The procedural ethics of discussion on the basis of universals has been carried to a high speculative level by Jean-Marc Ferry,[23] and the Collège de Philosophie in general, led by his brother Luc Ferry and Alain Renaut, has contributed much to ethical reflection in philosophy.

The renewal of moral questioning, just as tangible in the social sciences as in philosophy, enables one to institute, as we will see later on, new relations, more fruitful and less conflictual, between philosophers and specialists in the social sciences. At the articulation of phenomenology and cognitive science, Francisco Varela thus affirms the primordial character of ethics for a modern world that is prey to the uncertainties and disarray deriving from the discovery of the absence of foundations. "The realization of groundlessness as nonegocentric responsiveness . . . requires that we acknowledge the other with whom we dependently originate."[24]

Social interpellation through normativity is a sign of scientific effectiveness. When society calls on experts to rule on the social consequences of one scientific innovation or another, it is the sign of the importance accorded by the public powers to the sector that is asked to intervene. This is clearly the case in the areas of artificial intelligence, robotics, and molecular biology, which have thus acquired their status of mature sciences. Ethics therefore accompanies the scientific innovations that require a philosophical response as essential stakes of the social bond.

# Part VIII

## *Historicity*

*Twenty-eight*

# The Evenementalization of Meaning

The new attention of modern science to the notions of chaos, irreversibility, and the fractal has enabled a break with evolutionist determinism and an entry into a new form of temporality that privileges the event. This general context removes us from the time when Braudel was hunting "fireflies," the evenemental scum, which he consigned to the level of insignificance. The current political situation responds on this level, like an echo, to the current scientific situation with the radicality of evenemental discontinuities that render null and void any enclosure within explanatory schemata that saturated their meaning. The very idea of a contingent process excludes explanation and leads one to follow the evenemental framework, "each situation being both extension and reinvention."[1] Time becomes the leading strand with which the narration of the new is constructed.

This connection between the new scientific objectivity and the narrative register enables a departure from the objectivism of a causation that bound causality and its effect in a relation of reversible equivalence. "With the notion of the chaotic attractor, for example, the question is no longer that of opposing determinism and unforeseeability, but rather of attempting to understand why evolution is unforeseeable."[2] This new temporality, a product of the reflections on the discoveries of quantum physics and Ilya Prigogine's dissipative structures, has the effect of tracing an organic link between the arrow of time and its human dimension. "Movement as we conceive it today gives a thickness to the instant and articulates it as becoming. Each instantaneous 'state' is the memory of a past that allows only the definition of a limited future, marked off by the intrinsic temporal horizon."[3]

## The Time of Consciousness

The solidarity between the time of things and that of beings situates our contemporary relationship to temporality in close proximity with the Augustinian and then Husserlian conception of time.[4] The initial paradox that Saint Augustine puts forward is in asking how time can be, while the past is no more and the future is not yet. To this paradox is added another one, that of measuring what is not. Augustine finds a way out of this aporia in the valorization of a present that is found in an overarching position: "If future and past events exist, I want to know where they are. If I have not the strength to discover the answer, at least I know that wherever they are, they are not there as future or past, but as present."[5] So there are past and future only through a present. This is internal time, the memory that is the very foundation of time's arrow. This making-present situates time on the side of the speaker, of enunciation.

This psychological approach is later taken up in Husserl's phenomenological program, in the philosopher's concern with bringing out the meaning of internal consciousness, of intentionality, the "*immanent time* of the flow of consciousness."[6] To attempt to resolve the aporetic character of an internal time cut off from cosmological time, Husserl places the instant within a "longitudinal intentionality"[7] that allows one to find a connection with duration, as well as to establish a relation between the repetition of the same and the rise of the new.

This insertion of lived time into the definition of time also gives the present a preeminent place as a moment of remembering and a realization of remembered anticipations. It allows a conception of temporal unity. The event is a creator of actors and, as Isabelle Stengers says, of inheritors who speak in its name, interested in realizing the propagation of ideas or innovations carried by the discontinuity that it involves. "For its inheritors, the event effects a difference between the past and the future."[8] This constitutive bond between the event and its inheritors opens up the becoming of evenemental rupture to an original indeterminacy of its reach, which is no longer a priori but rather what the actors who will propagate its shock wave will make of it.

The event therefore involves a new temporality for the actors, brings on new practices. It cannot, therefore, shut away in its chrono-logical closure, take place as cause, because the inventors—whether Galileo, Newton, Boyle, or someone else—do not have the power to explain what follows. The proliferation of practices whose surfacing they have enabled will allow a measurement of the reach of the event that they incarnate. "The cause doesn't preexist its effects, but, on the contrary, the effects of the event are what will give it, will constitute for it an indefinitely proliferating status and, in some cases, a status of cause."[9]

## The Poietics of Time

The event therefore requires a new viewpoint, related to the way Paul Valéry defined the science of creative behaviors, poietics, to the Collège de France in 1937. René Passeron advocates this poietic approach to history, that is, the particular attention to creative activity as individual or collective singularity: "Who will deny that changes of conception in the sciences (including history), the arts, mores, religions, and philosophies are the result of the spark of an unforeseen event?"[10] If we are to believe the preface to his *Histoire de France,* it was in fact the flash of July 1830 that incited in Jules Michelet a passion for history in a quasi-Christlike sense. The required spark here is the one that causes breakage; it is situated on the side of risk, of the temporal crack, of the beginning of a new adventure. This evenementalization reopens the horizon of the future to unforeseeability. It introduces uncertainty in predictive projections: "Openness to future surprises introduces a gap into futurology."[11]

## Jewish Messianism

This discontinuist conception of history, which privileges the irre-ducible character of the event, leads to a questioning of the teleologi-cal vision of a historical Reason completing itself according to a speci-fied direction. Today, philosopher Alain Badiou advocates attention to evenementalization.[12] This attention echoes the reflection developed in Germany in the 1920s by Franz Rosenzweig, Walter Benjamin, and Gershom Sholem, with their idea of a time of today, discontinuous, outside progressive continuism and the idea of causality. What they have in common, as Stéphane Mosès has shown, is moving from a "time of necessity to a time of possibility."[13]

Jewish messianism, found in these three authors who were prey to the disappointments of the direct experience of their own time, escapes finalism to privilege the cracks in history. For Walter Benjamin, the aesthetic paradigm thus serves to define, among the various moments of time, a "link that is not a relation of causality."[14] Beginning from a discontinuous temporality, meaning is unveiled on the basis of a hermeneutic effort that strongly contributes to the course of the present, which finds itself in a prevalent situation, truly constitutive of the past. Only in the aftermath, in the trace, can one pretend to recapture a meaning that is not an a priori. "The aesthetic model of history questions the basic postulates of historicism: the continuity of historical time, the causality governing the chain of events between the past and the present and between the present and the future."[15]

This creativist approach to history implies a renewed questioning of the distance instituted by most historiographical traditions between a dead past and the historian charged with objectifying it. On the contrary, history is to be re-created, and the historian is the mediator, the conductor of this re-creation. History is achieved in the very effort of the hermeneut who reads the real as a writing whose meaning shifts in the course of time as a function of the various phases of actualization of the real. The object of history, then, is a construction forever reopened by this writing.

History is therefore first of all evenementality as inscription in a present that confers on it an actuality, ever new because situated in a singular configuration. Walter Benjamin already saw in historicism the mere transposition of a model borrowed from mechanical causality, in which the cause of an effect is sought in the position of immediate anteriority on the temporal chain. To this scientist model Benjamin opposed a "hermeneutic model, tending toward the interpretation of events—that is, toward the illumination of their meaning."[16] The evenementality that is returning is therefore not that of the methodical-positivist school of the nineteenth century, of history-as-battle that of course has more virtues than the demonized image of it left by the *Annales,* but whose entirely indispensable labor of internal and external source criticism was indeed limited to a purely factual summary.

## The End of Cold History

The current orientation is quite different, as it privileges the reading of these sources on the level of their signifiance,[17] and in this regard "all history is to be rewritten as a function of this. The sources speak to us differently."[18] The fact is examined in the trace of meaning, as Georges Duby exemplified it in relation to the famous battle of Bouvines.[19] So Fernand Braudel was wrong to wish to enclose the event within the short period. He denounced the "delusive smoke"[20] of the event and affirmed that "social science has almost what amounts to a horror of the event. And not without some justification, for the short time span is the most capricious and the most delusive of all."[21] On the contrary, the long period, set up as structural causality, offered itself as an infrastructure whose core was located in geohistory, a history with a geological rhythm, progressively evacuating the human dimension.

This tendency to the repression of the event was accentuated in the 1960s with Braudel's direct heirs. Emmanuel Le Roy Ladurie no longer spoke then of a quasi-immobile history, but of an immobile history. "The [Annales] school is like the societies it studies: it takes its time. It views its own life-span within the long-term context of the century. . . . And . . . it . . . displays a rather remarkable indifference to what is happening on the surface."[22]

Even if he saw no contradiction between these great socles of cold history and his own epistemological prejudice in favor of a discontinuist conception of the history of science borrowed from Bachelard and Canguilhem, Michel Foucault greatly contributed to the return of evenementality. His radical critique of all continuist temporality, of all absolutization and naturalization of values, enabled him to develop an attention to the caesuras in discursive space between epistémēs separated by fault lines that no longer allowed a reconnection of false constancies or illusory permanencies. "Necessarily, we must dismiss those tendencies that encourage the consoling play of recognitions."[23]

Foucault called himself a "happy" positivist, practicing the Nietzschean avoidance of research in terms of causality or origin and instead examining the discontinuities, the description of material positivities, the singularity of the event: " 'Effective' history . . . deals with events in terms of their most unique characteristics, their most acute manifestations."[24]

## Under Fire from the Media

Among historians, against the current of the vogue for the long period, Pierre Nora announced very early on, in 1972, the "return of the event."[25] He perceived this "return," which had the old-fashioned scent of the old generation of positivist historians, through the angle of the media. To be is to be perceived—and with this, the various media became master to the point of holding a monopoly on the production of events. In the Dreyfus Affair, Nora thus discerned the first event in the modern sense, which owed everything to the press.

An affair of the mass media, the contemporary event is quickly involved with the fluff media, which create out of nothing a sensitivity to current events and give it the sensation of historicity. Some of these contemporary events are perceived auditorily (the barricades of May 1968, General de Gaulle's speech on May 30, 1968), others are links to the image (the invasion of Prague, the Apollo moon landing, the oppression at Tiananmen Square). "The mass media have thus made history an aggression and rendered the event a monstrosity."[26] The immediacy makes deciphering the event easier, because it strikes with one blow, and more difficult, because it delivers everything with one blow. This paradoxical situation requires, according to Nora, a deconstruction of the event, which the historian must undertake in order to grasp how the media produce the event.

## The Oversignified Event

Between its dissolution and its exaltation, according to Ricoeur, the event undergoes a metamorphosis resulting from its hermeneutic renewal. Reconciling the continuist and discontinuist approaches, Ricoeur proposes that one distinguish three levels of approach to the event: "(1) an infrasignificant event; (2) the order and reign of meaning, ultimately nonevenemental; (3) the emergence of suprasignificant, oversignifying events."[27] The first use simply corresponds to describing "what happens" and evokes surprise, the new relation to what is instituted. It also corresponds with the orientations of the methodical school of Langlois and Seignobos, that of the establishment of source criticism.

In the second place, the event is held within explanatory schemes that correlate it with regularities, laws. This second moment tends to subsume the singularity of the event under the register of the law from which it springs, to the point of being at the limits of the negation of the event. Here we may recognize the orientation of the *Annales*. At this second stage of analysis, there must follow a third, interpretive moment renewing the event as emergence, but this time oversignified. The event is then an integral part of a narrative construction that constitutes a founding identity (the storming of the Bastille) or negative identity (Auschwitz). The event that returns is therefore not the same as the one reduced by explanatory meaning, and not the undersignified one that was outside discourse. It alone engenders meaning. "This salutary recovery of the *oversignified event* prospers only at the limits of meaning, at the point where it fails both through excess and through failure: an excess of arrogance and a failure to grasp."[28]

## The Aftermath

From this active relation between present and past, there results a possible involvement between the discipline of history and psychoanalysis. As Conrad Stein has shown, the psychoanalytic cure has the paradoxical aim of changing the past.[29] This is just as impossible for the historian, forever cut off from the past by an unsealable breach—that which holds the living and the dead generations in opposition—as for the psychoanalyst, who runs into the analyzing subject's structure of incompleteness.

There are similarities between the two procedures on the level of the place of the event for both the historian and the psychoanalyst. For the latter, the event is not reducible to an external traumatism. "Trauma should not be defined merely as an external event, as violent or trying as it may be, but rather as the tie between internal and external peril, between present and past."[30] In Freud, the trauma is an aftermath; it involves the past incorporated in the present, cleared paths, cross-checking. The task of the analyst is therefore to hold the two ends of the signifying chain outside simplistic determinisms.

The historian and the analyst are both faced with the same impasse. They can revive the past only through the mediation of its traces. It is just as impossible for the analyst to gain access to the real as it is for the historian to revive the reality of the past. They must both take into account external reality as well is its internal impact in attempting to approach their respective objects. For her part, the historian still has to learn from the analyst the fundamentally split character of the human being, and therefore the latter's incapacity to master his consciousness. From Freud's experiments she may draw the lesson of a procedure that privileges the unexpected character of discovery, the dazzle of the incidental idea. "The place that is then offered to us is Freud's theoretical imaginary: like the fantasy for the individual, this imaginary gives the lines of force in thought, indicates its requirements, and pushes into the field of narrative the metaphors designated to account for the labor of thought."[31] As for the psycho-analyst, he must cease to believe in the existence of transhistorical cate-gories. Jean-Pierre Vernant shows this very well by reminding Pierre Kahn that the ancient subject is very different from the modern one. Self-consciousness in antiquity is not yet that of an "I," but passes through a "He."[32]

## Fixing the Event

Events are discernible only by their traces, discursive or not. Without reducing the historical real to the sole dimension of language, we can say that fixing the event, crystallizing it, is effected through naming it. Gérard Noiriel's research on the construction of national identity shows this, in a nonessentialist perspective. "I work mainly in that perspective—on the social question of designation, or recording, which gives way to potential reuses."[33] Thus, he observes, with regard to immigration, that social phenomena may exist without for all that having attained a visibility. During the Second Empire, France already counted more than a million immigrants, who, according to Frédéric Le Play's studies, were easily assimilated into the regions of France without being perceived as immigrants. Only in the 1880s does the word *immigrant* attain its true fortune, become fixed as an event, laden with subsequent consequences. Therefore, a very essential relation is constituted between language and event, which today is broadly taken into account and problematized by the currents of ethnomethodology, interactionism, and, of course, the hermeneutic approach.

All these currents contribute to casting the foundation of a histori-cal semantics. The latter takes into consideration the sphere of acting, and breaks with the physicalist and causalist conceptions. The consti-tution of the event is, as we have seen with Paul Ricoeur, a part of its emplotment. It is the mediation that assures the materialization of the meaning of the human experience of time "at the following three levels: its *practical prefiguration,* its *epistemic configuration,* and its *hermeneutic reconfiguration.*"[34] Emplotment plays the role of opera-tor, of a relation of heterogeneous events. It is substituted for the causalist relation of physicalist explanation.

The hermeneutics of historical consciousness situates the event in an internal tension between two metahistorical categories that Koselleck gauges, the space of experience and the horizon of expecta-tion: "This then is a matter of epistemological categories which assist in the foundation of the possibility of a history."[35] These two categories permit a thematization of the historical time that can be read in concrete experience, with shifts of signification such as that of the progressive dissociation between experience and expectation in the modern Western world. The meaning of the event, according to Koselleck, is therefore constitutive of an anthropological structure of the temporal experience and of historically instituted symbolic forms. Koselleck, then, develops a "problematic of the individuation of events that places their identity under the auspices of temporalization, action, and dynamic individuality."[36] He targets a deeper level than that of mere description by examining the conditions of possibility of evenementality. His approach has the merit of showing the workability of historical concepts, their capacity to structure and to be structured by singular situations.

These concepts, which support experience and expectation, are not mere epiphenomena of language to be opposed to "true" history; they have "their own mode of existence within the language. It is on this basis that they affect or react to particular situations and occurrences."[37] The concepts are neither reducible to some rhetorical figure nor mere equipment to be classified by category. They are anchored in the field of experience in which they are born in order to subsume a multiplicity of significations. Can one then affirm that these concepts succeed in saturating the meaning of history to the point of allowing a total fusion between history and language? Like Paul Ricoeur, Koselleck does not go that far, and, on the contrary, holds that historical processes are not limited to their discursive dimension: "history is never identical with its linguistic registration and formulated experience."[38] It is, as Ricoeur thinks, the practical field that is the final rooting of the activity of temporalization.

## The Spokespersons

An example of the fecundity of this new approach to the evenemental trace, recaptured through a configurational procedure along the lines of Norbert Elias's work, is manifest in the studies of Jacques Guilhaumou, a historian with the journal *Raisons pratiques*. A linguist as well as a historian, he participated in the project of discourse analysis of the Pêcheux group in the early 1980s. At the time, it was a question of analyzing the political discourses constituted by parties and associations.

This linguistic opening was there only to confirm or deny certain hypotheses regarding a valid historical knowledge.

Guilhaumou was suddenly distanced from this orientation, having chosen to work on the discourse of the newspaper Le Père Duchesne from the time of the French Revolution—a burlesque discourse, outside the apparatuses. Next, he introduced the idea of the archive, "which caused the enclosure of the corpus, the relation to doctrinaire discourse, to burst."[39] Guilhaumou shows that, from the moment one works on the archive, one can no longer restrict oneself to the judgment of the historian; it is then necessary to examine the degrees of reflexivity of discourse.

Today, the system of reading archives that he has undertaken takes both actors and evenementality seriously. This has been the case since late 1985, when he was working on the death of Jean-Paul Marat.[40] On the occasion of the bicentennial of the French Revolution, he published a study on Marseilles from 1791 to 1793, done from the departmental archives.[41] He showed that in Provence, Republican partisanship was connected with the federalist experience. In 1792, Marseilles appears as an island of Republicanism within a Provence that was essentially royalist. Attention to the archive led Guilhaumou to follow step by step the extraordinary adventure of two young Republicans from Marseilles, Isoard and Tourneau, who succeeded in bringing down the royalist city of Sisteron by creating around sixty popular societies in around forty days, without arms, without combat—with only the argument of the expression of the "people armed with the Constitution": "The act of having the law speak is at the very center of the activity of the 'patriot missionaries.' It allowed, through its multiple concretizations, the formation of a public space consistent with the Constitution."[42] What interests Guilhaumou is showing how the spokespersons, the intermediaries, legitimate themselves as actors and themselves elaborate their own practical reason even within the event.

This shift of evenementality to its trace and its inheritors has incited a true return of the discipline of history to itself, within what one might term the hermeneutic circle or the historiographical turn. This new moment invites us to follow the metamorphoses of meaning in the successive mutations and slippages of the historian's writing, between the event itself and the present position. The historian then examines the various modalities of the creation and perception of the event on the basis of its textual frame.

This movement, which leads to revisiting the past through the writing of history, accompanies the exhumation of national memory and still confirms the current memorial moment. Through the renewal of historiography and memory, historians take on the task of mourning a past in itself and bring their contribution to the current reflexive and interpretive effort in the social sciences.

# Twenty-nine

# Situated Action

The attempt to surpass the alternative between the valorization of structures and that of events is well under way, thanks to the discovery of intellectual means allowing one to abandon those artificial splits that have until now inspired the social sciences. This is the whole direction of the research in progress on the meaning of appearance, linked to the realm of acting.

A microsociology of action explores this field of the historicity of the everyday. The connection to the question of time in sociological research came into favor when the question of the organization of the experience of everyday life was asked anew. This is particularly the case with the efforts of Louis Quéré, who has been strongly inspired in this area by the work of the American pragmatist George Herbert Mead.[1] Mead's work has enabled Quéré to make the link between the temporalization and the organization of action. Mead shows in fact that the nature of the past does not exist in itself, but that it remains a strong contributor to the relation maintained with the present. The emergence of the present always gives rise to new pasts, and so makes the past totally relative to the present.

In Mead, this relativization of the past and the primacy accorded to the present in its restoration are based "on a central notion, that of the event."[2] It is around the event itself as situated action that the structuration of time operates. The event, by its very discontinuity with respect to what precedes it, binds one to the distinction and articulation of the notions of past and future.

Mead's pragmatic perspective led him to view this temporalization as an essential component of action. He gives the example of what might be represented by the evocation of our childhood as it might have been lived—not as a past relative to our present, but as a past cut off from its future. This would have no other interest than an exotic one. This aporia demonstrates that "the reality of what the past, present, and future are is made up of praxeological dimensions to designate involvement in action."[3]

## The Tradition Revived

The second source of inspiration for this new sociology of action in its relation with temporality, evenementality, is hermeneutics, which has emphasized the eminently historical character of human experience: "Time is no longer primarily a gulf to be bridged, because it separates, but it is actually the supportive ground of process (*Geschehen*) in which the present is rooted. Hence temporal distance is not something that must be overcome. . . . In fact the important thing is to recognize the distance in time as a positive and productive possibility of understanding."[4] Contrary to the objectivist conception, it is belonging to a tradition that makes understanding possible, and not merely the objectifying scientistic posture.

Besides, the hermeneutic project does not view historical distance as a handicap, but on the contrary as an asset that facilitates historical cognition, because it enables us, thanks to the work of deciphering and interpreting what has happened between the event itself and the present from which we study, to enrich our understanding.

The hermeneutic dimension, which gives new life to tradition and access to a deeper understanding of the past, was a genuine discovery for the sociologists of Louis Quéré's generation. It offered a contrast to the epistemological discourse conducted in the social sciences in general, which conceived of their regime of scientificity in terms of an epistemological break, of the researcher's disengagement as the source of the necessary objectification.

Another suggestive dimension of hermeneutics is its very particular attention to language, to a semantics of action. "But tradition is not simply a process . . . ; it is language."[5] The role of language in experience is not reducible to the domain of representations; it is an integral part of reality, constitutive of it, and a factor in historicity. Social and political concepts incorporate a temporal dimension, as Koselleck has shown.

## A Progressive Unveiling of Meaning

On the basis of these sources of information, Louis Quéré advocates developing new categorial inquiries into time. For a sociologist, the latter are not only speculative but also empirical. They aim to "apprehend the social world within the structures of experience. This is a point of view that has been very strongly defended by the ethnomethodological current, which, for me, is a form of phenomenology."[6]

On this level, phenomenology is a source of two new aspects of the apprehension of evenementality. In the first place, it enables a consideration of time as constitutive of the identity and meaning of the event. The unveiling of meaning occurs only progressively, over the course of time, which confers on it an identity in gestation. So there is not a meaning of the event that would be given once and for all when it occurs. "We can reopen the proceedings of identification and the attribution of meaning to the event."[7] In the second place, the phenomenon of communication, of "working speech," as Merleau-Ponty puts it, is also essentially a phenomenon of temporalization. "Expression itself assumes a process of constitution of a past and a future that are intertwined with each other."[8]

On the basis of these multiple sources of inspiration, Quéré has envisaged the concrete study of the event constituting itself as a public event. Attentive to the social construction of the event, he then begins with the presupposition that the identity, the signification, of the event in the process of manifesting itself is not constituted a priori, but responds to an emergent process that is constructed in duration: "It's a temporal process, not an instantaneous one."[9] Of course, the identity of the event ends up by stabilizing, but without ever becoming saturated, remaining open to continually renewed interpretations.

From this perspective, Quéré has worked on the desecration of the Carpentras cemetery. This event has particularly held his attention, for, "depending on the description given of it, it is inscribed in absolutely different semantic fields. Each semantic field is open to different explanations and completely different possibilities of emplotment."[10] In fact, if this act is defined as a desecration, it affects a religious community. If it is attested as an anti-Semitic act, it has a different bearing and calls for a response of another scale. If it is only the morbid manifestation of a macabre game of young misfits, it belongs to yet another register of possible responses.

Quéré has also worked on suburban issues, notably those involving the incidents of Vaulx-en-Velin in 1990–91. It was a matter of understanding by what mechanisms a motorbike accident involving violent demonstrations became a thematized public event that posed the social question of the suburbs: "What is it about play that this event gains access to the public scene?"[11]

The empirical study of these events illustrates the way they are involved with a process of construction. They are very quickly brought back to the attempt at typology through which a "causal texture"[12] is constructed, thanks to a return of causalities and effects, between a before and an after, to a temporal situation. According to the selection effected by the event itself, a field of experience and a horizon of expectation are mobilized, very specific to the event.

Besides, the event is associated with a practical field, with a problematic field that involves one community of citizens or another. So it is not seen "in a situation of contemplation, of disengaged observation."[13] The public event derives from a particular register, that of the public action articulated around real or virtual collective entities. "This is Michel de Certeau's idea, according to which narratives move ahead of practices in order to open up a field for them."[14] The event does not depend on just any narrative; on this level, it undergoes the strong determination of situated action, of the context that limits its identification. In the last instance, it contributes to the description of the event that defines its identity on the basis of the semantic constraints proper to the context of its emergence.

## Reflexive Elaboration

Max Weber analyzed the loss of all foundation of an ontological order in modern society; Weber's diagnosis comes down to observing the loss of a federating common sense, the disenchantment of a world with plural values that has lost the religious source on which its political authority was based. Atomization and individualization have progressed together, with a rationalization that disenchants and desacralizes the religious images of the world. There results a loss of substance and understanding of representations.

This Weberian observation does not ineluctably imply the diagnosis made of the current conjuncture as an era of emptiness.[15] On the contrary, with Jean-Marc Ferry one may consider this labor of Reason's dissolution as leading to a "reflexive elaboration that formalizes Reason without for all that being a synonym of vacuousness. Meaning is certainly less visible, much less substantial, palpable, and tangible, but that doesn't mean it's empty."[16] Meaning is to be recaptured, says Ferry, thanks to its new placement in a contextual situation. It appeals, therefore, to the resources of pragmatism. The formation of common sense, of processes of agreement and mutual understanding, defines the singularity of situations according to the communicative process.

It is by recognizing the contextuality of the resources of meaning, the chains of pertinence that allow agreement in a situation, that one may restore the meaning of an action. These are procedures that, beyond their formal character, are bearers of a substantial common sense. "There is something substantial that allows one to begin from a contextual basis to elaborate formations of compromise and consensus."[17]

But, in many cases, there is an incommensurability of argumentative positions, as in the difficult debates of bioethics when it is a matter of seizing on a position common to the participants in a commission whose anthropological, ethical, and religious anchorings are totally different. In this case, consensus may be achieved only at the moment when each decides to defer her resources of semantic content of argumentation in order to substitute for them—or rather articulate them with—rules and pragmatic procedures.

Such a slippage appeals to an ethic of responsibility whose object is agreement on the procedural conditions of the formation of consensual contents. This pragmatic shift "consists of considering the price of the renunciation of the valorization of one's own positions, compared with the frustrations that would be imposed on the other if you imposed your positions."[18] It is then no longer a matter of a rationality directed toward the ego, but of a decentered calculation that takes the detour of considering the position of others. The meaning that then results is a mixture between the good and the just, thanks to a decentered ethic of responsibility.

## Popper's Logic of Situations

As Raymond Aron said, "We must accord to the past the uncertainty of the future." Such a defatalization leads the historian to come back to singular situations in order to attempt to explain them without presupposing an a priori determinism. This is the procedure advocated by the philosopher Alain Boyer, a member of the CREA. He supports his radical critique of positivism through the works of Weber and Popper along several axes. In the first place, and in opposition to positivism, he holds that what is not scientific is not for all that stripped of meaning, and that observable reality does not cover all of the real, which is woven of shadow zones. Faced with the inductivist model of positivism, Boyer opposes the "Popperian hypothesis of the primacy of theory over experience, which nonetheless conserves a crucial role that consists of testing the hypotheses."[19]

Contrary to the thesis developed by Jean-Claude Passeron, according to which the Popperian paradigm defines only a space proper to the natural sciences, Boyer holds that there is no Popperian scientific model. The latter corresponds only to the aspiration to establish a scientific institution based on a critical rationalism, in which debates and controversies may be settled. The only point of agreement between Popper's positions and those of positivism are situated in the defense of a common epistemology of science. "But this unity is considered only from a methodological point of view, not from an ontological point of view."[20]

What Boyer retains from Popper's analysis in the area of evenementality is the latter's attention to the logic of situations. The historian must pose the problem of the nature of the environment of the agents' problems at a given moment, and this enables him to give explanatory hypotheses of actions in terms of the attempts at solution under constraint: "The objective of situational analysis is the explanation of human behavior as a set of attempts at solutions to problems."[21]

This situational analysis presents itself as a generalized ecology with the objective of constructing a theory of decisions. It presupposes a postulation that the agents determine themselves in a rational manner—not that their action refers to Reason, but more simply that it is "directed toward a goal."[22] The notion of situation does not function as a determinism; it does not refer to any fixity. Thus, the same mountain will be perceived differently and even contradictorily by the tourist, the Alpinist, the military person, or the farmer. Besides, the situational constraints on human action are more or less strong. The more society is open, as Popper has shown, the more individual dispositions may be deployed within a broad field of possibilities.[23] This indeterminacy is quite essential in conceiving several possibilities in the choices of the agents of history. "Explaining a historical situation comes down to displaying its potentialities and explaining why the dispositions of the agents have led them to act in such a manner that certain consequences of their actions have transformed the situations in a way they could not foresee."[24] Such an approach, then, implies a break with the current forms of determinism.

The Popperian approach impugns all theodicy or sociodicy, and therefore any form of historicism that would presuppose the deployment of historical laws in history. Here Popper is aiming for an essentialist conception of historical explanation by which the historian could reach "self-explanatory descriptions of an essence."[25] For these laws that pretend to subsume historical situations, Boyer substitutes an attention to the long-neglected notion of intentionality.

## The Sphere of Possibilities

The studies of Jon Elster[26] and Philippe Van Parijs[27] in this area enable one to ask the complex question of individual rationality, of intentionality. It is fitting to rediscover the sphere of possibilities in the past so as to clarify the reasons that led to the choice of a certain direction. The constraints that weigh on action first bear on the situation that makes it possible or not, and this is the structural constraint. In the second place, the rules, the norms or conventions, orient the choice of the actors. The sociology of Elster and Van Parijs offers the interest of introducing a third filter, that of rational choice, of the motivation of the actors. The intentional horizon makes it possible to account for the notion of the unexpected effect and thereby to avoid the pitfall of psychologism. On this level, we also find the function that Popper accords to the theoretical social science whose primary objective would be to "determine the unintentional social repercussions of intentional human actions."[28]

One can, in fact, multiply the unexpected cases. So it is with self-fulfilling prophecies. Already in 1936, Robert King Merton showed how the attitude of American unions, which impeded the hiring of black workers on the pretext that they had a tendency to break strikes, had the perverse effect that, jobless, these black workers effectively became what the unions wanted to avoid. "This is the most famous self-fulfilling prophecy. Popper more elegantly calls it the 'Oedipus effect.'"[29]

More frequently, one may also have what is called the Cournot effect—that is, the fortuitous encounter of several independent causal series that provoke an unexpected effect.[30] This type of chance is a matter of a purely descriptive approach, as one may only notice the contingent fact without being able to reconnect it with some causal system or human reason in order to explain it.

## The Time of the Project

This situationalist approach is also very pregnant in cognitive science, which relates its investigations to what amounts to situated rationality. This theme contributes to reinvigorating the question of temporality, all too often removed from the cognitive perspective. Jean-Pierre Dupuy thus demonstrates that rational choice in the broad sense and the paradoxes it comes up against reveal, in spite of themselves, the existence of a double temporality.

Most commonly, one relies on a metaphysical principle of the fixity of the past in relation to free action, as one may find it in the principle of rationality that Maurice Allais deploys, according to which "only the future counts." But, most often, the actors contravene this principle, which would then have no claim to universal validity.

Dupuy therefore distinguishes two forms of rationality, irreducible to one another, which derive from two different conceptions of time.[31] These two modes of temporality differ on the question of the nature of the past. On the one hand, its fixity seems to constitute the very essence of rationality. Dupuy terms this temporality the "time of history"—somewhat abusively, for if this consequentialist relation that defines a past as a fixed object and a future as open corresponds well to a moment of production and definition of the historian's trade, the latter has for a long time not been based on such a dichotomy. In comparison to this fixity of the past, Dupuy defends the thesis that the human being has the experience of another temporality, which he terms the "time of the project." The latter has a demiurgical character and is open to a more paradoxical temporality, to the point that it has usually been situated on the side of irrationality. The actor is placed in a location of exteriority with respect to himself in order to endow himself with a power over his past based on a "retrograde reasoning through the horizon" (backwards induction). Dupuy defines this time of the project as a properly human apprehension of temporality. It enables one to find an articulation between rationality and the ethical horizon of acting.

On the basis of this link, one can detect a rationality in social practices that would be termed irrational manifestations with regard to the traditional conception of temporality. According to this conception, it is in effect irrational on the level of the individual to go to vote in a modern democracy, because the probability of bringing a change in the course of the polling by one's own vote is infinitesimal. This "paradox of the vote" may not be resolved within the causalist paradigm. Only the ethical reflex and a temporality of the project make it possible to conceive of the attitude of the electors as deriving from a different temporality, termed "evidentialist" reasoning.[32]

## A Surface Temporality

The temporality induced by the study of situated action is most often a short temporality in the current studies, which are in the tradition of interactionism and ethnomethodology. The plasticity assumed in the model of the competency of the actors implies a use of short sequences of observation. It is the means to bring all necessary attention to bear on the changes of level by which one passes from one situation to another. The pertinent temporality from Boltanski and Thévenot's model[33] is extended so that these changes may be conceived. It contains a surface temporality corresponding to the declared motives of action and a deep temporality that defines the dispositions, the competencies of the actor, located on an unconscious level of action.

This model accords such a privilege to the situation that it has a tendency to forget historical rooting. "It's not a position of rejection with regard to history, not at all";[34] rather, it corresponds to a refusal of a history that would substitute for an analytic effort. Now, on this level, Boltanski and Thévenot examine the analytic categories of history so as better to understand how time is inserted within the collective artifacts of action. "One might say that we are then only interested in the instant, since we ask how the past may function as a reference."[35]

Forgetting history therefore becomes a necessary methodological moment in valorizing the perceptible mutations and in refraining from presupposing artificial fixities. But it still remains to articulate and redistribute the various types of temporality. The latter are not postulated; they are mediated by the deployment of narrative, by the justifications of the persons engaged in the present. In addition, the model of the Cities revisits the tradition, not in a historicist perspective, but in order to "make the tie between a tradition of texts and a pragmatics of judgment."[36] In this area, the sociology of action articulates its studies on what Gadamer calls the "historical-effective."[37] It also has, for Gadamer, the very structure of experience.

The economists of convention also participate in the reflection on the various modes of temporality. Contrary to the economists of the standard model, for whom historicity has no status because at any moment the individual may in full freedom make a choice that seems preferable, the economists of convention have deepened the reflection on the role of historicity in the fabrication of irreversible situations, of stabilized institutional configurations.

They have brought to light formalized models, such as that of "path dependency" or the notion of "little events." These notions enable them to reconcile the unexpected, the contingent, the irreversibilities, with the fabrication of stabilized configurations. "From this point of view, the economics of technical change has brought something very interesting by showing the role played by technical choices in what the economists call 'locked situations.'"[38] The technical choices made without concert end up by fabricating, through their proper dynamic, irreversibilities that predetermine subsequent behaviors. Without a linear bond of interaction between two moments of decision, it is the very logic of technical choices that most often influences the choices that will follow. So observation and description of what happens become the most appropriate form of accounting for the concrete effects of this situational logic, as is shown by Michel Callon's studies on technological innovation.

Here, where the orientation of the anthropology of science is removed from the economists of convention and the CREA, it is deeming that there is no need to elaborate a theory of the transposable actor that permits a qualification of all situations and all forms of interaction. "This dialectic of opening, of diversity, of irreversibility leads to the idea that there is not a model of the actor but rather a model of action."[39] In this regard, it would be fitting to distinguish the majority of the situations in which the actors would follow only behaviors that are essentially preinscribed in their material environment and other situations in which the actors play a more elaborate role of elaboration, arbitration.

Competency may therefore be situated on the side of the situation or on the side of the actor; and this enables one to surmount the false alternative generally posed between structure and actor, as indeed they adjust to one another: "And this is not the same thing as the situation in which each of the elements is known by way of a fixed ontology."[40]

## A Situated Rationality

One of the postulates of the economists of convention is that of a dynamic, of a process to recapture, in the various constitutive and deconstructive modalities, the various coordinations of action. "The forms of coordination are articulated in time according to three modes: simultaneity, succession, and confrontation."[41] The economists of convention also prefer the notion of situated rationality to that of limited rationality, which presupposes a model of perfect rationality of which it would be only the incomplete realization: "In reality, there is no perfect rationality. There are only rationalities under construction."[42]

Deprived of a theory of situation, of context, the economists of convention have turned to analytic philosophy, to cognitive science, in order to find the bases of a semantics of situations—no longer situating it within a causal chain, but perceiving it as the source of its own intelligibility: "I believe in the sociocognitive interpretation of the French Revolution."[43]

This interpretive effort valorizes the notion of situation, that of actor. The event engenders its own representation, which becomes an indissociable part of it; and this presupposes a shift of cognitive competency, hitherto the monopoly of the historian himself, by restoring it to the protagonists, without for all that stopping at this interpretive stratum that remains open to the becoming of other subsequent representations.

This rootedness in the very situation of operative concepts enables the historical sciences to distinguish a specific epistemology that does not concern the discipline of history alone. Thus, Jean-Claude Passeron defines three types of epistemology: "There is the formal archetype of logic and mathematics; the archetype of experimental research; and the archetype of historical research, which I say is our issue."[44] An anchoring in historical contexts, in singular configurations, defines the singularity of sciences that can only illusorily aim to construct transhistorical modelizations, nomological assertions. This specificity does not for all that reduce these sciences to empiricism. As Weber has shown, they study the real thanks to the mediation of ideal types, of conceptualizations. Meanwhile, these concepts, as we have already noted, are proper seminouns. The generalizing explanations that these historical sciences advance "can never lose sight of the fact that the assertory validity of their reasoning always rests on singular and irreplaceable developments."[45]

The prevalence of the lived experience of temporality, of the attention to the rise of the new, is also found in Francisco Varela's theory of enaction, whose privileged object, as with Husserl, is the cognitive present, emergent processes, on the basis of a new theorization of situated action.

This instant, this present, is to be relinked, says Pierre Lévy, with the very historicity of our techniques of communication, which today is giving birth to a prevalence of "real time," tied to a cognitive ecology that belongs to the progressive computerization of communication. The latter allows one to envision a new type of temporality, that of a "real time, without relation to a before or an after, immediate and interactive."[46] This notion of real time provokes a condensation on the present, a presentification. "One may speak of a sort of chronological implosion, of a punctual time instituted by computer networks."[47] This returning present is not the purely psychological, individual, and intimate present of Saint Augustine, but a social, interactive intimate time that serves to coordinate individuals, who are producers of a collective intelligence.

The event-situation pair is therefore fundamental in this new configuration, mediated by individuals who give meaning to the event at the same time as they incite it. This reconstruction in the act itself shifts the center of gravity of subjectivity toward intersubjectivity, and invites us to take stock of the pragmatic turn in the apprehension of the notion of historicity.

# Thirty

# The Political

The political as a horizon of analysis has had a paradoxical destiny. In the sixties and seventies, it was agreed that everything was political according to a radical critique carried out by a philosophy of suspicion, which enabled one to release and unleash the scientific from underneath its ideologico-political gangue. Nevertheless, at the time when the political was everywhere, it was above all nowhere, having lost its autonomy. It was reduced, in the name of class interests or libidinal phantasms, to being only the veil without thickness of an always hidden truth, forever outside consciousness. It was the moment when, for the *Annales* school of history and in the tradition of its founding masters, the history of the political was assimilated to mere chronicle without the signification of a battle history, which François Simiand had banished from the territory of science when, in 1903, he denounced the three idols of the historian's tribe: biography, chronology, and . . . politics.[1] So the political was everywhere, polyformal, polymorphous. With Michel Foucault's concept of power, it was in everyone, and so nowhere, unassignable, without autonomy.

We have been witnessing a spectacular renaissance since the 1980s. It was manifest with the publication of the first issue of the journal *Le Débat* in 1980, which bore the subtitle "History, Politics, Society." This resurgence is concomitant with the global turn of the social sciences, which have begun to examine the "reflected role of human action."[2] The relativization of the role of the unconscious, which had

been the royal road of access to the truth for structuralism, and the rehabilitation of the explicit role of action have put back in the saddle a
political horizon that had been cast as the most old-fashioned, obso-
lete part of analysis in the social sciences.

This does not mean that prior to this shift there was no profound
political reflection. Such reflection was especially the case, in the area
of political philosophy, of the studies in the Socialism or Barbarism
current of Cornelius Castoriadis and Claude Lefort, in which the to-
talitarian phenomenon was analyzed. It is significant that Alain Caillé,
today denouncing the abdication of the clerics, the scholars, in *La
Démission des clercs*[3] for their forgetting of politics, dedicated his
book to Lefort. This dedication is less a remembrance of his former
teacher than the homage to the one who was able not to desert the
field of investigation of the political as such, as the publication of his
*Democracy and Political Theory* attests.[4]

The condemnation of totalitarianism had the perverse effect of
condemning any form of innovation, of voluntarism, and of taking
politics as a whole down with it. The originality of Lefort's thought
consisted of deepening his critique of totalitarianism by preserving the
political, the interrogation of the new, shifting the problematization to
"what came into being with the formation and development of modern democracy."[5] The political, reattached to a historical sensibility
and to an attention to the way it may impregnate social acting, enables a detection of the "symbolic dimension of the social."[6] It again
becomes a source of reflection on our present.

## The Disentanglement of the Religious and the Political

It is in the process of disentangling the political and the religious that
analysis must direct its attention to seizing the articulations and disar-
ticulations of the relation between these two levels. Now, the totalitar-
ian enterprise provokes a new investigation of the relation between
the religious and the political.[7] Power in modern democracy is defined, according to Claude Lefort, by an unexpected "shaping." It
turns out to be a system of representation that attests to the existence
of an empty place that maintains the "impossibility of precipitating
the symbolic into the real."[8] It is the only system to bring society to
the test of its institution, insofar as it cannot incarnate the empty and
central place, this necessary gap.

This relation of disentanglement between the political and the religious has been one of Marcel Gauchet's privileged objects of analysis. In it he sees the very singularity of the modern West. Gauchet takes his study back to the early times of Christianity, whose revolutionary vocation, bearer of our Western singularity, was to assure the break with immanence, thereby permitting the liberation of the political. Hence, "will Christianity be the religion of the abandonment of religion?"[9] Gauchet has applied himself to gauging the discontinuities and the reformulations that they imply in the relation between the political and the religious. The West knows a twofold process of reduction of alterity and of promotion of interiority with Christianity, which assures the passage from the immanence that assumed a split with the foundation to the transcendence that approaches and makes the foundation accessible. This mutation may be gauged by the new relation with temporality. It enables the "leap from the past to the present"[10] by reuniting the original and the actual thanks to the idea of creation. Divine transcendence frees, for its part, the human community delivered to itself, reunited around an absence, around a pure symbolic place. This separation enables the progressive autonomization of the political body.

The political will take charge of the question of the social bond and of the relations with nature. Gauchet therefore accords a prevalent place to the political, which is nonetheless not that of determination in the last instance, but rather the possible place of a globalization of the intelligibility of the social, of a reprise of meaning. "Political history won't be global history in the sense that it would exercise a sort of imperialism. It's a matter of constructing a theory of coherency."[11]

There is no question, therefore, of substituting a political causality for an economic causality, long used in a mechanical way, but rather of restoring this immanent coherence to social formation through the political. It is this "bringing into form" of the social by the political that Claude Lefort speaks of, that Gauchet explores with his notion of "bringing to coherency" in order to mean that he does not attribute any determined place to it.

The political, then, is at a level that is at once the most encompassing and the most concealed. In effect, the political is the sector in which the most explicit part of the functioning of society is expressed, the place of reasoned confrontations; but, at the same time, it represents a symbolic, hidden, unconscious level. Now, Gauchet explores this last stratum in his relations with religion. There results a reversal of perspective by which the infrastructure would in fact be a narrow tributary of the superstructure. The effectuating vision of society is situated at the principle of its signifying mutations. "The mainspring, in this case, is not the control of things but rather the hold over people."[12]

The return of the relation with nature does not come from some political agency assignable to a precise place, but more profoundly from the ontological duality that has provoked an investment of the energies of the social, of acting, on the appropriation of the resources of the world here below. This new mode of problematization, which has the objective of examining the deep symbolic mutations of society, has given up on simple causalisms, not proper to its object—"a problematic task, as it permanently faces the undecidable. It is indeed impossible, on this ground, ever to decide what belongs to the order of determination and what to the order of correspondence."[13]

It is erroneous to reproach Gauchet, as Roger Chartier has done,[14] for being content with the explicit part of human action and for having the desire of detaching the political from the social sciences. All the more so, as liberal society, according to Gauchet, is par excellence the social framework in which the actors have a false representation of the political, because they deem that social coherency is situated in the market (the invisible hand), or in civil society, while political function is in a position of maximal exercise. "The more liberal societies are, the more the state plays a role. Now, the latter is not understood by the actors, who never stop denouncing the fact that it does too much, all the while demanding that it do more."[15]

The mode of interlocking the various levels of a social formation remains the horizon of a program of total history whose principle is to understand the articulations, and not to reduce one level to another. Historicizing the great divisions is the central problem that this political history intends to pose in the symbolic sense. This historicization makes manifest the process of desymbolization in progress in modern society. This mutation permits one further to accord a place to the explicit, conscious part of thought, which coexists with an always important though latent symbolic register, which conceals itself from the direct gaze.

## The Autonomy and the Duality of the Political

The view on politics can no longer be content with an instrumentalizing vision—whether in its Leninist variant, for which the state is directly manipulated by the ruling class, or in its Althusserian variant of the ISA (ideological state apparatuses), which remain subject to their exteriority to assure the same function of social hegemony. Elias showed already in the 1930s that the political is more complex. Avoiding an instrumentalized conception, he analyzed power as an attempt to balance social tensions according to continually reborn configurations. According to him, the political plays a nodal role, as he shows with his study of the court society,[16] around the process of the courtization[17] of warriors, which is at the origin of the "trial of civilization," the pacification of behaviors, and the control of affects.

The political is the privileged entry in understanding the basis of the social bond. It allows an escape from physical causalism and, at the same time, it limits the freedom of individuals. Elias takes the metaphor of the chessboard to describe this tension, this interdependence: "As in a game of chess, every action achieved in relative independence represents a blow to the social chessboard, which, unfailingly, unleashes a counterblow from another individual, limiting the first player's freedom of action."[18]

A complex system is put in place in which the balancing of tensions is managed by a sovereign who constructs a more and more absolutist state on the basis of the rivalries between the aristocracies *de robe* and *d'épée,* too opposed to put the position of the sovereign in peril, and too much in solidarity to contest the bases of the social formation. Social relations are therefore ambivalent, and the state is no longer in the position of an instrument of an aristocracy that would use it from the outside. Elias thus demonstrates that the political grasped over the long period may be the place of a reglobalization of history and of an elucidation of the meaning of the fundamental evolutions of a society.

The autonomy of the political was strongly emphasized by Paul Ricoeur in an analysis that followed the Soviet Army's suppression of the revolution of Budapest in 1956. This event incited Ricoeur to a still very current reflection on the nature of the political: "Like every event worthy of this name, the event of Budapest has an infinite capacity for shocking. It has touched us and stirred us at several levels of our existence: at the level of historical compassion, caught by the unexpected; at the level of ordinary political strategy; at the level of reflection on the abiding political structures of human existence."[19] In the midst of the cold war, Ricoeur took a position that questioned anew the point of view of those who reduced the political to class conflict as well as that of those who, denouncing the regimes of the East, advocated the renunciation of all validity for the political.

The understanding of the event and its relativization with respect to the very nature of the political led Ricoeur to underscore the dual and paradoxical character of the political. It derives, through its autonomy, from a specific rationality that is irreducible to the economic and social bases. At the same time, it is characterized by two specific evils. The analysis of the political implies this double dimension, whereas the tradition of political philosophy has had a tendency either to overestimate the rationality of the political without integrating its other side—this is the case for Aristotle, Rousseau, Hegel—or, to the contrary, to insist on the mendacious and violent aspect of power; the latter is the tradition that goes from Plato to Marx by way of Machiavelli.

Now, the political is in the first place that agency that intends to assure the public good, the common happiness. To reflect on its autonomy is therefore to "find in the teleology of the State its irreducible manner of contributing to the humanity of man."[20] Such a conception renders vain frontal oppositions such as that between the state and the citizen, because the individual becomes human only in the totality of citizenship. The truth of the political is found, therefore, in the notion of equality: "This is what constitutes the *reality* of the State."[21] The point of view of the state, then, cannot be assigned a singularity such as that of the domination of such and such a social category.

But there is, in the second place, the other face of the political, that of the alienation it implies. Political evil is not an exogenous element, linked to contingency, to bad governors. "Not that power is evil. But power is one of the splendors of man that is eminently prone to evil."[22] So it is also legitimate to denounce, to unveil the lie, the fiction of the state because that is one of its dimensions. Marx's radical critique is therefore admissible, but its weakness derives from the failure to understand the alienation proper to the political and from reducing this dimension to a "mere superstructure,"[23] for lack of conceiving the autonomous character of the contradiction inherent in the political.

Ricoeur's critique of the limits of the philosophy of suspicion is not the sign of any pessimism or defeatism. Quite to the contrary, it allows one to continue to emphasize the political in its dual dimension and not to reject it in the name of the disillusions strewn throughout human history. "Henceforth, man cannot evade politics under penalty of evading his humanity. Throughout history, and by means of politics, man is faced with *his* grandeur and *his* culpability."[24]

## The Deficits of the Political

The 1960s, to the contrary, developed at leisure the vision of a maleficent power, everywhere present, and to it they opposed the figure of the free individual in revolt, seeking to escape her quartering by gauging its interstices, its flaws. Thinking the political in its autonomy and ontological duality has been pursued by only a few isolated currents. It is rather a lack that characterized those years in the area of thought on the political. Hence, Jean-Marc Ferry today observes the absence of vitality in the fundamental elements that should constitute the political base of the large European nations: "The civility of the sixteenth century with Erasmus; the principle of equality of the seventeenth century with Locke, and publicity in the noble sense of the term in the eighteenth century with Kant, the formation of a public sphere."[25] Now, if these three ingredients necessary for the good workings of a Western political democracy continue to be left in negligence, Ferry sees the risk of a more or less savage recommunitarianization of society. The latter could take two forms. The first would be that of small cities folded in on themselves, in the manner of ancient cities, and therefore exclusionist communities. It could be even worse, with the degeneration of the social in the form of a multiplication of sects, with their charismatic leaders organizing a communitarian violence on the basis of an intense affective bond.

Alain Caillé also attests to the observation of this turning away from the political and its grievous effects; he incriminates the responsibility of the clerics, and in particular of the social scientists, who have forgotten their civic function by exacerbating their constitutive break.[26]

This relegation of the political to a specialized sector, that of political science, has been favored, we have already seen, by the domination in the social sciences of paradigms that lead them to consider this level of study to be a matter of the ephemeral, of the illusory. The evolution of the discipline of history on this point is exemplary. The transformation is radical: "There are now instruments of study and research in political history that are much more sophisticated than before. The current studies remove themselves from the danger that threatens political history, that is, from coming back to a purely evenemental history. We immediately plunge into weighty tendencies."[27]

What dominates is incontestably the return of the political, which was the great domain abandoned by the tradition of the *Annales*; the latter considered this domain as bearing on the singular, the accidental, against which the historian, as a scientist, had to protect himself, so as to devote himself, on the contrary, to what lasts. For the genealogy of the national according to Lavisse, one substituted a genealogy of the social, often economistic. Today, we are to the contrary witnessing a firm renewal of political history, whose initiator in France was René Rémond, with the 1954 publication of his thesis, *The Right Wing in France*.[28]

## When History Interpellates the Political

History itself knocks on the door of the political when one cannot explain events as important as the fall of the Soviet regime and then of the Berlin Wall by economic curves alone—when the economists themselves seem powerless to model the longest economic crisis of our modernity.

Today, around René Rémond, of the National Foundation of Political Science and the University of Paris X-Nanterre, not to mention the Institute for the History of the Present Time, a new political history has been born: it is rich in contributions to a fertile dialogue with the other social sciences, in particular with political science, electoral sociology, legal studies. In this regard, the recent publication, in 1988, of a collective work edited by Rémond, *Pour une histoire politique,* is symptomatic of this reorientation in historiographical conjuncture. The lessons of the new history have been retained by the authors of the twelve contributions to the book.

The political is here conceived in a sense broadened to include the study of the words, manifestations, and foundational myths of the social imaginary and is supported by a meticulous attention to electoral fluctuations. Rémond observes, "Political history is seeing an astonishing reversal of fortune whose importance historians have not always seen."[29] Jean-Pierre Azéma reviews the panorama of the conceptions of war in their relations with rationality and violence. Elections, parties, associations, biographies, opinion, the media, intellectuals, political ideas, words, religion in its relation to the political, the relations between domestic and foreign policy—one by one these are studied by Rémond, Serge Bernstein, Jean-Pierre Rioux, Philippe Levillain, Jean-Jacques Becker, Jean-Noël Jeanneney, Jean-François Sirinelli, Michel Winock, Antoine Prost, Aline Coutrot, and Pierre Milza.

What results is that the political once again irrigates the field of history, but with a new vision, and as a site of management of the global society, not as a subcontinent disconnected from social history. This is witnessed by the recent editorial undertaking of a team united around Jean-François Sirinelli and the editor-historian Éric Vigne. This task has achieved an obvious demonstration: political history reintegrates the "territory" of the historian with a flash. Those who conceived the project of a new *Histoire des droites en France*[30] have not returned to the historicizing and reductive history of the Lavissian era. They have constructed a global history in which politics (la *politique*) opens onto the political (le *politique*). Far from being exclusive, this is an inclusive history. It is organized in a threefold register, which allows one to open the general analysis of phenomena to the micro-events of the everyday.

In the first place, the properly political dimension, that of the various forms of power, is conceived on the basis of a differentiation between its institutional aspects and a new dimension, borrowed from Reinhart Koselleck, that of ideological horizons as horizons of expectation. The second stratum of analysis is that of cultural policy through its channels of diffusion, various sieves that filter doctrines on the basis of the circles of inventors and the circles of mediators. Finally, and still more recently, Luc Boltanski and Laurent Thévenot's work on the justification of the actors here finds an extension into the discipline of history through an accounting for the realm of sensibilities in the third volume.

We then gain access to the sphere of the subjective, that of the essential solidarities that found being-together in the City on the level of individual and collective lived experience: "Our use of the term *City* is obviously inspired by the conceptual sense that Luc Boltanski and Laurent Thévenot give to it."[31] The book that Sirinelli and Vigne have edited takes up the pluralist conception of the phenomenon of rightism, which Rémond brought into evidence in 1954. But it especially opens the political to the cultural: it accounts for Maurice Agulhon's studies of political sociability, its networks, its places and milieus, as well as the recent development of studies on memory that is completely renewing historiography.

The event is grasped as a trace in the evolution of a collective memory. It can serve, however distant it may be, as a major marker for a generation. It was thus for the right wing of the French Revolution, an essential structuring event, but also—and this is better known—for the key moment constituted by the rallying to the Republic in the late nineteenth century. The project of this series of works goes back to 1986. The date is not insignificant, as it corresponds to the new rise of the extreme right, that of a national populism whose roots had to be found again in the depths of French history. It was also the moment when certain hasty commentators began to theorize the end of French exceptionalism, the end of the left-right split, in the name of a conjuncture that also required a resituating of the moment within a longer period.

Among the pioneers of the extension of the political to the field of the imaginary was Maurice Agulhon, with his key concept of sociability.[32] Defined by Agulhon as an aptitude for living in a group and for consolidating groups through a constitution of voluntary associations, the notion of sociability has made possible the opening up of a vast new field of research, as is illustrated by the recent publication of *Histoire vagabonde,* which collects around twenty articles from the period between 1968 and 1987.[33] Unsatisfied with traditional political history, Agulhon deeply scrutinizes the foundations of civic behavior and republicanism during the nineteenth century. Behind the laws and scenography of the politician's caste, he valorizes an underground circulation, that which continues a relation of adherence to an entire demonstration of republican faith around a specific statuary, inscriptions, and fountains, which allow the gathering together and expression of a collective fervor.

This return of the political puts the historians of the political on the center stage of the media. René Rémond has become the most expert commentator of election nights on television, Michel Winock tells us in detail about 1789, Jean-Pierre Azéma has us relive the dark hours of 1939 on the occasion of its fortieth anniversary, and Jean-Pierre Rioux directs *XXe siècle, revue d'histoire,* published by the Presses de la Fondation des Sciences Politiques. Illuminating the temporal thickness of the stakes of the present is their common ambition. The place conferred to the political is preponderant, without for all that selling out on problematic investigation for the profit of a mere chronological narrative.

The renewal of political history has been made possible thanks to a fertile dialogue with the other social sciences, through a pluridisciplinarity in action. Hence, in the new version, it is not presented as a separate sector, with hegemonic pretensions: "The political does not constitute a separate sector, but is rather a modality of social practice."[34] The history of the political presupposes the existence of an autonomous realm, but requires a globalizing horizon in which the point is a condensation. The political, in its indeterminacy and primary ambivalence, teaches us the limits of explanatory schemata, their incompleteness. "We must recognize that in the political there are more things than in the systems of explanation."[35] The human sacrifice offered in the phenomenon of war remains irreducible to the analyses of pure utilitarian rationalization. The history of the political is therefore a good school in which the researcher may acquire modesty. It is nothing less than the basis of a vast pluridisciplinary workshop.[36]

*Thirty-one*

# The Present Time

The implication the historian recognizes with regard to his writing has burst the objectivism claimed by those who defined history on the basis of the break between a fixed past to be exhumed and a present considered as a site of a possible overarching scientific practice. This indivisibility between past and present has brought the past deep within the historian's field of investigation. The investigations of contemporary history have long been concentrated on an earlier twentieth century whose end point was the archivistic workshops of World War II. Besides, the research on this period was at the origin of the creation of the Institute for the History of the Present Time (IHTP) in 1978.

In the 1950s and 1960s, the Committee on the History of the Second World War, then led by Henri Michel, gathered and collected testimonies and did many inquiries, essentially oriented toward the study of the various forms of resistance. In the seventies, they progressively left the heroic discourse on this episode in French history with the 1973 publication of the work of American historian Robert Paxton.[1] Besides the taboos it succeeded in lifting, it opened a necessary investigation into the bonds woven by history with memory. Marcel Ophuls's film on the chronicle of everyday life during the Occupation, *The Sorrow and the Pity,* long banned from television but a great success in the cinemas, invites a similar reflection and participates in a veritable overthrow, a return of the repressed.

Then the necessity of rethinking the relationship with World War II imposed itself, within a broader perspective, reinserting it into a present time that largely contributed to its effects. In addition, the Thirty Years' Law made quicker access to the archives possible, and so permitted an investigation of the event, previously kept out by the Braudelian long period, and now bolstered by an archivistic basis.

Pierre Nora then wrote, we have seen, on the "return of the event,"[2] and in 1978 received, at the very moment the IHTP was created, headed by François Bédarida, a directorship of studies titled "History of the Present." Bédarida then incarnated the success of an enterprise, until then underground, of renewing very contemporary history. Institutionally, the IHTP is achieving the difficult marriage between time and the present.

## From Christian Presence to the Present

Against the current of the orientations of the *Annales* in the 1950s, an entire current of Christian intellectuals was already asking the questions about the categories of contemporaneity that had particularly intense echoes within a painful present situation. In this regard, "the concept of the present is here to be taken in the very strong sense of presence to the world."[3] This real presence has roots in the personalism of the 1930s, which seeks to define the responsibilities of the person in a reflection on the act and the present. Michel Trebitsch rightly insists on the links between the spiritual engagement of the principal actors in the foundation of the IHTP and their stance in the field of history.

René Rémond himself has recalled the importance of his Catholic experience. "Belonging to the Catholic church has been and remains paramount for me."[4] He was an active militant in the JEC[5] and had important responsibilities in it. François and Renée Bédarida were militantly active in *Témoignage chrétien.*[6] This involvement gave them a particularly acute consciousness of the historian's responsibility. For them, it is not located in a mere timely response to a media-related social demand. It must be a "source of values."[7] This ethical vigilance is as precious as the risks of instrumentalization are great in an institute strongly called on by the immediacy of the needs of an information increasingly permeated by the media.

From this leftist Christian current came a reflection, in the 1950s, on a political history and a history of the present left behind by dominant historiography. The tragic context of decolonization, that of the wars in both Indochina and Algeria, constitutes the initial traumatism that seemed to assure the bases of this necessary recapturing of the historian by the demands of his time. In 1957, Rémond pleaded for this "abandoned history."[8] He rejected all the traditional criticisms of very contemporary history based on the necessary distance a historian must take in order to engage in work. His plea was heard in the framework of a basic reflection on the subjective implication of the historian in relation to his object of study.[9]

## Reopening Possibilities

Prey to the globalization of information, the acceleration of its rhythm, the contemporary world is seeing an "extraordinary dilation of history, a growth of a deep historic feeling."[10] This presentification has had the effect of a specifically modern experience of historicity. It has implied a redefinition of evenementality as an approach to a multiplicity of possibilities, virtual situations, and potentials, and no longer as what is accomplished in fixity.

The movement lays hold of the present time to the point of modifying the modern relation to the past. The historical reading of the event is no longer reducible to the event studied, but viewed in its trace, situated in an evenemental chain. All discourse on a vehicle event connotes a series of previous events, and this gives quite an importance to the discursive web that binds them together in an emplotment. As one can measure it, the history of the present time not only involves the opening of a new period, what is very near being opened to the historian's gaze. It is also a different history, participating in the new orientations of a paradigm that is sought in a break with unique and linear time, and pluralizing the modes of rationality.

Arguments presenting a certain number of insurmountable obstacles have been opposed to the history of the present time. In the first place, there is the handicap of proximity that does not allow a hierarchization according to an order of relative importance in the mass of available sources. One may not, according to this criticism, define what is a matter of the historical and what belongs to the epiphenomenon. In the second place, it is reproached with using a time cut off from its future. The historian does not know the temporal destiny of the facts studied, while most often meaning is revealed only in the aftermath.

In this regard, Paul Ricoeur, who places his intervention in the framework of a defense of the legitimacy of the history of the present time, directs attention to the difficulties of a configuration inscribed in the perspective of a short temporal distance. He advocates distinguishing incomplete time in the recent past, becoming in progress, when one speaks of it in the midst of its passage—"what constitutes a handicap for this historiography is the considerable place given to predictions and anticipations in the understanding of history in progress"[11]—from closed time, that of World War II, decolonization, the end of communism . . . And in this regard, 1989 becomes an interesting date of closure that allows one to configure intelligible sets once a certain cycle is complete. Added to these handicaps is the Thirty Years' Law, which does not allow immediate access to the archives. We must add the traditional reproach of the lack of critical distance that characterizes the historian's procedure.

## Indeterminacy

But the history of the present time also has the capacity to turn some of these inconveniences into advantages, as is demonstrated by Robert Frank, François Bédarida's successor in the directorship of the IHTP until 1994.[12] The work of investigating the incomplete contributes to defatalizing history, relativizing its causal chains, which constitute reading grids, the historian's ready-to-wear. In this regard, the history of the present time is a good laboratory for crushing causal fatalism. In addition, even if its handling poses serious methodological problems, the historian has the fortune of being able to work under control of the witnesses to the events he is analyzing. He has oral sources, a definite asset, at his disposal, even if they must be handled with care and critical distance, as they are "a source on a past time and not, like many written sources, contemporary with the event."[13] This interactivity of the historian confronted with her field study, in the manner of the sociologist, puts her in a good position "to do an objective history of subjectivity."[14]

This history of the present time has contributed to reversing the relation between history and memory. The traditional opposition between a critical history located on the side of science and a memory deriving from fluctuating and phantasmic sources is in transformation. Whereas history is losing a part of its scientificity, the problematization of memory leads to according an essential role in the construction of critical knowing to the notion of memory, the latter now essential in the work of demythologization. The two notions are close to each other, and the role of oral sources in the writing of the present time makes a history of memory possible. "We erect memory itself as a historical object."[15]

This reversal has a heuristic value, as it allows a better understanding of the indeterminate character of the possibilities opened for the actors of a past that was their present. So the history of the present time modifies the relation to the past, its vision, and its study. It is a significant rupture in the practice of the historian, and in its scale surpasses the significance of other locutions such as those of near history or immediate history. The latter notion acquired its letters of nobility in 1978 when it figured as an entry in the *Nouvelle Histoire* encyclopedia. It represented a history of the immediate marked by the seal of good journalism, in this case that of Jean Lacouture. Besides the fact that he makes consonant two notions that seem antinomic, history and the immediate, this genre, child of the press and the importance of media information, "is more in line with the techniques of journalism than with those of historical science."[16]

## The Present as a "Lacuna"

The historian of the present time inscribes the historiographical operation in duration. She does not limit her object to the instant and must make prevalent a self-conscious practice, and that prohibits the frequent naiveties of the historical operation. Belonging to the time she studies, the historian is required to situate herself, to conceive herself in relation to her object as an agent of cognition and not as a mere vector or ectoplasm. This retrospective view induces a rereading of all of the historian's production, a reevaluation of chance, of the event in its singularity and so in the direction of its defatalization. What therefore results is an entirely new problematic of the choices of the actors in the sense of a middle path between contingency and sequence, between narrative and structure. The present is no longer conceived so much as the site of a continuous passage between a before and an after, but as Hannah Arendt conceives it, as a "lacuna" between past and future.[17] This Arendtian notion enables one better to understand what the present may bear in the way of discontinuity, rupture, beginning of the possible. It refers to the generational notion that allows one to structure the lived of the present in a collective manner. "According to this conception, time is not a continuum; rather, it is interrupted at the point where the human being is found and where he or she must take a position against both past and future."[18]

Inscribed in time as discontinuity, the present is labored by the one who must historicize it by an effort to apprehend its presence as an absence, in the way that Michel de Certeau defined the historiographical operation.[19] This dialectic is all the more difficult to realize because one must proceed to a voluntary disengagement for the history of the present time, more natural when it is a question of past time. "The question is whether, in order to be historical, the history of the present time does not presuppose a similar movement of falling into absence, from the depths of which the past was calling us with the strength of a past that was recently present."[20] Here we grasp to what point the history of the present time is driven by deeper motivations than those of a mere access to something more contemporary. The quest for meaning guides its research as much as the refusal of the ephemeral—a meaning that is no longer a telos, a preconstructed continuity, but a reaction to "contemporary a-chronia."[21]

The history of the present time is radically differentiated, therefore, from classically contemporary history. It is looking for a temporal thickness and seeks to anchor an all too often lived present in a sort of temporal weightlessness. Through its conciliatory will, in the heart of the lived, of discontinuity, and of discontinuities, the history of the present as a constant telescoping between past and present allows a "vibrato of the incomplete that suddenly colors an entire past, a present delivered little by little from its autism."[22]

# Thirty-two

# The Historicity of the Sciences
## The Principle of Symmetry

A dichotomy has most often been postulated, in the name of a modern process of purification, between what derives from scientific truth removed from its gangue and ideology, the social. This mode of thinking found its culmination with Althusser and the Althusserians. It privileged a way of thinking in terms of epistemological breaks. Such a position was situated asymmetrically in order to allow the completion of the division between error and truth. The merit of this perspective was to break with the continuism of the old, purely linear history of ideas. But the privilege accorded to the internal logic of the concept brought about an underestimation of the weight of contextualization in scientific innovations.

At the time, scientific history presented itself as the succession of the point of view of the victors, and the historian of science could only laugh at the vague scientific impulses of the vanquished. The sociology of science opposed to this form of history what David Bloor calls the principle of symmetry,[1] which enables a realization of what François-André Isambert defined as a strong program in the sociology of science.[2] Nonetheless, Bloor's sociology achieves only one deontologization, that of nature, to bring all the explanatory elements to bear on society.

Michel Callon and Bruno Latour's anthropology of science, in Bloor's "strengthist" tradition, as Isambert calls it, advocates going further with a generalized principle of symmetry that prohibits it both from using external reality to explain the laboratory and from alternating natural realism and sociological realism at the whim of explanatory needs. It is fitting, therefore, to come back to the great division between a society considered in its historicity and an immutable nature whose laws of functioning it would suffice to discern, which themselves would escape historicity. On the contrary, humans and nonhumans are modified by their historicity: "With historicization, we will insist on the notions of event, circumstance, contingency, and locality."[3] It is a radical historicism that is defended insofar as it deals not only with human beings, but also with objects, natural elements. In this sense, it is common to the anthropology of science and the sociology of Boltanski and Thévenot.

## Pouchet/Pasteur

Latour provides an exemplary illustration of the application he intends to make of his principle of generalized symmetry when he takes up the controversy of Pasteur and Pouchet under the Second Empire. The terms of the dispute are concentrated on the question of spontaneous generation, whose existence is attested by Pouchet and denied by Pasteur. Classical history of science, in the face of such a controversy, tends to place itself in an overarching position, that of the end of the debate. It begins with the end point, by which Pasteur is right. The position of Pasteur the innovator, then, derives from the emergence of the true in his laboratory alone. All the rest, including Pouchet, are only parasites who delay the awaited discovery.

Latour leads us to another narrative.[4] He effectively distinguishes four forms of historicization in the sciences: "History as discovery, history as conditioning, history as formation and finally, history as construction."[5] The first form, the most classical, is that of history as discovery. It is a continual and heroicized series of inventors. In such a narrative, the stake is purely chronological. It is merely a matter of situating the moment of discovery on the temporal axis. Henceforth, there is irreversibility and incommensurability between two paradigms, those of error and truth. A mere chronicle of discoveries, this history is reduced to a series of "pearls strung into obituary narrative, without there being any history to tell."[6]

On the other end of the chain, history as construction applies a principle of generalized symmetry. The historian here must go back in time and in the demonstration by applying a procedure similar to those of Pasteur and Pouchet. If an explanation for one is advanced, its reliability for the other must be tested. Hence, one can disqualify Pouchet as a provincial, a professor at Rouen, only at the moment one can demonstrate that Pasteur's Parisianness is a decisive asset. The true identity of history as construction "is history itself, but extended to the things themselves."[7]

One must therefore submit everything to the principle of the transportation of forces, according to which, between the beginning and the end of the narrative, all the elements will be modified and the constants will have to be explained. The classical procedure of the epistemology of science was to disqualify error and its spokespersons by unveiling the perverse influences weighing on them. Thus, Pouchet as the loser could be delivered to history as a provincial, a believer, a rhetorician, and therefore incapable of achieving the level of scientific rationality that Pasteur achieved. This is the position of Bourdieu's so-called scientific sociology, according to which the radical critique of its own determinisms places it on the plane of the truth of knowledge. Now, "the social context is the ether of sociologists and historians."[8] It is in its turn to be historicized, pluralized.

Emperor Napoleon III was not the same for Pouchet and Pasteur, as is witnessed by the two letters he received in the year 1862. Pouchet's letter conveys a radically different conception of the relations between politics and science from Pasteur's. Pouchet appealed to the emperor to cut through the controversy and prove him right on the basis of science. "It is the principle of one king, one religion. Give me a prince for spontaneous generation, and the organization of ideas will follow the position of the prince";[9] whereas Pasteur appealed to power only incidentally, in order to procure the material means he needed to pursue his research. At no time did he solicit the opinion of Napoleon III on the content of the controversy. The historian, therefore, cannot postulate what a scientific policy was in 1862. He owes it to himself to compare the two conceptions without consigning them to a common contextual ether.

Another dimension to historicize is the virulence of the controversy itself, its stakes. When Pouchet wrote to Joly, a professor in the medical school at Toulouse, it was in these terms: "I don't want some scientist, born at Carpentras or Domfront, just like me, to lord it over me just because luck rather than merit has taken him to Paris. He will pay dearly for such an insult. . . . I will not let him go until he is crushed beneath the rock of heterogenesis."[10]

The conditionings that weighed on the two researchers did not stop at the laboratory door. Microbes themselves are to be historicized. "Microbes for Pouchet are not the same thing as microbes for Pasteur."[11] Microbes, as a culture for Pasteur and not as spontaneous generation with Pouchet, become a real event. They are considerably transformed before the sterilization experiment that Pasteur undertook: "What happened to Pasteur's microbes had never happened to microbes since the world began."[12] Pasteur himself was also metamorphosed by the success of his experiment. He became a great scholar recognized by his peers. This historicization is substituted for an analysis in essentialist terms. It involves society just as much as nature. The conception it puts forward of the relations between subjects and objects is completely original; it gives birth to new readings of the past, new narratives.

## Humor and Irony

Of course, the problem in this type of analysis is the danger of absolute relativism, for which the new anthropology of science has been reproached. Steve Woolgar has termed the relativist type of sociological reading of the sciences an "ironist" position.[13] The British sociologists have adopted a radicalized position contesting the possibility of establishing criteria of legitimacy on the basis of a verdict emanating from nature. By locating their criteria of truth in society alone, they reduce it to the single level of the relations of social forces and of the interests they involve. The fact of putting forth a scientific truth, then, has no more validity than some Bororo myth.

The sociologist of science engages a new relation with temporality. When the scientists retort with the irreversibility of scientific discoveries, he answers that he can reduce them to zero by bringing them back to their initial situation of uncertainty. For the relativist sociologist, in fact, an agreement on scientific truth results from the fact that socially weaker adversaries have been reduced. "It's very difficult to say that the fact that we know microbes exist isn't progress with respect to the theory of miasmas."[14]

At the risk of an ironist position, Isabelle Stengers opposes another attitude, that of humor: "Humor is an art of immanence."[15] It allows the past not to be reduced to a mere joust between powers, and controversies to be inscribed on the dividing line between science and nonscience within a tradition, a heritage in relation to past generations.

In this sense, Stengers, with the notion of an heir, leaves behind the relativist aporia by inscribing our century as an heir to Pasteur and not to Pouchet. The division between a before and an after is difficult to question, as there is certainly a cumulativeness of knowledge— more precise cognition of the relief patterns of the world. To escape the history of science as a linear continuum of progress, it is necessary to take up the course of historical narrative in its opening, so as to show that the role of the history undergone by the actors in scientific innovation is more pregnant than they say, whereas they have the tendency to maximize the role of the construction, of the self-production of historicity. "History is the very matter of scientific productivity."[16]

# Part IX

## *The New Alliance*
### *A Threefold Understanding*

# Thirty-three

# A Transdisciplinarity

If the time when the death of philosophy was proclaimed is past—and with it that battle of the trenches over whether the field researcher or the specialist of the concept would hold legitimate knowledge—it remains to be seen how the three-way dialogue may occur between the natural sciences, philosophy, and the social sciences.

Isabelle Stengers advocates defining the mode of relation among these three poles as transdisciplinarity rather than claiming an already traditional interdisciplinarity: "Interdisciplinarity is something of a division among property owners."[1] On the other hand, transdisciplinarity locates the relation at the heart of the sciences, of their elaboration. It involves a meeting of several specialists around the attempt to solve a common problem. Transdisciplinarity has the advantage, according to Stengers, of emerging from the routinization and false securities with which the disciplines adorn themselves. Indeed, it allows a problematization of the objects constituted as obstacles by this or that discipline as an obstacle to the fact of its intrinsic limits. In this spirit, Stengers has gone back to hypnosis as belonging to the field of psychoanalysis, all the while resisting psychoanalytic theory. Interdisciplinarity has had the tendency to be content with a mere juxtaposition of points of view, whereas pluridisciplinarity finds in its components a taste for risk, for the restlessness that belongs to all discovery. This does not for all that mean that one must postulate an indifference with regard to procedures: "Transdiscipline is the search for a type of alliance in which one uses the other to learn for one's own subject, so as better to understand the meaning of what one is doing by recognizing the choice from which one proceeds."[2] This type of procedure permits one to favor a new mode of coexistence between philosophers and scientists, whether the latter are natural or social scientists.

## Laterality, Intersubjectivity, Irreversibility

The mode of analysis of the scientific practice that Isabelle Stengers conducts aims to bring its stakes to the forefront by linking philosophy with science, but in a relationship of laterality by means of indirect alliances. That implies a recognition of the singularity of problems before one may see how they might interplay. This dialogue, a more demanding one, impugns the various forms of soft interdisciplinarity and substitutes a concern with conceptualization that may today be found among a growing number of historians.[3] Two philosophers have prepared Stengers for the risks involved in speculative production and philosophizing generalizations on the sciences: Gilles Deleuze and Alfred North Whitehead, the latter a philosopher of mathematics who, like many, emigrated to the United States, where late in life he constructed a rational cosmology in the tradition of Leibniz.[4] In *La Nouvelle Alliance,* Stengers has a tendency to cross Prigogine's arguments with Whitehead's: "The task of philosophy would then be, for Whitehead, to reconcile permanency with becoming, to think of things as processes, to think of becoming as constitutive of identifiable entities."[5] But facing the risk of bolstering Prigogine's arguments through a demonstration that derived from quite another register, Stengers henceforth intends to separate the domains better so as to avoid the deceptive gaps between one argumentative mode and another.

Transdisciplinarity, therefore, does not signify the confusion of genres. It is even against the latter that Stengers has acted in denouncing the claims of classical physics to incarnate a more general and valid truth in all the other fields of knowledge, beginning with the closest, chemistry. The alliance prescribed among disciplines must thus avoid the pitfall of reductionism.

From this point of view, the importance of the resonance that *La Nouvelle Alliance* met with bears on the questioning of the model of classical mechanical physics. Prigogine's studies on nonequilibrium thermodynamics, and notably his theory of dissipative structures, enable one to introduce the arrow of time into scientific discourse and to pass from a model in which invariance is the sign of a scientific law to the recognition of irreversibility at the very heart of matter, surpassing the age-old alternative between determinism and the aleatory. The notion of law constituted by classical mechanics has been upset by the discoveries of Niels Bohr and Werner Heisenberg, since quantum mechanics was substituted for the Galilean paradigm. Even if the quantum model should not be mechanically substituted for the older one so as to offer a new, valid paradigm in all the other fields of knowledge, one is forced to notice that a certain number of discoveries in any case allow for a disturbance of the old model of scientificity that belongs to classical physics; hence, the abandonment of the notion of linear trajectory, with what it implied for determinism, introduced to the concept of the operator and to Heisenberg's uncertainty relation: "Classical objectivity identifies the objective description of the system 'as in itself' and complete description. In this sense, quantitative mechanics of course requires us to redefine the notion of objectivity."[6] The relation between the observer and his objects and the relation with time are both transformed, and this permits the opening of a broad field of possibilities.

The classical problems discussed in philosophy, but also research in the social sciences, are posed in new terms. As a physicist, Bernard d'Espagnat deduces that one may no longer view an observation of objects as independent of the one who observes. Quantum mechanics reverses the schema of separability between, on the one hand, a system of elements studied in its intrinsic interactions and, on the other, a man who applies the measuring devices.[7] When, in 1928, Bohr opposed term for term the symbolic and the intuitive, he designated the question of the elaboration of ideas: "The situation . . . bears a deepgoing analogy to the general difficulty in the formation of human ideas, inherent in the distinction between subject and object."[8]

Foundationalism in all its forms, whether logical or transcendental, is disturbed—and so, with it, is the Kantian conception of objectivity. In the same manner, "the problem also becomes that of reconstructing a coherent concept of the subject."[9] Bernard d'Espagnat advances in this direction by considering science to be more "objective" than epistemologists of science such as Thomas Kuhn or Paul Feyerabend think; but he deems it a matter of a weak objectivity, "precisely what I call intersubjectivity."[10] In the debate, which is usually presented classically, and somewhat caricaturally—as that of an alternative between positivist theses (Bohr) and realist theses (Einstein)—d'Espagnat places himself in the middle of the road and proposes the notion of "veiled reality."

These disturbances resulting from discoveries in the natural sciences have effects, which are often delayed, in the social sciences. The current epistemological shift in this realm leads one to investigate, in an interdisciplinary manner, the notions of "chaos," "complexity," and self-organization, and is situated in the tradition of the work of René Thom, Ilya Prigogine, and Henri Atlan. The determinist ideal of Pierre-Simon de Laplace is upset, and the social sciences then feel authorized to depart from a fatalism in which they had a tendency to see the very criterion of scientificity. So-called hard-scientific accounting for the notions of evenementality, irreversibility, creative disorder, or interaction allows one to be no longer blocked by the required implication of the observer, which is more and more recognized today. The interpretive scheme and the meaning given to human acting here find issues in common with what is happening in the natural sciences. From here on, transdisciplinarity opens a new field to knowledge, in which notional schemata circulate from philosophy to the natural and social sciences without establishing a hierarchy among the various modes of experimentation and problematization.

## The Ethical Horizon of Science

The studies of a researcher such as Henri Atlan are symptomatic of this contemporary knowledge under construction on the basis of an opening to transdisciplinarity. A medical doctor, biologist, and theoretician of complexity and self-organization, he is also a member of the National Consultative Committee on Ethics for the Life Sciences and a great appreciator of the Talmud. In the same way that Francisco Varela attempts a cross-fertilization of Buddhist tradition and the latest discoveries in cognitive science, Atlan has sketched a dialogue between Jewish tradition and scientific reflection. "Through comparisons and differences the dialogue may get interesting, more so than through similitudes and analogies."[11] For Atlan, transdisciplinarity is an essential requirement: the new concepts brought into focus by molecular and cellular biology must be elucidated by philosophy, as the classical dilemmas of the history of philosophy are posed in a new fashion. This cross-fertilization implies no reductionism. Quite to the contrary, the relations between values and truths are to be rethought, says Atlan—marking his difference with Hilary Putnam—as ontologically different: "Scientific truth does not furnish us with any moral value. These values are always inherited."[12] With this caesura accepted, the discussion must take place in public. The latter may take the form of an "intercritique":[13] the scientific method allows one to take distance from myth, but conversely tradition must be reactivated so as to be removed from the products of science. From this dialogue there may result an ethical point of view elaborated at the price of provisional compromises and pragmatics between positions rooted in different traditions.

This exchange had been interrupted in the name of the parcelization of knowledges, of their ever more advanced degree of specialization, which no longer permitted dialogue. Meanwhile, at the beginning of the twentieth century there still existed a scholarly community that took account of the various conceptual advances. Thus, Gérard Noiriel could, in studying the minutes of the meetings of the French Society of Philosophy, remark on the proximity of historians, sociologists, physicists, and other specialists in the natural sciences. Noticeable, among other things, is the assiduous presence at these meetings of one Charles Seignobos, who, decidedly, barely corresponds to the caricature that the founders of the *Annales* wanted to circulate. The project of Henri Berr, a philosopher converted to history and battling for the erasure of the disciplinary boundaries, when in 1900 he launched the *Revue de synthèse historique,* was also from the outset transdisciplinary.

When Marc Bloch and Lucien Febvre founded the *Annales d'histoire économique et sociale* in 1929, a decisive enterprise of renovating French historiography, they kept informed of the most recent evolutions of science. Their intention was to bring the benefits of these to a discipline of history that seemed condemned to the study of the singular, the contingent, in order to enable it to integrate into true laboratories of collective research. Thus the passage from classical to quantum physics broadly contributed to the historiographical shift of the 1930s. The latter favored the flowering of a "possibilitism" disengaged from the causal mechanism that held sway then. "The attempt at explaining the world through Newtonian or rational mechanics ended in brutal failure."[14] "Our mental atmosphere is no longer the same."[15]

Here there was quite a rupture with regard to the preceding

intellectual and scientific climate, of which the *Annales,* in defining a paradigm, took measure, or rather half-measure, for the implications of quantum physics were not totally accounted for. It was a matter of the new place accorded to the observer, but also to the unforeseeable, to singular situations, to indeterminacy and irreversibility. Karl Popper's anti-inductionism is emblematic of this evolution, and it has rapidly affected all the sciences. Nonetheless, this program was only partially taken up by the *Annales* school: its members then viewed things especially from the side of the Durkheimian sociologists, whose orientations appeared more scientific to them than those of the historians. But those orientations were still broadly impregnated by the model of classical physics. Indeed, it was always a matter of accounting for regularities, universal laws, and permanencies—to surpass singular situations.

It is only today, with the hermeneutic turn, that we begin to take the true measure of the disturbance that the quantum revolution presented, not only in history but also throughout the social sciences.

The initiators of the *Annales* wished to depart from the simplistic reductionisms of causal history in use in the methodical school, on behalf of the approach to a reality perceived as complex, irreducible to a monocausal schema. Meanwhile, the scientistic horizon, in search of invariant laws from Durkheimian sociology, did not really allow a departure from reductionism, as it had in fact passed from one determinism to another: for the positive history of a purely political causality was substituted a fetishism of the quantitative.

## The Cognitivist Confluence

The transdisciplinary confluence is in the course of being realized, but it has been shifted to other fronts. It has its privileged places, its specialists. The cognitivist wave that today affects a large portion of the social sciences is the most salient aspect of these confluences. In this spirit, Pascal Engel advocates rethinking the link between the psychological and the philosophical elucidations of a concept such as that of belief, according to a model less inspired by the nineteenth century than by the eighteenth, "a period during which philosophy and science were not yet separated";[16] this does not for all that imply a confusion of procedures.

In this regard, the effort of cognitive science takes up, for a price, the phenomenological project of integrating scientific discoveries within a globalizing and philosophical view. Maurice Merleau-Ponty already devoted great attention to the discoveries of the most advanced psychologists of his time. Today it is the same for those in the new paradigm: "I think the sciences of the living today have an enormous amount to teach us about humanity. Now, in cognitivism, there is the program that requires a coupling of the exact sciences and the human, in particular everything concerning the superior processes."[17] The historian, confronted with the problem of belief, viewed otherwise than as the mere expression of a mystified consciousness, turns to the studies of cognitive science in order to revisit the past and reinterpret it from a new perspective.

The cognitivist wave contributes to bringing the question of consciousness to the forefront. Even if its inspiration is essentially Anglo-Saxon, by way of analytic philosophy, "the enormous difference between the analytic philosophy practiced on the Continent and American analytic philosophy is the passage through history."[18] This cross-fertilization is at the origin of a proper problematization, thanks to its openness to a historicity without historicism. Perhaps the configuration that may result has a chance to escape a mere return to functional schemata. By relocating the search for meaning even within the functional schemata, by trying to conjoin the semantic and the syntactic levels, the cognitivist detour, articulated with a historian's procedure, may enable a restoring of trajectories and an accounting for the various levels of meaning.

Will cognitive science for all that have the capacity to answer all the questions asked by the social sciences? Certainly not, and there are many who intend to temper any premature enthusiasm. "If cognitivism is interesting in certain areas of reflection, there's a limitation, for there exist observable facts that cognitive anthropology is totally powerless to explain. So it is for the incest prohibition and the sexual division of labor."[19] The blind horizon of the cognitivist orientation—despite the fertility of a transdisciplinarity in action—and its incapacity for totalization essentially stem from the fact that it tries to conjoin two incommensurable ontologies. Of course, the disciplinary boundaries do not derive from any naturalness. They are most often tied to institutional divisions that, despite their constant petitioning of principles, do not have any specific objects or notions. Nonetheless, we may think, with Jean-Marc Ferry, that certain partitions have a proper conceptual pertinence: "It is established, from the grammatical point of view, that the sciences of nature have a different methodology from that of the sciences of society, which themselves have a different methodology from the cultural sciences."[20] We also find this *distinguo,* in another form, with Jean-Claude Passeron when he distinguishes the "non-Popperian" sciences—history, sociology, anthropology—from the natural sciences.

## The Singularity of the Social Sciences

The Popperian principle that defines, as a criterion of scientificity, the capacity to utter a "falsifiable" affirmation is nonetheless not to be rejected from the realm of the social sciences. It may even find an application in the field of historical investigation,[21] but on condition of no longer being impregnated, as for Popper, by the specific methodology of the experimental sciences. According to Popper, falsification may be valid only on the basis of arguments that refer to experiments involving observation and measure. In the area of the apriorities of experimentation, the falsificationist principle is entirely acceptable and operational in the social sciences, but it is not in the area of the apriorities of experiment; "it becomes perverse when one reduces it to an experimental reference that is valid only in the realm of the exact or natural sciences."[22]

Transdisciplinarity must therefore presuppose a singularity of the social sciences. This is also the best remedy against any reductionist undertaking. The essential discriminating factor that distinguishes the social sciences is the implication of competencies attributed to the acting individual. This autonomy of the social sciences has its source, says Max Weber, in its specific object, which is action endowed with meaning, individuals' capacity for symbolization. Transdisciplinarity may allow a supplementary complexity to be given to the social sciences, and renders null and void any mechanistic causalist undertaking. That must lead the social sciences to free themselves from the inferiority complex that has made them adopt a model, already outmoded, considered proper to the exact sciences. As we have just seen, it is not only the case that quantum physics has questioned this model, but also that the "privilege of age, importance, and success of the natural sciences is a trap,"[23] as Sylvain Auroux says, reminding us that the sciences of language go back to the turns of the third and second millennia before our era.

In this way, done with dated complexes, Bruno Latour, defining his procedure as the articulation between the real (nature without substantialism), the narrated (discourse without narrativism), and the collective as society (without reification), places himself "firmly within the social sciences."[24] Of course, the anthropology of science is not far from the natural sciences, for it has introduced itself in the labs of the physicists, chemists, and biologists, and takes into consideration their instruments and discoveries; but it is first interested in them because they construct a collective. It does not aim therefore for some illusory synthesis between the natural and the social sciences on the basis of disparate elements; it experiments with concepts proper to the social sciences for a better understanding of the social.

## Two Ontologies

Beginning with the postulate of the differentiation of two ontologies (those of the natural and the social sciences) does not come down to impugning transdisciplinarity. The latter is all the more indispensable in that certain disciplines are frontally traversed by this caesura. Thus, anthropology is situated at the intersection of a search for the human mind, mental enclosures, invariants proper to the human species, and of a search for singularities, differences, variations. This internal tension has always traversed anthropological discourse, which with Lévi-Strauss knew a strong period because of his temptation by an integral structural realism, notably in his later work, when he postulated an isomorphism between the semantic and nature. But the current predominant tendency carries anthropology toward a more historical horizon, a greater accounting for the lived, the contingent, the spoken, even if the explanatory schemata must then suffer.

Sociologist Jean-Claude Passeron, as we have seen, opposes two epistemologies, one corresponding to the Galilean sciences and the other to the historical sciences—while, for his part, ethnologist Alain Testart envisions only one regime of scientificity belonging to both the natural and the social sciences. Nevertheless, they both end up, paradoxically, with the same conclusion of a prevalence of the contextualized, situated character of the heuristic instruments of the social sciences. "In each case, it must be specified how the general law applied. In this regard, I would like to speak of specifiable generality"[25]—whereas for Passeron the social sciences sketch out two different epistemologies and Testart defends the thesis of a unique epistemology.[26] So as better to discern the shifts of these internal tensions, Jean-Luc Jamard poses the prolegomena of an anthropology of anthropologists that enables one better to restore the conditions of validity of the discourse of one's discipline.[27] Thus, he succeeds in defining the opposition between science and history that belongs to anthropology, and that corresponds to a "thematic dyad: stability versus change, the nomological world versus the historical world."[28]

Even in postulating the existence of two different ontologies, Dany-Robert Dufour is not hindered from using a certain number of symbolic figures in the most diverse fields of knowledge, as these figures traverse diverse modes of scientificity, the natural as well as the social sciences. Thus, Dufour created, along with Serge Leclaire (who died, sadly, in 1994), a site of discussion (a seminar) where philosophers, psychoanalysts, and specialists in the "technosciences" such as artificial intelligence work together, to understand better the deployment of the symbolic function. All the researchers examine hypotheses relative to the forms that labor the grand discourses, and so the subject in its personal bond. The need for this transdisciplinarity in action is defined as an attempt to respond to the current discontent of civilization.

Thus, they investigate the unseen relation between this discontent and the modernism of our Western societies, which continue to engender new forms of human suffering. The most modern technologies have a tendency to displace the traditional notion of the subject, to create technosubjective prostheses, or, as Bruno Latour terms them, "hybrids." The investigation of this constant activity of prosthetic creation is at the basis of new and necessary alliances between the sciences of nature and those of the mind. For Dufour, this encounter of three components has the objective of elaborating a problematic of prosthetic invention in its relations with the symbolic universe. It should mobilize the protagonists of prosthetic mutation (the scientists), those intimately familiar with their effects on the personal bond (the psychoanalysts), and finally the sociologists and philosophers who envision the consequences of these mutations in the area of the social bond.

The pulverization of knowledge into numerous parcels, more and more technical and sophisticated, may find its necessary counterpoint thanks to the multiplication of these sites of confluence, attentive to the rise of the new, capable of transgressing the traditional disciplinary boundaries. These sites may allow the beginning of a synthesis of the particular knowledges of the various social sciences, a possible articulation of their various dimensions, so as to render intelligible the human phenomenon, the relations between desire and the law, and so on. This necessitates that one postulate a complexity of this knowledge and put in place transdisciplinary research programs. The CNRS has begun to realize such a program, by launching three large programs in recent years that have in common their transdisciplinarity. "Today there is a questioning common to natural and social science: it is Aristotle's revenge on Plato."[29]

Epistemology, having lost its overarching position, is today further constructing itself in the course of the research process. In this regard, cognitive science is a good example of the possible fertility of the transdisciplinary opening, of a possible new alliance between philosophers and scientists on the basis of a methodological choice. Nevertheless, it postulates an epistemological monism including in the same set the sciences of nature and those of the mind, with which not all scholars are in agreement. The play of disciplinary boundaries may be at the origin of tangible advances in knowledge. "We don't know very well where a cognitive psychology might go, with a strong neuroscientific connection, with a strong physicalist connection."[30] The communications in the research programs common to biologists and specialists in self-organization have already allowed advances in the area of the inferior cognitive functions: vision, perception, and so on. Psychology thus tends to be transformed with the current of the new questions asked of it. It is situated in a position of tension between a physicalist tendency and another explanatory angle even further directed toward interpretation, toward evaluation. In this experimental epistemology, certain cognitivists find the questions that phenomenology has asked. These questions allow one to take up important questions for the sociology of action, such as that of situated action, and to conceive better, for example, the mode of functioning of artifacts, of robots that behave intelligently thanks to their faculty to adapt to new situations.

## Thirty-four

# An Experimental Epistemology

The transdisciplinarity that tends to impose itself as a new requirement does not signify the return to the epistemological quarrel over the conditions of scientificity. If we follow Bruno Latour, research in the social sciences must work toward a "slimming treatment" of its explanations. The idea that "everything is epistemological" is no longer the index of scientific reliability—as was the case in the time of structuralism's triumph, when every field study had to be reduced to a few lessons of an epistemological order.

Epistemology "is too loaded with what I want to avoid, the ideas of objectivity, authority, neutrality, rationality."[1] The pitfall of epistemology is in deriving its particular field of study from general considerations and in functioning in the mode of the stereotype, whereas the domain of scientific innovation is essentially local, contingent, and within the scope of a chain of punctual decisions. It is by transgressing the great divisions between practices and theories that science invents. An epistemology is elaborated in the course of this process, but in an experimental form. The latter is in rupture with the positivist tradition, which led to the Althusserian "break," whose effectiveness consisted of delimiting the space of nonscience in order to disqualify it. In this schema, science was constructed "against" the obstacle of ideology, of opinion, of common knowledge: "In this sense, Bachelard is closer to the 'grand positivism' associated with Auguste Comte than to the epistemological positivism associated with the Vienna Circle."[2]

There had already been a firebrand against objectivism, Paul Feyerabend. "The idea that science can, and should, be run according to fixed and universal rules, is both unrealistic and pernicious."[3] The lesson he drew from this, according to which "anything goes,"[4] was a scandal in scientific circles. His relativist positioning was nonetheless caricatured when it was reduced to its deliberately provoking analogies. When he impugns any form of superiority for science with respect to other forms of knowledge, he is not seeking to oppose scientific practice, but the "assimilation of objectivity to the product of an objective procedure."[5] So Feyerabend does not turn his back on science. He criticizes positivism and its assimilation of objectivity to the product of an objective procedure that refers to an indefinite play of subject and object. It is in this framework that his questioning of epistemology is inscribed, when he invokes the distinction between science and myth: "Both science and myth cap common sense with a theoretical superstructure."[6]

## Field Sciences/Experimental Sciences

Isabelle Stengers pursues the work of disentanglement and, in the same spirit, she retains from Karl Popper something other than the discriminating position by which a science is a science only from the moment when its propositions are refutable, falsifiable. Against the image generally given of Popper, she compares her position to that of an "art critic."[7] Popper's major thesis was put forth, in 1934, in *The Logic of Scientific Discovery*. Indeed, Popper took on irrefutability, which he considers a vice. At the time he opposed the theses of the Vienna Circle (stated in 1929), defending a unified conception of the world based on the alignment of the sciences of mind with the sciences of nature. On this point Popper developed an entire critique of Gottlob Carnap's theses. What Popper essentially reproaches positivism for is its lack of novelty, the singular moment of scientific discovery. He opposes, to the closure within an unfalsifiable theory, incapable of producing anything new, an epistemology of risk, of daring, for the purpose of science is of course the production of novelty. It is precisely this epistemology of risk, this experimental epistemology, that Stengers defends against the various temptations to routinization and sterilization.

Nevertheless, Stengers advocates differentiating two regimes of scientificity. Indeed, she distinguishes, even within the natural sciences, the experimental sciences (physics, chemistry, molecular biology, in which discovery is produced on the basis of experiment) and the sciences with Darwinian ancestry, such as geology, meteorology, and climatology, which have no experimental object but try to reconstitute experimental processes. It would therefore be fitting to differentiate the field sciences, which do not lend themselves to an establishment of experimental devices enabling the researcher to test his hypotheses, but only offer the possibility of gathering indexes, traces, from the laboratory sciences; the latter could gain access to the Galilean paradigm. "Irreducible uncertainty is the mark of the field sciences. It does not hold to an inferiority, but rather to a modification of the relations between 'subject' and 'object.'"[8]

This distinction between field sciences and experimental sciences is not for all that irreducible, according to Stengers, for whom it is rather of the order of the model of the Cities, in Boltanski and Thévenot's sense, than a definitive split between two modes of scientificity. The difference resides above all in the mode of positioning of the subject with respect to the question she poses. In the laboratory sciences, the theoretical, experimental sciences, the scientist is the one who decides, as Kant emphasized. Stengers, by isolating the singularity of these experimental sciences, has the objective of disqualifying them as a universalizable model. In this regard, she hails the work of Stephen Jay Gould when he insists on the novelty, the singularity of evolutionary biology, Darwin's heir, and whose criteria differ from those of the experimental sciences.[9] By escaping this model, Gould shows that there are other regimes of scientificity, more directed toward historicity and narrativity.

This distinction has therefore strengthened the project that Stengers has had since La Nouvelle Alliance, which is to track down the univocal modelization, the sources of reduction, and the obstacles to innovation. It is a matter of avoiding a repeat of the destiny of chemistry, subjugated by a triumphant physics imposing its model and annexing the former as auxiliary knowledge.[10] What is common to both the field sciences and the theoretical and experimental sciences must be their sense of risk, which, according to Stengers, constitutes the nodal criterion for belonging to the scientific field. The notion of risk must incite the social sciences not to enclose themselves in preestablished objects or theoretical frameworks shut in on themselves, but rather to be open to the eruption of novelty, of irreversibility.

## Hypnosis: A Problem at a Crossroads

The crisis of causalism and the current interest in unsayable border zones are also noticeable in another field of knowledge, psychoanalysis, with the rediscovery of hypnosis. This practice, repressed by Freud, who substituted for it the scene of the cure, allows one to pose anew the problem of the social bond. Jean-Paul Escande discovered just how fascinating the question of hypnosis is, when he read an interview that the great specialist on the question, Léon Chertok, gave in 1985 to *L'Autre Journal*. He concluded with this sentence from Isabelle Stengers: "Hypnosis raises the problem of the affective bond that allows us to live." For Escande, that was "one of the most violent shocks of [his] life."[11] We are far removed from Lacan's matheme and Borromean knots, when the pure symbolic had to empty any manifestation of affect. Quite the contrary, today this dimension is being reevaluated. It is what incited Stengers's interest, as much as the meeting with Chertok in 1984. Hypnosis is a "problem at a crossroads"[12] that traces in the negative the positivity of a new moral economy. It has given the hope of defeating, in the laboratory, the opposition between truth and fiction, the possible experimentation with a becoming true. "The question is whether Freud's abandonment of this hope . . . signifies that the institution of psychoanalysis marks the end of the analogy between therapy, henceforth analytic, and the laboratory."[13]

Freud preferred to work on the artifact constituted by the analytic protocol as a controllable area that he substituted for Charcot's hypnosis. The psychoanalyst then created his object, in the manner of nineteenth-century chemists. Hypnosis also touches on a moral problem. It was disavowed as a practice and accused of not addressing the individual as a conscious, free, and rational being. "The lived experience of scientists with hypnosis interests me more than the lived experience of hypnosis itself."[14] On this level, hypnosis plays the role of the test, of the risk in psychoanalytic practice as a practice with an uncertain status. It is therefore a good test of Stengers's point of view, which defines scientificity by its capacity to take risks on the road of innovation.

Now, the question seems to have been reopened even by Freud's own statements in 1937, when he recognized certain limits to the practice he had established.[15] He said then that transference was not sufficient to make psychic reality a theoretical object. Now, hypnosis remains an undecidable, a risk, a challenge to be reactivated as a "narcissistic wound, just as much for experimenters as for therapists."[16] A site of osmosis between rationality and irrationality, hypnosis enables one to ask anew the question of the bond, of suggestion. Here one finds oneself not in the confines but at the heart of what may allow an interrogation of the social bond in its most opaque manifestation. "Isn't it time we stop criticizing suggestion so as to understand that what we call suggestion in fact designates what gives humans the possibility of thinking and living together?"[17]

## Reconnecting to the Tradition of the Social Sciences

Jean-Pierre Dupuy has succeeded in constructing bridges between disciplines on the basis of modelization. Through the angle of mathematical and logical models on autonomy, self-organization, and self-reference, he manages to make a transdisciplinary link between the natural or life sciences and the social sciences. He does not have the object of transposing a model produced by the exact sciences in order to make it function in the social sciences, or the other way around, but rather of making the modelizations resonate among themselves. Differently from those who gaze from the side of physics to detect the immutable rules of a scientificity valid for all fields of knowledge, Dupuy has shown, with self-organization, that this model "was in the social sciences, in social philosophy well before the natural sciences. It was at the root of my work on Adam Smith on the theme of the invisible hand."[18] According to Dupuy, the current bent of the social sciences toward investigations into the notions of disorder, chaos, and irreversibility comes less from the late accounting for the lessons of quantum physics than from the traditions proper to the social sciences. Durkheim already staged a tension between order and disorder when he began with the idea of a transcendence of the social with respect to individuals.[19] It is above all in René Girard that Dupuy finds this tension, because the transcendence of the social is effected in the very course of the sacrificial crisis. "It's a disorder that produces a new order."[20]

## The "Experimental" Path

Herbert Simon's idea of an experimental epistemology, which he gets from ethnomethodology, is therefore broadly practiced in the social sciences today. It comes down to considering the fundamental episte-

mological problems as questions of cognition that leave the epistemological framework to become objects of study, which may then be observed. With this reversal in respect to the notion of epistemological
rupture, which to the contrary emphasized the line of division, the
overarching position of the epistemologist is common to ethnomethodology, the sociology of action, cognitive science, the anthropology of science, and history conceived as an inquiry according to
the indexical paradigm.

Besides, certain historians have become engaged in this "experimental" path,[21] which seeks to exalt the multiplicity of possibilities.
They call on the imagination, the creativity of the historian to restore
the proliferation of the past when it was present: "Every order is an
artifact."[22] Leaving behind passivity conceived as a traditional virtue
of science, experimenting so as to make human creativity spring forth:
"Thus defined, science belongs to avant-garde art."[23] Historical experimentation then opens onto an alliance with literary fiction—whose
ties with historical writing have been amply demonstrated[24]—without
ever being reduced to it.

Daniel S. Milo and Alain Boureau have also reacted against the
distrust manifested by an entire generation of historians with regard
to surface phenomena, which have been accused of deriving from
mere contingency and so of being exterior to scientific exigency. "The
primacy of structures in history thus goes together with the evacuation, or at least the neutralization, of the subject/actor. In practice it
leads to an accrued indifference to intentionality."[25] As an alternative,
they propose the idea of an experimental history that would allow an
emphasis on the active role of the historian, her imagination, her capacity to reactivate the field of unrecognized multiple possibilities of
the past by putting it into play as the present. As a heuristic model,
they use comparatism and the anthropological method of transforming the everyday and familiar universe into a strange world.

*Thirty-five*

# Pacified Relations between Philosophy
# and the Social Sciences

The relations between the social sciences and philosophy have always been ambivalent. Born in the lap of the philosophy of the Enlightenment, the social sciences endowed themselves with the great project whose dual end was to explain the nature of the social and to build a better world in a progressive perspective. The French Revolution of 1789 sanctioned this innovative ambition by abandoning the traditional denomination of "moral and political sciences" so as to give a clear place to the new sciences of the human. Throughout the nineteenth century, new disciplines succeeded in cutting the umbilical cord that bound them to philosophy in order to assure their development on the basis of a specific object and method, legitimating their taking flight. The new adventurers' gazes were then oriented toward the natural sciences. If reason must govern the world, it is thanks to the scientific method that it may deploy.

The lengthy emergence of the social sciences as installed, institutionalized disciplines has taken place in the twentieth century with a strong period in France, that of structuralist thought. The institutional breakthrough of anthropology, linguistics, and psychoanalysis was achieved at the price of proclamations on the end of philosophy and the irreversible advent of a thought of the concept. The rupture seemed to be consummated. This break between the social sciences and philosophy, besides its dimension as a stake of power and legitimate knowledge, has been particularly accentuated in France in the twentieth century insofar as the social sciences have had difficulties imposed on them. What was needed was the structuralist lightning bolt/coup d'état to win a finally decentralized university (the EHESS) to their cause.

In addition, the two dominant philosophies of the 1960s, Marxism and Heideggerianism, strongly contributed to the ambivalence of the relations between philosophy and the social sciences. For Marxism, philosophy was supposed to be either surpassed by the social sciences or erected (with Althusser and the Althusserians) into a scientific theory of empirical practices in order to unveil in them the role of ideology. As for the Heideggerian theses, they demonstrated a deep contempt for the swarming activity of the social sciences condemned to the inauthenticity of the being. Onto these two postures, contradictory but impugning dialogue a priori, was grafted the tradition of French positivism, which insisted on the notion of rupture (Bachelard), or even of epistemological break (Foucault, Althusser), as a weapon of war against the continuism of the history of ideas.

## A Reconfiguration

Today, the decline of the great unifying paradigms and the legitimation acquired by the various knowledges constituted as the disciplines of the social sciences have caused an evolution of the relations between the latter and philosophy, to the point where one may speak of pacified relations. "The proposed theory no longer gives a place to carry on the tense relations with philosophy that characterized the previous period."[1] We are even witnessing a spectacular reversal, because in the 1960s philosophers had to nourish their reflections on the basis of empirical studies and laboratory results, whereas today we have seen that scholars in the social sciences most often seek in philosophy the concepts they need to analyze better their empirical material.

Philosophy is finding again its dual role of a "purveyor of concepts"[2] and of a reflexive reworking of scientific contents. The latter dimension, traditional to philosophy, had become all the more necessary by the atomization of knowledges and terminologies, ever more technical, too specialized for communication among themselves. This evolution toward a parceling of the sciences has particularly negative consequences that may lead "to a feudalization, a tribalization that can be surmounted only by a knowledge of a reflexive type to reappropriate scientific contents."[3]

This task first comes back to philosophy, which may thus find again its vocation to develop a second-level problematization with a globalizing scope. Insofar as the organon of philosophy is reflection, the appropriation it allows of the production of knowledge is felt by the various social sciences to be indispensable, especially as this function is not part of an imperialist aim to demonstrate the absolute mastery of philosophy in the often cacophonous concert of the social sciences. Philosophy is lived more and more as the becoming of the social sciences, whereas previously the latter saw it as their past, their archaeology. Within this new configuration, philosophy may play an essential communicative role, "to surmount the excommunication that scientific production has been struck with as a broad aspect of cultural production, and thus to bring culture into the process of recognizing the contents that have been produced. Only a reflexive power may do that."[4]

## Renouncing the Philosopher-King

The pacification of relations between the social sciences and philosophy is therefore the fruit of a twofold evolution: that of philosophy, which no longer claims the place of mastering meaning, and that of the social sciences, which are no longer inscribed in a dynamic of falsely surmounting philosophical investigations. The beginning of this shift is contemporary in France with the rediscovery of Max Weber's major contribution. Weber in fact initiated the progressive renunciation of a recourse to an abstract, total, and unique reason, in order to oppose the multiplicity of plural rationalities, practices, and complexes to it. Weber inaugurated the great transformation of the passage from reason to rationalities, without being well received by a philosophical world that was deprived of its position of mastery and kept him away, as a sociologist, outside the most legitimate scholarly City. That contributed to conceiving philosophy and the social sciences as two incommensurable paths. With Weber, comparatism was articulated with the finitude of concrete societies, and broke with the idea of an absolute to be conquered. This secularization would allow a deployment of the effectiveness of practical thought and a new possible relation between empirical studies and their problematization.[5]

So the figure of the philosopher-king disappears. That in no way reduces the historical task of philosophical discourse as a reflexive discourse called on to render intelligible a more and more complex, disparate, and shattered reality. This reflexivity of the aftermath corresponds to a broader task than that of the so-called tradition of reflexive philosophy. At this level, we may deem that we are entering a new philosophical age of modernity, which no longer corresponds to the construction of great systems or to what succeeded modernity, the era of the deconstruction of philosophy as a metaphysical project.

Refitting the question of meaning implied by the new task of contemporary philosophy is leading the latter to form relations with the social sciences that were hitherto thought of in terms of antagonism. Of course, the social sciences were born in the extension of the project of the Enlightenment and from a faith in the progress achieved by reason, but they defined their enterprise as that of a critique of the naiveties inherent in the belief in a possible mastery or transparent apprehension of human history by its subjects. Their historical role was therefore to show the various unseen determinations that weighed on the individual and the social and to objectify social practices. Investigations in the social sciences have brought to the surface the effectiveness of a social unconscious behind the naiveties of the Enlightenment that postulated a possible transparency. That is the major and irreversible contribution of the social sciences in general and the structuralist moment in particular. There is appearing today a new phase marked by the reactivation of the Weberian project of understanding the consciousness of the actors, which may allow a reconciliation of those who hold to the specificity of the philosophical stance and those who hold to the critical project of the positive sciences.

## Reglobalizing

This perspective opens the way to a "reglobalization" of parceled knowledges through a philosophy capable of reappropriating what has been objectified outside it, what the Hegelian tradition calls "positivities." Thus is affirmed a philosophy that is more and more receptive to questions of ethics, law, and politics, and to social questions. So the conditions of the dialogue are more favorable between these two traditions. A new generation feels this dialogue to be a necessity. "Philosophy students really want to learn politics and law and know what economics is, or else they have the anguishing feeling of being cut off from reality."[6] For their part, the sociologists who leave the tradition of comprehensive sociology are oriented toward the works of Peter L. Berger, Alfred Schutz, Thomas Luckmann, Edmund Husserl, and others. There may result a dynamic proper to the social sciences such that they promote themselves in opposition to the preceding period. Instead of seeking to rid themselves of their philosophical origin and presenting themselves as surpassing the philosophical horizon in the name of their scientific capacity, they may work "for the philosophical becoming of these sciences."[7]

Such a perspective of opening enables the philosophers, for their part, to reconnect with a long tradition in the history of philosophy based on an active dialogue, a problematization of scientific discoveries. It may contribute to keeping philosophers from withdrawing into a mutilating, impoverishing conception of a "restricted philosophy" that has retreated into its little estate. Sylvain Auroux, an epistemologist of the sciences of language, whose itinerary is aligned with the tradition of his mentor Jean-Toussaint Desanti, is firmly placed at the articulation of philosophy and the social sciences. A philosopher, he has worked within a particular "positivity," linguistics. On the basis of this dual competency, he reconnects with the encyclopedic spirit of the eighteenth century[8] and defends the idea that philosophy can be only a secondary activity in relation to scientific practices: "As Desanti said, to be a philosopher of mathematics is to put oneself in the field of mathematics."[9] An initiator of this rapprochement of philosophy and science, he harshly judges all the efforts at distancing that confine philosophical investigation to the literary humanities. Recalling to what point philosophers such as Descartes, Spinoza, Leibniz, and more recently Russell, Carnap, and Quine conduct both a philosophical interrogation and a mastery of scientific knowledge, Auroux deplores the retreat to a "restricted philosophy."[10]

Philosophers have had the tendency to withdraw into the little estate that constitutes their disciplinary and institutional anatomy. After losing the battle between the philosophy of nature and the progress of the physical sciences, they found a base of retreat in the sciences of the human, defined as an ontological rupture that would assure them an autonomy. But, like the army, philosophy has all too often become the "great silent one" in the area of contemporary problems. For Auroux, the philosopher today must once again be in touch with the present as much as with the past and show how innovations participate in a singular historical moment and so are to be referred to their contextual conditions of emergence. The historical requirement also leads Auroux to revisit the Aristotelian categories in which he perceives the first interesting definitions in linguistics and grammar.[11] So he places himself in opposition to the French epistemological tradition of ruptures and breaks, which refers to the past in a prescientific or ideological manner. Thus, the historian's procedure allows one better to perceive the third revolution in progress before our eyes, that of the "automatization of the means of human communication."[12] It is intervening after two other revolutions, those of writing and grammaticization. It is therefore vain to search for a date of decisive rupture, a radical break on the basis of which the sciences of language would be constituted. Whether it is 1816 with Bopp, 1916 with Saussure, or 1957 with Greimas, these refittings should be resituated in a longer period.

For Auroux, the tension whose primary vocation is that of a universalist project that has led it to impugn the dispersion of knowledges, even while recognizing a commonality with the various positive knowledges—this tension is proper to philosophy—may be surpassed or displaced. It is fitting to revive an epistemology on new bases, not those of the break or the overarching position, but rather by replacing the "critical and reflexive function at the heart of knowledge,"[13] reconnecting thereby with the freshness of the philosophy of the Enlightenment,[14] and renouncing the imperial position. For their part, the social sciences broadly call on the philosophers. Thus, in the journal founded by Claude Lévi-Strauss, *L'Homme,* "the authors most often cited in the articles are not the anthropologists, but Quine, Wittgenstein, Strawson, and others."[15]

## The Program of Modernity

Philosophy's status as a resource for the social sciences is explicit in the assessment that Alain Caillé gives of ten years of evolution in the social sciences, in which he presents a "plea for a political philosophy that has the look of science."[16] He begins with the observation that the function of the social sciences has been to accompany the advent of modernity, to contribute to the symbolic and ideological liquidation of the aftereffects of traditional society. This historical task of eviction of any foundation outside society itself, of any transcendence other than what is immanent to human rationality, is in the course of realization: "This program of modernity in developed Western societies is almost totally realized in its outlines."[17]

Modernity has succeeded in unburdening itself of the particularisms of traditional society so as to impose the three universals that characterize it: the market, the representative state, and science. This very success explains the breathlessness experienced today by the social sciences, less in phase with political stakes insofar as their adventure has ended in this area. Are they for all that condemned to disappear? Of course not, but on the condition that they recharge their program with new ambitions. They may revisit the three universals of modernity to attempt to respond to the always unresolved question: what is the essence of the social bond, of what holds human beings together?[18] For this it is important to question anew the break considered as constituting the specificity of the social sciences. "The first hurdle is that which organizes the untenable dichotomy between judgments of fact and judgments of value."[19] In these conditions, the split between the social sciences and philosophy must be surpassed—notably in the implicit division that made the philosopher the guardian of normative judgment, whereas the specialist in the social sciences was the guarantor of the veracity of the fact. To achieve this rapprochement, Caillé suggests going back in time to reinvestigate the situation and the problematics from before the disentanglement of philosophy and the social sciences.

Of course, this is not an issue of questioning knowledges in their strict specialization, nor of returning to a distant past. But it is possible to conduct, with respect "to the movement of parcellization and atomization of knowledge, a reverse movement of resynthesization that would allow the social sciences to return to their common origin, political philosophy."[20] Such an orientation presupposes revisiting the texts of the tradition in a hermeneutic perspective of dialogue between what they meant in their time and what they mean today. In this perspective of opening a common space that would be the horizon of political philosophy, we find the positions of the one who inspired Alain Caillé's critical work, Claude Lefort. The latter's trajectory, from sociology to political philosophy, began with the observation of the basic indeterminacy of the truth of the social relation. This observation made a positive grasp impossible.

Caillé first borrowed a critical procedure from the dominant utilitarian paradigm. By denouncing the four divinities (Reason, Interest, Individualism, and Evolution), he sought the ways of an antipositivist paradigm. According to Philippe Chanial, at this stage "the social sciences are then a modern form of ethics and must ask the question of the just, the desirable, and the true."[21] Today, Caillé is seeking the bases of an "adisciplinary" discipline, a federating site that recalls the era of moral and political science. But where may this site of unity be located? If we follow Claude Lefort, this place may be incarnated by political philosophy insofar as it leads to society's own interrogation of itself. As the political is a constitutive axis of the social, political philosophy sketches the space of questioning on the institutional variants of society. "Political philosophy is, finally, a questioning of the conditions of social unity."[22]

This possible reconstitution of a unitary questioning is all the more achievable as more and more philosophers contribute to desacralizing the philosophical enterprise and make a path in the direction of the social sciences, such as Habermas, Rorty, Ricoeur, Taylor, and others. Caillé's idea of an "adisciplinary discipline" nonetheless leaves Chanial skeptical; the latter opposes to this "discipline" the indeterminate character of a political philosophy referring to a mode of questioning more than to a tradition, and to an immaterial theoretical space more than to empirical studies. "We must finally take political philosophy as a forum, the space of a properly modern tension between, on the one hand, this horizon maintained by the unity whose economy we cannot gauge, and, on the other hand, the respect for the plurality of terminologies, discourses, and disciplines."[23]

## The Difficult Dialogue between History and Philosophy

The dialogue between history and philosophy has not really taken place, and this absence of an opening has given way to many misunderstandings, as can be measured by the ambivalent relations between historians and the work of Michel Foucault. The French historians of the *Annales* school, who dominated during the sixties and seventies, had a tendency to emphasize a methodology, the rules of a profession, instead of an epistemology of the historian's practice. Roger Chartier, one of the rare historians to have carried on a true dialogue with philosophy, essentially attributes the responsibility for this absence of dialogue to the philosophers alone, "who incorporate a hierarchy of disciplines"[24] within a field where they have the impression of occupying a mastering position. This observation is not false, even if the current "secularization" of the philosophers henceforth allows one to envision a renewal of the dialogue.

The second reason Chartier invokes is the very tradition of the history of philosophy in France, marked by an ahistorical approach, that of Martial Guéroult.[25] It is true that the purely structural, systematic approach adopted by Guéroult turns its back on history so as better to gauge the purely internal coherence of a work. At the basis of his method, "dianoematics," Guéroult revisits the monuments of the history of philosophy (the work of Fichte, Descartes, Spinoza, and others) as autonomous structures, independent of time. "The philosophical objective applied to the objects of the history of philosophy is a function of viewing the material of this history—that is, the systems—as objects with their own value, their own reality that belongs only to them and may be explained through them alone."[26] But the great architectures that Guéroult constructs represent only one current among the philosophers, even if it is the one that has most strongly marked philosophical discourse in the time of structuralism. These obstacles are surmountable, because they belong to a past epoch, and today historians may reformulate certain historical problems by engaging in philosophical reflection.

The dialogue recently begun between Paul Ricoeur and certain historians attests to the potentialities of certain concepts for a better understanding of the various modes of writing history, the status of historical cognition, and the nature of the forms of appropriation. Here an entire common workshop becomes possible, that of a history of philosophical ideas that takes into account at once the literalness of the works and their inscription in a broader cultural framework. "To give back to the history of philosophy its historicity is to inscribe in it the history of the reception of doctrines."[27] With philosophers leaving the systematic closure of the work that is bound up in its internal logic, with historians freeing themselves of the prejudices of a guild given over to empiricism, the search for conceptual circulation throughout the disciplinary boundaries finally becomes possible.

## Sociology's Resource in Philosophy

In the field of sociology, the philosophical categories evidently circulate more easily. Philosophy is often a spectacular resource on this terrain, as is illustrated, for example, by the "sociology of action," which borrows from the categories of common sense deriving from the sphere of action, of relations, of feelings on the empirical plane, as well as from the philosophical stance of a theoretical notional labor: this approach defines a new field of investigation, that of a "categorical sociology, trying to put to the test local theories on the categories of common sense, and so to elaborate them."[28] This field implies a relationship of proximity with philosophy, and in this framework the work of Luc Boltanski and Laurent Thévenot on denunciation takes place, as do that of Boltanski on *agapē* or suffering, that of Bernard Conein on invitation, that of Patrick Pharo or Denis Duclos on civility, and so on. "As a sociologist, I consume much more philosophy than the sociologists, but I pose myself the problem of understanding singular social situations of one category or another. So I remain a sociologist."[29]

Indeed, the danger is of leaving one's starting discipline to escape it "upwards" by abandoning the field of empirical studies—especially because sociology has not sufficiently constructed its own categorical space, lacking a tradition rooted in objects deriving from interpersonal relations. A better understanding of intersubjectivity in an earlier period valorized the relations with linguistics, in the pragmatic tradition of Austin and Searle. Then the categories came to take the task of renewing sociological investigation. "For me, the interest in philosophers has been a means of giving this conceptual elaboration back to sociology."[30]

Louis Quéré values just as much his sociologist's stance—to be sure, nourished by philosophy—but he intends to remain clear on the latter's use. He observes that one of the major problems of French sociology is its deficit in the area of conceptual elaboration; to remedy this, he surmises, the philosophical detour is essential. It enables one to proceed to clarifications in analysis and to bring to emergence new modes of reasoning to treat action, the event. "One must appropriate the result of these reflections for one's own discipline."[31] All this assumes a conservation of the vitality of the specific mode of questioning of one's own disciplinary tradition and hence an avoidance of the frequent disconnection from one's specialization of origin to the profit of a pure theoretical speculation. "It's clear that one is impugning the two radical breaks that brought on the birth of sociology. But one must still do social science."[32]

## A Cross-Fertilization

This relationship of proximity with philosophy is common to the CREA, the CSI, and the new investigations in the discipline of history. There is quite an important disturbance on the basis of which one can affirm that "the prohibition in the social sciences against philosophy has been lifted."[33] This opening may be found in the investigations of a new geography, which has for a long time already been out of its descriptive bed in search of the paths of an axiomatization.[34]

This new relationship of cross-fertilization between philosophy and the social sciences is facilitated by the trajectory of certain philosophers, who are little by little leaving their position of mastery to problematize the outside of philosophy. We have already evoked such a trajectory with Sylvain Auroux. This is also the constant requirement of the philosophical trajectory of Paul Ricoeur, as he is in dialogue with semiology, history, and psychoanalysis, before revisiting the sphere of law. For his part, Michel Serres, a true border crosser, has devoted himself to problems of society such as the school and ecology.[35] Beginning with the observation that philosophy has overvalued the role attributed to language and lost contact with things, he advocates a reappropriation of things in a globalizing and almost encyclopedic scope.

The evolution of a philosopher such as Alain Badiou is also symptomatic. After being a convinced Althusserian, a defender of the primacy of the One, today he affirms that one "must, on the contrary, recognize, from the beginning, that there exist many places where thoughts are constituted."[36] He renounces the overarching posture that would aim for a retotalization of entities as heterogeneous as science, art, politics, and sexual experience, which are as many places of thought, but heterogeneous with respect to one another. Today, he conceives the work of philosophy as a recognition of that plurality of emergence of the places of thought, of truth, and of understanding the way in which they constitute an epoch, a historical moment:

> Philosophy undertakes to think its time through the common placement of the state of the procedures that condition it. Its operators, whatever they may be, always aim to think "together," to configure in a single exercise of thought the epochal disposition of the matheme, the poem, political invention, and love (or the evenemental status of the Two). In this sense, philosophy's only question is very much that of the truth, not that it produces one, but rather because it proposes a mode of access to the unity of a moment of truths.[37]

This task comes down to gauging the evolution of singular configurations and, to achieve it, Badiou gives philosophy the objective of "drawing the map of what derives effectively from thought"[38]—this requires a particular attention to novelty, breaks, the plays and replays of evenementality.[39]

# Conclusion

The world moves, and the social sciences whose object is to conceive of this change undergo the same disturbance of their categories of making the present understandable, carrying in their wake the exhaustion of previously dominant paradigms: functionalism, structuralism, Marxism, and so on.

The concern that aims to understand the foundations of the social bond, what holds a society together, is of course not new. Innovation is gauged from the angle of analysis of many studies that leave behind the dominant models: the one that exclusively privileges the utilitarian considerations of the market, the individual, and her strategic singularity, as well as the opposite/complementary model in which the schemata of reproduction, the internal logic of the work in manipulative and reductive institutions, are prevalent. The latter practices a philosophy of suspicion with regard to the justifications of the actors, a strategy of unveiling their presuppositions conceived as the expression of their bad faith.

The new investigation of the social bond implies another scale of analysis, closer to the social actors. The everyday and representations play the role of methodological levers that allow a greater interest in the instituter than in the instituted. The notions of situation, moment, generation, and so on, are thus revisited on the basis of the narrative procedures of construction and reconstruction, of reconfiguration, of "emplotment" of the social actors themselves.

The great new fact is the reconciliation of previously antinomic positions, between the natural sciences, the social sciences, and philosophy, to build relationships of alliance, often at the initiative of the social sciences themselves, which have renounced the culture of resentment that was theirs when they were emancipated from philosophical speculation.

Stengthened today by their own tradition, the social sciences may again open themselves to dialogue. The new configuration that is emerging from current research cannot be reduced to a single current of thought with an encompassing vocation. It is traversed, we have seen, by multiple polarities. Behind this diversity, two divergent philosophical orientations irrigate the investigative workshops of the social sciences. In the first place, it appears that the modern, rationalist program remains incomplete and still inspires the works in progress. It is aligned with the tradition of critical philosophy, that of Kant, pursued and displaced by Husserl, finding in France its continuation with Maurice Merleau-Ponty and Paul Ricoeur. The second youth that the phenomenological program is seeing, enriched by the hermeneutic "graft," attests to the fertility of this orientation. This tradition may escape the relativist temptation, thanks to an anthropological and social history of meaning and subjectivity, by impugning the arbitrary antievolutionism of the great Foucauldian *epistēmē*s as well as the great teleological narratives.

The tradition that takes its source of inspiration from Nietzsche is manifestly different. It finds its extensions in France with Gilles Deleuze or Michel Serres. This perspective, more transversal, notably nourishes the studies in the new anthropology of science. The anthropology of networks that it carries within it offers the possibility of sketching a rhizomatic history of modernity on the basis of the notion of the "extension of networks" and may make its honey from the historical anthropology of communication and of intellectual technologies.

Beyond this opposition, one may deem that the social sciences in their entirety take into account a conception that is no longer either that of the deification of the subject or that of its dissolution. Today, they have in common a vision of the growing complexity of problems and a refusal of any form of dogmatism, reductionism, in postulating a certain form of indeterminacy that makes impossible and vain the enclosure of humanity in an exclusivist logic, whether moral, national, genetic, or neuronal.

Of course, the programmatic orientations of the emergent paradigm entail a few risks of blind spots. Thus, the emphasis on interactionism, narrativity, and the latter's cognitive supports tends to focus its attention exclusively on individual agents and "instituting" plots, most often forgetting the resistance of "instituted" plots. The interest in justification and, in general, the effort to construct a grammar of intersubjective agreement may have the perverse effect of somewhat rapidly emptying the various forms of conflictuality, of material or symbolic imposition, the structuring relations of force, by reconnecting them either to a passing cognitive dissonance, a mere defect of coordination, or, on the contrary, to an insurmountable schism, an originary noncoincidence of society with itself.

In the same way, as we have already evoked, the register of temporality used by most scholars is a surface one. The attention rightly recentered on situational singularity, after the excesses of immobile history, may nevertheless have the negative effect of missing the historical thickness of social phenomena.

Noticing the fertility of the recent orientations must incite us to an accrued vigilance so that we do not forget yesterday's achievements. The very existence, inevitable as it is, of these blind spots in the emergent paradigm is an invitation to a more sedimented practice of accumulated knowledge in the social sciences so that we may avoid returning to a precritical humanism.

The disappointment in the great systemic alternatives has led to a legitimate caution and to an "interstitial" approach to the social bond. There is no "other world" of utopia, but a "lower world" of the gift, of recovered or preserved civility. But if society is incomprehensible without its interstices and ecological niches, it is not made only of interstices. Between the slack "depth" of the fundamental social bond (civility, primary sociality, the symbolic order) and micro-objects, the quick cuts of micro-*storia* or of ethnomethodological, interactionist, or neophenomenological sociology, there are many other horizontal, vertical, and transversal planes, among them that of intermediary macro-objects and great structuring and periodizing scansions.

The social sciences therefore pursue, by other paths, their modern mission of clarifying decisions thanks to the light shed on the various forms of rationality. They contribute in this way to closing the authoritarian paths, such as that which consists of settling the complexity of problems by imposing such and such a solution from above. To the contrary, their pragmatic function today consists of clarifying the public debate, valorizing a cautious judgment issuing from the conflictuality of points of view and from the uncertain character of the questions asked of society. Also, the complexity of the questions today is such that, as with the question of where the human begins (in bioethics, for example), a single specialist, even of exceptional competency, can in no case take the totality of aspects into account. Nonetheless, complexity must not exclude the "laypeople" from the procedures of debate and decision. The rediscovery by the social sciences of the competency belonging to "common sense" leads to not conceiving committees of experts isolated from the rest of society, and, to the contrary, makes possible the projection of a new, broadened public sphere of communication.

The lone expert in his laboratory must therefore place his knowledge at the disposal of public debate. In this regard, behind the effervescence of current research, there is an outline of the emergence of the definition of a participatory democracy that Bruno Latour terms the "Parliament of Things," conceived as the reunion of delegates and problems, of hybrid objects, of everything deriving from the various realms of biopolitics. This parliament of spokespersons, of parties concerned by the question debated in the City, casts the foundations of a complex democracy in which points of view that would remain minoritarian coexist and are debated. This new democracy is not based on mere past compromises between divergent interests, but on a collective process perpetually reflecting on the basis of a staging of the conflict of interpretations in the public sphere.

It is here, on the basis of this redefinition of politics, which has finally become the political in a broader sense, that the two traditions may meet. Indeed, they both contribute to redynamizing a public sphere articulated around the diversity of expressions. Hermeneutics, as Paul Ricoeur understands it, as an art of questioning, may represent a way of surpassing the still perceptible antinomies.

This hermeneutic procedure may indeed allow an assimilation of the critical moment and thereby a reestablishment of a communication jammed by temporal and spatial distance and by the various effects of domination or manipulation, as Habermas has shown. So it integrates a methodological time, that of explanation, that of the procedural and formal rules of discussion. But it especially leads to a second moment, that of belonging, comprehension, and appropriation, which permits the construction of a common space, produced by common questions. What is then postulated has nothing to do with unformed eclecticism, or with a new dogmatism imposed in the name of tradition; it is the necessary dialogic conducted by the spokespersons whose convictions, testimonies, and "ontological vehemence," to borrow Paul Ricoeur's terms, reveal the force of attestation.

# Notes

[In the case of works whose original is not in English, I refer to English versions if they are available, on occasion altering the translation; if they are not, the translation is in each case mine.—*Trans.*]

## Introduction

1. [The City (*la Cité*) is an innovative concept in ethnomethodology formulated by Luc Boltanski and Laurent Thévenot, which Dosse explains in chapter 15. The City constitutes an individual's model of greatness: greatness is the status an individual must attain, in an act of protest, in order to gain access to the public sphere. To do this, the individual appeals to higher principles of justice and commonly accepted values. The movement toward greatness is driven by the "ambition to universality"; the City is the ensemble of principles and values that is invoked. Boltanski and Thévenot propose six different Cities or sets of general principles. The innovative quality of this concept, according to Dosse, lies in its valorization of the particular with respect to the general, through its maintenance of the individual by a recognition of a plurality of collectivities. Drawing on sources as diverse as Saint Augustine (the "City of God"), Thomas Hobbes (the "City of renown"), Adam Smith (the "mercantile City"), and the Comte de Saint-Simon (the "industrial City"), Boltanski and Thévenot identify the following Cities or models of greatness: civic greatness, domestic greatness, inspired greatness, the greatness of renown, mercantile greatness, and industrial greatness.—*Trans.*]

2. Marcel Gauchet, "Changement de paradigme en sciences sociales," *Le Débat* 50 (May–August 1988): 165–70.

3. François Dosse, *History of Structuralism,* 2 vols., trans. Deborah Glassman (Minneapolis: University of Minnesota Press, 1997).

4. [In French, Centre de Recherche en Épistémologie Appliquée.—*Trans.*]

5. Olivier Mongin, *Face au scepticisme* (Paris: La Découverte, 1994).

6. Anthony Giddens, *Social Theory and Modern Sociology,* (Stanford, Calif.: Stanford University Press, 1987).

7. See Paul Ricoeur, *From Text to Action: Essays in Hermeneutics*, vol. 2, trans. Kathleen Blamey and John B. Thompson (Evanston, Ill.: Northwestern University Press, 1991).

8. To borrow the words of Henri Atlan, *Le Cristal et la Fumée. Essai sur l'organisation du vivant* (Paris: Seuil, 1979).

## Part I. One Generation

## One. The Galaxy of Michel Serres's Disciples

1. Michel Serres, *Feu et Signaux de brume. Zola* (Paris: Grasset, 1975).

2. Michel Serres, *Le Système de Leibniz et ses modèles mathématiques*, 2 vols. (Paris: Presses Universitaires de France, 1968).

3. Michel Serres, *Hermès*, vol. 1, *La Communication* (Paris: Minuit, 1969); vol. 2, *L'Interférence* (Minuit, 1972); vol. 3, *La Traduction* (Paris: Minuit, 1974); vol. 4, *La Distribution* (Paris: Minuit, 1977); vol. 5, *Le Passage du Nord-Ouest* (Paris: Minuit, 1980).

4. Michel Serres, with Bruno Latour, *Conversations on Science, Culture, and Time*, trans. Roxanne Lapidus (Ann Arbor: University of Michigan Press, 1995), 105.

5. Ibid., 81.

6. [In French, Centre de Sociologie de l'Innovation.—*Trans.*]

7. [The *grandes écoles* are the elite schools of France's system of higher education, differing from the universities in that they are specialized and require prospective students to pass a competitive entrance exam. The most well known of these is the École Normale Supérieure (ENS), which trains educators. Among the others are the École Nationale de l'Administration (ENA), which trains high government officials; the École Polytechnique; and the École des Mines. The students in these schools have long had an activist organization, the Union des Grandes Écoles, which is part of the UNEF (Union Nationale des Étudiants de France—National Union of Students of France.—*Trans.*]

8. Michel Callon, interview with the author.

9. Alain Touraine, *The Self-Production of Society*, trans. Derek Coltman (Chicago: University of Chicago Press, 1977).

10. Ibid., 65.

11. *1967–1992: comprendre la création scientifique, technique et culturelle* (CSI pamphlet, 1992), 11.

12. Ibid., 12.

13. Haroun Jamous, *Sociologie de la décision. La réforme des études médicales et des structures hospitalières* (Paris: Éditions du CNRS, 1969).

14. Michel Crozier, *Le Problème bureaucratique* (Paris: Seuil, 1963).

15. Robert King Merton, *Science, Technology and Society in Seventeenth Century England* (New York: H. Fertig, 1938).

16. Michel Callon, interview with the author.

17. Ibid.

18. Ibid.

19. Ibid.

20. Jean-Marc Lévy-Leblond and Alain Jaubert, *Autocritique de la science* (Paris: Seuil, 1973).

21. [The expression in French is *empêcheuse de penser en rond*, a play on *empêcheur de danser en rond*, someone who keeps others from dancing around or from enjoying themselves, a spoilsport. *Penser en rond*, "to think in a round," suggests the

totalizing thinking that has been the target of much French critical thought since World War II.—*Trans.*]

22. Philippe Roqueplo, *Le Partage du savoir: science, culture, vulgarisation* (Paris: Seuil, 1974).

23. We may also note among the participants in the seminar under the scientific direction of Claude Gruson and under the responsibility, in the area of research, of Philippe Roqueplo and Pierre Thuillier, the following: Anita Bensaïd, Hubert Brochier, François Chesnais, Benjamin Coriat, Elisabeth Crawford, Jacques de Cutaines, André Gauron, Baudoin Jurdant, Ludovic Lebart, Philippe Mallein, Christos Passadeos, Michaël Pollak, Joseph Pouget, Georges Thill, and Dominique Wolton.

24. CORDES: Comité d'Organisation des Recherches Appliquées sur le Développement Économique et Social (Committee on the Organization of Applied Research on Economic and Social Development).

25. [The Commissariat Général du Plan was founded by Charles de Gaulle in 1946 for the purpose of extensive state involvement in economic and social planning.—*Trans.*]

26. Michel Callon, interview with the author.

27. Serres, *Hermès,* vol. 3, *La Traduction.*

28. Michel Callon, interview with the author.

29. Ibid.

30. Michel Callon, "L'Opération de traduction comme relation symbolique," in *Incidence des rapports sociaux sur le développement scientifique et technique* (Paris: CORDES, 1976), 105–41.

31. Ibid., 123.

32. See Michel Callon, "Struggles and Negotiations to Define What Is Problematic and What Is Not: The Sociologic of Translation," in Karin D. Knorr, Roger Krohn, and Richard Whitley, eds., *The Social Process of Scientific Investigation* (Dordrecht: R. Reidel, 1980), 197–219.

33. Michel Callon, interview with the author.

34. [EDF = Électricité de France—the French national power company.—*Trans.*]

35. Michel Callon, interview with the author.

36. Claude Gruson, *Origines et espoirs de la planification française* (Paris: Dunod, 1968).

37. Michel Callon, interview with the author.

38. Ibid.

39. Ibid.

40. Michel Callon and Bruno Latour, "Unscrewing the Big Leviathan; or How Actors Macrostructure Reality, and How Sociologists Help Them to Do So," in Karin Knorr-Cetina and Aaron Cicourel, eds., *Advances in Social Theory and Methodology* (London: Routledge and Kegan Paul, 1981), 277–303.

41. Michel Callon, interview with the author.

42. Bruno Latour, interview with the author.

43. [The *agrégation* is the exam, preceded by a course, that anyone entering the teaching position in a public institution in France must take.—*Trans.*]

44. [ORSTOM: originally, Office de la Recherche Scientifique et Technique Outre-Mer (Office of Overseas Scientific and Technical Research). Although the organization still uses the same acronym, with decolonization its official title is now Institut Français de Recherche Scientifique pour le Développement en Coopération (French Institute of Scientific Research for Cooperative Development).—*Trans.*]

45. Bruno Latour, interview with the author.

46. Ibid.

47. Ibid.

48. Ibid.

49. The semiotic square, according to Greimas, is the elementary unit of signification. It is a reworking of the Aristotelian square—the square of contraries and contradictions—that Greimas used as a matrix to explain an indefinite number of narrative structures. Meaning is then directly derived from a structure that is immanent to it.

50. Bruno Latour, interview with the author.

51. Bruno Latour and Steve Woolgar, *Laboratory Life: The Social Construction of Scientific Facts* (Los Angeles and London: Sage, 1979).

52. Bruno Latour, interview with the author.

53. Ibid.

54. Latour, speaking in *Le Bon Plaisir d'Isabelle Stengers,* a program produced by Antoine Spire, France Culture, March 5, 1994.

55. Michel Serres, speaking in *Le Bon Plaisir.*

56. Isabelle Stengers, speaking in *Le Bon Plaisir.*

57. Ibid.

58. Ibid.

59. Bernadette Bensaude-Vincent and Isabelle Stengers, *A History of Chemistry,* trans. Deborah van Dam (Cambridge: Harvard University Press, 1996).

60. Isabelle Stengers, interview with the author.

61. Ibid.

62. Gilles Deleuze and Félix Guattari, *Anti-Oedipus,* trans. Robert Hurley, Mark Seem, and Helen R. Lane (Minneapolis: University of Minnesota Press, 1983).

63. Gilles Deleuze, *Difference and Repetition,* trans. Paul Patton (New York: Columbia University Press, 1994).

64. Isabelle Stengers, interview with the author.

65. Stengers, speaking in *Le Bon Plaisir.*

66. Ibid.

67. Isabelle Stengers, interview with the author.

68. Ilya Prigogine and Isabelle Stengers, *La Nouvelle Alliance* (Paris: Gallimard, 1979); reissued in the "Folio-Essais" series (Paris: Gallimard, 1986).

69. Isabelle Stengers, interview with the author.

70. Ibid.

71. Stengers, speaking in *Le Bon Plaisir.*

72. Ilya Prigogine and Isabelle Stengers, *Entre le temps et l'éternité* (Paris: Fayard, 1988); reissued in the "Champs" series (Paris: Flammarion, 1992).

73. Isabelle Stengers, interview with the author.

74. Léon Chertok and Isabelle Stengers, *Le Cœur et la Raison. L'hypnose en question, de Lavoisier à Lacan* (Paris: Payot, 1989). Stengers, in collaboration with Didier Gille, would also work with Chertok on his memoirs, *Mémoires d'un hérétique* (Paris: La Découverte, 1991).

75. [In French, "Les empêcheurs de penser en rond"; see note 21.—*Trans.*]

76. Philippe Pignarre, speaking in *Le Bon Plaisir.*

77. Stengers, speaking in *Le Bon Plaisir.*

78. Michel Serres, ed., *A History of Scientific Thought: Elements of a History of Science* (Oxford: Blackwell, 1995).

79. Pierre Lévy, *La Machine univers. Création, cognition et culture informatique* (Paris: La Découverte, 1987).

80. Pierre Lévy, interview with the author.

81. Ibid.

82. Ibid.

83. Ibid.

84. [DEA: *Diplôme d'études approfondies,* the diploma preliminary to the doctorate in the French university system.—*Trans.*]

85. Pierre Lévy, interview with the author.

86. Ibid.

87. See Jean-Pierre Dupuy, *Aux origines des sciences cognitives* (Paris: La Découverte, 1994).

88. Pierre Lévy, interview with the author.

## Two. The Cognitivist Pole

1. Saint Geneviève was the patron saint of Paris. She boosted the courage of the inhabitants of Lutetia during the invasion of Attila.

2. Jean-Pierre Dupuy, interview with the author.

3. [SAGEM is among the largest high-tech and telecommunications companies in Europe.—*Trans.*]

4. Ibid.

5. Jean-Pierre Dupuy, *Ordres et Désordres. Enquête sur un nouveau paradigme* (Paris: Seuil, 1982), 274.

6. Ibid.

7. [CIDOC: Centro Intercultural de Documentación.—*Trans.*]

8. Dupuy, *Ordres et Désordres,* 86.

9. Jean-Pierre Dupuy, interview with the author.

10. The "group of ten" was formed in 1967 and from the beginning included more than ten members: Robert Buron, Henri Laborit, Edgar Morin, Jacques Robin, René Passet, Alain Laurent, Jacques Sauvan, Jack Baillet, Gérard Rosenthal, Jean-François Boissel, David Rousset, and Bernard Weber. In the early 1970s, it expanded to include Joël de Rosnay, Jacques Attali, Jacques Piette, and Henri Atlan. The group ceased its activities in 1979.

11. Dupuy, *Ordres et Désordres,* 18.

12. Paul Dumouchel and Jean-Pierre Dupuy, eds., *L'Auto-organisation* (Paris: Seuil, 1983). The participants in the conference were Henri Atlan, Yves Barel, Julien Bok, Cornelius Castoriadis, Paul Dumouchel, Jean-Pierre Dupuy, Françoise Fogelman, René Girard, Roger Guesnerie, Michel Gutsatz, Jean-Louis Le Moigne, Pierre Livet, Maurice Milgram, Philippe Mongin, Thierry de Montbrial, Edgar Morin, Jacques Paillard, Pierre Rosanvallon, Benny Shanon, Isabelle Stengers, Jean-Claude Tabary, Francisco Varela, Jean-Louis Vullierme, Bernard Walliser, and Gérard Weisbuch.

13. Ibid., 13.

14. Paul Dumouchel and Jean-Pierre Dupuy, *L'Enfer des choses* (Paris: Seuil, 1979).

15. René Girard, *Deceit, Desire, and the Novel: Self and Other in Literary Structure* (Baltimore: Johns Hopkins University Press, 1976); *Resurrection from the Underground: Feodor Dostoevsky* (New York: Crossroad, 1997); *Violence and the Sacred,* trans. Patrick Gregory (Baltimore: Johns Hopkins University Press, 1993); *Things Hidden since the Foundation of the World,* trans. Stephen Bann and Michael Meteer (Stanford, Calif.: Stanford University Press, 1987); *The Scapegoat* (Baltimore: Johns Hopkins University Press, 1989); *A Theater of Envy: William Shakespeare* (Oxford and New York: Oxford University Press, 1991).

16. Jean-Pierre Dupuy, interview with the author.

17. [The "rose wave" (*la vague rose*) refers to the triumph of the Socialist Party in the French parliamentary elections, which enabled President Mitterrand to appoint a Socialist prime minister and a cabinet made up of a coalition drawn from several parties on the left.—*Trans.*]

18. Jean-Pierre Dupuy, interview with the author.

19. Ibid.

20. CESTA: Centre d'Étude des Systèmes Techniques Avancés—Center for the Study of Advanced Technical Systems.

21. The members of the Science-Culture group were Henri Atlan, Jacques Attali, Cornelius Castoriadis, Jean-Marie Domenach, Jean-Pierre Dupuy, Françoise Fogelman, Jacques Lesourne, Edgar Morin, René Passet, Jacques Robin, Joël de Rosnay, Isabelle Stengers, and Gérard Weisbuch.

22. Jean-Pierre Dupuy, interview with the author.

23. Ibid.

24. Connectionism is a current in cognitive science in which every cognitive process is viewed as a simultaneous treatment of partial information within a network, and not within a series of simple operations. Connectionism is thus opposed to the computational approach.

25. Jean-Pierre Dupuy, interview with the author.

26. See Part V, "Representations," chapter 19, "The Neuronal Temptation and Its Limits."

27. Jean-Pierre Dupuy, interview with the author.

28. Ibid.

29. Francisco Varela, interview with the author.

30. Francisco Varela, *Principles of Biological Autonomy* (New York: Elvesier North Holland, 1980).

31. Francisco Varela, interview with the author.

32. Humberto Maturana and Francisco Varela, *The Tree of Knowledge: The Biological Roots of Human Understanding* (Boston: New Science Library, 1987).

33. Daniel Andler, interview with the author.

34. Ibid.

35. Daniel Andler, "Mouvements de l'esprit," *Le Débat* 72 (November–December 1992): 7.

36. Ibid., 9.

37. Hubert Dreyfus, *What Computers Can't Do: Critique of Artificial Reason* (New York: Harper and Row, 1972); French translation by Daniel Andler, *Intelligence artificielle: mythes et limites* (Paris: Flammarion, 1984).

38. Andler, "Mouvements de l'esprit," 11.

39. Daniel Andler, interview with the author.

40. Pascal Engel, interview with the author.

41. Ibid.

42. Jacques Bouveresse, *Wittgenstein: la rime et la raison* (Paris: Minuit, 1973); *Le Mythe de l'intériorité* (Paris: Minuit, 1976). *Critique* 567–69 (August–September 1994) was devoted to Bouveresse.

43. Pascal Engel, interview with the author.

44. Ibid.

45. Ibid.

46. Ibid.

47. See especially Jacques-Paul Dubucs, "La fabrique de la preuve," *EspacesTemps* 47–48 (1991): 35–52.

48. See especially Jacques Hoarau, "Description d'une conjoncture en sociologie," *EspacesTemps* 49–50 (1992): 6–23; "Jon Elster et les conventions artistiques," *Espaces-Temps* 55–56 (1994): 30–35.

49. Claudine Engel-Tiercelin, *C. S. Peirce et le pragmatisme* (Paris: Presses Universitaires de France, 1993).

50. Jacques Bouveresse, *La Parole malheureuse. De l'alchimie linguistique à la grammaire philosophique* (Paris: Minuit, 1971).

51. Gottlob Frege, *The Foundations of Arithmetic: A Logico-Mathematical Enquiry into the Concept of Number*, trans. J. L. Austin (Evanston, Ill.: Northwestern University Press, 1986).

52. Pascal Engel, *Identité et référence. La théorie des noms propres chez Frege et Kripke* (Paris: Presses de l'École Normale Supérieure, 1985).

53. [Until 1984, there were two levels of the doctorate in the French university system, the first being the *doctorat d'université* and the second the *doctorat d'État.—Trans.*]

54. Pascal Engel, *Davidson et la philosophie du langage* (Paris: Presses Universitaires de France, 1994).

## Three. The Pragmatist Pole

1. Jean-Marc Ferry, interview with the author.

2. Ibid.

3. Ibid.

4. Ibid.

5. Ibid.

6. Jean-Marc Ferry, *Habermas. L'éthique de la communication* (Paris: Presses Universitaires de France, 1987).

7. See Part IV, "At the Risk of Acting," chapter 17, "The Social Sciences: Pragmatic Sciences."

8. Luc Boltanski, interview with the author.

9. Ibid.

10. The concept of "habitus" in Bourdieu allows a mediation between objective relations and individual behaviors. It expresses the interiorization on the part of the "agents" of objective conditions. Within this tension, the definition that Bourdieu gives of this concept has not ceased to fluctuate between the simple relation of production and a more complex interpretation. On this point, see François Dosse, *History of Structuralism*, vol. 2, *The Sign Sets, 1967–Present*, trans. Deborah Glassman (Minneapolis: University of Minnesota Press, 1997), 301–11.

11. Luc Boltanski, interview with the author.

12. Ibid.

13. Luc Boltanski, *Les Cadres. La formation d'un groupe social* (Paris: Minuit, 1982).

14. Luc Boltanski, interview with the author.

15. Ibid.

16. [INSEE: Institut National de la Statistique et des Études Économiques— National Institute of Statistics and Economic Study.—*Trans.*]

17. Eleanor Rosch and B. B. Lloyd, eds., *Cognition and Categorization* (New York: Erlbaum, 1978).

18. Luc Boltanski and Laurent Thévenot, "Finding One's Way in Social Space: A Study Based on Games," *Social Science Information* 22:4–5 (1983): 631–79.

19. Luc Boltanski, interview with the author.

20. Ibid.

21. Harold Garfinkel, its founder, defines ethnomethodology as the empirical science of methods by which individuals give meaning to their everyday actions. Thus, the interpretation of social realities is reduced to the observation of the discourses on their actions provided by actors capable of accounting for these actions.

22. Luc Boltanski, interview with the author.

23. Ibid.

24. Luc Boltanski, *L'Amour et la Justice comme compétences* (Paris: Métailié, 1990), 38.

25. Luc Boltanski, interview with the author.

26. Ibid.

27. Ibid.

28. Ibid.

29. Ibid.

30. Luc Boltanski and Laurent Thévenot, *Les Économies de la grandeur* (Paris: Presses Universitaires de France, 1987); reissued as *De la justification. Les économies de la grandeur* (Paris: Gallimard, 1991).

31. [ENSAE: École Nationale de la Statistique et de l'Administration Économique.—*Trans.*]

32. Laurent Thévenot, interview with the author.

33. Ibid.

34. Ibid.

35. Ibid.

36. Ibid.

37. Laurent Thévenot, "Les Investissements de forme," in *Conventions économiques* (Paris: Presses Universitaires de France, 1985), 21–65.

38. Ibid., 22.

39. Laurent Thévenot, *Économie et formes conventionnelles,* report presented at the INSEE–CNRS roundtable, November 22–23, 1984; published in Robert Salais and Laurent Thévenot, eds., *Le Travail: marchés, règles, conventions* (Paris: INSEE, Économica, 1986).

40. Thévenot, "Les investissements de forme," 25.

41. *Revue économique* 40:2 (March 1989), special issue on the topic "The Economics of Convention."

42. [ENA: École Nationale de l'Administration.—*Trans.*]

43. Olivier Favereau, interview with the author.

44. Ibid.

45. Peter B. Doeringer and Michael J. Piore, *Internal Labor Markets and Manpower Analysis* (Armonk, N.Y.: M. E. Sharpe, 1971).

46. Olivier Favereau, interview with the author.

47. [CEPREMAP: Centre d'Études Prospectives d'Économie Mathématique Appliquée à la Planification—Center for Prospective Studies in Mathematical Economics Applied to Planification.—*Trans.*]

48. Olivier Favereau, "L'incertain dans la 'révolution keynésienne': l'hypothèse Wittgenstein," *Économies et Sociétés* 3 (1985): 29–72.

49. Olivier Favereau, interview with the author.

50. *Revue économique* 40:2 (March 1989).

51. Olivier Favereau, interview with the author.

52. *Revue économique* 40:2 (March 1989): 142.

53. Olivier Favereau, interview with the author.

54. Ibid.

55. Ibid.

56. FORUM: Fondements des Organisations et des Régulations de l'Univers Marchand—Foundations of the Organizations and Regulations of the World of Commerce. It includes several groups: LAEDIX (employment, job market), MINI (the theory of money, money policy in an open economy), CEREM, IREP (corporate behavior, forms of competition), CERED (development), CAESAR (the history of economic thought,

the epistemology and history of the monetary/market bond), and MUERS (industrial relations and social protection).

57. Olivier Favereau, interview with the author.

58. Jean-Yves Calvez, *La Pensée de Karl Marx* (Paris: Seuil, 1970).

59. Louis Quéré, interview with the author.

60. Alain Touraine, *The Self-Production of Society,* trans. Derek Coltman (Chicago: University of Chicago Press, 1977), 105.

61. Louis Quéré, interview with the author.

62. Ibid.

63. Jürgen Habermas, *The Structural Transformation of the Public Sphere: An Inquiry into a Category of Bourgeois Society,* trans. Thomas Burger and Frederick Lawrence (Cambridge: MIT Press, 1991); *Legitimation Crisis,* trans. Thomas McCarthy (Boston: Beacon Press, 1975).

64. Louis Quéré, "Le sociologue et le touriste," interview with Jacque Hoarau, *EspacesTemps* 49–50 (1992): 42.

65. Louis Quéré, *Des miroirs équivoques* (Paris: Aubier, 1982).

66. Louis Quéré, interview with the author.

67. Quéré, *Des miroirs équivoques,* 12.

68. Erving Goffman, *Interaction Ritual: Essays on Face-to-Face Behavior* (New York: Pantheon, 1982).

69. *Arguments ethnométhodologiques, problèmes d'épistémologie en sciences sociales* (Paris: EHESS, 1985).

70. Patrick Pharo, interview with the author.

71. Max Weber, *The Theory of Social and Economic Organization,* trans. A. M. Henderson and Talcott Parsons (New York: Free Press, 1964).

72. Patrick Pharo, interview with the author.

73. Ibid.

74. Patrick Pharo, *Phénoménologie du lien civil. Sens et légitimité* (Paris: L'Harmattan, 1992).

75. Bernard Conein, interview with the author. [The term *Soboulians* refers to the disciples of Albert Soboul, a leading historian of the French Revolution, associated with the *Annales* school.—*Trans.*]

76. Michel Pêcheux, who was close to Althusser, honed a program of automatic discourse analysis in 1969. He located discourse analysis within the Althusserian conception of ideology. For the history of this period, see Denise Maldidier, paper presented at the meeting "Linguistics and Materialism" at Rouen (October 1988), *Cahiers de linguistique sociale* (1989); reprinted in Jacques Guilhaumou, Denise Maldidier, and Régine Robin, *Discours et Archive* (Liège: Mardaga, 1994), 173–83.

77. Bernard Conein, interview with the author.

78. Ibid.

79. Nicolas Herpin, *Les Sociologues américains et le siècle* (Paris: Presses Universitaires de France, 1973).

80. Bernard Conein, interview with the author.

81. Warner Ackermann, Bernard Conein, Christiane Guigues, Louis Quéré, and Daniel Vidal, eds., *Décrire: un impératif? Description, explication, interprétation en sciences sociales,* 2 vols. (Paris: EHESS, 1985).

82. Bernard Conein, interview with the author.

83. Ibid.

84. Gérard Noiriel, "Pour une approche subjectiviste du social," *Annales* 44 (November–December 1989): 1435–59.

85. Ibid., 1453.

86. Gérard Noiriel, with Benaceur Azzaoui, *Vivre et lutter à Longwy* (Paris: Maspero, 1980).

87. Gérard Noiriel, interview with the author.

88. Ibid.

89. Ibid.

90. Gérard Noiriel, "Les Ouvriers sidérurgistes et les mineurs de fer dans le bassin de Longwy (1919–1939)," doctoral thesis, University of Paris VIII, 1982, typescript.

91. Gérard Noiriel, interview with the author.

92. Gérard Noiriel, *The French Melting Pot: Immigration, Citizenship, and National Identity*, trans. Geoffroy de Laforcade (Minneapolis: University of Minnesota Press, 1996); *La Tyrannie du national, le droit d'asile en Europe: 1793–1993* (Paris: Calmann-Lévy, 1991).

93. Gérard Noiriel, interview with the author.

94. Ibid.

## Four. The Pole of Reglobalization through the Political

1. [Ernest Lavisse (1842–1922) was a historian whose principal work on France (*L'Histoire contemporaine de la France*, 1920–22) was very widely read and whose many manuals were universally adopted in the French educational system. His version of French history, with which many have taken serious issue, is still arguably the predominant one.—*Trans.*]

2. Marcel Gauchet, interview with the author.

3. Ibid.

4. Ibid.

5. Ibid.

6. Ibid.

7. Ibid.

8. Alain Caillé, *La Démission des clercs. La crise des sciences sociales et l'oubli du politique* (Paris: La Découverte, 1993).

9. Alain Caillé, interview with the author.

10. Ibid.

11. Ibid.

12. Ibid.

13. Ibid.

14. Alain Caillé, *Splendeurs et misères des sciences sociales* (Geneva: Droz, 1986).

15. The *Bulletin du MAUSS* would be published by La Découverte under the name *Revue de MAUSS* beginning in 1988.

16. Alain Caillé, interview with the author.

17. Dany-Robert Dufour, *Les Mystères de la trinité* (Paris: Gallimard, 1990).

18. Dany-Robert Dufour, interview with the author.

19. Ibid.

20. Ibid.

21. Ibid.

22. Ibid.

23. Ibid.

24. Dany-Robert Dufour, *Le Bégaiement des maîtres* (Paris: François Burin, 1988).

25. See Part III, "The Social Bond," chapter 12, "Gift and Countergift."

26. Dany-Robert Dufour, "Le structuralisme, le pli et la trinité," *Le Débat* 56 (September–October 1989): 132–53.

27. Dany-Robert Dufour, interview with the author.

28. See note 17.

29. IHTP: Institut d'Histoire du Temps Présent—Institute for the History of the Present Time.

30. Henry Rousso, *The Vichy Syndrome: History and Memory in France since 1944*, trans. Arthur Goldhammer (Cambridge: Harvard University Press, 1994).

31. Michel Trebitsch, interview with the author.

32. Michel Trebitsch, "La quarantaine et l'an 40," days of study in homage to François Bédarida, in IHTP, *Écrire l'histoire du temps présent* (Paris: CNRS, 1993), 63–76.

33. In 1954, no fewer than three books illustrate this sensitivity to the present: Robert Aron, *The Vichy Regime, 1940–44*, trans. Humphrey Hare (Philadelphia: Dufour Editions, 1966); René Rémond, *La Droite en France de 1815 à nos jours. Continuité et diversité d'une tradition politique* (Paris: Aubier, 1954); and Pierre Renouvin, *Histoire des relations internationales de 1870 à 1914* (Paris: Centre de Documentation Universitaire, 1954).

34. Michel Trebitsch, interview with the author.

35. Ibid.

36. Ibid.

## Part II. The "American" Detour

1. See *EspacesTemps* 53–54 (1993), special issue on the topic "The German Connection."

## Five. Ethnomethodology

1. Alfred Schutz, *The Phenomenology of the Social World,* trans. George Walsh and Frederick Lehnert (Evanston, Ill.: Northwestern University Press, 1967).

2. Louis Quéré, interview with the author.

3. Ibid.

4. Charles Taylor, *Philosophical Papers* (Cambridge: Cambridge University Press, 1985); *Sources of the Self: The Making of Modern Identity* (Cambridge: Harvard University Press, 1989).

5. Patrick Pharo, interview with the author.

6. Nicolas Herpin, *Les Sociologues américains et le siècle* (Paris: Presses Universitaires de France, 1973).

7. Erving Goffman, *The Presentation of Self in Everyday Life* (New York: Anchor Books, 1959).

8. The paradigm of symbolic interactionism was first formulated in 1937 by Herbert Blumer, a disciple of George Herbert Mead. See Herbert Blumer, *Symbolic Interactionism: Perspective and Method* (Berkeley and Los Angeles: University of California Press, 1986).

9. Herpin, *Les Sociologues américains et le siècle,* 71.

10. Harold Garfinkel, "A Conception of, and Experiments with, 'Trust' as a Condition of Stable Concerted Action," in O. J. Harvey, ed., *Motivation and Social Interaction* (New York: Ronald Press, 1963), 187–238.

11. Harold Garfinkel, *Studies in Ethnomethodology* (Englewood Cliffs, N.J.: Prentice Hall, 1967).

12. Peter L. Berger and Thomas Luckmann, *The Social Construction of Reality: A Treatise in the Sociology of Knowledge* (London: A. Lane, 1971).

13. Patrick Pharo, interview with the author.

14. Ibid.

15. Ibid.

16. Aaron V. Cicourel, *Cognitive Sociology: Language and Meaning in Social Inter-action* (New York: Free Press, 1974).

17. Bernard Conein, interview with the author.

18. Ibid.

19. Bruno Latour and Steve Woolgar, *Laboratory Life: The Construction of Scientific Facts* (Princeton, N.J.: Princeton University Press, 1986); revised French edition, *La Vie de laboratoire,* trans. Michel Biezunski (Paris: La Découverte, 1988). [Dosse quotes from sections added to the original in the French edition.—*Trans.*]

20. Bruno Latour, interview with the author.

21. Ibid.

22. Ibid.

23. Latour and Woolgar, *La Vie de laboratoire,* 17.

24. Ibid., 25.

25. Barry Barnes, *Scientific Knowledge and Sociological Theory* (London: Routledge and Kegan Paul, 1974); Harry Collins, "The T.E.A. Set: Tacit Knowledge and Scientific Networks," *Science Studies* 4: 165–86; Steven Shapin and Simon Schaffer, *Leviathan and the Air-Pump: Hobbes, Boyle, and the Experimental Life* (Princeton, N.J.: Princeton University Press, 1985).

26. Michel Callon, interview with the author.

27. Ibid.

28. Karin Knorr-Cetina, *The Manufacture of Knowledge: An Essay on the Constructivist and Contextual Nature of Science* (Oxford: Pergamon Press, 1981).

29. Michael Lynch, *Art and Artifact in Laboratory Science: A Study of Shop Work and Shop Talk in a Research Laboratory* (London: Routledge and Kegan Paul, 1985).

30. Laurent Thévenot, interview with the author.

31. Ibid.

32. Ibid.

33. Ibid.

34. The holistic procedure rests on an epistemological doctrine according to which each scientific statement is a tributary of the entire domain in which it appears. In the social sciences, holism refers to the idea of a globality, of a totality in principle.

## Six. Analytic Philosophy

1. Jean-Marc Ferry, interview with the author.

2. Jürgen Habermas, *Knowledge and Human Interests,* trans. Jeremy J. Shapiro (Boston: Beacon Press, 1972).

3. Jürgen Habermas, *The Theory of Communicative Action,* trans. Thomas McCarthy (Cambridge: Polity Press, 1989).

4. Jean-Marc Ferry, interview with the author.

5. Ibid.

6. Jean-Marc Ferry, *Les Puissances de l'expérience,* vol. 1, *Le Sujet et le Verbe,* vol. 2, *Les Ordres de la reconnaissance* (Paris: Cerf, 1992).

7. Jean-Marc Ferry, interview with the author.

8. See François Dosse, *History of Structuralism,* vol. 2, *The Sign Sets, 1967–Present,* trans. Deborah Glassman (Minneapolis: University of Minnesota Press, 1997).

9. John Rawls, *A Theory of Justice* (Oxford: Oxford University Press, 1971).

10. Jean-Pierre Dupuy, *Le Sacrifice et l'Envie* (Paris: Calmann-Lévy, 1992).

11. See David Hume, *An Enquiry concerning the Human Understanding; and, an Enquiry concerning the Principles of Morals* (Oxford: Clarendon Press, 1983).

12. Jean-Pierre Dupuy, interview with the author.

13. Ibid.

14. The oxymoron is a figure of style that unites two apparently contradictory words. For example, black sun, eloquent silence, and so on.

15. Jean-Pierre Dupuy, interview with the author.

16. Ibid.

17. Bernard Conein, interview with the author.

18. Dorothy L. Cheney and Robert M. Seyfarth, *How Monkeys See the World: Inside the Mind of Another Species* (Chicago: University of Chicago Press, 1990).

19. A cognitive artifact is an artificial tool conceived for conserving, displaying, and processing information with the aim of satisfying a representational function. According to Donald A. Norman, artifacts occupy an important place in human action, as the support for human activities, and also as the means to understand human cognition.

20. In distributed cognition, the object of study is the distribution of actions among persons according to the configuration of the artifacts.

21. Donald A. Norman, *The Psychology of Everyday Things* (New York: Basic Books, 1988).

22. Michael E. Bratman, *Intention, Plans, and Practical Reason* (Cambridge: Harvard University Press, 1987).

23. Daniel Dennett, *Consciousness Explained* (Boston: Little, Brown, 1991); Donald Davidson, *Essays on Actions and Events* (Oxford: Oxford University Press, 1980).

24. Jacques Bouveresse, *La Parole malheureuse* (Paris: Minuit, 1971); *Wittgenstein: la rime et la raison* (Paris: Minuit, 1973).

25. Ludwig Wittgenstein, *Philosophical Investigations,* trans. G. E. M. Anscombe (Oxford: Blackwell, 1958).

26. Ludwig Wittgenstein, *The Blue and Brown Books,* ed. R. Rhees (Oxford: Blackwell, 1969), 18.

27. See Claudine Engel-Tiercelin, *C. S. Peirce et le pragmatisme* (Paris: Presses Universitaires de France, Paris, 1993).

28. Jean-Marc Ferry, *Philosophie de la communication* (Paris: Cerf, 1994), 9.

29. Wilfred Sellars, *Science, Perception and Reality* (New York: Humanities Press, 1963), 160; quoted in Richard Rorty, *Philosophy and the Mirror of Nature* (Princeton, N.J.: Princeton University Press, 1979), 182.

30. Rorty, *Philosophy and the Mirror of Nature,* 157.

31. Richard Rorty, "Dewey entre Hegel et Darwin," *Rue Descartes* 5–6 (1992): 65.

32. See John Rajchman and Cornel West, eds., *Post-Analytic Philosophy* (New York: Columbia University Press, 1985).

33. Hilary Putnam, *Reason, Truth and History* (Cambridge: Cambridge University Press, 1981), 49–74.

34. Ibid.

35. Hilary Putnam, "Wittgenstein, la vérité et le passé de la philosophie," *Rue Descartes* 5–6 (1992): 85.

36. See Jean-Marc Ferry, *Philosophie de la communication* (Paris: Cerf, 1994), 24.

37. Putnam, "Wittgenstein, la vérité et le passé de la philosophie," 88.

38. Jacques Poulain, *L'Âge pragmatique ou l'Expérimentation totale* (Paris: L'Harmattan, 1990); Jacques Poulain, ed., *Critique de la raison phénoménologique. La transformation pragmatique* (Paris: Cerf, 1991).

39. Joëlle Proust, "De l'histoire de la logique à la philosophie de l'esprit," *Le Débat* 72 (November–December 1992).

40. Olivier Favereau, interview with the author.

41. Ibid.

42. Modal logic, formulated by the Megarians and Stoics, is not an ontology. By way of the question of language, it broaches the question of the "mode" in which being is given and so takes into account the modality of propositions.

43. David K. Lewis, *Convention: A Philosophical Study* (Cambridge: Harvard University Press, 1969).

44. In modal logic, the "semantic of possible worlds" consists of an ingenious use of set theory to characterize the conditions of truth of statements of the form "it is possible that," "it is necessary that," and so on. Of interest, then, is the set of "possible worlds" in which a determined proposition is true.

45. Peter B. Doeringer and Michael J. Piore, *Internal Labor Markets and Manpower Analysis* (Lexington, Mass.: Heath, 1971).

46. Olivier Favereau, interview with the author.

## Seven. The Philosophy of Science

1. Kurt Gödel was an American logician, born in Brno in 1906. With his two incompleteness theorems, he demonstrated the aporia of David Hilbert's research; Hilbert wanted to reveal the consistency of a formal system of analysis. For Gödel, a whole formal system powerful enough to include a minimum of arithmetic, of set theory, includes undecidable propositions. Next he put an end, thanks to his second incompleteness theorem (1931), to the "finitist" hopes of Hilbert, by showing that a noncontradictory arithmetic, as Hilbert hoped for, would not form a complete system, because in this system noncontradiction constitutes an "undecidable" statement.

2. Thomas Kuhn, *The Structure of Scientific Revolutions* (Urbana: University of Illinois Press, 1973).

3. Paul Feyerabend, *Against Method: Outline of an Anarchistic Theory of Knowledge* (London: New Left Books, 1975).

4. Isabelle Stengers, interview with the author.

5. Karl Popper, *The Logic of Scientific Discovery* (London: Hutchison, 1980); *Conjectures and Refutations: The Growth of Scientific Knowledge* (London and New York: Routledge, 1989); *Objective Knowledge: An Evolutionary Approach* (Oxford: Clarendon Press, 1981); *The Open Society and Its Enemies,* 2 vols. (Princeton, N.J.: Princeton University Press, 1971).

6. Karl Popper, *The Open Universe: An Argument for Indeterminism* (London and New York: Routledge, 1992); see Renée Bouveresse, ed., *K. Popper et la science d'aujourd'hui* (Paris: Aubier, 1989).

7. Jean-Michel Besnier, *Histoire de la philosophie moderne et contemporaine* (Paris: Grasset, 1993), 429.

8. Daniel Andler, interview with the author.

9. Alain Boyer, *L'Explication en histoire* (Lille: Presses Universitaires de Lille, 1992).

10. Jon Elster, *Ulysses and the Sirens* (Cambridge: Cambridge University Press, 1984).

11. Philippe van Parijs, *Le Modèle économique et ses rivaux* (Geneva: Droz, 1990).

12. Theodor Adorno, Karl Popper, Jürgen Habermas, et al., *The Positivist Dispute in German Sociology,* trans. Glyn Adney and David Frisby (New York: Harper and Row, 1976).

13. Alain Boyer, *EspacesTemps* seminar, European Research University, February 7, 1994.

14. Ibid.

## Eight. The Chicago School, Elias, and Weber

1. Michel Trebitsch, interview with the author.

2. Daniel Bertaux, "L'Histoire orale en France: fin de la préhistoire," *International Journal of Oral History* 2 (June 2, 1981): 121–27.

3. Michaël Pollak, "Signes de crise, signes de changement," in *Mai 68 et les sciences sociales* (Paris: Institut d'Histoire du Temps Présent, 1989).

4. Michel Trebitsch, "La Bouche de la vérité?" *Cahiers de l'IHTP* 21 (November 1992): 17.

5. Alain Coulon, *L'École de Chicago* (Paris: Presses Universitaires de France, 1992).

6. William I. Thomas and Florian Znaniecki, *The Polish Peasant in Europe and America* (1918); reprint, (New York: Dover, 1958).

7. Charles Henri Cuin and François Gresle, *Histoire de la sociologie*, vol. 2, *Depuis 1918* (Paris: La Découverte, 1992), 29.

8. Gérard Noiriel, *The French Melting Pot: Immigration, Citizenship, and National Identity*, trans. Geoffroy de Laforcade (Minneapolis: University of Minnesota Press, 1996).

9. Gérard Noiriel, interview with the author.

10. Danièle Voldman, "La Bouche de la vérité?" 33.

11. Roger Chartier, interview with the author.

12. Ibid.

13. Roger Chartier, "Elias, une pensée de relations," *EspacesTemps* 53–54 (1993): 44–60.

14. Ibid., 44.

15. Norbert Elias, remarks written for the French translation of volume 1 of *Über den Prozess der Zivilisation* (Basel: Haus zum Falken, 1939): *La Civilisation des mœurs* (Paris: Union Générale d'Éditions, 1982), 446–47.

16. Chartier, "Elias, une pensée de relations," 49.

17. Noiriel, *The French Melting Pot*, 268.

18. Norbert Elias, *The Society of Individuals*, trans. Edmund Jephcott (Oxford: Blackwell, 1991), 55.

19. Jean-Pierre Olivier de Sardan, "L'espace wéberien des sciences sociales," *Genèses* 10 (January 1993): 146–60.

20. Gérard Noiriel, interview with the author.

21. Raymond Aron, *Essai sur une théorie de l'histoire dans l'Allemagne contemporaine, la philosophie critique de l'histoire* (Paris: Vrin, 1938).

22. Julien Freund, *The Sociology of Max Weber*, trans. Mary Ilford (New York: Vintage Books, 1969).

23. Laurent Muchielli, "La Guerre n'a pas eu lieu: les sociologues français et l'Allemagne (1870–1940)," *EspacesTemps* 53–54 (1993): 5–18.

24. Monique Hirschhorn, *Max Weber et la sociologie française* (Paris: L'Harmattan, 1988).

25. *Rechtssoziologie* was only translated into French in 1959, by Julien Freund; *Gesammelte Aufsätze der Wissenschaftslehre* in 1965; and *The Protestant Ethic and the Spirit of Capitalism* in 1964.

26. Michaël Pollak analyzed this publishing situation in "Max Weber en France, l'itinéraire d'une œuvre," *Cahiers de l'IHTP* 3 (1986).

27. Sylvie Mesure, "Sociologie allemande, sociologie française: la guerre a eu lieu . . . ," *EspacesTemps* 53–54 (1993): 19–27.

28. Jean-Claude Passeron, *Le Raisonnement sociologique, l'espace non poppérien du raisonnement naturel* (Paris: Nathan, 1991).

29. The nomological sciences are those sciences capable of formulating their knowledge in the form of "universal laws" from which one may deduce "basic statements" that contradict "statements that prove something false." This is the case for the experimental sciences. They are opposed to the idiographic sciences, the sciences of the singular.

30. A *deictic* is a term that serves to designate or show.

31. Passeron, *Le Raisonnement sociologique,* 384.

32. Ibid., 61.

33. Ibid., 62.

34. Ibid., 369.

## Part III. The Social Bond

1. See Olivier Mongin, *Face au scepticisme* (Paris: La Découverte, 1994).

2. Marcel Gauchet, interview with the author.

## Nine. A New Triad: Nature/Society/Discourse

1. *1967–1992: comprendre la création scientifique, technique et culturelle* (CSI pamphlet, 1992), 26.

2. Ibid., 33.

3. Ibid., 34.

4. Ibid., 36.

5. Ibid., 40.

6. Bruno Latour, *We Have Never Been Modern,* trans. Catherine Porter (Cambridge: Harvard University Press, 1993), 6.

7. Michel Callon, ed., *La Science et ses réseaux* (Paris: La Découverte, 1989), 32.

8. Ibid., 31.

9. Michel Callon, interview with the author.

10. Michel Callon, "L'agonie d'un laboratoire," in *La Science et ses réseaux,* 173–214.

11. Michel Callon, interview with the author.

12. Bruno Latour, interview with the author.

13. Michel Callon, interview with the author.

14. Ibid.

15. Antoine Hennion, *Les Professionnels du disque. Une sociologie des variétés* (Paris: Métailié, 1981).

16. Antoine Hennion, *La Passion musicale: une sociologie de la médiation* (Paris: Métailié, 1993).

17. Bruno Latour, interview with the author.

18. Michel Callon, interview with the author.

19. Ibid.

20. Michel Serres, ed., *A History of Scientific Thought: Elements of a History of Science* (Oxford: Blackwell, 1995), with Bernadette Bensaude-Vincent, Catherine Goldstein, Françoise Micheau, Isabelle Stengers, Michel Authier, Paul Benoit, Geof Bowker, Jean-Marc Drouin, Bruno Latour, Pierre Lévy, and James Ritter.

21. Latour, *We Have Never Been Modern,* 56.

22. Ibid., 58.

23. Ibid., 63.

24. Ibid., 64.

25. Ibid., 78.

26. Ibid., 79.

27. David Bloor, *Knowledge and Social Imagery* (Chicago: University of Chicago Press, 1991).

28. Latour, *We Have Never Been Modern*, 93.

29. Ibid.

30. Christian Delacroix, *EspacesTemps* seminar, European Research University, March 7, 1994.

31. François Chateauraynaud, "Forces et faiblesses de la nouvelle anthropologie des sciences," *Critique* 529–30 (June–July 1991): 464.

32. Jacques Hoarau, "Description d'une conjoncture en sociologie," *EspacesTemps* 49–50 (1992): 15.

33. Latour, *We Have Never Been Modern*, 144.

34. Isabelle Stengers, *L'Invention des sciences modernes* (Paris: La Découverte, 1993), 173.

35. Ibid., 180.

36. Isabelle Stengers, with Olivier Ralet, *Drogues. Le défi hollandais* (Paris: Éditions des Laboratoires Delagrange, 1991).

37. Latour, in a debate with Stengers organized by Synthé-Labo, moderated by Philippe Pignarre, March 8, 1994.

38. Bruno Latour, "Moderniser ou écologiser? À la recherche de la 'septième' cité," *Écologie politique* 13 (spring 1995): 19.

39. Bruno Latour, "Esquisse d'un parlement des choses," *Écologie politique* 10 (1994): 110.

## Ten. A Great Innovation: The Introduction of Objects

1. Bruno Latour, interview with the author.

2. Ibid.

3. Michel Callon, interview with the author.

4. Ibid.

5. To gauge the interest in thinking of the world of objects in its relations with that of actors, see Bruno Latour and Pierre Lemonnier, eds., *De la préhistoire des missiles balistiques* (Paris: La Découverte, 1994).

6. Philippe Pignarre, *Les Deux Médecines* (Paris: La Découverte, 1995), 14.

7. Ibid., 16.

8. Ibid., 18.

9. Bruno Latour, *La Clef de Berlin* (Paris: La Découverte, 1993), 214.

10. This seminar led to an issue of *Raisons pratiques* on the theme of objects, *Les Objets dans l'action* 4 (1993).

11. Donald A. Norman, *The Design of Everyday Things* (New York: Doubleday, 1988).

12. Donald A. Norman, "Les artefacts cognitifs," *Raisons pratiques* 4 (1993): 19.

13. Bernard Conein, interview with the author.

14. Phil Agre and D. Chapman, "Pengi: An Implementation of a Theory of Activity," *Proceedings of the Sixth National Annual Conference on Artificial Intelligence* (Los Altos, Calif.: Morgan Faufman, 1987), 261–72.

15. Bernard Conein and Eric Jacopin, "Les objets dans l'espace," *Raisons pratiques* 4 (1993): 79.

16. Ibid., 82.

17. Laurent Thévenot, "Essai sur les objets usuels," *Raisons pratiques* 4 (1993): 96.

18. Ibid., 85.

19. Luc Boltanski and Laurent Thévenot, *De la justification. Les économies de la grandeur* (Paris: Gallimard, 1991), 30.

20. Ibid.

21. Laurent Thévenot, interview with the author.

22. This is the object of a study launched in 1991, in relation to Thévenot's teaching at the EHESS, on the forms of engagement of objects. Emmanuel Kessous, François Mouliérac, and Nicolas Auray directed their attention to the following areas: the normalization of infant care products and particularly of strollers; the customer service departments of two manufacturers of photographic and video cameras; the quarrels over computing, "user-friendly" and expert uses. Thévenot participated in the first two studies conducted in the context of the "Conventions and Coordination of Action" program, developed at the International Institute of Paris-La Défense; this program also includes the international seminar "Objects in Action," organized by Bernard Conein, Nicolas Dodier, and Laurent Thévenot. Information is provided in Thévenot, "Essai sur les objets usuels," *Raisons pratiques* 4 (1993): 86–87.

23. Pierre Lévy, *Les Technologies de l'intelligence* (Paris: La Découverte, 1990), 209.

24. Lévy defines hypertext as a set of worlds of signification characterized by six abstract principles: the principle of metamorphosis, the principle of heterogeneity, that of multiplicity and fitting of scales, the principle of exteriority, that of typology, and that of the mobility of centers.

25. Pierre Lévy, interview with the author.

26. Lévy, *Les Technologies de l'intelligence,* 212.

27. Ibid., 215.

28. Ibid., 220.

29. Michel Authier and Pierre Lévy, *Les Arbres de connaissances* (Paris: La Découverte, 1992).

30. Ibid., 109.

31. Ibid., 138.

## Eleven. Civility

1. Robert Castel, "Le roman de la désaffiliation. À propos de Tristan et Iseut," *Le Débat* 61 (September–October 1990): 152–64.

2. Gérard Mendel, *54 Millions d'individus sans appartenance* (Paris: Laffont, 1983).

3. Denis Duclos, *De la civilité* (Paris: La Découverte, 1993), 83.

4. Patrick Pharo, interview with the author.

5. Patrick Pharo, *Le Civisme ordinaire* (Paris: Méridiens-Klincksieck, 1985); *Politique et Savoir-vivre* (Paris: L'Harmattan, 1991).

6. Marcel Gauchet, interview with the author.

7. Patrick Pharo, *Phénoménologie du lien civil* (Paris: L'Harmattan, 1992), 11.

8. Ibid., 18.

9. Ibid., 19.

10. Georg Simmel, *The Problem of Sociology* (Philadelphia: American Academy of Political and Social Science, 1895).

11. Louis Quéré, interview with the author.

12. Claude Lefort, *Democracy and Political Theory*, trans. David Macey (Minneapolis: University of Minnesota Press, 1988).

13. Norbert Elias, *The Court Society*, trans. Edmund Jephcott (New York: Pantheon, 1983).

14. Pharo, *Phénoménologie du lien civil*, 78.

15. Paul Dumouchel and Jean-Pierre Dupuy, *L'Enfer des choses* (Paris: Seuil, 1979).

16. Jean-Pierre Dupuy, *Ordres et Désordres. Enquête sur un nouveau paradigme* (Paris: Seuil, 1982), 229.

17. Jean-Pierre Dupuy, *La Panique* (Paris: Synthé-Labo, "Les empêcheurs de penser en rond," 1991), 10.

18. John William Nevil Watkins, "Historical Explanation in the Social Sciences," in John O'Neill, ed., *Modes of Individualism and Collectivism* (London: Heinemann, 1973), 171.

19. Dupuy, *La Panique*, 92–93.

20. See Jean-Michel Saussois, "La force des liens faibles," *Sciences humaines,* special issue, *Les Liens sociaux invisibles* 5 (May–June 1994).

21. Mark Granovetter, "Threshold Models of Collective Behavior," *American Journal of Sociology* 83:6 (1978): 1442.

22. Jean-Pierre Dupuy, *Introduction aux sciences sociales. Logique des phénomènes collectifs* (Paris: Ellipses, École Polytechnique, 1992), 15.

23. Alain Caillé, *La Démission des clercs* (Paris: La Découverte, 1993), 149.

24. Pascal Engel, interview with the author.

25. Bernard Conein, interview with the author.

26. Edmond Marc and Dominique Picard, "La logique cachée des relations sociales," *Sciences humaines,* special publication, *Les Liens sociaux invisibles* 5 (1994).

27. Ibid., 10.

28. Dominique Picard, *Du code au désir* (Paris: Dunod, 1983).

29. Duclos, *De la civilité.*

30. Ibid., 125.

31. Ibid., 294.

32. Ibid., 21.

33. Ibid., 33.

34. Pierre Lévy, interview with the author.

35. Ibid.

36. Isabelle Stengers, interview with the author.

37. [Généthon is the French Human Genome Research Center.—*Trans.*]

38. Isabelle Stengers, *EspacesTemps* seminar, European Research University, January 10, 1994.

## Twelve. Gift and Countergift

1. A philosophical controversy arose over the use of this concept of utilitarianism, extending into *La Revue du Mauss*. In effect, in Jeremy Bentham's sense, utilitarianism is not necessarily synonymous with *homo economicus* or the theory of interested rational choice. Alain Caillé finally resolved it through a broadened definition of utilitarianism encompassing the normative position that puts forth that actions and norms are just if they work toward maximizing happiness. Utilitarianism is thus more than an epistemological position—it is the "basis of Western thinking," in three variations: practical utilitarianism, theoretical utilitarianism, and normative utilitarianism. See Alain Caillé, "Le principe de raison, l'utilitarisme et l'antiutilitarisme," in *La Démission des clercs* (Paris: La Découverte, 1993), 109–39.

2. Alain Caillé, *Critique de la raison utilitaire* (Paris: La Découverte, 1989), 61.

3. Alain Caillé, interview with the author.

4. Caillé, *Critique de la raison utilitaire*, 93.

5. Weber distinguishes four principles of action: the affective, the traditional, that of axiological rationality, and that of instrumental, strategic rationality.

6. Jacques Godbout, with Alain Caillé, *L'Esprit du don* (Paris: La Découverte, 1992), 32.

7. Alain Caillé, interview with the author.

8. Caillé, *Critique de la raison utilitaire*, 107.

9. Godbout, with Caillé, *L'Esprit du don*.

10. Marcel Mauss, *The Gift: The Form and Reason for Exchange in Archaic Societies,* trans. W. D. Halls (New York: W. W. Norton, 1990).

11. Godbout, with Caillé, *L'Esprit du don*, 30.

12. Ibid., 291.

13. Ibid., 276.

14. Ibid., 298.

15. Ibid., 32.

16. Luc Boltanski, *L'Amour et la Justice comme compétences* (Paris: Métailié, 1990).

17. *Agapē* is a Greek term, especially developed in the Pauline literature of the New Testament. It enunciates a manner of loving that is not identified with either *philia* in Aristotle or *eros* in Plato. The most common term for defining *agapē* is charity, but this is still an unsatisfying definition for this polysemous term.

18. Claude Lefort, *Les Formes de l'histoire* (Paris: Gallimard, 1978), 15-29.

19. Ibid.

20. Paul Ricoeur, *Freedom and Nature: The Voluntary and the Involuntary,* trans. Erazim V. Kohák (Evanston, Ill.: Northwestern University Press, 1966).

21. Jacques Derrida, *Given Time,* vol. 1, *Counterfeit Money,* trans. Peggy Kamuf (Chicago: University of Chicago Press, 1992), 13.

22. Jacques Derrida, *The Gift of Death,* trans. David Wills (Chicago: University of Chicago Press, 1995), 113.

23. Dany-Robert Dufour, interview with the author.

24. Samuel Beckett, *The Unnamable* (New York: Grove Press, 1970), 3.

25. Dany-Robert Dufour, *Le Bégaiement des maîtres* (Paris: François Bourin, 1988).

26. Dany-Robert Dufour, *Les Mystères de la trinité* (Paris: Gallimard, 1990), 9.

27. Ibid., 24.

28. Ibid., 59.

29. Ibid., 63.

30. Ibid., 278.

31. Dany-Robert Dufour, interview with the author.

32. Dufour, *Les Mystères de la trinité*, 165.

33. Alain Caillé, "Le don de paroles," *Ce que donner veut dire,* MAUSS (Paris: La Découverte, 1993), 194–218.

## Part IV. At the Risk of Acting

## Thirteen. The Paradigm Shift

1. Marcel Gauchet, "Changement de paradigme en sciences sociales," *Le Débat* 50 (May–August 1988): 165–70.

2. Marcel Gauchet, *EspacesTemps* seminar, European Research University, April 5, 1993.

3. François Dosse, *History of Structuralism,* 2 vols., trans. Deborah Glassman (Minneapolis: University of Minnesota Press, 1997).

4. Gauchet, "Changement de paradigme en sciences sociales," 165.

5. Gauchet, *EspacesTemps* seminar, European Research University, April 5, 1993.

6. Gauchet, "Changement de paradigme en sciences sociales," 165.

7. Gauchet, *EspacesTemps* seminar, European Research University, April 5, 1993.

8. Ibid.

9. Ibid.

10. Ibid.

11. Luc Boltanski, interview with the author.

12. Ibid.

13. Luc Boltanski, *EspacesTemps* seminar, European Research University, December 14, 1992.

14. Ibid.

15. Luc Boltanski, *L'Amour et la Justice comme compétences* (Paris: Métailié, 1990), 49–50.

16. See Part 1, "Itineraries," chapter 3, "The Pragmatist Pole."

17. Boltanski, *L'Amour et la Justice comme compétences,* 23.

18. Boltanski, *EspacesTemps* seminar, European Research University, December 14, 1992.

19. Boltanski, *L'Amour et la Justice comme compétences,* 53.

20. Ibid., 57.

21. Alain Caillé, "Plaidoyer pour une philosophie politique qui aurait des allures de science," in *La Démission des clercs* (Paris: La Découverte, 1993), 60.

22. Ibid., 62.

23. Hilary Putnam, *Reason, Truth and History* (Cambridge: Cambridge University Press, 1981).

## Fourteen. A Philosophy of Acting: Paul Ricoeur

1. Paul Ricoeur, *Freedom and Nature: The Voluntary and the Involuntary,* trans. Erazim V. Kohák (Evanston, Ill.: Northwestern University Press, 1966); *The Symbolism of Evil,* trans. Emerson Buchanan (New York: Harper and Row, 1967).

2. Paul Ricoeur, *De l'interprétation* (Paris: Seuil, 1965).

3. Jean-Marc Ferry, interview with the author.

4. Ibid.

5. Olivier Mongin, *Paul Ricœur* (Paris: Seuil, 1994), 26.

6. Paul Ricoeur, *From Text to Action: Essays in Hermeneutics,* vol. 2, trans. Kathleen Blamey and John B. Thompson (Evanston, Ill.: Northwestern University Press, 1991), 275.

7. In Husserl, the eidetic quest corresponds to the quest for the essence of the object, constituted by ideal contents capable of fulfilling many variable signifying intentions. Essence is experienced in a lived intuition, an originary giving. So it is a matter of seeking the laws that guide empirical knowledge, thanks to a procedure of eidetic reduction.

8. Ricoeur, *From Text to Action,* 16.

9. Mongin, *Paul Ricœur,* 137–44.

10. Ibid., 47.

11. Ricoeur, *The Conflict of Interpretations: Essays in Hermeneutics* (Evanston, Ill.: Northwestern University Press, 1974), "Religion, Atheism, and Faith," trans. Charles Freilich, 440–67.

12. Gottlob Frege introduced a distinction, a major one in semantics, between

meaning (*Sinn*) and reference (*Bedeutung*). He thus allowed a place for something extralinguistic, which is reference.

13. Ricoeur, *From Text to Action*, 17.

14. Paul Ricoeur, "The Model of the Text: Meaningful Action Considered as a Text," in *From Text to Action*, 144–67.

15. Louis Quéré, interview with the author.

16. Ibid.

17. Paul Ricoeur, *Philosophie et sociologie. Histoire d'une rencontre* (Paris: EHESS, 1985), 24.

18. Ibid., 26.

19. Ibid., 37.

20. Ricoeur, *The Conflict of Interpretations*, 99–159.

21. An allusion to the book Luc Boltanski wrote with Laurent Thévenot, *De la justification. Les économies de la grandeur* (Paris: Gallimard, 1991).

22. Luc Boltanski, interview with the author.

23. G. E. M. Anscombe, *Intention* (Oxford: Blackwell, 1957).

24. Paul Ricoeur, *Oneself as Another*, trans. Kathleen Blamey (Chicago: University of Chicago Press, 1992), 56.

25. Ibid., 67.

26. Ricoeur, *From Text to Action*, 134.

27. Ibid., 137–38.

28. Ricoeur, *Oneself as Another*, 72.

29. Michel Callon, interview with the author.

30. Ibid.

31. Bruno Latour, interview with the author.

32. Ibid.

33. *Esprit* 12:7–8 (July–August 1988).

34. Eric Vigne, "L'intrigue mode d'emploi," *Esprit* 12:7–8 (July–August 1988): 253.

35. Roger Chartier, "Débat sur l'histoire," *Esprit* 12:7–8 (July–August 1988): 258.

36. Ibid., 258–59.

37. Roger Chartier, interview with the author.

38. Chartier, "Débat sur l'histoire," 261.

39. Ibid., 262.

40. Roger Chartier, interview with the author.

41. Ibid.

42. Paul Ricoeur, *Esprit* 12:7–8 (July–August 1988): 304.

## Fifteen. The Descriptive Turn

1. Louis Quéré, "Le tournant descriptif en sociologie," *Current Sociology* 40:1 (spring 1992): 139.

2. [Throughout, I have translated the French *événémentiel* and its variations as "evenemental," as there is no standard adjective in English that means "pertaining or relative to an event or events." Evenemental history refers to the history based on events, rather than on the long period that the *Annales* school insisted on. Although *événémentiel* is often translated as "event-based" or "event-centered," Renée Baernstein, a historian, has informed me that "evenemental" is a word accepted in her discipline.— *Trans.*]

3. Michel Foucault, in Michelle Perrot, *L'Impossible Prison* (Paris: Seuil, 1980), 44–45.

4. Patrick Pharo, "L'ethnométhodologie et la question de l'interprétation," in *Arguments ethnométhodologiques* (Paris: EHESS, 1985), 150.

5. Ibid., 152.

6. Quéré, "Le tournant descriptif en sociologie," 141–42.

7. Ibid., 142.

8. Werner Ackermann, Bernard Conein, Christiane Guigues, Louis Quéré, and Daniel Vidal, eds., *Décrire: un impératif?* 2 vols. (Paris: EHESS, 1985).

9. Harold Garfinkel and Harvey Sacks, "On Formal Structures of Practical Actions," in J. C. McKinney and E. A. Tiryakian, eds., *Theoretical Sociology: Perspectives and Developments* (New York: Appleton-Century-Crofts, 1970), 342.

10. Harold Garfinkel, *Studies in Ethnomethodology* (Englewood Cliffs, N.J.: Prentice Hall, 1967), 47.

11. Bernard Conein, "L'enquête sociologique et l'analyse du langage: les formes linguistiques de la connaissance sociale," in *Arguments ethnométhodologiques,* 17.

12. Garfinkel, *Studies in Ethnomethodology.*

13. Louis Quéré, "L'argument sociologique de Garfinkel," in *Arguments ethnométhodologiques,* 102.

14. Ibid.

15. Ibid., 110.

16. Garfinkel, *Studies in Ethnomethodology.*

17. Quéré, "L'argument sociologique de Garfinkel," 105.

18. Ibid., 106.

19. Quéré, "Le tournant descriptif en sociologie," 147.

20. Ibid., 151.

21. Quéré, "L'argument sociologique de Garfinkel," 135.

22. Louis Quéré, "Le sociologue et le touriste," interview with Jacques Hoarau, *EspacesTemps* 49–50 (1992): 54.

23. Hans-Georg Gadamer, *Truth and Method,* trans. Garrett Barden and John Cumming (New York: Crossroad, 1975).

24. Quéré, "Le sociologue et le touriste," 54.

25. This is a thesis discussed in *La Revue du MAUSS* 4 (1989), in a debate between Michel Freitag, who contends that the social world is a matter for description, and Quéré. See Freitag, "La quadrature du cercle. Quelques remarques sur le problème de la description de l'activité significative"; Quéré, "L'impératif de la description: remarques sur la position de Michel Freitag"; Freitag, "'Vous avez bien dit transcendantal?' Réponse à Louis Quéré, en défense de la connaissance sociologique et historique contre la réduction sémiotique et pragmatique," *Cahiers de recherche du Groupe interuniversitaire d'étude de la postmodernité* 23 (Montreal) (1994).

26. Harvey Sacks, "Perspectives de recherche," in *Arguments ethnométhodologiques,* 143.

27. Louis Quéré, interview with the author.

28. Ibid.

29. Luc Boltanski and Laurent Thévenot, *De la justification. Les économies de la grandeur* (Paris: Gallimard, 1991).

30. Luc Boltanski, interview with the author.

31. Luc Boltanski, *L'Amour et la Justice comme compétences* (Paris: Métailié, 1990), 72.

32. Luc Boltanski, interview with the author.

33. Ibid.
34. Ibid.
35. Boltanski and Thévenot, *De la justification*, 26.
36. Luc Boltanski, interview with the author.
37. Michael Walzer, *Spheres of Justice: A Defense of Pluralism and Equality* (New York: Basic Books, 1983).
38. Boltanski and Thévenot, *De la justification*, 28.
39. Luc Boltanski, interview with the author.
40. Boltanski and Thévenot, *De la justification*, 183.
41. Ibid., 340.
42. Ibid., 425–38.
43. Ibid., 430.
44. Luc Boltanski, interview with the author.
45. Ibid.
46. Ibid.
47. Jean-Marc Ferry, interview with the author.

## Sixteen. The Hermeneutic Horizon

1. Patrick Pharo, "La question du pourquoi," *Raisons pratiques* 1 (1990): 270.
2. Patrick Pharo, "L'ethnométhodologie et la question de l'interprétation," in *Arguments ethnométhodologiques* (Paris: EHESS, 1985), 146.
3. *Epochē*: for the Stoics, a suspension of judgment; a stance taken up by Husserl in the perspective of a phenomenological reduction that suspends judgment with regard to the problem of the existence of the external world, thus placed in parentheses.
4. Harvey Sacks, "Sociological Descriptions," *Berkeley Journal of Sociology* 8 (1963): 7.
5. Hans-Georg Gadamer, *Truth and Method*, trans. Garrett Barden and John Cumming (New York: Crossroad, 1975), 236.
6. Pharo, "L'ethnométhodologie et la question de l'interprétation," 159.
7. Edmund Husserl, *The Crisis of European Sciences and Transcendental Phenomenology: An Introduction to Phenomenological Philosophy,* trans. David Carr (Evanston, Ill.: Northwestern University Press, 1970), 189.
8. Patrick Pharo, interview with the author.
9. Ibid.
10. Ibid.
11. Ibid.
12. Patrick Pharo, *Phénoménologie du lien civil* (Paris: L'Harmattan, 1992), 30.
13. Ibid., 42.
14. G. E. M. Anscombe, *Intention* (Oxford: Blackwell, 1957).
15. Pharo, "La question du pourquoi," 267–309.
16. Max Weber, *Gesammelte Aufsätze zur Wissenschaftslehre* (1917); this passage does not appear in the selection of essays from this volume published in English, *The Methodology of the Social Sciences,* trans. Edward A. Shills and Henry A. Finch (New York: Free Press, 1949); *Essais sur la théorie de la science,* trans. Julien Freund (Paris: Plon, 1965), 475.
17. Alfred Schutz, *The Phenomenology of the Social World,* trans. George Walsh and Frederick Lehnert (Evanston, Ill.: Northwestern University Press, 1967). On the phenomenological approach to comprehensive sociology, see Robert Williame, *Les*

*Fondements phénoménologiques de la sociologie compréhensive: Alfred Schutz et Max Weber* (The Hague: Martinus Nijhoff, 1973).

18. Patrick Pharo, *Le Sens de l'action et la compréhension d'autrui* (Paris: L'Harmattan, 1993), 26.

19. Schutz, *The Phenomenology of the Social World*, 42.

20. Charles Taylor, *Philosophical Papers* 2 vols. (Cambridge: Cambridge University Press, 1985), vol. 1, *Human Agency and Language*, 45.

21. Paul Ricoeur, *Oneself as Another*, trans. Kathleen Blamey (Chicago: University of Chicago Press, 1992), 179.

22. Ibid., 180.

23. Charles Taylor, *The Explanation of Behaviour* (London: Routledge and Kegan Paul, 1954), 9; quoted in Ricoeur, *Oneself as Another*, 78.

24. Paul Ricoeur, *Time and Narrative*, trans. Kathleen McLaughlin and David Pellauer, 3 vols. (Chicago: University of Chicago Press, 1984, 1985, 1988).

25. Louis Quéré, "Agir dans l'espace public," *Raisons pratiques* 1 (1990): 90.

26. Ibid.

27. Ibid., 110.

28. Nicolas Dodier, "Représenter ses actions, le cas des inspecteurs et des médecins du travail," *Raisons pratiques* 1 (1990): 115–48.

29. Ibid., 118.

30. Nicolas Dodier, "Le travail d'accommodation des inspecteurs du travail en matière de sécurité," in *Justesse et justice dans le travail* (Paris: Presses Universitaires de France, 1989), 281–306.

31. Ibid., 282.

32. Ibid., 304.

33. Jean-Claude Coquet, interview with the author, for François Dosse, *History of Structuralism*, 2 vols., trans. Deborah Glassman (Minneapolis: University of Minnesota Press, 1997).

34. Ibid.

35. Pierre Lévy, *Les Technologies de l'intelligence* (Paris: La Découverte, 1990), 81.

36. Ibid., 213.

37. François Furet, "From Narrative History to Problem-Oriented History," in *In the Workshop of History*, trans. Jonathan Mandelbaum (Chicago: University of Chicago Press, 1984).

38. Signed *Annales* editorial, "Tentons l'expérience," in *Annales* 44.6 (November–December 1989): 1319.

39. Ibid., 1320.

40. Marcel Gauchet, *La Pratique de l'esprit humain* (Paris: Gallimard, 1980).

41. Michel Foucault, *Madness and Civilization*, trans. Richard Howard (New York: Vintage Books, 1988).

42. Marcel Gauchet, interview with the author.

43. Jacques Guilhaumou, *EspacesTemps* seminar, European Research University, December 5, 1994.

44. Émile Benveniste, *Problems in General Linguistics*, trans. Mary Elizabeth Meek (Coral Gables: University of Miami Press, 1971), 236.

45. Guilhaumou, *EspacesTemps* seminar, European Research University, December 5, 1994.

46. Francisco Varela, Evan Thompson, and Eleanor Rosch, *The Embodied Mind: Cognitive Science and Human Experience* (Cambridge: MIT Press, 1991), xv.

47. Maurice Merleau-Ponty, *Phenomenology of Perception,* trans. Colin Smith (London: Routledge and Kegan Paul, 1962), 405.

48. Maurice Merleau-Ponty, *The Structure of Behavior,* trans. Alden L. Fisher (Boston: Beacon Press, 1967).

49. Varela, Thompson, and Rosch, *The Embodied Mind,* 16.

50. Ibid., 173.

51. Ibid., 149.

52. Ibid.

53. Mark Johnson, *The Body in the Mind: The Bodily Basis of Imagination, Reason, and Meaning* (Chicago: University of Chicago Press, 1987), 14.

54. Daniel Andler, interview with the author.

55. Patricia Smith Churchland, *Neurophilosophy: Towards a Unified Theory of the Mind-Brain* (Cambridge: MIT Press, 1986).

56. Bernard Conein, "Peut-on observer l'interprétation?" *Raisons pratiques* 1 (1990): 313.

57. Daniel Dennett, *The Intentional Stance* (Cambridge: MIT Press, 1987), 271.

58. Pascal Engel, *Introduction à la philosophie de l'esprit* (Paris: La Découverte, 1994), 75.

59. Dorothy L. Cheney and Robert M. Seyfarth, *How Monkeys See the World: Inside the Mind of Another Species* (Chicago: University of Chicago Press, 1990).

60. Conein, "Peut-on observer l'interprétation?" 316.

61. Bernard Conein, interview with the author.

62. Ibid.

63. Donald Davidson, *Inquiries into Truth and Interpretation* (Oxford: Oxford University Press, 1984).

64. Engel, *Introduction à la philosophie de l'esprit,* 74.

65. Donald Davidson, *Essays on Action and Events* (Oxford: Oxford University Press, 1980).

66. Pascal Engel, "Le rêve analytique et le réveil naturaliste," *Le Débat* 72 (November–December 1992): 113.

67. Engel, *Introduction à la philosophie de l'esprit,* 75.

68. Donald Davidson, interview with Christian Delcampagne, *Le Monde,* June 28, 1994.

69. Ibid.

70. Ricoeur, *Oneself as Another,* 73–87.

71. Ibid., 74.

72. Davidson, *Essays on Action and Events.*

73. Davidson, "Actions, Reasons, and Causes," in *Essays on Actions and Events,* 3–19.

74. Ricoeur, *Oneself as Another,* 80–81.

75. Davidson, "Intending," in *Essays on Action and Events,* 83–102.

76. Ricoeur, *Oneself as Another,* 87.

77. Pascal Engel, interview with the author. The phrase "interpretation without hermeneutics" refers to Engels's "Interpretation without Hermeneutics," *Topoi* 10 (1991): 137–46.

78. Peter Frederick Strawson, *Individuals* (London: Methuen, 1959).

79. Pascal Engel, "Le rêve analytique et le réveil naturaliste," *Le Débat* 72 (November–December 1992): 114.

80. Pascal Engel, interview with the author.

## Seventeen. The Social Sciences: Pragmatic Sciences

1. Charles Sanders Peirce, *Peirce on Signs: Writings on Semiotics* (Chapel Hill: University of North Carolina Press, 1991).

2. Immanuel Kant, *Anthropology from a Pragmatic Point of View,* trans. Victor Lyle Dowdell (Carbondale: Southern Illinois University Press, 1996).

3. Vincent Descombes, "En guise d'introduction," *Critique* 529–30 (June–July 1991): 420.

4. *Pragmatica sanctio*—a pragmatics as a sanction in the area of law.

5. Wilhelm Dilthey, *Der Aufbau der geschichtlichen Welt in den Geisteswissenschaften* (Frankfurt am Main: Suhrkamp, 1981).

6. Jean-Marc Ferry, interview with the author.

7. Ibid.

8. Ibid.

9. Ibid.

10. Ricoeur establishes a fundamental difference between the two usages of the concept of identity: identity as the same (in Latin, *idem;* French, *même;* German, *gleich*) and identity as self (in Latin, *ipse;* French, *soi;* German, *selbst*).

11. Paul Ricoeur, *Oneself as Another,* trans. Kathleen Blamey (Chicago: University of Chicago Press, 1992), 140.

12. Jean-Marc Ferry, interview with the author.

13. Ibid.

14. Jürgen Habermas, *The Theory of Communicative Action,* trans. Thomas McCarthy (Boston: Beacon Press, 1987).

15. Louis Quéré, "Raison, action sociale et intersubjectivité," in *Langage, action sociale et communication* (Paris: EHESS, 1987), 90.

16. Jean-Marc Ferry, interview with the author.

17. Jean-Marc Ferry, *Les Puissances de l'expérience,* 2 vols. (Paris: Cerf, 1992).

18. Ludwig Wittgenstein, *Philosophical Investigations,* trans. G. E. M. Anscombe (Oxford: Blackwell, 1958), section 373.

19. Louis Quéré, "Langage de l'action et questionnement sociologique," in Quéré, ed., *La Théorie de l'action. Le sujet pratique en débat* (Paris: Presses du CNRS, 1993), 55.

20. Émile Benveniste, "Le langage et l'expérience humaine," in *Problèmes de linguistique générale* (Paris: Gallimard, 1966), vol. 2, 78.

21. Mikhail Bakhtin, *Problems of Dostoevsky's Poetics,* trans. Caryl Emerson (Minneapolis: University of Minnesota Press, 1984), 40.

22. Mikhail Bakhtin, *Speech Genres and Other Late Essays,* trans. Vern W. McGee (Austin: University of Texas Press, 1986), 160.

23. Francis Jacques, *Difference and Subjectivity: Dialogue and Personal Identity,* trans. Andrew Rothwell (New Haven: Yale University Press, 1991); *L'Espace logique de l'interlocution* (Paris: Presses Universitaires de France, 1985).

24. Jacques, *Difference and Subjectivity,* 42–43.

25. Luc Boltanski, *La Souffrance à distance. Morale humanitaire, médias et politique* (Paris: Métailié, 1993), 9.

26. Ibid., 27.

27. Ibid., 101.

28. Élisabeth Claverie, "Sainte indignation contre indignation éclairée: L'affaire du chevalier de La Barre," *Ethnologie française* 22:3 (1993): 271–90.

29. Boltanski, *La Souffrance à distance,* 139.

30. Ibid., 171.

31. Pierre Pachet, *Le Premier Venu. Essai sur la politique baudelairienne* (Paris: Denoël, 1976).

32. Luc Boltanski, interview with the author.

33. Ibid.

34. Gérard Mendel, *La Société n'est pas une famille* (Paris: La Découverte, 1992), 8.

35. Ibid., 14.

36. Ibid., 176.

37. Ibid., 179.

## Part V. Representations

## Eighteen. Mental Representations: The Cognitivist Orientation

1. Edgar Morin, *Le Paradigme perdu. La nature humaine* (Paris: Seuil, 1973).

2. Warren McCulloch and Walter Pitts, "A Logical Calculus of Ideas Immanent in Nervous Activity," in Warren McCulloch, *Embodiments of Mind* (Cambridge: MIT Press, 1965), 19–39.

3. See Jean-Pierre Dupuy, *Aux origines des sciences cognitives* (Paris: La Découverte, 1994).

4. Francisco Varela, Evan Thompson, and Eleanor Rosch, *The Embodied Mind: Cognitive Science and Human Experience* (Cambridge: MIT Press, 1991), 38–39.

5. John von Neumann, *The Computer and the Brain* (New Haven: Yale University Press, 1958).

6. Daniel Andler, ed., *Introduction aux sciences cognitives* (Paris: Gallimard, 1992), 31.

7. Georges Vignaux, *Les Sciences cognitives: une introduction* (Paris: La Découverte, 1992), 7.

8. Andler, *Introduction aux sciences cognitives,* 13.

9. Daniel Andler, "À quoi pensent les sciences cognitives?" *Raison présente* 109 (1994): 30.

10. Ibid., 35.

11. Paul D. MacLean, *The Triune Brain in Evolution* (New York: Plenum Press, 1990).

12. André Bourguignon, "Cerveau et complexité," *Sciences humaines* 8 (July 1991): 25.

13. Jean-Didier Vincent, *Biologie des passions* (Paris: Odile Jacob, 1986).

14. Gérard Edelman, *Neural Darwinism: The Theory of Neuronal Group Selection* (New York: Basic Books, 1987).

15. Achille Weinberg, "Où en sont les neurosciences?" *Sciences humaines* 8 (July 1991): 18.

16. Jean-Pierre Changeux, *Neuronal Man,* trans. Laurence Garey (Oxford: Oxford University Press, 1986).

17. Jean-Pierre Vernant, debate with Andler and Changeux, at the Collège de France, February 15, 1993, *Raison présente* 109 (1994): 68.

18. Vignaux, *Les Sciences cognitives,* 316.

19. Julian Feldman and D. Ballard, "Connectionist Models and Their Properties," *Cognitive Science* 6 (1982): 205–54.

20. Andler, "À quoi pensent les sciences cognitives?" 42.

21. Daniel Andler, interview with Bernard Conein, *Préfaces* 10 (November–December 1988): 71.

22. Ibid., p. 48.

23. "Cognition et complexité," *Cahiers du CREA* 9 (March 1986): 1.

24. Dan Sperber and Deirdre Wilson, *Relevance: Communication and Cognition* (Oxford: Blackwell, 1986).

25. Jean-Pierre Dupuy, interview with the author.

26. Vignaux, *Les Sciences cognitives*, 27.

27. See Part IV, "At the Risk of Acting," chapter 15, "The Descriptive Turn."

28. Varela, Thompson, and Rosch, *The Embodied Mind*, 46.

29. Claude Bonnet, Rodolphe Ghiglione, and Jean-François Richard, *Traité de psychologie cognitive* (Paris: Dunod, 1989).

30. Jerome-Seymour Bruner, "On Voluntary Action and Its Hierarchical Structure," *Intentional Journal of Psychology* 3 (1968): 239–55.

31. Vignaux, *Les Sciences cognitives*, 223.

32. Marcel Gauchet, *L'Inconscient cérébral* (Paris: Seuil, 1992).

33. Eduard von Hartmann, *Philosophy of the Unconscious* (New York: MacMillan, 1884).

34. Gauchet, *L'Inconscient cérébral*, 32.

35. Louis Quéré, interview with Jacques Hoarau, *EspacesTemps* 49–50 (1992): 51.

36. Marcel Gauchet, *Esprit* 17:10 (October 1993): 71.

37. Daniel Widlöcher, "Inconscient cognitif et inconscient psychanalytique," *Annales médico-psychologiques* 147:9 (1989): 1008–10.

38. Serban Ionescu, "Inconscient: les pistes du futur," *Sciences humaines* 29 (June 1993): 24.

39. M. Eagle, "Revisioning the Unconscious," *Canadian Psychology* 28:2 (1987): 113–16.

40. André Bourguignon, *Sciences humaines* 29 (June 1993): 29.

41. Marie Bonnafé, "Et la neurobiologie?" *Revue française de psychanalyse* 63 (1990): 1673–76.

42. Pierre Fédida, debate at the Maison des Écrivains, with Pascal Engel, Daniel Andler, and Pierre Jacob, February 2, 1993.

43. Vignaux, *Les Sciences cognitives*, 274.

44. Pierre Lévy, *Les Technologies de l'intelligence* (Paris: La Découverte, 1990).

45. Terry Winograd and Fernando Flores, *Understanding Computers and Cognition* (Norwood, N.J.: Ablex, 1986), 143–62.

46. Lévy, *Les Technologies de l'intelligence*, 72.

47. François Récanati, "Du tournant linguistique au tournant cognitif: l'exemple de la pragmatique," *Préfaces* 10 (November–December 1988): 80–83.

48. Jerry Alan Fodor, *The Modularity of Mind: An Essay on Faculty Psychology* (Cambridge: MIT Press, 1983).

49. Récanati, "Du tournant linguistique au tournant cognitif," 83.

## Nineteen. The Neuronal Temptation and Its Limits

1. Georges Canguilhem, "Mort de l'homme ou épuisement du cogito," *Critique* 242 (July 1967): 559–618.

2. Daniel Andler, "À quoi pensent les sciences cognitives?" *Raison présente* 109 (1994): 50.

3. Jean-Pierre Dupuy, interview with the author.

4. Ibid.

5. Jean-Pierre Changeux, ed., *Les Fondements naturels de l'éthique* (Paris: Odile Jacob, 1993).

6. Jean-Didier Vincent, interview, *Sciences humaines* 8 (July 1991): 22.

7. Ibid.

8. Pascal Engel, "Le rêve analytique et le réveil naturaliste," *Le Débat* 72 (November–December 1992): 113.

9. Pascal Engel, *Introduction à la philosophie de l'esprit* (Paris: La Découverte, 1994), 9.

10. Ibid., 10–11.

11. Patricia Smith Churchland, *Neurophilosophy: Towards a Unified Theory of the Mind-Brain* (Cambridge: MIT Press, 1986).

12. See Part IV, "At the Risk of Acting," chapter 16, "The Hermeneutic Horizon."

13. Hilary Putnam, *Reason, Truth and History* (Cambridge: Cambridge University Press, 1979).

14. Pascal Engel, interview with the author.

15. Ibid.

16. Ibid.

17. Ibid.

18. Ibid.

19. Francisco Varela, interview, *Sciences humaines* 31 (August–September 1993): 52–55.

20. Francisco Varela, Evan Thompson, and Eleanor Rosch, *The Embodied Mind: Cognitive Science and Human Experience* (Cambridge: MIT Press, 1991), 157.

21. Francisco Varela, interview with the author.

22. Ibid.

23. Dan Sperber, "Les sciences cognitives, les sciences sociales et le matérialisme," in Daniel Andler, ed., *Introduction aux sciences cognitives* (Paris: Gallimard, 1992), 397–420.

24. Dan Sperber and Deirdre Wilson, *Relevance: Communication and Cognition* (Cambridge: Harvard University Press, 1986).

25. Dan Sperber, interview with François Dosse, for *History of Structuralism,* 2 vols., trans. Deborah Glassman (Minneapolis: University of Minnesota Press, 1997).

26. Ibid.

27. Dan Sperber, "Le structuralisme en anthropologie," in *Qu'est-ce que le structuralisme?* (Paris: Seuil, 1968).

28. Sperber, "Les sciences cognitives, les sciences sociales et le matérialisme," 406.

29. Ibid., 412.

30. Ibid., 416.

31. Jean-Luc Jamard, *Anthropologies françaises en perspective* (Paris: Kimé, 1993), 186.

32. Dan Sperber, interview with Bernard Conein, "De l'anthropologie structurale à l'anthropologie cognitive," *Préfaces* 10 (1988): 104.

33. Lucien Scubla, "Sciences cognitives, matérialisme et anthropologie," in Andler, ed., *Introduction aux sciences cognitives,* 421–46.

34. Ibid., 430.

35. Ibid., 444.

36. Daniel Andler, interview with the author.

37. Ibid.

38. Laurent Thévenot, interview with the author.

39. Luc Boltanski and Laurent Thévenot, *De la justification. Les économies de la grandeur* (Paris: Gallimard, 1991).

40. Laurent Thévenot, interview with the author.

41. Ibid.

42. Olivier Favereau, interview with the author.

43. Ibid.

44. Herbert Simon, "A Formal Theory of the Employment Relationship," *Econometrica* 19:3 (July 1951): 293–305. See also Herbert Simon, *The Sciences of the Artificial* (Cambridge: MIT Press, 1969), and *Reason in Human Affairs* (Oxford: Blackwell, 1983).

45. D. Kahneman, P. Slovic, and A. Tversky, eds., *Judgement under Uncertainty: Heuristics and Biases* (Cambridge: Cambridge University Press, 1974).

46. Olivier Favereau, interview with the author.

47. Dorothy L. Cheney and Robert M. Seyfarth, *How Monkeys See the World: Inside the Mind of Another Spicies* (Chicago: University of Chicago Press, 1990).

48. D. Premack, "The Infant's Theory of Self-Propelled Objects," *Cognition* 36 (1990).

49. Bernard Conein, interview with the author.

50. Jérôme H. Barkow, "Règles de conduite et conduite de l'évolution," in Changeux, ed., *Les Fondements naturels de l'éthique*, 89.

51. Bernard Conein, interview with the author.

52. See Part III, "The Social Bond," chapter 10, "A Great Innovation: The Introduction of Objects."

53. Jean-Pierre Dupuy, interview with the author.

54. Ibid.

55. Michel Callon, interview with the author.

56. Ibid.

57. Bruno Latour, interview with the author.

58. Ibid.

## Twenty. Collective Representations: Leaving the History of Mentalities

1. Alain Corbin, "Le vertige des foisonnements, esquisse panoramique d'une histoire sans nom," *Revue d'histoire moderne et contemporaine* 36 (January–March 1992): 117.

2. Roger Chartier, "Le monde comme représentation," *Annales* 44:6 (November–December 1989): 1505–20.

3. The other two are the economic and the social levels.

4. François Dosse, *New History in France: The Triumph of the* Annales, trans. Peter V. Conroy Jr. (Urbana: University of Illinois Press, 1994).

5. Chartier, "Le monde comme représentation," 1508.

6. Ibid., 1509.

7. Roger Chartier, interview with the author.

8. Ibid.

9. See Part 11, "The 'American' Detour," chapter 8, "The Chicago School, Elias, and Weber."

10. Michel Foucault, "The Order of Discourse," in Robert Young, ed., *Untying the Text: A Post-Structuralist Reader* (Boston and London: Routledge and Kegan Paul, 1981), 64.

11. Chartier, "Le monde comme représentation," 1511.

12. Ibid., 1518.

13. Michel de Certeau, *The Practice of Everyday Life,* vol. 1, trans. Steven Randall (Berkeley: University of California Press, 1984).

14. Michel Foucault, *Discipline and Punish: The Birth of the Prison,* trans. Alan Sheridan (New York: Vintage Books, 1979).

15. Roger Chartier, interview with the author.

16. Ibid.

17. Chartier, "Le monde comme représentation," 1511.

18. Ibid., 1512.

19. Roger Chartier, interview with the author.

20. Chartier, "Le monde comme représentation," 1514.

21. Marcel Gauchet, *EspacesTemps* seminar, European Research University, April 5, 1993.

22. Marcel Gauchet, interview with the author.

23. Marcel Gauchet, *Le Désenchantement du monde* (Paris: Gallimard, 1985).

24. Ibid., xviii.

25. Marcel Gauchet, interview with the author.

26. Gauchet, *EspacesTemps* seminar, European Research University, April 5, 1993.

27. Ibid.

28. Arlette Farge, *Le Goût de l'archive* (Paris: Seuil, 1989).

29. Marcel Gauchet, interview with the author.

30. Robert Bonnaud, *Le Système de l'histoire* (Paris: Fayard, 1989).

31. Marcel Gauchet, interview with the author.

32. Alain Corbin, *The Lure of the Sea: The Discovery of the Seaside in the Western World, 1750–1840,* trans. Jocelyn Phelps (Berkeley: University of California Press, 1994).

33. Alain Corbin, *The Village of Cannibals: Rage and Murder in France, 1870,* trans. Arthur Goldhammer (Cambridge: Harvard University Press, 1992).

34. Alain Corbin, "Désir, subjectivité et limites, l'impossible synthèse . . . ," *Espaces-Temps,* special issue on the topic "Reflected Time: History at the Risk of Historians" (1995): 40–46.

35. Ibid.

36. Alain Corbin, "Le vertige des foisonnements," *Revue d'histoire moderne et contemporaine* 36 (January–March 1992): 117.

37. Gérard Noiriel, "Pour une approche subjectiviste du social," *Annales* 44:6 (November–December 1989): 1435–59; "Histoire: la perspective pragmatique," *Espaces-Temps* 49–50 (1992): 83–85.

38. Noiriel, "Pour une approche subjectiviste du social," 1437.

39. Ibid., 1443.

40. Ibid., 1451.

41. Gérard Noiriel, *The French Melting Pot: Immigration, Citizenship, and National Identity,* trans. Geoffroy de Laforcade (Minneapolis: University of Minnesota Press, 1996).

42. Alain Boureau, "Propositions pour une histoire restreinte des mentalités," *Annales* 44:6 (November–December 1989): 1491–1504.

43. Ibid., 1493.

44. Ibid., 1496.

45. John Henry Newman, *An Essay in Aid of a Grammar of Assent* (Oxford: Oxford University Press, 1985).

46. Michel Foucault, *The Archaeology of Knowledge,* trans. A. M. Sheridan Smith (New York: Pantheon, 1982).

47. Boureau, "Propositions pour une histoire restreinte des mentalités," 1501.

48. Alain Boureau, "La croyance comme compétence," *Critique* 529–30 (June–July 1991): 513.

49. Bruno Latour, *The Pasteurization of France,* trans. Alan Sheridan and John Law (Cambridge: Harvard University Press, 1988).

50. Aline Rousselle, *Croire et Guérir. La foi en Gaule dans l'Antiquité tardive* (Paris: Fayard, 1990); Denis Crouzet, *Les Guerriers de Dieu. La violence au temps des troubles de religion. Vers 1525–vers 1610,* 2 vols. (Paris: Champvallon, 1990); Carlo Ginzburg,

*Ecstasies: Deciphering the Witches' Sabbath,* trans. Raymond Rosenthal (New York: Pantheon, 1991).

51. Claude Lévi-Strauss, "The Effectiveness of Symbols," in *Structural Anthropology,* trans. Claire Jacobson and Brooke Grundfest Schoepf (New York: Basic Books, 1963), 186–205.

52. Ernst Kantorowicz, *Frederick the Second, 1194–1250,* trans. E. O. Lorimer (New York: Ungar, 1967); *The King's Two Bodies: A Study in Mediaeval Political Theology* (Princeton, N.J.: Princeton University Press, 1985).

53. Marcel Gauchet, interview with the author.

54. Edoardo Grendi, "Micro-analisi e storia sociale," *Quaderni Storici* 35 (1972): 506–20.

55. Carlo Ginzburg, *The Cheese and the Worms: The Cosmos of a Sixteenth-Century Miller,* trans. John and Anne Tedeschi (Baltimore: Johns Hopkins University Press, 1992).

56. Roger Chartier, interview with the author.

57. Giovanni Levi, *Inheriting Power: The Story of an Exorcist,* trans. Lydia G. Cochrane (Chicago: University of Chicago Press, 1988).

58. Emmanuel Le Roy Ladurie, *Montaillou: Cathars and Catholics in a French Village,* trans. Barbara Bray (Harmondsworth, England: Penguin, 1981); *Carnival in Romans: A People's Uprising at Romans 1579–1580,* trans. Mary Feeney (Harmondsworth, England: Penguin, 1981).

59. See Jacques Revel, "L'histoire au ras du sol," preface to the French translation of Giovanni Levi, *Inheriting Power*: Levi, *Le Pouvoir au village* (Paris: Gallimard, 1989), i–xxxiii.

60. Carlo Ginzburg, *The Night Battles: Witchcraft and Agrarian Cults in the Sixteenth and Seventeenth Centuries,* trans. John and Anne Tedeschi (Baltimore: Johns Hopkins University Press, 1992).

61. Ginzburg, *Ecstasies,* 22.

62. Boureau, "La croyance comme compétence," 519.

63. See Alain Boureau, *La Papesse Jeanne* (Paris: Aubier, 1988).

64. Giovanni Levi, "Usages de la biographie," *Annales* 44:6 (November–December 1989): 1329.

65. Ibid., 1333.

## Twenty-one. The Memorial Moment

1. Peter Lasslet, *Un monde que nous avons perdu* (Paris: Flammarion, 1969).

2. Pierre Nora, *Les Lieux de mémoire,* vol. 1 (Paris: Gallimard, 1984), xvii.

3. Ibid., vol. 3 (Paris: Gallimard, 1993), 22.

4. Maurice Halbwachs, *On Collective Memory,* trans. Lewis A. Coser (Chicago: University of Chicago Press, 1992).

5. Nora, *Les Lieux de mémoire,* vol. 1, xix.

6. Suzanne Citron, *Le Mythe national* (Paris: Éditions Ouvrières, 1987).

7. Olivier Mongin, *Face au scepticisme. Les mutations du paysage intellectuel ou l'invention de l'intellectuel démocratique* (Paris: La Découverte, 1994).

8. Nora, *Les Lieux de mémoire,* vol. 3, 26.

9. Ibid., 24.

10. Georges Duby, *The Legend of Bouvines: War, Religion and Culture in the Middle Ages,* trans. Catherine Tihanyi (Berkeley: University of California Press, 1990).

11. Ibid., 5.

12. Ibid., 6.

13. Philippe Joutard, *La Légende des camisards. Une sensibilité au passé* (Paris: Gallimard, 1977), 356.

14. Henry Rousso, *The Vichy Syndrome: History and Memory in France since 1944,* trans. Arthur Goldhammer (Cambridge: Harvard University Press, 1994).

15. Benjamin Stora, *Le Gangrène et l'Oubli* (Paris: La Découverte, 1991).

16. Michaël Pollak, *L'Expérience concentrationnaire. Essai sur le maintien de l'identité sociale* (Paris: Métailié, 1990).

17. Michaël Pollak, "Mémoire, oubli, silence," in *Une identité blessée* (Paris: Métailié, 1993), 38.

18. Nathalie Heinich, "Motifs d'une recherche: hommage à Michaël Pollak," *Bulletin trimestrial de la fondation Auschwitz* 35 (January–March 1993): 101.

19. Ibid., 103.

20. Marie-Claire Lavabre, "Génération et mémoire," in *Génération et Politique,* Congress of the Association Française de Science Politique, October 1981, typescript; *Le Fil rouge, sociologie de la mémoire communiste* (Paris: Presses de la Fondation Nationale des Sciences Politiques, 1994).

21. Pierre Vidal-Naquet, *Assassins of Memory: Essays on the Denial of the Holocaust* (New York: Columbia University Press, 1992).

22. Henry Rousso, "La mémoire n'est plus ce qu'elle était," in *Écrire l'histoire du temps présent* (Paris: CNRS, 1993), 105.

23. Nora, *Les Lieux de mémoire,* vol. 3, 1012.

24. Paul Ricoeur, *Du texte à l'action* (Paris: Seuil, 1986), 391. [A somewhat different version of the essay "Ideology and Utopia" appears in the English translation of this book, *From Text to Action.—Trans.*]

## Part VI. Conventions: A Third Way?

## Twenty-two. From Regulation to Convention

1. See François Dosse, *History of Structuralism,* vol. 2, *The Sign Sets, 1967–Present,* trans. Deborah Glassman (Minneapolis: University of Minnesota Press, 1997), 288–300.

2. On the regulationist current, see Robert Boyer and Yves Saillard, eds., *Théorie de la régulation. L'État des savoirs* (Paris: La Découverte, 1995).

3. See Michel Aglietta and Alain Lipietz, "Braudel dans tous ses états," *Espaces-Temps* 34–35 (1986).

4. Robert Boyer, *The Regulation School: A Critical Introduction,* trans. Craig Charney (New York: Columbia University Press, 1990).

5. Olivier Favereau, interview with the author.

6. Ibid.

7. Ibid.

8. Ibid.

9. Laurent Thévenot, interview with the author.

10. See André Orléan, ed., *Analyse économique des conventions* (Paris: Presses Universitaires de France, 1994), a collective work in which may be found, among others, Michel Aglietta and Robert Boyer; and Boyer and Saillard, eds., *Théorie de la régulation,* a collective work in which Favereau appears.

11. See Alain Desrosières, *La Politique des grands nombres* (Paris: La Découverte, 1993).

12. Luc Boltanski and Laurent Thévenot, *De la justification. Les économies de la grandeur* (Paris: Gallimard, 1991).

13. Robert Salais, Nicolas Baverez, and Bénédicte Reynaud, *L'Invention du chômage* (Paris: Presses Universitaires de France, 1986).

14. The committee responsible for the roundtable included Robert Boyer, François Eymard-Duvernay, Robert Salais, Jean-Jacques Sylvestre, and Laurent Thévenot.

15. Laurent Thévenot, interview with the author.

16. Robert Salais and Laurent Thévenot, eds., *Le Travail: marchés, règles, conventions* (Paris: Économica, 1986).

17. Laurent Thévenot, "Les investissements de forme," in *Conventions économiques*, cahiers du Centre d'Études de l'Emploi (Paris: Presses Universitaires de France, 1986), 21–71.

18. Ibid., 63.

19. Laurent Thévenot, interview with the author.

20. Ibid.

21. Pierre Boisard and Marie-Thérèse Letablier, "Le camembert: normand ou normé. Deux modèles de production dans l'industrie fromagère," in *Entreprises et Produits* (Paris: Presses Universitaires de France, 1987), 1–29.

22. Laurent Thévenot, interview with the author.

23. Thévenot, introductory remarks, in *Conventions économiques*, vi.

24. See Part I, "Itineraries: One Generation," chapter 3, "The Pragmatist Pole."

25. *Revue économique* 40:2 (March 1989), special issue on the topic "The Economics of Convention." Introduction signed by Jean-Pierre Dupuy, François Eymard-Duvernay, Olivier Favereau, André Orléan, Robert Salais, and Laurent Thévenot.

26. Ibid., 143.

27. Ibid.

28. Ibid., 145.

29. See Richard Swedberg, *Histoire de la sociologie économique* (Paris: Desclée de Brouwer, 1995); Jean-Jacques Gislain and Philippe Steiner, *La Sociologie économique: 1890–1920* (Paris: Presses Universitaires de France, 1995).

30. "Appel à la création d'un enseignement universitaire de socio-économie," *MAUSS, Pour une autre économie* 3 (1994): 282–84.

## Twenty-three. Beyond the Opposition between Holism and Methodological Individualism

1. Laurent Thévenot, "À quoi convient la théorie des conventions?" *Réseaux* 62 (November–December 1993): 137.

2. Ibid., 138.

3. See Part III, "The Social Bond."

4. Alain Rallet, "La théorie des conventions chez les économistes," *Réseaux* 62 (November–December 1993): 48.

5. Ibid., 51.

6. David K. Lewis, *Convention: A Philosophical Study* (Cambridge: Harvard University Press, 1969).

7. Ibid., 97.

8. Jean-Pierre Dupuy, "Convention et *common knowledge*," *Revue économique* 40:2 (March 1989): 361–400.

9. Ibid., 397.

10. Laurent Thévenot, interview with the author.

11. Ibid.

12. H. P. Grice, "Meaning," *Philosophical Review* 66 (1957): 377–88.

13. Dupuy, "Convention et *common knowledge*," 375.

14. Ludwig Wittgenstein, *Philosophical Investigations,* trans. G. E. M. Anscombe (Oxford: Blackwell, 1958), section 581.

15. Louis Quéré, "A-t-on vraiment besoin de la notion de convention?" *Réseaux* 62 (November–December 1993): 38.

16. Robert Salais, "Convention et mondes possibles," *Réseaux* 62 (November–December 1993): 133.

17. Quéré, "A-t-on vraiment besoin de la notion de convention?" 32.

18. Salais, "Convention et mondes possibles," 135.

19. Quéré, "A-t-on vraiment besoin de la notion de convention?" 26.

20. André Orléan, "Pour une approche cognitive des conventions économiques," *Revue économique* 40:2 (March 1989): 243.

21. Ibid., 244.

22. Quéré, "A-t-on vraiment besoin de la notion de convention?" 26.

23. Ibid., 34.

24. Olivier Favereau, "Marchés internes, marchés externes," *Revue économique* 40:2 (March 1989): 273.

25. Olivier Favereau, "L'incertain dans la 'révolution keynésienne': l'hypothèse Wittgenstein," *Économies et Sociétés* 3 (1985): 30.

26. John Maynard Keynes, "The General Theory of Employment," *Quarterly Journal of Economics* 52 (February 1937): 209–23.

27. Favereau, "L'incertain dans la 'révolution keynésienne,'" 64.

28. Olivier Favereau, "La théorie générale: de l'économie conventionnelle à l'économie des conventions," *Cahiers d'économie politique* 14–15 (1988): 214.

29. Olivier Favereau, interview with the author.

30. Olivier Favereau, "Règle, organisation et apprentissage collectif: un paradigme non standard pour trois théories hétérodoxes," in André Orléan, ed., *Analyse économique des conventions* (Paris: Presses Universitaires de France, 1994), 127.

31. G. A. Akerlof, "Labor Contracts as Partial Gift Exchange," *Quarterly Journal of Economics* 96 (November 1982): 543–69.

32. Favereau, "Règle, organisation et apprentissage collectif," 132.

33. Kenneth J. Arrow, *The Limits of Organization* (New York and London: W. W. Norton, 1974), 23.

34. Hervé Defalvard, "Critique de l'individualisme méthodologique revu par l'économie des conventions," *Revue économique* 43:1 (1992): 127–43.

## Twenty-four. A Historicized Interpretive Theory

1. André Orléan, "Un savoir dynamique," *Le Monde des débats,* December 1993, 7.

2. Laurent Thévenot, interview with the author.

3. Ibid.

4. Laurent Thévenot, "Rationalité ou normes sociales: une opposition dépassée?" in L.-A. Gérard Varet and Jean-Claude Passeron, eds., *Principes de rationalité dans les sciences sociales* (Paris: EHESS, forthcoming).

5. Herbert Simon, "Rationality as Process and as Product of Thought," *American Economic Review* 68:2 (1978):1–16.

6. Laurent Thévenot, interview with the author.

7. Pierre Livet, "Les limites de la communication," *Les Études philosophiques* 2–3 (1987): 255–75.

8. Saul A. Kripke, *Wittgenstein on Rules and Private Language: An Elementary Exposition* (Oxford: Oxford University Press, 1982).

9. Laurent Thévenot, interview with the author.

10. Ibid.

11. Ibid.

12. Pierre Livet and Laurent Thévenot, "Les catégories de l'action collective," in André Orléan, ed., *Analyse économique des conventions* (Paris: Presses Universitaires de France, 1994), 139–67.

13. Ibid., 145.

14. Ibid.

15. Pierre Livet and Laurent Thévenot, "Modes d'action collective et construction éthique. Les émotions dans l'évaluation," paper presented at the international conference at Cerisy, June 5–12, 1993, "Limiting Rationality and Constituting the Collective"; proceedings in Jean-Pierre Dupuy and Pierre Livet, eds., *Les Limites de la rationnalité*, 2 vols. (Paris: La Découverte, 1997).

16. Richard S. Lazarus, A. D. Kanner, and S. Folkman, "Emotions: A Cognitive-Phenomenological Analysis," in R. Plutchik and H. Kellerman, eds., *Emotion: Theory, Research, and Experience*, vol. 1 (San Diego: Academic Press, 1980), 189–217.

17. Livet and Thévenot, "Modes d'action collective et construction éthique."

18. Robert Boyer, "Économie et histoire: vers de nouvelles alliances," *Annales* 44:6 (November–December 1989): 1397–1426.

19. Ibid., 1405.

20. Ibid., 1414.

21. Laurent Thévenot, interview with the author.

22. See Christian Delacroix, "La falaise et le rivage: histoire du tournant critique," *EspacesTemps*, special issue on the topic "Reflected Time: History at the Risk of Historians" (1995): 86–111.

23. Bernard Lepetit, "L'histoire prend-elle les acteurs au sérieux?" ibid., 112–22.

24. Bernard Lepetit, ed., *Les Formes de l'expérience* (Paris: Albin Michel, 1995), 14.

25. Ibid., 17.

26. Ibid., 21.

27. Lepetit, "L'histoire prend-elle les acteurs au sérieux?" 114.

28. Ibid., 283.

29. Alain Coutereau, "Esprit public et capacité de juger. La stabilisation d'un espace public en France aux lendemains de la Révolution," *Raisons pratiques* 3 (1992): 239–73.

## Part VII. Underdetermination

## Twenty-five. The Unsayable, or the Crisis of Causalism

1. Pierre Duhem, *The Aim and Structure of Physical Theory*, trans. Philip P. Wiener (Princeton, N.J.: Princeton University Press, 1991).

2. Bruno Latour, "Irreductions," trans. John Law, in *The Pasteurization of France* (Cambridge: Harvard University Press, 1988).

3. Ibid., 167.

4. Daniel Andler, interview with the author.

5. Michel de Certeau, "L'histoire, une passion nouvelle," roundtable with Paul Veyne and Emmanuel Le Roy Ladurie, *Magazine Littéraire* 123 (April 1977): 19–20.

6. Michel de Certeau, *The Writing of History*, trans. Tom Conley (New York: Columbia University Press, 1988), 68.

7. Paul Veyne, *Writing History: Essay on Epistemology*, trans. Mina Moore-Rinvolucri (Middletown, Conn.: Wesleyan University Press, 1984).

8. François Furet, "From Narrative History to Problem-Oriented History," in *In the Workshop of History,* trans. Jonathan Mandelbaum (Chicago: University of Chicago Press, 1984), 60.

9. Lawrence Stone, "The Revival of Narrative: Reflections on a New Old History," *Past and Present* 85 (November 1979): 3–24.

10. Paul Ricoeur, *History and Truth,* trans. Charles A. Kelbley (Evanston, Ill.: Northwestern University Press, 1965), 27.

11. Ibid., 43.

12. Paul Ricoeur, *Time and Narrative,* trans. Kathleen McLaughlin and David Pellauer, 3 vols. (Chicago: University of Chicago Press, 1984, 1985, 1988).

13. Ibid., vol. 1, 208.

14. Ibid., 214.

15. Ibid., vol. 3, 241.

16. Ibid., 209.

17. Ibid., 216.

18. Ibid., 221.

19. Ibid., 274.

20. Ibid.

21. Jean-Claude Passeron, *Le Raisonnement sociologique. L'espace non-poppérien du raisonnement naturel* (Paris: Nathan, 1991).

22. Ibid., 358.

23. Jean-Pierre Olivier de Sardan, "L'unité épistémologique des sciences sociales," in *L'Histoire entre épistémologie et demande sociale,* proceedings of the Blois summer university, September 1993 (Toulouse and Versailles: IUFM de Créteil, 1994), 16. The emic designates autochthonous representations.

24. Ibid., 17.

25. Ibid., 18.

26. Ibid., 20.

27. Anthony Giddens, *Social Theory and Modern Sociology* (Stanford, Calif.: Stanford University Press, 1987).

28. Jean-Pierre Olivier de Sardan, "L'espace webérien des sciences sociales," *Genèses* 10 (January 1993): 160.

29. Olivier de Sardan, "L'unité épistémologique des sciences sociales," 32.

30. Alain Corbin, "Le vertige des foisonnements," *Revue d'histoire moderne et contemporaine* 39 (January–March 1992): 103.

31. Alain Corbin, *Women for Hire: Prostitution and Sexuality in France after 1850,* trans. Alan Sheridan (Cambridge: Harvard University Press, 1990).

32. Alain Corbin, "Désir, subjectivité et limites, l'impossible synthèse . . . ," *Espaces-Temps,* special issue on the topic "Reflected Time: History at the Risk of Historians" (1995): 40–46.

33. Alain Corbin, *The Foul and the Fragrant: Odor and the French Social Imagination,* trans. Miriam L. Kochan, Roy Porter, and Christopher Prendergast (Cambridge: Harvard University Press, 1986), 1–8.

34. Ibid., 230.

35. Alain Corbin, *The Lure of the Sea: The Discovery of the Seaside in the Western World, 1750–1840,* trans. Jocelyn Phelps (Berkeley: University of California Press, 1994).

36. Corbin, "Désir, subjectivité et limites," 42.

37. Corbin, *The Lure of the Sea,* 283–84.

38. Paul Ricoeur, *Oneself as Another,* trans. Kathleen Blamey (Chicago: University of Chicago Press, 1992).

39. Carol Zisowitz-Stearns and Peter N. Stearns, *Emotion and Social Change: Toward a New Psychohistory* (New York: Holmes and Meier, 1988).

40. Marcel Gauchet, interview with the author.

41. Roger Chartier, interview with the author.

42. Roger Chartier, *Lectures et Lecteurs dans la France d'Ancien Régime* (Paris: Seuil, 1987), 7.

43. Roger Chartier, interview with the author.

44. Alain Caillé, interview with the author.

45. Ibid.

46. Ibid.

## Twenty-six. A Poetics of Knowledge

1. Jacques Rancière, *The Names of History,* trans. Hassan Melehy (Minneapolis: University of Minnesota Press, 1994), 103.

2. Jacques Rancière, interview with the author, *Politis,* January 21, 1993.

3. Rancière, *The Names of History,* 208.

4. Arlette Farge, *Le Cours ordinaire des choses. Dans la cité du XVIII^e siècle* (Paris: Seuil, 1994), 151.

5. Paul Ricoeur, *Time and Narrative,* vol. 1, trans. Kathleen McLaughlin and David Pellauer (Chicago: University of Chicago Press, 1984), 121–74.

6. William Dray, *Laws and Explanation in History* (Oxford: Oxford University Press, 1957).

7. Georg Henrik von Wright, *Explanation and Understanding* (London: Routledge and Kegan Paul, 1971).

8. Ricoeur, *Time and Narrative,* vol. 1, 142.

9. Arthur Danto, *Analytical Philosophy of History* (Cambridge: Cambridge University Press, 1965).

10. Hayden White, *Metahistory: The Historical Imagination in Nineteenth-Century Europe* (Baltimore and London: Johns Hopkins University Press, 1973).

11. Ricoeur, *Time and Narrative,* vol. 1, 178.

12. Régine Robin, *Le Naufrage du siècle* and *Le Cheval blanc de Lénine, ou l'Histoire autre* (Paris: Berg International, 1995); *Le Roman mémoriel* (Montreal: Le Préambule, 1989).

13. Olivier Mongin, *Paul Ricœur* (Paris: Seuil, 1994), 132.

14. Rogier Chartier, *Le Monde,* March 18, 1993.

15. Roger Chartier, interview with the author.

16. Paul-André Rosental, "Métaphore et stratégie épistémologique: *La Méditerranée* de Fernand Braudel," in Daniel S. Milo and Alain Boureau, eds., *Alter-histoire. Essais d'histoire expérimentale* (Paris: Les Belles Lettres, 1991).

17. Ibid., 125.

18. See of course Paul Ricoeur, *The Rule of Metaphor,* trans. Robert Czerny with Kathleen McLaughlin and John Costello (Toronto: University of Toronto Press, 1977); also Alain Boissinot, "Comparaison est-elle raison?" and François Dosse "Oxymore, le soleil noir du structuralisme," *EspacesTemps* 47–48 (1991): 113–28 and 129–43.

19. See Yveline Lévy-Piarroux, "Les notes donnent le ton," *EspacesTemps* 47–48 (1991): 21–33.

## Twenty-seven. A Horizon More Ethical than Epistemological

1. Jean-Marc Ferry, interview with the author.

2. Ibid.

3. Amartya Sen, *On Ethics and Economics* (Oxford: Blackwell, 1988).

4. Pierre Cahuc, *La Nouvelle Microéconomie* (Paris: La Découverte, 1993).

5. Olivier Favereau, interview with the author.

6. Olivier Favereau, "L'incomplétude n'est pas le problème, c'est la solution," paper presented at the international conference at Cerisy, June 5–12, 1993, "Limiting Rationality and Constituting the Collective"; proceedings in Jean-Pierre Dupuy and Pierre Livet, eds., *Les Limites de la rationnalité*, 2 vols. (Paris: La Découverte, 1997), 219–33.

7. Ibid.

8. Herbert Simon, *Reason in Human Affairs* (Stanford, Calif.: Stanford University Press, 1983), 57–58.

9. Patrick Pharo, interview with the author.

10. Bernard Conein, interview with the author.

11. Jean-Pierre Dupuy, interview with the author.

12. See Georges Duby, *History Continues,* trans. Edmund Jephcott (New York: Pantheon, 1983); and Pierre Chaunu and François Dosse, *L'Instant éclaté* (Paris: Aubier, 1994).

13. Marcel Gauchet, interview with the author.

14. Paul Ricoeur, *History and Truth,* trans. Charles A. Kelbley (Evanston, Ill.: Northwestern University Press, 1965), 31.

15. Marcel Gauchet, interview with the author.

16. Gérard Noiriel, interview with the author.

17. Ibid.

18. Ibid.

19. Pierre Lévy, interview with the author.

20. Monique Canto-Sperber, "Pour la philosophie morale," *Le Débat* 72 (November–December 1992): 42.

21. Monique Canto-Sperber, *Le Monde,* March 11, 1994.

22. Ibid.

23. Jean-Marc Ferry, *Les Puissances de l'expérience* (Paris: Cerf, 1991).

24. Francisco Varela, Evan Thompson, and Eleanor Rosch, *The Embodied Mind: Cognitive Science and Human Experience* (Cambridge: MIT Press, 1991), 254.

## Part VIII. Historicity

## Twenty-eight. The Evenementalization of Meaning

1. Isabelle Stengers, *L'Invention des sciences modernes* (Paris: La Découverte, 1993), 85.

2. Ilya Prigogine and Isabelle Stengers, *Entre le temps et l'éternité* (Paris: Fayard, 1988), 180.

3. Ibid., 192.

4. See Pierre Chaunu's developments in Pierre Chaunu and François Dosse, *L'Instant éclaté* (Paris: Aubier, 1994).

5. Saint Augustine, *Confessions,* trans. Henry Chadwick (Oxford: Oxford University Press, 1991), book 11, chapter 18, 233.

6. Edmund Husserl, *On the Phenomenology of the Consciousness of Internal Time*

*(1893–1917)*, trans. John Barnett Brough (Dordrecht: Kluwer Academic Publishers, 1991), 5.

7. Paul Ricoeur, *Time and Narrative*, vol. 3, trans. Kathleen Blamey and David Pellauer (Chicago: University of Chicago Press, 1988), 26.

8. Isabelle Stengers, *EspacesTemps* seminar, European Research University, January 10, 1994.

9. Ibid.

10. René Passeron, "Poïétique et histoire," *EspacesTemps* 55–56 (1994): 103.

11. Ibid., 105.

12. Alain Badiou, *L'Être et l'événement* (Paris: Seuil, 1988).

13. Stéphane Mosès, *L'Ange de l'histoire* (Paris: Seuil, 1992), 23.

14. Ibid., 122.

15. Ibid., 126.

16. Ibid., 161.

17. [The word *signifiance* simply translates the French *signifiance*. This word has come to refer to the capacity of elements of language, in different combinations, to produce meaning—a meaning that will be different when the same set of elements (a phrase or sentence, for example) moves from context to context.—*Trans.*]

18. Marcel Gauchet, interview with the author.

19. Georges Duby, *The Legend of Bouvines: War, Religion and Culture in the Middle Ages,* trans. Catherine Tihanyi (Berkeley: University of California Press, 1990).

20. Fernand Braudel, *On History,* trans. Sarah Matthews (Chicago: University of Chicago Press, 1980), 27.

21. Ibid., 28.

22. Emmanuel Le Roy Ladurie, *The Mind and Method of the Historian,* trans. Siân Reynolds and Ben Reynolds (Chicago: University of Chicago Press, 1981), 7.

23. Michel Foucault, "Nietzsche, Genealogy, History," in *Language, Countermemory, Practice,* trans. Donald F. Bouchard and Sherry Simon (Ithaca, N.Y.: Cornell University Press, 1977), 153.

24. Ibid., 154.

25. Pierre Nora, "Le retour de l'événement," in Jacques le Goff and Pierre Nora, eds., *Faire de l'histoire,* vol. 1 (Paris: Gallimard, 1974), 210–28.

26. Ibid., 215.

27. Paul Ricoeur, "Événement et sens," *Raisons pratiques* 2 (1991): 51–52.

28. Ibid., 55.

29. Conrad Stein, *L'Enfant imaginaire* (Paris: Denoël, 1971).

30. Michèle Bertrand and Bernard Doray, *Psychanalyse et Sciences sociales* (Paris: La Découverte, 1989), 132.

31. Patrick di Mascio, "Freud hors contexte," *EspacesTemps,* special issue on the topic "Reflected Time: History at the Risk of Historians" (1995): 137–45.

32. Jean-Pierre Vernant, "D'une illusion des illusions," *Espaces* (spring 1986): 75–83.

33. Gérard Noiriel, interview with the author.

34. Jean-Luc Petit, "La constitution de l'événement social," *Raisons pratiques* 2 (1991): 15.

35. Reinhart Koselleck, *Futures Past: On the Semantics of Historical Time,* trans. Keith Tribe (Cambridge: MIT Press, 1985), 269.

36. Louis Quéré, "Événement et temps de l'histoire," *Raisons pratiques* 2 (1991): 267.

37. Koselleck, *Futures Past,* 232.

38. Ibid., 164.

39. Jacques Guilhaumou, *EspacesTemps* seminar, European Research University, December 5, 1994.

40. Jacques Guilhaumou, *1793. La mort de Marat* (Brussels: Complexe, 1989).

41. Jacques Guilhaumou, *Marseille républicaine* (Paris: Presses de la Fondation Nationale des Sciences Politiques, 1992).

42. Ibid., 77.

## Twenty-nine. Situated Action

1. George H. Mead, *The Philosophy of the Present* (Chicago: University of Chicago Press, 1980).

2. Louis Quéré, *EspacesTemps* seminar, European Research University, May 2, 1994.

3. Ibid.

4. Hans-Georg Gadamer, *Truth and Method,* trans. Garrett Barden and John Cumming (New York: Crossroad, 1975), 264.

5. Ibid., 321.

6. Louis Quéré, *EspacesTemps* seminar, European Research University, May 2, 1994.

7. Ibid.

8. Ibid.

9. Ibid.

10. Louis Quéré, interview with the author.

11. Ibid.

12. Quéré, *EspacesTemps* seminar, European Research University, May 2, 1994.

13. Ibid.

14. Ibid.

15. Georges Lipovetsky, *L'Ère du vide* (Paris: Gallimard, 1983).

16. Jean-Marc Ferry, interview with the author.

17. Ibid.

18. Ibid.

19. Alain Boyer, *EspacesTemps* seminar, European Research University, February 7, 1994; see also Alain Boyer, *Introduction à la lecture de Popper* (Paris: Presses de l'École Normale Supérieure, 1994).

20. Boyer, *EspacesTemps* seminar, European Research University, February 7, 1994.

21. Alain Boyer, *L'Explication historique* (Lille: Presses Universitaires de Lille, 1992), 171.

22. Ibid., 175.

23. Karl Popper, *The Open Society and Its Enemies,* 2 vols. (Princeton, N.J.: Princeton University Press, 1966).

24. Boyer, *L'Explication historique,* 182.

25. Karl Popper, *Objective Knowledge* (Oxford: Oxford University Press, 1979), 195.

26. Jon Elster, *Ulysses and the Sirens* (Cambridge: Cambridge University Press, 1984).

27. Philippe Van Parijs, *Le Modèle économique et ses rivaux* (Geneva: Droz, 1990).

28. Karl Popper, *Conjectures and Refutations* (London: Routledge and Kegan Paul, 1972), 342.

29. Boyer, *EspacesTemps* seminar, European Research University, February 7, 1994.

30. [Auguste Cournot (1801–77) was the economist who introduced the precision of mathematical formulas into all economic processes.—*Trans.*]

31. Jean-Pierre Dupuy, "Two Temporalities, Two Rationalities: A New Look at Newcomb's Paradox," in Paul Bourgine and B. Walliser, eds., *Economics and Cognitive Science* (New York: Pergamon Press, 1992), 191–220.

32. G. A. Quattrone and A. Tversky, "Self-Deception and the Voter's Illusion," in Jon Elster, ed., *The Multiple Self* (Cambridge: Cambridge University Press, 1987).

33. Luc Boltanski and Laurent Thévenot, *De la justification. Les économies de la grandeur* (Paris: Gallimard, 1991).

34. Laurent Thévenot, interview with the author.

35. Ibid.

36. Nicolas Dodier, "Agir dans plusieurs mondes," *Critique* 529–30 (June–July 1991): 457.

37. Gadamer, *Truth and Method,* 310.

38. Michel Callon, interview with the author.

39. Ibid.

40. Ibid.

41. Nicolas Dodier, "Les appuis conventionnels de l'action. Éléments de pragmatique sociologique," *Réseaux* 62 (November–December 1993): 73.

42. Olivier Favereau, interview with the author.

43. Bernard Conein, interview with the author.

44. Jean-Claude Passeron, "Les sciences humaines en débat (1)," *Raison présente* 108 (1993): 39.

45. Ibid., 8.

46. Pierre Lévy, interview with the author.

47. Pierre Lévy, *Les Technologies de l'intelligence* (Paris: La Découverte, 1990), 131.

## Thirty. The Political

1. François Simiand, "Méthode historique et science sociale," *Annales* 15 (1960): 139–69.

2. Marcel Gauchet, "Changement de paradigme en sciences sociales?" *Le Débat* 50 (May–August 1988): 169.

3. Alain Caillé, *La Démission des clercs* (Paris: La Découverte, 1993).

4. Claude Lefort, *Democracy and Political Theory,* trans. David Macey (Minneapolis: University of Minnesota Press, 1988).

5. Ibid., 5.

6. Ibid., 6.

7. Ibid., 233–35.

8. Ibid., 234.

9. Marcel Gauchet, *Le Désenchantement du monde* (Paris: Gallimard, 1985), ii.

10. Ibid., 54.

11. Marcel Gauchet, interview with the author.

12. Gauchet, *Le Désenchantement du monde,* 87.

13. Ibid., 113.

14. Roger Chartier, "Le monde comme représentation," *Annales* 44:6 (November–December 1989): 1505–20.

15. Marcel Gauchet, interview with the author.

16. Norbert Elias, *The Court Society,* trans. Edmund Jephcott (New York: Pantheon, 1983).

17. For Elias, the process of courtization corresponds to the construction of the

absolutist state around a court that transforms the social conditions, the mentalities, and the psychology of a good part of the *noblesse d'épée* and of a bourgeoisie transformed into a *noblesse de robe* that live in the confined universe of the royal court. Elias studies this process notably in *Power and Civility,* trans. Edmund Jephcott (New York: Pantheon, 1982).

18. Norbert Elias, *Power and Civility,* French edition, *La Dynamique de l'Occident* (Paris: Presses Pocket, 1990), 152–53.

19. Paul Ricoeur, *History and Truth,* trans. Charles A. Kelbley (Evanston, Ill.: Northwestern University Press, 1965), 247.

20. Ibid., 249–50.

21. Ibid., 252.

22. Ibid., 255–56.

23. Ibid., 259.

24. Ibid., 261.

25. Jean-Marc Ferry, interview with the author.

26. Caillé, *La Démission des clercs.*

27. Michel Trebitsch, interview with the author.

28. René Rémond, *The Right Wing in France from 1815 to De Gaulle,* trans. James M. Laux (Philadelphia: University of Pennsylvania Press, 1969).

29. René Rémond, *Pour une histoire politique* (Paris: Seuil, 1988), 12.

30. Jean-François Sirinelli and Eric Vigne, eds., *Histoire des droites en France,* 3 vols. (Paris: Gallimard, 1992).

31. Ibid., vol. 1, xli n.

32. Maurice Agulhon, *La République du village* (Paris: Seuil, 1979).

33. Maurice Agulhon, *Histoire vagabonde,* 2 vols. (Paris: Gallimard, 1988).

34. Rémond, *Pour une histoire politique,* 31.

35. Ibid., 384.

36. Denis Peschanski, Michaël Pollak, and Henry Rousso, *Histoire politique et sciences sociales* (Brussels: Complexe, 1991).

## Thirty-one. The Present Time

1. Robert O. Paxton, *Vichy France: Old Guard and New Order, 1940–1944* (New York: W. W. Norton, 1975).

2. Pierre Nora, "Le retour de l'événement," in Jacques Le Goff and Pierre Nora, eds., *Faire de l'histoire,* vol. 1 (Paris: Gallimard, 1974), 210–29.

3. Michel Trebitsch, "La quarantaine et l'an 40. Hypothèses sur l'étymologie du temps présent," in *Écrire l'histoire du temps présent* (Paris: IHTP, 1993), 70.

4. René Rémond, "Le contemporain du contemporain," in Pierre Nora, ed., *Essais d'ego-histoire* (Paris: Gallimard, 1987), 330.

5. [JEC: Jeunesse Étudiante Catholique—Catholic Student Youth.—*Trans.*]

6. Renée Bédarida, *Les Armes de l'esprit:* Témoignage chrétien, *1941–1944* (Paris: Éditions Ouvrières, 1977).

7. Trebitsch, "La quarantaine et l'an 40," 71.

8. René Rémond, "Plaidoyer pour une histoire délaissée. La fin de la III$^e$ République," *Revue française de sciences politiques* 7 (1957).

9. Henri-Irénée Marrou, *The Meaning of History* (Montreal: Palm Publishers, 1966); Paul Ricoeur, *History and Truth,* trans. Charles A. Kelbley (Evanston, Ill.: Northwestern University Press, 1965).

10. Pierre Nora, "De l'histoire contemporaine au présent historique," in *Écrire l'histoire du temps présent*, 45.

11. Paul Ricoeur, "Remarques d'un philosophe," in *Écrire l'histoire du temps présent*, 38.

12. Robert Frank, "Enjeux épistémologiques de l'enseignement de l'histoire du temps présent," *L'Histoire entre l'épistémologie et demande sociale*, proceedings of the Blois Summer University, September 1992 (1994), 161–69.

13. Ibid., 165.

14. Ibid., 166.

15. Ricoeur, "Remarques d'un philosophe," 37.

16. Agnès Chauveau and Philippe Tétart, in *Questions à l'histoire des temps présents* (Brussels: Complexe, 1992), 25–26.

17. Hannah Arendt, *Between Past and Future* (New York: Penguin, 1987).

18. Luisa Passerini, "La lacune du présent," in *Écrire l'histoire du temps présent*, 60.

19. Michel de Certeau, *L'Absent de l'histoire* (Paris: Repères, 1973).

20. Ricoeur, "Remarques d'un philosophe," 39.

21. Jean-Pierre Rioux, "Peut-on faire une histoire du temps présent?" in *Questions à l'histoire des temps présents*, 50.

22. Ibid., 54.

## Thirty-two. The Historicity of the Sciences: The Principle of Symmetry

1. David Bloor, *Knowledge and Social Imagery* (Chicago: University of Chicago Press, 1991).

2. François-André Isambert, "Un programme fort en sociologie de la science?" *Revue française de sociologie* 26 (1966): 485–508.

3. Bruno Latour, *EspacesTemps* seminar, European Research University, March 7, 1994.

4. Bruno Latour, "Pasteur and Pouchet: The Heterogenesis of the History of Science," in Michel Serres, ed., *A History of Scientific Thought: Elements of a History of Science* (Oxford: Blackwell, 1995), 526–55.

5. Ibid., 528.

6. Ibid., 534.

7. Ibid., 555.

8. Latour, *EspacesTemps* seminar, European Research University, March 7, 1994.

9. Ibid.

10. Félix-Archimède Pouchet, quoted in Latour, "Pasteur and Pouchet," 541.

11. Latour, *EspacesTemps* seminar, European Research University, March 7, 1994.

12. Ibid.

13. Steve Woolgar, "Irony in the Social Study of Science," in Karin Knorr-Cetina and Michael Mulkay, eds., *Science Observed* (London: Sage Publications, 1983), 239–66.

14. Isabelle Stengers, interview with the author.

15. Isabelle Stengers, *L'Invention des sciences modernes* (Paris: La Découverte, 1993), 79.

16. Isabelle Stengers, interview with the author.

*Part IX. The New Alliance: A Threefold Understanding*

## Thirty-three. A Transdisciplinarity

1. Isabelle Stengers, interview with the author.

2. Ibid.

3. Bernard Lepetit, "Propositions pour une pratique restreinte de l'interdisciplinarité," *Revue de synthèse* 60 (1990): 331–38.

4. Alfred North Whitehead, *Process and Reality: An Essay in Cosmology* (New York: Macmillan, 1969).

5. Ilya Prigogine and Isabelle Stengers, *La Nouvelle Alliance* (Paris: Gallimard, "Folio-Essais," 1979), 159.

6. Ibid., 312.

7. Bernard d'Espagnat, *Reality and the Physicist: Knowledge, Duration, and the Quantum World,* trans. Dr. J. C. Whitehouse and Bernard d'Espagnat (Cambridge: Cambridge University Press, 1989).

8. Niels Bohr, "The Quantum Postulate and the Recent Development of Atomic Theory," *Nature* 121 (1928): 590.

9. Catherine Chevalley, "Physique quantique et philosophie," *Le Débat* 72 (November–December 1992): 76.

10. Bernard d'Espagnat, interview with Guitta Pessis-Pasternak, in *Faut-il brûler Descartes?* (Paris: La Découverte, 1991), 119.

11. Henri Atlan, interview with Pessis-Pasternak, in ibid., 54.

12. Henri Atlan, *Le Monde,* November 19, 1991.

13. Ibid.

14. Lucien Febvre, *Combats pour l'histoire* (Paris: Armand Colin, 1953), 29.

15. Marc Bloch, *Apologie pour l'histoire* (Paris: Armand Colin, 1952), xvi.

16. Pascal Engel, interview with the author.

17. Marcel Gauchet, interview with the author.

18. Ibid.

19. Jean-Luc Jamard, *EspacesTemps* seminar, European Research University, January 4, 1993.

20. Jean-Marc Ferry, interview with the author.

21. See Alain Boyer, *L'Explication en histoire* (Lille: Presses Universitaires de Lille, 1992).

22. Jean-Marc Ferry, interview with the author.

23. Sylvain Auroux, *Sciences humaines* 24 (January 1993): 34.

24. Bruno Latour, interview with the author.

25. Alain Testart, *Essai d'épistémologie. Pour les sciences sociales* (Paris: Christian Bourgois, 1991), 151.

26. Jean-Claude Passeron, *Le Raisonnement sociologique* (Paris: Nathan, 1991).

27. Jean-Luc Jamard, *Anthropologies françaises en perspective* (Paris: Kimé, 1993).

28. Jamard, *EspacesTemps* seminar, European Research University, January 4, 1993.

29. Alain d'Iribarne, *Sciences humaines* 25 (February 1993): 24.

30. Daniel Andler, interview with the author.

## Thirty-four. An Experimental Epistemology

1. Isabelle Stengers, speaking in *Le Bon Plaisir d'Isabelle Stengers,* program produced by Antoine Spire, France Culture, March 5, 1994.

2. Isabelle Stengers, *L'Invention des sciences modernes* (Paris: La Découverte, 1993), 34.

3. Paul Feyerabend, *Against Method: Outline of an Anarchistic Theory of Knowledge* (London: New Left Books, 1975), 295.

4. Ibid., 296.

5. Stengers, *L'Invention des sciences modernes,* 46.

6. Feyerabend, *Against Method,* 297.

7. Stengers, *L'Invention des sciences modernes,* 38.

8. Ibid., 63.

9. Stephen Jay Gould, *The Flamingo's Smile: Reflections in Natural History* (New York: W. W. Norton, 1987); *The Panda's Thumb: More Reflections in Natural History* (New York: W. W. Norton, 1992); *Hen's Teeth and Horse's Toes* (New York: W. W. Norton, 1994); *Wonderful Life: The Burgess Shale and the Nature of History* (New York: Penguin, 1991).

10. Bernadette Bensaude-Vincent and Isabelle Stengers, *A History of Chemistry,* trans. Deborah van Dam (Cambridge: Harvard University Press, 1996).

11. Jean-Paul Escande, speaking in *Le Bon Plaisir.*

12. Isabelle Stengers, interview with the author.

13. Isabelle Stengers, *La Volonté de faire science* (Paris: Laboratoires Delagrange, "Les empêcheurs de penser en rond," 1992), 53.

14. Isabelle Stengers, interview with the author.

15. Sigmund Freud, "Analysis Terminable and Interminable," trans. James Strachey, in Joseph Sandler, ed., *On Freud's "Analysis Terminable and Interminable"* (New Haven: Yale University Press, 1991).

16. Isabelle Stengers and Léon Chertok, *L'Hypnose, blessure narcissique* (Paris: Laboratoires Delagrange, "Les empêcheurs de penser en rond," 1990), 47.

17. Ibid., 52.

18. Jean-Pierre Dupuy, interview with the author.

19. Émile Durkheim, *The Elementary Forms of Religious Life,* trans. Karen E. Fields (New York: Free Press, 1995).

20. Jean-Pierre Dupuy, interview with the author.

21. Alain Boureau and Daniel S. Milo, eds., *Alter-histoire. Essais d'histoire expérimentale* (Paris: Les Belles Lettres, 1991).

22. Boureau and Milo, in ibid., 10.

23. Ibid., 19.

24. Paul Ricoeur, *Time and Narrative,* vol. 2, trans. Kathleen McLaughlin and David Pellauer (Chicago: University of Chicago Press, 1985).

25. Boureau and Milo, in *Alter-histoire,* 16.

## Thirty-five. Pacified Relations between Philosophy and the Social Sciences

1. Jacques Hoarau, "Description d'une conjonction en sociologie," *EspacesTemps* 49–50 (1992): 11.

2. Nicolas Dodier, "Agir dans plusieurs mondes," *Critique* 529–30 (June–July 1991): 446.

3. Jean-Marc Ferry, interview with the author.

4. Ibid.

5. See Catherine Colliot-Thélène, *Le Désenchantement de l'État, de Hegel à Max Weber* (Paris: Minuit, 1992); and Sophie Ernct, "Weber, la philosophie déplacée," *EspacesTemps* 53–54 (1993): 28–42.

6. Jean-Marc Ferry, interview with the author.

7. Ibid.

8. Sylvain Auroux, *Encyclopédie philosophique universelle,* vol. 2, *Les Notions philosophiques* (Paris: Presses Universitaires de France, 1990); *Histoire des idées linguistiques* (Paris: Presses Universitaires de France, 1989–93).

9. Sylvain Auroux, interview with the author for François Dosse, *History of Structuralism,* 2 vols., trans. Deborah Glassman (Minneapolis: University of Minnesota Press, 1997).

10. Sylvain Auroux, *Barbarie et Philosophie* (Paris: Presses Universitaires de France, 1990), 20.

11. Aristotle, "De Interpretatione," trans. J. L. Ackrill, in *The Complete Works of Aristotle,* ed. Jonathan Barnes, vol. 1 (Princeton, N.J.: Princeton University Press, 1984): 25–38.

12. Sylvain Auroux, *Sciences humaines* 24 (January 1993): 32–35.

13. Auroux, *Barbarie et Philosophie,* 121.

14. Ibid.

15. Jean-Luc Jamard, *EspacesTemps* seminar, European Research University, January 4, 1993.

16. Alain Caillé, *La Démission des clercs* (Paris: La Découverte, 1993), 40.

17. Alain Caillé, *EspacesTemps* seminar, European Research University, February 1, 1993.

18. On this point, see the book by Denis Duclos, *De la civilité* (Paris: La Découverte, 1993) [discussed in chapter 11—*Trans.*].

19. Caillé, *La Démission des clercs,* 66.

20. Ibid., 69.

21. Philippe Chanial, *EspacesTemps* seminar, European Research University, February 1, 1993.

22. Ibid.

23. Ibid.

24. Roger Chartier, interview with the author.

25. Martial Guéroult, *Philosophie de l'histoire de la philosophie* (Paris: Aubier, 1979).

26. Ibid., 243.

27. François Azouvi, "Pour une histoire philosophique des idées," *Le Débat* 72 (November–December 1992): 28.

28. Patrick Pharo, interview with the author.

29. Ibid.

30. Louis Quéré, interview with the author.

31. Ibid.

32. Laurent Thévenot, interview with the author.

33. Bruno Latour, interview with the author.

34. Marie-Françoise Durand, Jacques Lévy, and Denis Retaillé, *Le Monde, espaces et systèmes* (Paris: Presses de la Fondation Nationale des Sciences Politiques, 1992).

35. Michel Serres, *The Troubadour of Knowledge,* trans. Sheila Glaser and William Paulson (Ann Arbor: University of Michigan Press, 1997); Michel Serres, *The Natural Contract,* trans. Elizabeth MacArthur and William Paulson (Ann Arbor: University of Michigan Press, 1995).

36. Alain Badiou, *Le Monde,* August 31, 1993.

37. Alain Badiou, *Manifeste pour la philosophie* (Paris: Seuil, 1989), 18.

38. Badiou, *Le Monde,* August 31, 1993.

39. Alain Badiou, *L'Être et l'Événement* (Paris: Seuil, 1988).

# Index

## Compiled by Hassan Melehy

*François Dosse* teaches at the University of Paris X-Nanterre and at the Political Science Institution in Paris. He is also a guest lecturer at the University of Lausanne, where he lectures on historiography, methodology, historical epistemology, and the relationship between history and the social sciences. He is the author of a rapidly growing list of publications, among them his first best-selling book, *L'Histoire en miettes: Des "Annales" à la "nouvelle histoire"* (published in English as *New History of France: The Triumph of the Annales*), and the two-volume *History of Structuralism* (Minnesota, 1997). He is on the editorial board of *EspacesTemps* and is currently working on an intellectual biography of Paul Ricoeur.

*Hassan Melehy* holds a Ph.D. in comparative literature and is assistant professor of French at the University of Connecticut. His research areas include early modern French, critical theory, and cinema. He is the author of *Writing Cogito: Montaigne, Descartes, and the Institution of the Modern Subject.* He has translated a number of books and articles, including *The Names of History* by Jacques Rancière (Minnesota, 1994).